BARRON'S
HOW TO PREPARE FOR

ADVANCED PLACEMENT
EXAMINATIONS
MATHEMATICS

Shirley O. Hockett
Professor of Mathematics
Ithaca College, New York

Barron's Educational Series • 113 Crossways Park Drive, Woodbury, N.Y.

All inquiries should be addressed to:
BARRON'S EDUCATIONAL SERIES, INC.
113 Crossways Park Drive
Woodbury, New York 11797

Library of Congress Catalog Card No. 77-149360

International Standard Book No. 0-8120-0354-3

PRINTED IN THE UNITED STATES OF AMERICA

9 10 11 M 9 8 7

CONTENTS

TOPICAL REVIEW CONTENTS

INTRODUCTION

This book is intended for students who are preparing to take one of the Advanced Placement Examinations in Mathematics offered by the College Entrance Examination Board ("CEEB"). It is based on the 1970-1971 Course Description published by CEEB,* and covers all the topics listed for either "Calculus AB" or "Calculus BC."

The Calculus AB syllabus is for a course in elementary functions and introductory calculus. The Calculus BC syllabus is for a year's course in calculus, and assumes that the student has previously studied not only geometry, trigonometry, and college algebra but also analytic geometry and elementary functions. Calculus BC includes topics in infinite series and in differential equations.

This book consists of three parts.

Part One has eleven sections with notes for review on the

---

*1970-1971 Advanced Placement Mathematics. Princeton, N. J.: College Entrance Examination Board (1970). Available from College Entrance Examination Board, Publications Order Office, Box 592, Princeton, N. J. 08540; price 50 cents. All direct quotations in this Introduction are from this document.

main topics of the calculus, with many illustrative examples.
Each section concludes with a set of multiple-choice questions,
for which the answers are supplied in the Solution Keys at
the back of the book. The section on series and the section on
differential equations cover the material on those topics
prescribed by CEEB.

Part Two has four Practice Examinations, each with forty-
five questions, designed to prepare the students for the first
half of the Advanced Placement Examination. The first half of
recent AP Examinations has been a "multiple-choice section
testing proficiency in a large variety of topics."

Part Three consists of fifteen Sample Essay Examinations,
designed to prepare the student for the second half of the
AP Examination. Recently this half, with seven questions,
has been "a problem section that requires solutions in detail,
giving the student an opportunity to demonstrate his ability
to carry out proofs and solve problems involving a more
extended chain of reasoning." The Solution Keys to the first
seven Sample Essay Examinations are detailed and complete;
some of those to the remaining eight are deliberately sketchy
so that the student may work out his own answers independently.

Students intending to take the Calculus AB Examination
may omit the following from Part One:

```
Section  1, E
   "     3, D, K
   "     4, C, D, E
   "     5, D
   "     8, A, B, E, F, G, H, I
   "     9 (all)
   "    10 (all).
```

Furthermore, multiple-choice questions and essay-type problems that are likely to occur only on the BC Examination are preceded by an asterisk ("*"); the AB course student can also omit these. The remaining questions are typical of those that could, in the opinion of the author, appear on either Examination. Whenever it was difficult to decide whether a specific question (or its equivalent) would occur on the AB Examination, the author has preferred to allow for the possibility that it might, thus not marking it with an asterisk. The examining committee of CEEB says, "Each Advanced Placement Examination in Mathematics . . . seeks to determine how well a student has mastered the concepts and techniques of the subject matter of the corresponding course. Since each examination is designed for full coverage of the subject matter, it is not expected that many students will be able to answer all the questions." It should also be pointed out here that the multiple-choice questions of Advanced Placement Examinations are confidential, and that the author has not seen any restricted items.

THE STUDENT WHO USES THIS BOOK INDEPENDENTLY will improve his performance if he studies illustrative examples carefully and tries to complete practice problems *before* referring to the Solution Keys.

THE TEACHER WHO USES THIS BOOK WITH A CLASS may profitably do so in any of several ways. If the book is used throughout a year's course, then the teacher can assign all or part of each section of multiple-choice problems after the topic has been covered. These sections can also be used for review purposes shortly before examination time. The Practice Examinations and Sample Essay Examinations will also be very helpful in reviewing towards the end of the year. The teacher who wishes to give his class "take-home" examinations throughout the year can assemble such examinations by appropriately choosing problems, on the material to be covered, from several of the Sample Essay Examinations.

Since many COLLEGES IN THEIR FIRST-YEAR MATHEMATICS COURSES follow syllabi very similar to that proposed by CEEB for Advanced Placement High School courses, college students and teachers will also find the book useful.

Many of the problems in this book were used by the author with her classes in Advanced Placement Mathematics at

Ithaca Senior High School, Ithaca, New York. Indeed, it was the success of these students on the AP Examination that inspired the preparation of this book.

The author wishes especially to thank Professor George B. Thomas for his help and encouragement in planning the book, Mr. Nathaniel Strout for his careful checking of the manuscript, and Mr. Ernest Noa of Barron's Educational Series, Inc., for his fine draftsmanship in the figures. The author is solely responsible for any errors that are still present.

Finally, the author bows deeply to her competent, skillful husband who, alone, double-handedly, typed the entire manuscript.

Shirley O. Hockett

Ithaca, New York

December 1970

Topical Review

Section 1: Limits

Review of Definitions and Methods

A. The important definitions of limit are the following:

1. $\lim\limits_{x \to c} f(x) = L$ if, for any positive number ε, however small, there exists a positive number δ such that if $0 < |x - c| < \delta$ then $|f(x) - L| < \varepsilon$.

Here c and L are finite numbers. Note that the function need not be defined at c and that x is *different* from c as x approaches c. This definition says precisely that if $f(x)$ approaches the limit L as x approaches c then the difference between $f(x)$ and L can be made arbitrarily small by taking x sufficiently close to c.

2. $\lim\limits_{x \to c} f(x) = \infty$ if, for any positive number N, however large, there exists a positive number δ such that if $0 < |x - c| < \delta$ then $|f(x)| > N$ [if $f(x) > N$ then $\lim\limits_{x \to c} f(x) = +\infty$, while if $f(x) < -N$ then $\lim\limits_{x \to c} f(x) = -\infty$].

Here, again, $f(c)$ may or may not exist, and x does not equal c as $x \to c$. The function $f(x)$ is said to become infinite as x approaches c if $f(x)$ can be made numerically arbitrarily large by taking x sufficiently close to c. Note carefully that if $\lim\limits_{x \to c} f(x) = \infty$, the limit *does not exist*.

3. (a) $\lim\limits_{x \to +\infty} f(x) = L$ if, for any positive number ε, however small, there exists a positive number N such that if $x > N$ then $|f(x) - L| < \varepsilon$.

(b) $\lim\limits_{x \to -\infty} f(x) = L$ if, for any positive number ε, however small, there exists a positive number N such that if $x < -N$ then $|f(x) - L| < \varepsilon$.

Here, L is again finite and $f(x)$ is said to approach the limit L as x becomes infinite. Under the notation "lim" the notation "$x \to \infty$" is sometimes used to mean indifferently "$x \to +\infty$" or "$x \to -\infty$".

4. $\lim\limits_{x \to \infty} f(x) = \infty$ if, for any positive number N, however large, there exists a positive number M such that if $|x| > M$ then $|f(x)| > N$.

$f(x)$ here is said to become infinite as x becomes infinite, and, as in 2 above, *no limit exists*.

B. The following theorems on limits are important. If c, k, R, S, U, and V are finite numbers and if

$$\lim_{x \to c} f(x) = R \qquad \lim_{x \to c} g(x) = S \qquad \lim_{x \to \infty} f(x) = U \qquad \lim_{x \to \infty} g(x) = V$$

then:

(1a) $\lim\limits_{x \to c} kf(x) = kR$ (1b) $\lim\limits_{x \to \infty} kf(x) = kU$

(2a) $\lim\limits_{x \to c} [f(x) + g(x)] = R+S$ (2b) $\lim\limits_{x \to \infty} [f(x) + g(x)] = U+V$

(3a) $\lim\limits_{x \to c} f(x)g(x) = RS$ (3b) $\lim\limits_{x \to \infty} f(x)g(x) = UV$

(4a) $\lim\limits_{x \to c} \dfrac{f(x)}{g(x)} = \dfrac{R}{S}$ (if $S \neq 0$)   (4b) $\lim\limits_{x \to \infty} \dfrac{f(x)}{g(x)} = \dfrac{U}{V}$ (if $V \neq 0$)

(5) (The "Squeeze Theorem.") If $f(x) \leqq g(x) \leqq h(x)$ and if $\lim\limits_{x \to c} f(x) = \lim\limits_{x \to c} h(x) = L$, then $\lim\limits_{x \to c} g(x) = L$.

EXAMPLES:

1. $\lim\limits_{x\to 2} (5x^2 - 3x + 1) = 5 \lim\limits_{x\to 2} x^2 - 3 \lim\limits_{x\to 2} x + \lim\limits_{x\to 2} 1$

$$= 5\cdot 4 \qquad - 3\cdot 2 \qquad + 1$$

$$= 15.$$

2. $\lim\limits_{x\to 0} (x \cos 2x) = \lim\limits_{x\to 0} x \cdot \lim\limits_{x\to 0} (\cos 2x)$

$$= 0 \qquad \cdot 1$$

$$= 0.$$

3. $\lim\limits_{x\to -1} \dfrac{3x^2 - 2x - 1}{x^2 + 1} = \lim\limits_{x\to -1} (3x^2 - 2x - 1) \div \lim\limits_{x\to -1} (x^2 + 1)$

$$= (3 + 2 - 1) \div (1 + 1)$$

$$= 2.$$

4. $\lim\limits_{x\to 3} \dfrac{x^2 - 9}{x - 3} = \lim\limits_{x\to 3} \dfrac{(x - 3)(x + 3)}{x - 3}$. Since $\dfrac{(x - 3)(x + 3)}{x - 3} = x + 3$

provided $x \neq 3$, and since by definition A1 above x must be different from

3 as $x \to 3$, it follows that $\lim\limits_{x\to 3} \dfrac{(x - 3)(x + 3)}{x - 3} = \lim\limits_{x\to 3} (x + 3) = 6$, where

the factor $x - 3$ is removed *before* taking the limit.

5. $\lim\limits_{x\to -2} \dfrac{x^3 + 8}{x^2 - 4} = \lim\limits_{x\to -2} \dfrac{(x + 2)(x^2 - 2x + 4)}{(x + 2)(x - 2)} = \lim\limits_{x\to -2} \dfrac{x^2 - 2x + 4}{x - 2}$

$= \dfrac{4 + 4 + 4}{-4} = -3.$

6. $\lim\limits_{x\to 0} \dfrac{x}{x^3} = \lim\limits_{x\to 0} \dfrac{1}{x^2} = \infty$. As $x \to 0$, the numerator approaches 1

while the denominator approaches 0; the limit does *not* exist.

7. $\lim\limits_{x\to 1} \dfrac{x^2 - 1}{x^2 - 1} = \lim\limits_{x\to 1} 1 = 1.$

8. $\lim\limits_{\Delta x\to 0} \dfrac{(3 + \Delta x)^2 - 3^2}{\Delta x} = \lim\limits_{\Delta x\to 0} \dfrac{6\Delta x + \Delta x^2}{\Delta x} = \lim\limits_{\Delta x\to 0} 6 + \Delta x$. This is,

of course, the definition of the derivative of $f(x) = x^2$ when $x = 3$.

Since $f'(x) = 2x$, one sees immediately that $f'(3) = 6$.

9. $\lim_{h \to 0} \dfrac{e^h - 1}{h} = 1$. This is $f'(0)$ where $f(x) = e^x$. (See also illustrative example 18 below.)

C. To find $\lim_{x \to \infty} \dfrac{P(x)}{Q(x)}$ where $P(x)$ and $Q(x)$ are polynomials in x, we can divide both numerator and denominator by the highest power of x that occurs and use the fact that $\lim_{x \to \infty} \dfrac{1}{x} = 0$.

10. $\lim_{x \to \infty} \dfrac{3 - x}{4 + x + x^2} = \lim_{x \to \infty} \dfrac{\dfrac{3}{x^2} - \dfrac{1}{x}}{\dfrac{4}{x^2} + \dfrac{1}{x} + 1} = \dfrac{0 - 0}{0 + 0 + 1} = 0.$

11. $\lim_{x \to \infty} \dfrac{4x^4 + 5x + 1}{37x^3 - 9} = \lim_{x \to \infty} \dfrac{4 + \dfrac{5}{x^3} + \dfrac{1}{x^4}}{\dfrac{37}{x} - \dfrac{9}{x^4}} = \infty$ (no limit).

12. $\lim_{x \to \infty} \dfrac{x^3 - 4x^2 + 7}{3 - 6x - 2x^3} = \lim_{x \to \infty} \dfrac{1 - \dfrac{4}{x} + \dfrac{7}{x^3}}{\dfrac{3}{x^3} - \dfrac{6}{x^2} - 2} = \dfrac{1 - 0 + 0}{0 - 0 - 2} = -\dfrac{1}{2}.$

We see from examples 10, 11, and 12 that: if the degree of $Q(x)$ is higher than that of $P(x)$, then $\lim_{x \to \infty} \dfrac{P(x)}{Q(x)} = 0$; if the degree of $P(x)$ is higher than that of $Q(x)$, then $\lim_{x \to \infty} \dfrac{P(x)}{Q(x)} = \infty$ (i.e., does not exist); and if the degrees of $P(x)$ and $Q(x)$ are the same then $\lim_{x \to \infty} \dfrac{P(x)}{Q(x)} = \dfrac{a_n}{b_n}$, where a_n and b_n are the coefficients of the highest powers of x in $P(x)$ and $Q(x)$ respectively.

13. $\lim_{x \to \infty} \dfrac{100x^2 - 19}{x^3 + 5x^2 + 2} = 0$; $\lim_{x \to \infty} \dfrac{x^3 - 5}{1 + 6x + 81x^2} = \infty$ (no limit);

$\lim_{x \to \infty} \dfrac{x - 4}{13 + 5x} = \dfrac{1}{5}$; $\lim_{x \to \infty} \dfrac{4 + x^2 - 3x^3}{x + 7x^3} = -\dfrac{3}{7}.$

D. Let $[x]$ be the greatest integer not greater than x. Then we have:

14. $\lim\limits_{x\to 1}\ [x]$ does not exist. For the left-hand limit $\lim\limits_{x\to 1-}\ [x]\ =\ 0$, while the right-hand limit $\lim\limits_{x\to 1+}\ [x]\ =\ 1$. If $\lim\limits_{x\to c-} f(x) = L$ and $\lim\limits_{x\to c+} f(x) = R$, L and R finite numbers, and if $L \ne R$, then $\lim\limits_{x\to c} f(x)$ fails to exist.

15. $\lim\limits_{x\to\frac{3}{2}}\ [x]\ =\ 1$. The "greatest integer" function has a limit except at the integers.

E. *L'Hôpital's Rule* is very useful in handling indeterminate forms of the type $\frac{0}{0}$ or $\frac{\infty}{\infty}$. Let a be a finite number. The rule says:

(a) If $\lim\limits_{x\to a} f(x)\ =\ \lim\limits_{x\to a} g(x)\ =\ 0$ and if $\lim\limits_{x\to a} \frac{f'(x)}{g'(x)}$ exists, then

$\lim\limits_{x\to a} \frac{f(x)}{g(x)}\ =\ \lim\limits_{x\to a} \frac{f'(x)}{g'(x)}$; if $\lim\limits_{x\to a} \frac{f'(x)}{g'(x)}$ does not exist, then neither does $\lim\limits_{x\to a} \frac{f(x)}{g(x)}$.

(b) If $\lim\limits_{x\to a} f(x)\ =\ \lim\limits_{x\to a} g(x)\ =\ \infty$, the same consequences follow as in case (a).

(c) If $\lim\limits_{x\to\infty} f(x)\ =\ \lim\limits_{x\to\infty} g(x)\ =\ 0$ and if $\lim\limits_{x\to\infty} \frac{f'(x)}{g'(x)}$ exists, then

$\lim\limits_{x\to\infty} \frac{f(x)}{g(x)}\ =\ \lim\limits_{x\to\infty} \frac{f'(x)}{g'(x)}$; if $\lim\limits_{x\to\infty} \frac{f'(x)}{g'(x)}$ does not exist, then neither does

$\lim\limits_{x\to\infty} \frac{f(x)}{g(x)}$. (Here the notation "$x \to \infty$" represents either $x \to +\infty$ or

$x \to -\infty$.)

(d) If $\lim\limits_{x\to\infty} f(x)\ =\ \lim\limits_{x\to\infty} g(x)\ =\ \infty$, the same consequences follow as in case (c).

16. $\lim\limits_{x\to 3} \frac{x^2 - 9}{x - 3}$ (example 4 above) is of type $\frac{0}{0}$ and thus equals

$\lim\limits_{x\to 3} \frac{2x}{1}\ =\ 6$, as before.

17. $\lim\limits_{x \to -2} \dfrac{x^3 + 8}{x^2 - 4}$ (example 5 above) is of type $\dfrac{0}{0}$ and thus equals

$\lim\limits_{x \to -2} \dfrac{3x^2}{2x}$ = -3, as before.

18. $\lim\limits_{h \to 0} \dfrac{e^h - 1}{h}$ (example 9 above) is of type $\dfrac{0}{0}$ and therefore equals

$\lim\limits_{h \to 0} \dfrac{e^h}{1}$ = 1.

19. $\lim\limits_{x \to \infty} \dfrac{x^3 - 4x^2 + 7}{3 - 6x - 2x^3}$ (example 12 above) is of type $\dfrac{\infty}{\infty}$, so that it

equals $\lim\limits_{x \to \infty} \dfrac{3x^2 - 8x}{-6 - 6x^2}$, which is again of type $\dfrac{\infty}{\infty}$. Apply L'Hôpital's

Rule twice more to get $\lim\limits_{x \to \infty} \dfrac{6x - 8}{-12x}$ = $\lim\limits_{x \to \infty} \dfrac{6}{-12}$ = $-\dfrac{1}{2}$, as before.

20. $\lim\limits_{x \to \infty} \dfrac{\ln x}{x}$ is of type $\dfrac{\infty}{\infty}$ and equals $\lim\limits_{x \to \infty} \dfrac{\frac{1}{x}}{1}$ = 0.

L'Hôpital's Rule can also be applied to indeterminate forms of the

types $0 \cdot \infty$ and $\infty - \infty$, if they can be transformed to either $\dfrac{0}{0}$ or $\dfrac{\infty}{\infty}$.

21. $\lim\limits_{x \to \infty} x \sin \dfrac{1}{x}$ is of type $\infty \cdot 0$. Since $x \sin \dfrac{1}{x}$ = $\dfrac{\sin \frac{1}{x}}{\frac{1}{x}}$ and

the latter is $\dfrac{0}{0}$ we see that $\lim\limits_{x \to \infty} x \sin \dfrac{1}{x}$ = $\lim\limits_{x \to \infty} \dfrac{-\frac{1}{x^2} \cos \frac{1}{x}}{-\frac{1}{x^2}}$ = $\lim\limits_{x \to \infty} \cos \dfrac{1}{x}$ = 1.

NOTE TO PROBLEM 21. Alternatively, of course, we can use here the

basic limit for trigonometric functions: $\lim\limits_{\theta \to 0} \dfrac{\sin \theta}{\theta}$ = 1.

Thus, $\lim\limits_{x \to \infty} x \sin \dfrac{1}{x}$ = $\lim\limits_{x \to \infty} \dfrac{\sin \frac{1}{x}}{\frac{1}{x}}$ = $\lim\limits_{\theta \to 0} \dfrac{\sin \theta}{\theta}$ = 1.

Other indeterminate forms, such as 0^0, 1^∞, and ∞^0, are handled by

taking the natural logarithm and then applying L'Hôpital's Rule.

22. $\lim\limits_{x\to 0} (1 + x)^{1/x}$ is of type 1^{∞}. Let $y = (1 + x)^{1/x}$, so that

$\ln y = \dfrac{1}{x} \ln (1 + x)$ and $\lim\limits_{x\to 0} \ln y$ is of type $\dfrac{0}{0}$. Thus $\lim\limits_{x\to 0} \ln y =$

$\lim\limits_{x\to 0} \dfrac{\dfrac{1}{1 + x}}{1} = \dfrac{1}{1} = 1$, and since $\lim\limits_{x\to 0} \ln y = 1$, $\lim\limits_{x\to 0} y = e^1 = e$.

23. $\lim\limits_{x\to\infty} x^{1/x}$ is of type ∞^0. Let $y = x^{1/x}$ and $\ln y = \dfrac{1}{x} \ln x$ (of

type $\dfrac{\infty}{\infty}$). Then $\lim\limits_{x\to\infty} \ln y = \dfrac{\dfrac{1}{x}}{1} = 0$, and $\lim\limits_{x\to\infty} y = e^0 = 1$.

All of the multiple-choice questions in Set One on Limits can be done without recourse to L'Hôpital's Rule. However, many of them can be handled more directly by applying it.

Multiple Choice Questions: Limits

1. $\lim\limits_{x\to 2} \dfrac{x^2 - 4}{x^2 + 4}$ is

   (A) 1   (B) 0   (C) $-\dfrac{1}{2}$ (D) −1   (E) ∞ .

2. $\lim\limits_{x\to\infty} \dfrac{4 - x^2}{x^2 - 1}$ is

   (A) 1   (B) 0   (C) −4   (D) −1   (E) ∞ .

3. $\lim\limits_{x\to 3} \dfrac{x - 3}{x^2 - 2x - 3}$ is

   (A) 0   (B) 1   (C) $\dfrac{1}{4}$ (D) ∞ (E) none of these.

4. $\lim\limits_{x\to 0} \dfrac{x}{x}$ is

   (A) 1   (B) 0   (C) ∞ (D) − 1   (E) nonexistent.

5. $\lim\limits_{x \to 2} \dfrac{x^3 - 8}{x^2 - 4}$ is

    (A) 4   (B) 0   (C) 1   (D) 3   (E) ∞ .

6. $\lim\limits_{h \to 0} \dfrac{(1 + h)^6 - 1}{h}$ is

    (A) 0   (B) 1   (C) ∞ (D) 6   (E) nonexistent.

7. $\lim\limits_{x \to \infty} \dfrac{5x^3 + 27}{20x^2 + 10x + 9}$ is

    (A) ∞ (B) $\dfrac{1}{4}$ (C) 3   (D) 0   (E) 1 .

8. $\lim\limits_{x \to \infty} \dfrac{3x^2 + 27}{x^3 - 27}$ is

    (A) 3   (B) ∞ (C) 1   (D) -1   (E) 0 .

9. $\lim\limits_{x \to \infty} \dfrac{2^{-x}}{2^{x}}$ is

    (A) -1   (B) 1   (C) 0   (D) ∞ (E) none of these.

10. If [x] is the greatest integer not greater than x, then $\lim\limits_{x \to \frac{1}{2}} [x]$ is

    (A) ½   (B) 1   (C) nonexistent   (D) 0   (E) none of these.

11. (With the same notation:) $\lim\limits_{x \to 2} [x]$ is

    (A) 0   (B) 1   (C) 2   (D) 3   (E) none of these.

12. $\lim\limits_{h \to 0} \dfrac{\sqrt[3]{8 + h} - 2}{h}$ is

    (A) ∞ (B) $\dfrac{1}{12}$ (C) 0   (D) 192   (E) 1 .

13. $\lim\limits_{x \to 0} \dfrac{\sin 2x}{x}$ is

    (A) 1   (B) 2   (C) ½   (D) 0   (E) ∞ .

14. $\lim\limits_{x\to\infty} \sin x$ (A) is nonexistent   (B) is infinity   (C) oscillates

between -1 and 1   (D) is zero   (E) is 1 or -1 .

15. $\lim\limits_{x\to 0} \dfrac{\sin 3x}{\sin 4x}$ is

(A) 1   (B) $\dfrac{4}{3}$ (C) $\dfrac{3}{4}$ (D) 0   (E) nonexistent.

16. $\lim\limits_{x\to 0} \dfrac{1 - \cos x}{x}$ is

(A) nonexistent   (B) 1   (C) 2   (D) ∞ (E) none of these.

17. $\lim\limits_{x\to 0} \dfrac{\sin x}{x^2 + 3x}$ is

(A) 1   (B) $\dfrac{1}{3}$ (C) 3   (D) ∞ (E) ¼ .

18. $\lim\limits_{x\to 0} \sin \dfrac{1}{x}$ is

(A) ∞ (B) 1   (C) nonexistent   (D) -1   (E) none of these.

19. $\lim\limits_{x\to 0} \dfrac{\tan \pi x}{x}$ is

(A) $\dfrac{1}{\pi}$ (B) 0   (C) 1   (D) π (E) ∞ .

20. $\lim\limits_{x\to\infty} x^2 \sin \dfrac{1}{x}$ is

(A) 1   (B) 0   (C) ∞ (D) oscillates between -1 and 1

(E) none of these.

21. $\lim\limits_{h\to 0} \dfrac{e^{-h} - 1}{h}$ is

(A) 1   (B) 0   (C) -1   (D) $\dfrac{1}{e}$ (E) ∞ .

22. $\lim\limits_{h\to 0} \dfrac{\ln (e + h) - 1}{h}$ is

(A) 0   (B) $\dfrac{1}{e}$ (C) 1   (D) e (E) nonexistent.

23. $\lim\limits_{x\to 0} |x|$ is

(A) 0   (B) nonexistent   (C) 1   (D) -1   (E) none of these.

24. $\lim\limits_{x \to \infty} x \sin \dfrac{1}{x}$ is

     (A) 0   (B) ∞ (C) nonexistent   (D) -1   (E) 1 .

25. $\lim\limits_{x \to \infty} \dfrac{\ln x}{x}$ is

     (A) 1   (B) 0   (C) ∞ (D) nonexistent   (E) none of these.

Section 2: Differentiation

Review of Definitions and Methods

A. The definition of the derivative of $y = f(x)$ (at any x in the domain of the function) is

$$\lim_{\Delta x \to 0} \frac{f(x + \Delta x) - f(x)}{\Delta x} \qquad \text{or} \qquad \lim_{\Delta x \to 0} \frac{\Delta y}{\Delta x} .$$

The function is said to be *differentiable* at every x for which this limit exists, and its derivative may be denoted by $f'(x)$, y', $\dfrac{dy}{dx}$, or $D_x y$. Frequently 'Δx' is replaced by 'h' or some other symbol.

The derivative of $y = f(x)$ at $x = x_1$, denoted by $f'(x_1)$ or $y'(x_1)$, may be defined as

$$\lim_{h \to 0} \frac{f(x_1 + h) - f(x_1)}{h} .$$

The second derivative, denoted by $f''(x)$ (or $\dfrac{d^2 y}{dx^2}$ or y''), is the (first) derivative of $f'(x)$.

B. The following formulas for finding derivatives are so important that familiarity with them is essential. If a and n are constants and u and v are differentiable functions of x, then

(1) $\dfrac{da}{dx} = 0.$
(2) $\dfrac{d}{dx} au = a\dfrac{du}{dx}.$

(3) $\dfrac{d}{dx} u^n = nu^{n-1}\dfrac{du}{dx}.$ (Note that $\dfrac{d}{dx} x^n = nx^{n-1}$ is a special case of this formula when $u = x$.)

(4) $\dfrac{d}{dx}(u+v) = \dfrac{d}{dx}u + \dfrac{d}{dx}v .$

(5) $\dfrac{d}{dx}(uv) = u\dfrac{dv}{dx} + v\dfrac{du}{dx} .$

(6) $\dfrac{d}{dx}\left(\dfrac{u}{v}\right) = \dfrac{v\dfrac{du}{dx} - u\dfrac{dv}{dx}}{v^2}$, provided $v \neq 0.$

(7) $\dfrac{d}{dx}\sin u = \cos u \dfrac{du}{dx} .$

(8) $\dfrac{d}{dx}\cos u = -\sin u \dfrac{du}{dx} .$

(9) $\dfrac{d}{dx}\tan u = \sec^2 u \dfrac{du}{dx} .$

(10) $\dfrac{d}{dx}\cot u = -\csc^2 u \dfrac{du}{dx} .$

(11) $\dfrac{d}{dx}\sec u = \sec u \tan u \dfrac{du}{dx} .$

(12) $\dfrac{d}{dx}\csc u = -\csc u \cot u \dfrac{du}{dx} .$

(13) $\dfrac{d}{dx}\ln u = \dfrac{1}{u}\dfrac{du}{dx} .$

($\ln x$, the "natural logarithm of x," is defined for positive x as follows:

$\ln x = \displaystyle\int_1^x \dfrac{1}{t}\, dt.$)

(14) $\dfrac{d}{dx} e^u = e^u \dfrac{du}{dx} .$ (e is the number whose natural logarithm is 1; i.e. $\ln e = 1$.)

(15) $\frac{d}{dx} a^u = a^u \ln a \frac{du}{dx}$.

(16) $\frac{d}{dx} \sin^{-1} u = \frac{1}{\sqrt{1 - u^2}} \frac{du}{dx}$.

(17) $\frac{d}{dx} \cos^{-1} u = - \frac{1}{\sqrt{1 - u^2}} \frac{du}{dx}$.

(18) $\frac{d}{dx} \tan^{-1} u = \frac{1}{1 + u^2} \frac{du}{dx}$.

(19) $\frac{d}{dx} \cot^{-1} u = - \frac{1}{1 + u^2} \frac{du}{dx}$.

(20) $\frac{d}{dx} \sec^{-1} u = \frac{1}{|u| \sqrt{u^2 - 1}} \frac{du}{dx}$.

(21) $\frac{d}{dx} \csc^{-1} u = - \frac{1}{|u| \sqrt{u^2 - 1}} \frac{du}{dx}$.

These formulas are applied in the following illustrative EXAMPLES:

1. If $y = 4x^3 - 5x + 7$ then $\frac{dy}{dx} = 12x^2 - 5$ and $\frac{d^2y}{dx^2} = 24x$.

2. If $u = \sqrt[3]{2x^2} - \frac{1}{\sqrt{3x}}$ then $u = (2x^2)^{1/3} - (3x)^{-1/2}$, and (for $x > 0$)

$\frac{du}{dx} = \frac{1}{3} (2x^2)^{-2/3}(4x) + \frac{1}{2} (3x)^{-3/2} \cdot 3 = \frac{4}{3\sqrt[3]{4x}} + \frac{1}{2x\sqrt{3x}}$.

3. If $y = \sqrt{3 - x - x^2}$ then $y = (3 - x - x^2)^{1/2}$ and

$\frac{dy}{dx} = \frac{1}{2}(3 - x - x^2)^{-1/2}(-1 - 2x) = - \frac{1 + 2x}{2\sqrt{3 - x - x^2}}$.

4. If $y = \frac{5}{\sqrt{(1 - x^2)^3}}$ then $y = 5(1 - x^2)^{-3/2}$ and $\frac{dy}{dx} =$

$\frac{-15}{2}(1 - x^2)^{-5/2}(-2x) = \frac{15x}{(1 - x^2)^{5/2}}$.

5. If $s = (t^2 + 1)^3(1 - t)^2$ then $\frac{ds}{dt} = (t^2 + 1)^3[2(1 - t)(-1)]$

$+ (1 - t)^2[3(t^2 + 1)^2(2t)] = 2(t^2 + 1)^2(1 - t)(3t - 1 - 4t^2)$.

6. If $f(t) = e^{2t} \sin 3t$ then $f'(t) = e^{2t}(\cos 3t \cdot 3) + \sin 3t (e^{2t} \cdot 2)$

$= e^{2t}(3 \cos 3t + 2 \sin 3t)$.

7. If $z = \dfrac{v}{\sqrt{1 - 2v^2}}$ then $\dfrac{dz}{dv} = \dfrac{\sqrt{1 - 2v^2} - \dfrac{v(-4v)}{2\sqrt{1 - 2v^2}}}{1 - 2v^2}$

$= \dfrac{\dfrac{(1 - 2v^2) + 2v^2}{\sqrt{1 - 2v^2}}}{1 - 2v^2} = \dfrac{1}{(1 - 2v^2)^{3/2}}$.

Since $\dfrac{dz}{dv}$ equals $(1 - 2v^2)^{-3/2}$, note that $\dfrac{d^2z}{dv^2} = -\dfrac{3}{2}(1 - 2v^2)^{-5/2}(-4v)$

$= \dfrac{6v}{(1 - 2v^2)^{5/2}}$.

8. If $f(x) = \dfrac{\sin x}{x^2}$, $x \neq 0$, then $f'(x) = \dfrac{x^2 \cos x - \sin x \cdot 2x}{x^4}$

$= \dfrac{x \cos x - 2 \sin x}{x^3}$.

9. If $y = \tan (2x^2 + 1)$ then $y' = 4x \sec^2 (2x^2 + 1)$ and

$y'' = 4[x \cdot 2 \sec (2x^2 + 1) \cdot \sec (2x^2 + 1) \tan (2x^2 + 1) \cdot 4x + \sec^2 (2x^2 + 1)]$

$= 4 \sec^2 (2x^2 + 1)[8x^2 \tan (2x^2 + 1) + 1]$.

10. If $x = \cos^3 (1 - 3\theta)$ then $\dfrac{dx}{d\theta} = -3 \cos^2 (1 - 3\theta) \sin (1 - 3\theta)(-3)$

$= 9 \cos^2 (1 - 3\theta) \sin (1 - 3\theta)$.

11. If $y = e^{\sin x + 1}$ then $\dfrac{dy}{dx} = \cos x \cdot e^{\sin x + 1}$.

12. If $y = (x + 1) \ln^2 (x + 1)$

then $\dfrac{dy}{dx} = (x + 1) \dfrac{2 \ln (x + 1)}{x + 1} + \ln^2 (x + 1) = 2 \ln (x + 1) + \ln^2 (x + 1)$.

13. If $f(\theta) = \tan^{-1} \dfrac{1 - \theta}{1 + \theta}$ then $f'(\theta) = \dfrac{\dfrac{(1 + \theta)(-1) - (1 - \theta)}{(1 + \theta)^2}}{1 + (\dfrac{1 - \theta}{1 + \theta})^2}$

$= \dfrac{-1 - \theta - 1 + \theta}{1 + 2\theta + \theta^2 + 1 - 2\theta + \theta^2} = -\dfrac{1}{1 + \theta^2}$.

14. If $y = \sin^{-1} x + x\sqrt{1 - x^2}$ then $y' = \dfrac{1}{\sqrt{1 - x^2}} + \dfrac{x(-2x)}{2\sqrt{1 - x^2}} + \sqrt{1 - x^2}$

$= \dfrac{1 - x^2 + 1 - x^2}{\sqrt{1 - x^2}} = 2\sqrt{1 - x^2}$.

15. If $u = \ln \sqrt{v^2 + 2v - 1}$ then $u = \dfrac{1}{2} \ln (v^2 + 2v - 1)$

and $\dfrac{du}{dv} = \dfrac{1}{2} \dfrac{2v + 2}{v^2 + 2v - 1} = \dfrac{v + 1}{v^2 + 2v - 1}$.

16. If $s = e^{-t}(\sin t - \cos t)$ then $s' = e^{-t}(\cos t + \sin t)$
$+ (\sin t - \cos t)(-e^{-t}) = e^{-t}(2 \cos t) = 2e^{-t} \cos t$.

C. Familiarity with the *Chain Rule* is also important: if $y = f(u)$ and $u = g(x)$ are differentiable functions of u and x respectively, then

$\dfrac{dy}{dx} = f'(u) \cdot g'(x) = \dfrac{dy}{du} \cdot \dfrac{du}{dx}$.

EXAMPLE:

17. Let $y = 2u^3 - 4u^2 + 5u - 3$ and $u = x^2 - x$. Then $\dfrac{dy}{dx} =$

$(6u^2 - 8u + 5)(2x - 1) = [6(x^2 - x)^2 - 8(x^2 - x) + 5](2x - 1)$.

D. *Parametric Equations.* If $x = f(t)$ and $y = g(t)$ are differentiable functions of t then

$$\dfrac{dy}{dx} = \dfrac{\dfrac{dy}{dt}}{\dfrac{dx}{dt}} \qquad \text{and} \qquad \dfrac{d^2y}{dx^2} = \dfrac{d}{dx}(\dfrac{dy}{dx}) = \dfrac{\dfrac{d}{dt}(\dfrac{dy}{dx})}{\dfrac{dx}{dt}} .$$

EXAMPLE:

18. If $x = 2 \sin \theta$ and $y = \cos 2\theta$, then $\dfrac{dy}{dx} = \dfrac{\dfrac{dy}{d\theta}}{\dfrac{dx}{d\theta}} = \dfrac{-2 \sin 2\theta}{2 \cos \theta}$

$= -\dfrac{2 \sin \theta \cos \theta}{\cos \theta}$, and $\dfrac{d^2y}{dx^2} = \dfrac{\dfrac{d}{d\theta}\left(\dfrac{dy}{dx}\right)}{\dfrac{dx}{d\theta}} = \dfrac{-2 \cos \theta}{2 \cos \theta} = -1.$

E. If y is not defined explicitly in terms of x but is differentiable,

then $\dfrac{dy}{dx}$ can be found by *implicit differentiation*. In the examples below

we differentiate both sides with respect to x, using appropriate formulas,

and then solve for $\dfrac{dy}{dx}$.

EXAMPLES:

19. If $x^2 - 2xy + 3y^2 = 2$, then $2x - 2(x \dfrac{dy}{dx} + y \cdot 1) + 6y \dfrac{dy}{dx} = 0$

and $\dfrac{dy}{dx}(6y - 2x) = 2y - 2x.$ So $\dfrac{dy}{dx} = \dfrac{y - x}{3y - x}$.

20. If $x \sin y = \cos (x + y)$,

then $x \cos y \dfrac{dy}{dx} + \sin y = -\sin (x + y)(1 + \dfrac{dy}{dx}),$

so that $\dfrac{dy}{dx} = -\dfrac{\sin y + \sin (x + y)}{x \cos y + \sin (x + y)}$.

Multiple Choice Questions: Differentiation

In each of problems 1-27 a function is given. In each problem, mark the alternative that is the derivative, $\frac{dy}{dx}$, of the function.

1. $y = (4x + 1)^2(1 - x)^3$

  (A) $(4x + 1)^2(1 - x)^2(5 - 20x)$

  (B) $(4x + 1)(1 - x)^2(4x + 11)$

  (C) $5(4x + 1)(1 - x)^2(1 - 4x)$

  (D) $(4x + 1)(1 - x)^2(11 - 20x)$

  (E) $-24(4x + 1)(1 - x)^2$.

2. $y = \frac{2 - x}{3x + 1}$

  (A) $-\frac{7}{(3x + 1)^2}$ (B) $\frac{6x - 5}{(3x + 1)^2}$

  (C) $-\frac{9}{(3x + 1)^2}$ (D) $\frac{7}{(3x + 1)^2}$

  (E) $\frac{7 - 6x}{(3x + 1)^2}$.

3. $y = \sqrt{3 - 2x}$

  (A) $\frac{1}{2\sqrt{3 - 2x}}$ (B) $-\frac{1}{\sqrt{3 - 2x}}$

  (C) $-\frac{(3 - 2x)^{3/2}}{3}$ (D) $-\frac{1}{(3 - 2x)}$

  (E) $\frac{2}{3}(3 - 2x)^{3/2}$.

4. $y = \frac{2}{(5x + 1)^3}$

  (A) $-\frac{30}{(5x + 1)^2}$ (B) $-30(5x + 1)^{-4}$ (C) $\frac{-6}{(5x + 1)^4}$

  (D) $-\frac{10}{3}(5x + 1)^{-4/3}$ (E) $\frac{30}{(5x + 1)^4}$.

5. $y = 3x^{2/3} - 4x^{1/2} - 2$

(A) $2x^{1/3} - 2x^{-1/2}$ (B) $3x^{-1/3} - 2x^{-1/2}$

(C) $\frac{9}{5}x^{5/3} - 8x^{3/2}$ (D) $\frac{2}{x^{1/3}} - \frac{2}{x^{1/2}} - 2$

(E) $2x^{-1/3} - 2x^{-1/2}$.

6. $y = 2\sqrt{x} - \frac{1}{2\sqrt{x}}$

(A) $x + \frac{1}{x\sqrt{x}}$ (B) $x^{-1/2} + x^{-3/2}$ (C) $\frac{4x - 1}{4x\sqrt{x}}$

(D) $\frac{1}{\sqrt{x}} + \frac{1}{4x\sqrt{x}}$ (E) $\frac{4}{\sqrt{x}} + \frac{1}{x\sqrt{x}}$.

7. $y = \sqrt{x^2 + 2x - 1}$

(A) $\frac{x + 1}{y}$ (B) $4y(x + 1)$ (C) $\frac{1}{2\sqrt{x^2 + 2x - 1}}$

(D) $- \frac{(x + 1)}{(x^2 + 2x - 1)^{3/2}}$ (E) none of these.

8. $y = \frac{x}{\sqrt{1 - x^2}}$

(A) $\frac{1 - 2x^2}{(1 - x^2)^{3/2}}$ (B) $\frac{1}{1 - x^2}$ (C) $\frac{1}{\sqrt{1 - x^2}}$

(D) $\frac{1 - 2x^2}{(1 - x^2)^{1/2}}$ (E) none of these.

9. $y = \cos x^2$

(A) $2x \sin x^2$ (B) $-\sin x^2$ (C) $-2 \sin x \cos x$

(D) $-2x \sin x^2$ (E) $\sin 2x$.

10. $y = \sin^2 3x + \cos^2 3x$

(A) $-6 \sin 6x$ (B) 0 (C) $12 \sin 3x \cos 3x$

(D) $6(\sin 3x + \cos 3x)$ (E) 1 .

11. $y = \ln \dfrac{e^x}{e^x - 1}$

(A) $x - \dfrac{e^x}{e^x - 1}$ (B) $\dfrac{1}{e^x - 1}$ (C) $\dfrac{1}{1 - e^x}$

(D) 0 (E) $\dfrac{e^x - 2}{e^x - 1}$.

12. $y = \tan^{-1} \dfrac{x}{2}$

(A) $\dfrac{4}{4 + x^2}$ (B) $\dfrac{1}{2\sqrt{4 - x^2}}$ (C) $\dfrac{2}{\sqrt{4 - x^2}}$

(D) $\dfrac{1}{2 + x^2}$ (E) $\dfrac{2}{x^2 + 4}$.

13. $y = \ln (\sec x + \tan x)$

(A) $\sec x$ (B) $\dfrac{1}{\sec x}$ (C) $\tan x + \dfrac{\sec^2 x}{\tan x}$

(D) $\dfrac{1}{\sec x + \tan x}$ (E) $- \dfrac{1}{\sec x + \tan x}$.

14. $y = \cos^2 x$

(A) $-\sin^2 x$ (B) $2 \sin x \cos x$ (C) $-\sin 2x$

(D) $2 \cos x$ (E) $-2 \sin x$.

15. $y = \dfrac{e^x - e^{-x}}{e^x + e^{-x}}$

(A) 0 (B) 1 (C) $\dfrac{2}{(e^x + e^{-x})^2}$

(D) $\dfrac{4}{(e^x + e^{-x})^2}$ (E) $\dfrac{1}{e^{2x} + e^{-2x}}$.

16. $y = \ln (x\sqrt{x^2 + 1})$

(A) $1 + \dfrac{x}{x^2 + 1}$ (B) $\dfrac{1}{x\sqrt{x^2 + 1}}$ (C) $\dfrac{2x^2 + 1}{x\sqrt{x^2 + 1}}$

(D) $\dfrac{2x^2 + 1}{x(x^2 + 1)}$ (E) none of these.

17. $y = \ln(x + \sqrt{x^2 + 1})$

(A) $\frac{1}{x} + \frac{x}{x^2 + 1}$ (B) $\frac{1}{\sqrt{x^2 + 1}}$ (C) 1

(D) $\sqrt{x^2 + 1}$ (E) $\frac{1}{x} + \frac{1}{2\sqrt{x^2 + 1}}$.

18. $y = x^2 \sin \frac{1}{x}$ $x \neq 0$

(A) $2x \sin \frac{1}{x} - x^2 \cos \frac{1}{x}$ (B) $-\frac{2}{x} \cos \frac{1}{x}$

(C) $2x \cos \frac{1}{x}$ (D) $2x \sin \frac{1}{x} - \cos \frac{1}{x}$

(E) $-\cos \frac{1}{x}$.

19. $y = \frac{1}{2 \sin 2x}$

(A) $-\csc 2x \cot 2x$ (B) $\frac{1}{4 \cos 2x}$

(C) $-4 \csc 2x \cot 2x$ (D) $\frac{\cos 2x}{2\sqrt{\sin 2x}}$

(E) $-\csc^2 2x$.

20. $y = x^{\ln x}$ $x > 0$

(A) $\frac{2}{x}$ (B) $2 \frac{\ln x}{x}$ (C) $\frac{2(\ln x)y}{x}$

(D) $\frac{2y}{x}$ (E) $(\ln x)x^{\ln x - 1}$.

21. $y = x \tan^{-1} x - \ln \sqrt{x^2 + 1}$

(A) 0   (B) $\frac{1}{\sqrt{1 - x^2}} - \frac{x}{x^2 + 1}$

(C) $\tan^{-1} x$ (D) $\frac{x}{1 + x^2} + \tan^{-1} x - x$

(E) $\frac{1 - x}{1 + x^2}$.

22. $y = e^{-x} \cos 2x$

    (A) $-e^{-x}(\cos 2x + 2 \sin 2x)$ (B) $e^{-x}(\sin 2x - \cos 2x)$

    (C) $2e^{-x} \sin 2x$ (D) $-e^{-x}(\cos 2x + \sin 2x)$

    (E) $-e^{-x} \sin 2x$.

23. $y = \sec^2 \sqrt{x}$

    (A) $\dfrac{\sec \sqrt{x} \tan \sqrt{x}}{\sqrt{x}}$ (B) $\dfrac{\tan \sqrt{x}}{\sqrt{x}}$

    (C) $2 \sec \sqrt{x} \tan^2 \sqrt{x}$ (D) $\dfrac{\sec^2 \sqrt{x} \tan \sqrt{x}}{\sqrt{x}}$

    (E) $2 \sec^2 \sqrt{x} \tan \sqrt{x}$.

24. $y = x \ln^3 x$

    (A) $\dfrac{3 \ln^2 x}{x}$ (B) $3 \ln^2 x$ (C) $3x \ln^2 x + \ln^3 x$

    (D) $3(\ln x + 1)$ (E) none of these.

25. $y = \dfrac{1 + x^2}{1 - x^2}$

    (A) $- \dfrac{4x}{(1 - x^2)^2}$ (B) $\dfrac{4x}{(1 - x^2)^2}$ (C) $\dfrac{-4x^3}{(1 - x^2)^2}$

    (D) $\dfrac{2x}{1 - x^2}$ (E) $\dfrac{4}{1 - x^2}$.

26. $y = \ln \sqrt{2} \, x$

    (A) $\dfrac{\sqrt{2}}{x}$ (B) $\dfrac{1}{\sqrt{2} \, x}$ (C) $\dfrac{1}{2x}$

    (D) $\dfrac{1}{x}$ (E) $\dfrac{1}{\sqrt{x}}$.

27. $y = \sin^{-1} x - \sqrt{1 - x^2}$

    (A) $\dfrac{1}{2\sqrt{1 - x^2}}$ (B) $\dfrac{2}{\sqrt{1 - x^2}}$ (C) $\dfrac{1 + x}{\sqrt{1 - x^2}}$

    (D) $\dfrac{x^2}{\sqrt{1 - x^2}}$ (E) $\dfrac{1}{\sqrt{1 + x}}$.

In each of problems 28-31 a pair of equations is given which represents a curve parametrically. In each, choose the alternative that is the derivative $\frac{dy}{dx}$.

28. $x = t - \sin t$ and $y = 1 - \cos t$

(A) $\dfrac{\sin t}{1 - \cos t}$ (B) $\dfrac{1 - \cos t}{\sin t}$ (C) $\dfrac{\sin t}{\cos t - 1}$

(D) $\dfrac{1 - x}{y}$ (E) $\dfrac{1 - \cos t}{t - \sin t}$.

29. $x = \cos^3 \theta$ and $y = \sin^3 \theta$

(A) $\tan^3 \theta$ (B) $-\cot \theta$ (C) $\cot \theta$ (D) $-\tan \theta$ (E) $-\tan^2 \theta$.

30. $x = 1 - e^{-t}$ and $y = t + e^{-t}$

(A) $\dfrac{e^{-t}}{1 - e^{-t}}$ (B) $e^{-t} - 1$ (C) $e^{t} + 1$

(D) $e^{t} - e^{-2t}$ (E) $e^{t} - 1$.

31. $x = \dfrac{1}{1 - t}$ and $y = 1 - \ln (1 - t)$ $t < 1$

(A) $\dfrac{1}{1 - t}$ (B) $t - 1$ (C) $\dfrac{1}{x}$

(D) $\dfrac{(1 - t)^2}{t}$ (E) $1 + \ln x$.

In each of problems 32-35, y is a differentiable function of x. In each, choose the alternative that is the derivative $\frac{dy}{dx}$.

32. $x^3 - xy + y^3 = 1$

(A) $\dfrac{3x^2}{x - 3y^2}$ (B) $\dfrac{3x^2 - 1}{1 - 3y^2}$ (C) $\dfrac{y - 3x^2}{3y^2 - x}$

(D) $\dfrac{3x^2 + 3y^2 - y}{x}$ (E) $\dfrac{3x^2 + 3y^2}{x}$.

33. $x + \cos(x + y) = 0$

    (A) $\csc(x + y) - 1$ (B) $\csc(x + y)$

    (C) $\dfrac{x}{\sin(x + y)}$ (D) $\dfrac{1}{\sqrt{1 - x^2}}$ (E) $\dfrac{1 - \sin x}{\sin y}$.

34. $\sin x - \cos y - 2 = 0$

    (A) $-\cot x$ (B) $-\cot y$ (C) $\dfrac{\cos x}{\sin y}$

    (D) $-\csc y \cos x$ (E) $\dfrac{2 - \cos x}{\sin y}$.

35. $3x^2 - 2xy + 5y^2 = 1$

    (A) $\dfrac{3x + y}{x - 5y}$ (B) $\dfrac{y - 3x}{5y - x}$ (C) $3x + 5y$

    (D) $\dfrac{3x + 4y}{x}$ (E)   none of these.

Individual instructions are given in full for each of the remaining problems of this set (problems 36-50).

36. If $x = t^2 - 1$ and $y = t^4 - 2t^3$ then when $t = 1$, $\dfrac{d^2y}{dx^2}$ is

    (A) 1   (B) -1   (C) 0   (D) 3   (E) ½.

37. If $f(x) = x^4 - 4x^3 + 4x^2 - 1$, then the set of values of x for which the derivative equals zero is

    (A) $\{1, 2\}$ (B) $\{0, -1, -2\}$ (C) $\{-1, +2\}$

    (D) $\{0\}$ (E) $\{0, 1, 2\}$.

38. If $f(x) = 16\sqrt{x}$, then $f'''(4)$ is equal to

    (A) $\dfrac{3}{16}$ (B) -4   (C) -½   (D) 0   (E) 6 .

39. If $f(x) = \ln x$, then $f^{iv}(x)$ is

    (A) $\dfrac{2}{x^3}$ (B) $\dfrac{24}{x^5}$ (C) $\dfrac{6}{x^4}$ (D) $-\dfrac{1}{x^4}$ (E) none of these.

40. If a point moves on the curve $x^2 + y^2 = 25$, then, at $(0,5)$, $\frac{d^2y}{dx^2}$ is

(A) 0   (B) $\frac{1}{5}$ (C) -5   (D) $-\frac{1}{5}$ (E) nonexistent.

41. If $y = a \sin ct + b \cos ct$, where a, b, and c are constants, then $\frac{d^2y}{dt^2}$ is

(A) $ac^2(\sin t + \cos t)$ (B) $-c^2y$ (C) $-ay$

(D) $-y$ (E) $a^2c^2 \sin ct - b^2c^2 \cos ct$.

42. If $f(x) = x^4 - 4x^2$, then $f^{iv}(2)$ equals

(A) 48   (B) 0   (C) 24   (D) 144   (E) 16.

43. If $f(x) = \dfrac{x}{(x - 1)^2}$ then the set of x's for which $f'(x)$ exists is

(A) all reals   (B) all reals except $x = 1$ and $x = -1$

(C) all reals except $x = -1$

(D) all reals except $x = \frac{1}{3}$ and $x = -1$

(E) all reals except $x = 1$.

44. If $y = (x - 1)^2e^x$, then $\frac{d^2y}{dx^2}$ is equal to

(A) $e^x(x - 1)^2$ (B) $e^x(x^2 - 2x - 1)$

(C) $e^x(x^2 + 2x - 1)$ (D) $2e^x(x - 1)$

(E) none of these.

45. If $f(x) = e^{-x} \ln x$ then, when $x = 1$, $\frac{df}{dx}$ is

(A) 0   (B) nonexistent   (C) $\frac{2}{e}$ (D) $\frac{1}{e}$ (E) e .

46. If $y = \sqrt{x^2 + 1}$, then the derivative of y^2 with respect to x^2 is

(A) 1   (B) $\dfrac{x^2 + 1}{2x}$ (C) $\dfrac{x}{2(x^2 + 1)}$

(D) $\dfrac{2}{x}$ (E) $\dfrac{x^2}{x^2 + 1}$.

47. If $f(x) = \dfrac{1}{x^2 + 1}$ and $g(x) = \sqrt{x}$, then the derivative of $f(g(x))$ is

     (A) $\dfrac{-\sqrt{x}}{(x^2 + 1)^2}$ (B) $-(x + 1)^{-2}$ (C) $\dfrac{-2x}{(x^2 + 1)^2}$

     (D) $\dfrac{1}{(x + 1)^2}$ (E) $\dfrac{1}{2\sqrt{x}(x + 1)}$.

48. If $x = e^\theta \cos \theta$ and $y = e^\theta \sin \theta$, then when $\theta = \dfrac{\pi}{2}$, $\dfrac{dy}{dx}$ is

     (A) 1   (B) 0   (C) $e^{\pi/2}$ (D) nonexistent   (E) -1 .

49. If $x = \cos t$ and $y = \cos 2t$, then $\dfrac{d^2 y}{dx^2}$ is

     (A) $4 \cos t$ (B) 4   (C) $\dfrac{4y}{x}$ (D) -4   (E) $-4 \cot t$.

50. If $y = x^2 + x$, then the derivative of y with respect to $\dfrac{1}{1 - x}$ is

     (A) $(2x + 1)(x - 1)^2$ (B) $\dfrac{2x + 1}{(1 - x)^2}$

     (C) $2x + 1$ (D) $\dfrac{3 - x}{(1 - x)^3}$ (E) none of these.

Section 3: Applications of Differential Calculus

Review of Definitions and Methods

    A. Continuity. The function $f(x)$ is said to be *continuous at* $x = c$ if (1) $f(c)$ is a finite number, (2) $\lim\limits_{x \to c} f(x)$ exists, and (3) $\lim\limits_{x \to c} f(x) = f(c)$. The function is continuous over the closed interval $[a, b]$ if it is continuous at each x such that $a \leqq x \leqq b$. A function which is not continuous at $x = c$ is said to be discontinuous at that point.

EXAMPLES:

1. $f(x) = \dfrac{x - 1}{x^2 + x}$ is not continuous if $x = 0$ or -1, since the function is not defined for either of these numbers. Note also that neither $\lim\limits_{x \to 0} f(x)$ nor $\lim\limits_{x \to -1} f(x)$ exists.

2. $f(x) = \dfrac{x^2 - 4}{x - 2}$ is not continuous at $x = 2$ because $f(2)$ does not exist. Since, here, $\lim\limits_{x \to 2} f(x) = \lim\limits_{x \to 2} (x + 2) = 4$, we can define a new function

$$f(x) = \frac{x^2 - 4}{x - 2} \qquad x \neq 2$$
$$f(2) = 4$$

which is continuous for all x *including* 2.

3. If $f(x) = [x]$ (where $[x]$ is defined as the greatest integer not greater than x), then $f(x)$ is discontinuous at each integer. For any integer n, $\lim\limits_{x \to n^+} f(x) \neq \lim\limits_{x \to n^-} f(x)$, so $\lim\limits_{x \to n} f(x)$ does not exist. Note that this greatest integer function is continuous *except* at the integers.

It is important to remember that (1) if a function has a finite derivative at a point then it is also continuous at that point, but that (2) a function may be continuous at a point without having a derivative at that point.

EXAMPLE:

4. $f(x) = |x - 1|$ is everywhere (that is, for all real x) continuous, but $f'(x)$ does *not* exist at $x = 1$.

Differentiability implies continuity, but continuity does not imply differentiability.

If $f(x)$ is continuous on the closed interval $[a,b]$ then it follows that

(1) the function attains a minimum value and a maximum value somewhere on the interval;

(2) if M is a number such that $f(a) \leqq M \leqq f(b)$, then there is at least one number c between a and b such that $f(c) = M$;

(3) if x_1 and x_2 are numbers between a and b and if $f(x_1)$ and $f(x_2)$ have opposite signs, then there is at least one number c between x_1 and x_2 such that $f(c) = 0$.

If the functions f and g are continuous at $x = a$, so is their sum, their difference, their product, and (if the denominator is not zero at a) their quotient; also kf, where k is a constant, is continuous at a. Polynomials are everywhere continuous and so are rational functions $\frac{P(x)}{Q(x)}$, where P and Q are polynomials, except where Q equals zero.

B. Slope. If the derivative of $y = f(x)$ exists at $P(x_1, y_1)$, then the *slope of the curve* at P (which is defined to be the slope of the tangent to the curve at P) is $f'(x_1)$, the derivative of $f(x)$ at $x = x_1$.

The *equation of the tangent* at P is $y - y_1 = f'(x_1)(x - x_1)$. Since the normal to the curve at P is the line through P which is perpendicular to the tangent, its slope is $-\frac{1}{f'(x_1)}$ and the *equation of the normal* is $y - y_1 = -\frac{1}{f'(x_1)}(x - x_1)$.

If the tangent to a curve is horizontal at a point then the derivative at the point is 0. If it is vertical at a point then the derivative does not exist at the point.

EXAMPLES:

5. Find the equations of the tangent and normal to the curve of $f(x) = x^3 - 3x^2$ at the point $(1, -2)$.

Since $f'(x) = 3x^2 - 6x$ and $f'(1) = -3$, the equation of the tangent is $y + 2 = -3(x - 1)$, or $y + 3x = 1$, and the equation of the normal is $y + 2 = \frac{1}{3}(x - 1)$, or $3y - x = -7$.

6. Find the equation of the tangent to the curve of $x^2y - x = y^3 - 8$ at the point where $x = 0$.

Here we differentiate implicitly to get $\frac{dy}{dx} = \frac{1 - 2xy}{x^2 - 3y^2}$. Since $y = 2$ when $x = 0$ and the slope at this point is $\frac{1 - 0}{0 - 12} = -\frac{1}{12}$, the equation of the tangent is $y - 2 = -\frac{1}{12}x$ or $12y + x = 24$.

7. Find the coordinates of any point on the curve of $y^2 - 4xy = x^2 + 5$ for which the tangent is horizontal.

Since $\frac{dy}{dx} = \frac{x + 2y}{y - 2x}$ and the tangent is horizontal when $\frac{dy}{dx} = 0$, then $x = -2y$. If we substitute this in the equation of the curve we get $y^2 - 4y(-2y) = 4y^2 + 5$. Thus $y = \pm 1$ and $x = \mp 2$. The points, then, are $(2,-1)$ and $(-2,1)$.

8. Find the abscissa of any point on the curve of $y = \sin^2 (x + 1)$ for which the tangent is parallel to the line $3x - 3y - 5 = 0$.

Since $\frac{dy}{dx} = 2 \sin (x + 1) \cos (x + 1) = \sin 2(x + 1)$ and since the given line has slope 1, we seek x such that $\sin 2(x + 1) = 1$. Then $2(x + 1) = \frac{\pi}{2} + 2n\pi$, n an integer, or $(x + 1) = \frac{\pi}{4} + n\pi$, and $x = \frac{\pi}{4} + n\pi - 1$.

C. **The Angle Between Curves.** The angle between two curves that intersect at $Q(x_0, y_0)$ is defined to be the angle between the tangents to the curves at Q. In Figure N3-1 α and α' denote the angles at which the curves of $f(x)$ and $g(x)$ intersect. These

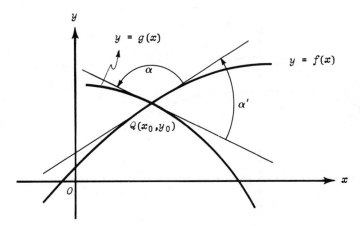

Figure N3-1

angles are, of course, supplementary. The formula for tan α is

$\dfrac{g'(x_0) - f'(x_0)}{1 + f'(x_0)g'(x_0)}$.   If $0 < \alpha < 90°$, tan α > 0, while if $90° < \alpha < 180°$,

tan α < 0; in either case tan α' = - tan α. If α = 90°, the curves

are said to intersect orthogonally and $f'(x_0)g'(x_0)$ = -1.

EXAMPLES:

9. Find the acute angles at which the ellipse $x^2 + 4y^2 = 208$

and the circle $x^2 + y^2 = 100$ intersect.

We solve simultaneously to find the point or points of

intersection. Then, $100 + 3y^2 = 208$ and $y = \pm6$. There are four

points of intersection: $P_1(8,6)$, $P_2(8,-6)$, $P_3(-8,6)$, and $P_4(-8,-6)$.

We find the slopes of the given curves by differentiating implicitly.

For the ellipse, $2x + 8yy' = 0$ and $y' = -\dfrac{x}{4y}$; for the circle,

$2x + 2yy' = 0$ and $y' = -\dfrac{x}{y}$. The table below shows the slopes of the

two curves at the four points of intersection:

	$P_1(8,6)$	$P_2(8,-6)$	$P_3(-8,6)$	$P_4(-8,-6)$
ellipse:	$-\dfrac{1}{3}$	$\dfrac{1}{3}$	$\dfrac{1}{3}$	$-\dfrac{1}{3}$
circle:	$-\dfrac{4}{3}$	$\dfrac{4}{3}$	$\dfrac{4}{3}$	$-\dfrac{4}{3}$.

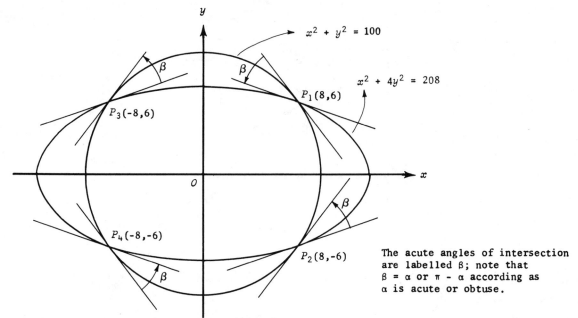

Figure N3-2

At P_1, for example, $\tan \alpha = \dfrac{-\frac{1}{3} - \left(-\frac{4}{3}\right)}{1 + \left(-\frac{1}{3}\right)\left(-\frac{4}{3}\right)} = \dfrac{9}{13}$. At each of the

other points of intersection $\tan \alpha = +\dfrac{9}{13}$ or $-\dfrac{9}{13}$. Therefore, at each

of these intersections the acute angle is $\tan^{-1} \dfrac{9}{13}$. See Figure N3-2.

10. Find a^2 so that the ellipse $a^2x^2 + y^2 = 1$ and the

parabola $y^2 = x$ intersect at right angles.

We find $\dfrac{dy}{dx}$; for the ellipse $2a^2x + 2y\dfrac{dy}{dx} = 0$ and $\dfrac{dy}{dx} = -\dfrac{a^2x}{y}$;

and for the parabola $2y\dfrac{dy}{dx} = 1$ and $\dfrac{dy}{dx} = \dfrac{1}{2y}$. For the curves to

intersect at $Q(x_0, y_0)$ at right angles, the product of the slopes at

Q must equal -1. So $-\dfrac{a^2x_0}{y_0} \dfrac{1}{2y_0} = -1$, or $2y_0{}^2 = a^2x_0$. But

Q lies on the parabola, so $y_0{}^2 = x_0$. Thus $2x_0 = a^2x_0$ and

$x_0(a^2 - 2) = 0$. Since x_0 is different from 0, $a^2 = 2$.

The ellipse $2x^2 + y^2 = 1$ and the parabola $y^2 = x$ are

sketched in Figure N3-3.

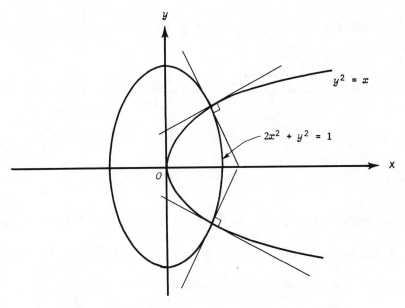

Figure N3-3

D. Differentials. If $y = f(x)$ is differentiable then the _differential dx_ is defined to be a real variable and the _differential dy_ is defined to be $f'(x)\ dx$. Every formula for derivatives in B of Section Two gives rise to one for differentials by the mere replacement of the word "derivative" by the word "differential." Thus, for example, we obtain from the rule "The derivative of a sum is the sum of the derivatives" the rule "The differential of a sum is the sum of the differentials"; in the same way, from "the derivative of a product is the first times the derivative of the second plus the second times the derivative of the first" we obtain "the differential of a product is the first times the differential of the second plus the second times the differential of the first."

EXAMPLES:

11. If $y = xe^{-x}$ then $dy = x d(e^{-x}) + e^{-x}\ dx = -xe^{-x}\ dx + e^{-x}\ dx$ or $e^{-x}(1 - x)\ dx$.

12. If $\ln \sqrt{x^2 + y^2} = \tan^{-1} \dfrac{x}{y}$ then we can find $\dfrac{dy}{dx}$ by using

differentials. Since $\ln \sqrt{x^2 + y^2} = \frac{1}{2} \ln (x^2 + y^2)$ we get

$$\frac{1}{2} \frac{2x\ dx + 2y\ dy}{x^2 + y^2} = \frac{\dfrac{y\ dx - x\ dy}{y^2}}{1 + \dfrac{x^2}{y^2}}, \quad \frac{x\ dx + y\ dy}{x^2 + y^2} = \frac{y\ dx - x\ dy}{y^2 + x^2},$$

$x\ dx + y\ dy = y\ dx - x\ dy$, and $dy(y + x) = dx(y - x)$, so that

$$\frac{dy}{dx} = \frac{y - x}{y + x}.$$

Approximations Using Differentials. If dx is taken equal to
Δx (and is sufficiently small), then dy is a reasonable approximation
to Δy, as can be seen from Figure N3-4.

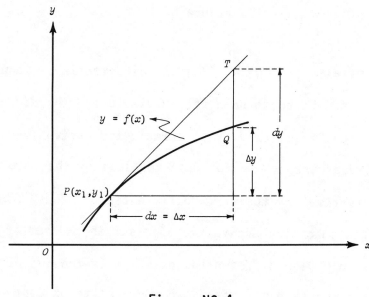

Figure N3-4

Examples:

13. By approximately how much does the volume of a sphere of radius
4 inches change if the radius is decreased by 0.1 inches?

Here the volume V of the sphere equals $\frac{4}{3} \pi r^3$ and $dV = 4\pi r^2\ dr$.

If we take $r = 4$ and $dr = -0.1$, then $dV = 4\pi(4)^2 \cdot (-0.1) = -6.4\pi$ in^3.

14. If the edge of a cube is increased by approximately 1%, find
the approximate error in the surface area.

If we let S be the surface area and x the edge, then $S = 6x^2$ and $dS = 12x\ dx$. Since $dx = 0.01x$, $dS = 12x(0.01x) = 0.12x^2$. The relative error in S is thus $\frac{0.12x^2}{6x^2} = 0.02$, and the percentage error is 2%.

E. Related Rates. If several variables which are functions of time t are related by an equation, we can obtain a relation involving their (time) rates of change by differentiating with respect to t.

EXAMPLE:

15. If one leg AB of a right triangle increases at the rate of 2 in/sec, while the other leg AC decreases at 3 in/sec, find how fast the hypotenuse is changing when $AB = 6$ ft and $AC = 8$ ft.

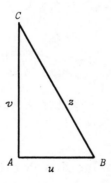

Figure N3-5

See Figure N3-5. Let u, v, and z denote the lengths respectively of AB, AC, and BC. We know that $\frac{du}{dt} = \frac{1}{6}$ (ft/sec) and $\frac{dv}{dt} = -\frac{1}{4}$.

Since (at any time) $z^2 = u^2 + v^2$, then $2z\frac{dz}{dt} = 2u\frac{du}{dt} + 2v\frac{dv}{dt}$,

and $\frac{dz}{dt} = \dfrac{u\frac{du}{dt} + v\frac{dv}{dt}}{z}$. At the instant in question, $u = 6$, $v = 8$,

and $z = 10$. So $\frac{dz}{dt} = \dfrac{6(\frac{1}{6}) + 8(-\frac{1}{4})}{10} = -\frac{1}{10}$ ft/sec.

F. **Sign of the First Derivative, applied to curve-sketching.** A function $y = f(x)$ is said to be $\begin{smallmatrix}\text{increasing}\\\text{decreasing}\end{smallmatrix}$ at $P(x_1, y_1)$ if its derivative $f'(x_1)$, the slope at P, is $\begin{smallmatrix}\text{positive}\\\text{negative}\end{smallmatrix}$. To find intervals over which $f(x)$ $\begin{smallmatrix}\text{increases}\\\text{decreases}\end{smallmatrix}$, that is, over which the curve $\begin{smallmatrix}\text{rises}\\\text{falls}\end{smallmatrix}$, compute $f'(x)$ and determine where it is $\begin{smallmatrix}\text{positive}\\\text{negative}\end{smallmatrix}$.

EXAMPLE:

16. If $f(x) = x^4 - 4x^3 + 4x^2$, then $f'(x) = 4x^3 - 12x^2 + 8x$ $= 4x(x^2 - 3x + 2) = 4x(x - 1)(x - 2)$. Since this derivative changes sign only at $x = 0, 1,$ or 2, it has a constant sign in each of the intervals between these numbers. Thus

$$\begin{array}{ll} \text{if} \quad x < 0 & \text{then} \quad f'(x) < 0 \\ 0 < x < 1 & f'(x) > 0 \\ 1 < x < 2 & f'(x) < 0 \\ 2 < x & f'(x) > 0. \end{array}$$

G. **Maximum, Minimum, and Inflection Points.**

DEFINITIONS:

The curve of $y = f(x)$ has a *relative* $\begin{smallmatrix}maximum\\minimum\end{smallmatrix}$ at a point where $x = c$ if $\begin{smallmatrix}f(c) \geq f(x)\\f(c) \leq f(x)\end{smallmatrix}$ for all x in the immediate neighborhood of c.

If a curve has a relative $\begin{smallmatrix}\text{maximum}\\\text{minimum}\end{smallmatrix}$ at $x = c$ then the curve changes from $\begin{smallmatrix}\text{rising to falling}\\\text{falling to rising}\end{smallmatrix}$ as x increases through c. If a function is differentiable on the closed interval $[a,b]$ and has a relative maximum or minimum at $x = c$ $(a < c < b)$, then $f'(c) = 0$. The converse of this statement is not true.

The *absolute* $\frac{maximum}{minimum}$ of a function on $[a,b]$ occurs at $x = c$

if $\begin{array}{l} f(c) \geqq f(x) \\ f(c) \leqq f(x) \end{array}$ for all x on $[a,b]$.

A curve is said to be *concave* $\frac{upward}{downward}$ at a point $P(x_1,y_1)$ if

the curve lies $\frac{above}{below}$ its tangent. If $\begin{array}{l} y'' > 0 \\ y'' < 0 \end{array}$ at P, the curve is

concave $\frac{up}{down}$. In Figure N3-6, the curves sketched in (a) and (b) are

concave downward at P while in (c) and (d) they are concave upward at P.

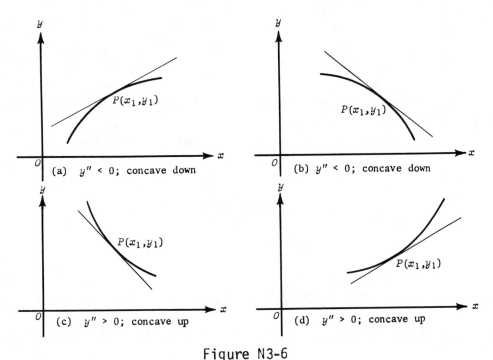

Figure N3-6

A *point of inflection* is a point where the curve changes its
concavity from upward to downward or from downward to upward.

PROCEDURE FOR CURVE-SKETCHING:

The following procedure is suggested when seeking to determine any
maximum, minimum, or inflection points of a curve and to sketch the curve.

(1) Find y' and y''.

(2) Find all x for which $y' = 0$; at each point corresponding to
these abscissas the tangent to the curve is horizontal.

(3) Let c be a number for which y' is 0; investigate the sign of y'' at c. If $y''(c) > 0$, the curve is concave up and c yields a relative minimum; if $y''(c) < 0$ the curve is concave down and c yields a relative maximum. See Figure N3-7. If $y''(c) = 0$, the second-derivative test fails and we must use the test in step (4) below.

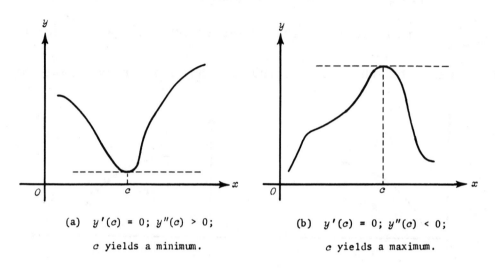

(a) $y'(c) = 0$; $y''(c) > 0$;

c yields a minimum.

(b) $y'(c) = 0$; $y''(c) < 0$;

c yields a maximum.

Figure N3-7

(4) If $y'(c) = 0$ and $y''(c) = 0$, investigate the signs of y' as x increases through c. If $y'(x) > 0$ for x's (just) less than c but $y'(x) < 0$ for x's (just) greater than c then the situation is that indicated in Figure N3-8a, where the tangent lines have been sketched as x increases through c; here c yields a relative maximum. If the situation is reversed and the sign of y' changes from - to + as x increases through c then it yields a relative minimum. Figure N3-8b shows this case. The schematic sign patterns of y', + 0 - or - 0 +, describe each situation completely. If y' does not change sign as x increases through c, then c yields neither a relative maximum nor a relative minimum. Two examples of this appear in Figures N3-8c and N3-8d.

(a)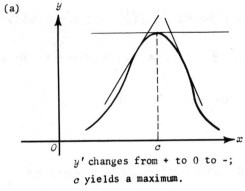

y' changes from + to 0 to -;
c yields a maximum.

(b)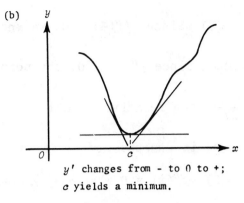

y' changes from - to 0 to +;
c yields a minimum.

(c)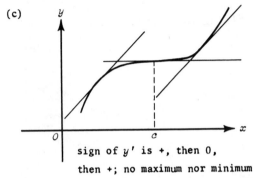

sign of y' is +, then 0,
then +; no maximum nor minimum

(d)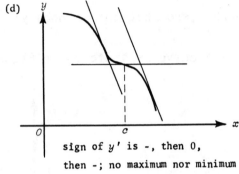

sign of y' is -, then 0,
then -; no maximum nor minimum

Figure N3-8

(5) Find all x for which $y'' = 0$; these are abscissas of possible points of inflection. If c is such an x and the sign of y'' changes (from + to - or from - to +) as x increases through c, then c is the x-coordinate of a point of inflection. If the signs do not change then c does *not* yield a point of inflection.

The crucial points found as indicated in (1) through (5) above should be plotted along with the intercepts. Care should be exercised to insure that the tangent to the curve is horizontal whenever $\frac{dy}{dx} = 0$ and that the curve has the proper concavity.

EXAMPLES:

17. Find any maximum, minimum, or inflection points of $f(x) = x^3 - 5x^2 + 3x + 6$ and sketch the curve.

Steps: (1) Here $f'(x) = 3x^2 - 10x + 3$ and $f''(x) = 6x - 10$.

(2) $f'(x) = (3x - 1)(x - 3)$, which is zero when $x = \frac{1}{3}$ or 3.

(3)   Since $f''(\frac{1}{3}) < 0$, we know that the point $(\frac{1}{3}, f(\frac{1}{3}))$ is a relative maximum; since $f''(3) > 0$, the point $(3, f(3))$ is a relative minimum. Thus, $(\frac{1}{3}, \frac{175}{27})$ is a relative maximum and $(3, -3)$ a relative minimum.

(4) is unnecessary for this problem.

(5) $f''(x) = 0$ when $x = \frac{5}{3}$, and f'' does change sign as x increases through $\frac{5}{3}$, so that this x does yield an inflection point.

The curve is sketched in Figure N3-9.

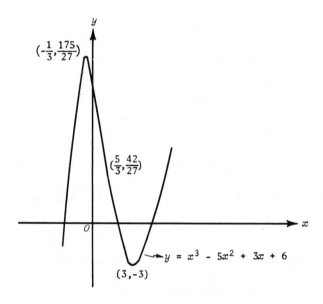

Figure N3-9

18.   If we apply the procedure to $f(x) = x^4 - 4x^3$ we see that

(1) $f'(x) = 4x^3 - 12x^2$ and $f''(x) = 12x^2 - 24x$.

(2) $f'(x) = 4x^2(x - 3)$, which is zero when $x = 0$ or $x = 3$.

(3)   Since $f''(x) = 12x(x - 2)$ and $f''(3) > 0$, the point $(3, -27)$ is a relative minimum. Since $f''(0) = 0$, the second-derivative test fails to tell us whether 0 yields a maximum or minimum.

(4)   Since $f'(x)$ does not change sign as x increases through 0, 0 yields neither a maximum nor a minimum.

(5) $f'' = 0$ when x is 0 or 2. It changes sign (+ 0 -) as x increases through 0, and also (- 0 +) as x increases through 2. Thus both (0,0) and (2,-16) are inflection points.

The curve is sketched in Figure N3-10.

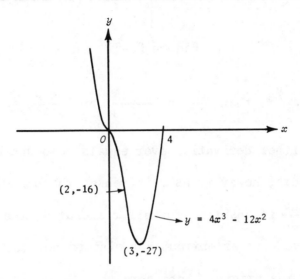

Figure N3-10

ADDITIONAL NOTE ON PROCEDURE: If there are values of x for which $\frac{dy}{dx}$ or $\frac{d^2y}{dx^2}$ does not exist, we can consider these values separately, recalling that a relative maximum or minimum point is one of transition between intervals of rise and fall and that an inflection point is one of transition between intervals of upward and downward concavity.

EXAMPLES:

19. If $y = x^{2/3}$ then $\frac{dy}{dx} = \frac{2}{3x^{1/3}}$ and $\frac{d^2y}{dx^2} = -\frac{2}{9x^{4/3}}$.

Neither derivative is zero anywhere; both derivatives fail to exist when $x = 0$. As x increases through 0, $\frac{dy}{dx}$ changes from - to +; (0,0) is therefore a minimum. Note that the tangent is vertical at the origin, and that since $\frac{d^2y}{dx^2}$ is negative everywhere except at 0, the curve is everywhere concave down. See Figure N3-11.

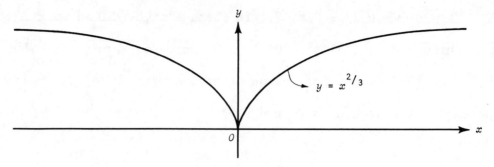

Figure N3-11

20. If $y = x^{1/3}$ then $\dfrac{dy}{dx} = \dfrac{1}{3x^{2/3}}$ and $\dfrac{d^2y}{dx^2} = -\dfrac{2}{9x^{5/3}}$.

As in Example 19, neither derivative ever equals zero and both fail to exist when $x = 0$. Here, however, as x increases through 0, $\dfrac{dy}{dx}$ does not change sign. Since $\dfrac{dy}{dx}$ is positive for all x except 0, the curve rises for all x and can have neither maximum nor minimum points. The tangent is again vertical at the origin. Note here that $\dfrac{d^2y}{dx^2}$ does change sign (from + to -) as x increases through 0, so that (0,0) is a point of inflection. See Figure N3-12.

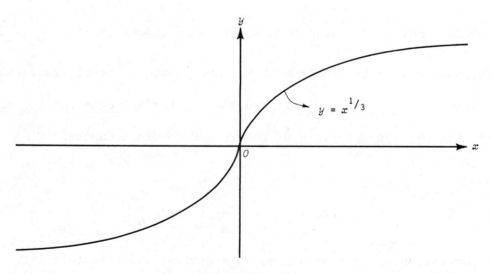

Figure N3-12

H. Problems Involving Maxima and Minima. The techniques described in G can be applied to problems in which a function is to be maximized (or minimized). Often it helps to draw a figure. If y, the quantity to be maximized (or minimized), can be expressed explicitly in terms of x, then the procedure outlined in G can be used. If the domain of y is restricted to some closed interval one should always check the endpoints of this interval so as not to overlook possible extrema. Often, implicit differentiation, sometimes of two or more equations, is indicated.

EXAMPLES:

21. The region in the first quadrant bounded by the curves of $y^2 = x$ and $y = x$ is rotated about the y-axis to form a solid. Find the area of the largest cross-section of this solid which is perpendicular to the y-axis.

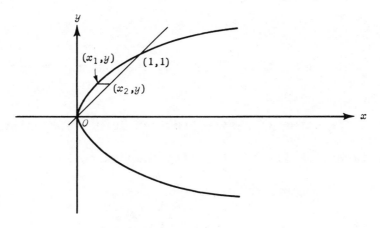

Figure N3-13

See Figure N3-13. The curves intersect at the origin and at $(1,1)$, so $0 < y < 1$. A cross-section of the solid is a ring whose area A is the difference between the areas of two circles, one with radius x_2, the other with radius x_1. Thus $A = \pi x_2{}^2 - \pi x_1{}^2 = \pi(y^2 - y^4)$; $\frac{dA}{dy} = \pi(2y - 4y^3)$ $= 2\pi y(1 - 2y^2)$. The only relevant zero of the first derivative is $y = \frac{1}{\sqrt{2}}$. The maximum area A is thus $\pi(\frac{1}{2} - \frac{1}{4}) = \frac{\pi}{4}$.

Note that $\frac{d^2A}{dy^2} = \pi(2 - 12y^2)$ and that this is negative when $y = \frac{1}{\sqrt{2}}$, assuring a maximum there. Note further that A equals zero at each endpoint of the interval $[0,1]$ so that $\frac{\pi}{4}$ is the absolute maximum area.

22. The volume of a cylinder equals k in^3, where k is a constant.

Find the proportions of the cylinder that minimize the total surface area.

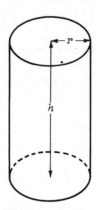

Figure N3-14

See Figure N3-14. We know that the volume is

$$V = \pi r^2 h = k, \tag{1}$$

where r is the radius and h the height. We seek to minimize S, the total

surface area, where

$$S = 2\pi r^2 + 2\pi rh = 2\pi (r^2 + rh). \tag{2}$$

We can differentiate both (1) and (2) with respect to r, getting, from (1),

$$\pi (r^2 \cdot \frac{dh}{dr} + 2rh) = 0, \tag{3}$$

where we use the fact that $\frac{dk}{dr} = 0$, and, from (2),

$$2\pi (2r + r \cdot \frac{dh}{dr} + h) = 0 \tag{4}$$

where $\frac{dS}{dr}$ is set equal to zero because S is to be a minimum.

From (3) we see that $\frac{dh}{dr} = -\frac{2h}{r}$, and if we use this in (4) we get

$2r + r(\frac{-2h}{r}) + h = 0$, or $h = 2r$. The total surface area of a cylinder

of fixed volume is thus a minimum when its height equals its diameter.

(Note that we need not concern ourselves with the possibility that

the value of r which renders $\frac{dS}{dr}$ equal to zero will produce a maximum

surface area rather than a minimum one. With k fixed, we can choose

r and h in such a way as to make S as large as we like.)

I. **Mean Value Theorem.** If the function $f(x)$ is continuous at each point on the closed interval $a \leq x \leq b$ and has a derivative at each point on the open interval $a < x < b$, then there is a number c, $a < c < b$, such that $\frac{f(b) - f(a)}{b - a} = f'(c)$. This important theorem is illustrated in Figure N3-15. For the function sketched in the Figure there are two numbers, c_1 and c_2, between a and b where the slope of the curve equals the slope of the chord PQ (i.e., where the tangent to the curve is parallel to the chord).

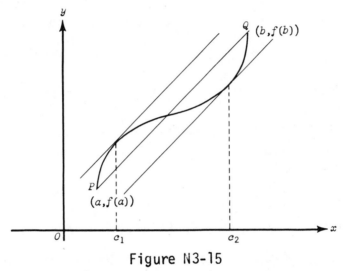

Figure N3-15

A special case of this theorem is that embodied in *Rolle's Theorem*. If in addition to the hypotheses of the Mean Value Theorem it is given that $f(a) = f(b) = 0$, then there is a number c between a and b such that $f'(c) = 0$. See Figure N3-16.

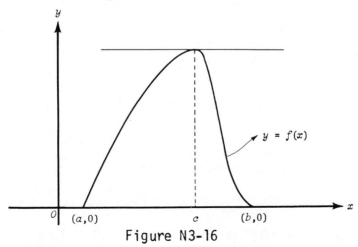

Figure N3-16

The Mean Value Theorem is one of the most useful laws when properly applied.

EXAMPLE:

23. If $x > 0$, prove that $\sin x < x$.

Note that $\sin x \leqq 1$ for all x and consider the following cases if $x > 0$:

(1) $x > 1$. Here $\sin x < x$.

(2) $0 < x < 1$. Since $\sin x$ is continuous on $[0,1]$ and since its derivative $\cos x$ exists at all x and therefore on the open interval $(0,1)$, the Mean Value Theorem can be applied to the function, with $a = 0$ and $b = x$. Thus there is a number c, $0 < c < x < 1$, such that $\dfrac{\sin x - \sin 0}{x - 0} = \cos c$. Since $\cos c < 1$ if $0 < x < 1$, therefore $\dfrac{\sin x}{x} < 1$, and since $x > 0$ therefore $\sin x < x$.

J. Motion Along a Line. If a particle moves along a line according to the law $s = f(t)$, where s represents the position of the particle P on the line at time t, then the *velocity* v of P at time t is given by $\dfrac{ds}{dt}$ and its *acceleration* a by $\dfrac{dv}{dt}$ or by $\dfrac{d^2s}{dt^2}$. The *speed* of the particle is $|v|$, the magnitude of v. If the line of motion is directed positively to the right then the motion of the particle P is subject to the following: At any instant,

(1) if $v > 0$ then P is moving to the right and its distance s is increasing; if $v < 0$ then P is moving to the left and its distance s is decreasing;

(2) if $a > 0$ then v is increasing; if $a < 0$ then v is decreasing;

(3) if a and v are both positive or both negative then (1) and (2) imply that the speed of P is increasing or that P is accelerating;

if a and v have opposite signs then the speed of P is decreasing or P is decelerating;

(4) if s is a continuous function of t, then P reverses direction whenever v is zero but a is different from zero; note that zero velocity does *not* imply a reversal in direction.

EXAMPLES:

24. A particle moves along a line according to the law $s = 2t^3 - 9t^2 + 12t - 4$, where $t \geqq 0$.

(a) Find all t for which the distance s is increasing.

(b) Find all t for which the velocity is increasing.

(c) Find all t for which the speed of the particle is increasing.

(d) Find the speed when $t = \frac{3}{2}$.

(e) Find the total distance travelled between $t = 0$ and $t = 4$.

We have $v = \dfrac{ds}{dt} = 6t^2 - 18t + 12 = 6(t^2 - 3t + 2) = 6(t - 2)(t - 1)$,

and $a = \dfrac{dv}{dt} = \dfrac{d^2s}{dt^2} = 12t - 18 = 12(t - \frac{3}{2})$.

The sign of v behaves as follows:

$$\begin{array}{lll} \text{if} & t < 1 & \text{then } v > 0 \\ & 1 < t < 2 & v < 0 \\ & 2 < t & v > 0. \end{array}$$

For a, we have:

$$\begin{array}{lll} \text{if} & t < \frac{3}{2} & \text{then } a < 0 \\ & \frac{3}{2} < t & a > 0. \end{array}$$

These immediately yield the answers, as follows:

(a) s increases when $t < 1$ or $t > 2$.

(b) v increases when $t > \frac{3}{2}$.

(c) The speed $|v|$ is increasing when v and a are both > 0, i.e., for $t > 2$, and when v and a are both < 0, i.e. for $1 < t < \frac{3}{2}$.

(d)   The speed when $t = \frac{3}{2}$ equals $|v| = |-\frac{3}{2}| = \frac{3}{2}$.

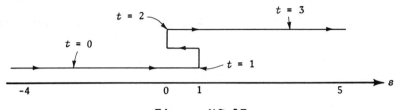

Figure N3-17

(e) P's motion can be indicated as shown in Figure N3-17. P moves to the right if $t < 1$, reverses its direction at $t = 1$, moves to the left when $1 < t < 2$, reverses again at $t = 2$, and continues to the right for all $t > 2$. The position of P at certain times t is shown in the following table:

t:	0	1	2	4
s:	-4	1	0	28.

Thus P travels a total of 34 units between times $t = 0$ and $t = 4$.

25. Answer the questions of Example 24 if the law of motion is
$$s = t^4 - 4t^3.$$

Since $v = 4t^3 - 12t^2 = 4t^2(t - 3)$ and $a = 12t^2 - 24t = 12t(t - 2)$, the signs of v and a are

if	$t < 3$	then	$v < 0$
	$3 < t$		$v > 0$;
if	$t < 0$	then	$a > 0$
	$0 < t < 2$		$a < 0$
	$2 < t$		$a > 0.$

Thus:

(a) s increases if $t > 3$.

(b) v increases if $t < 0$ or $t > 2$.

(c) Since v and a have the same sign if $0 < t < 2$ or if $t > 3$, the speed increases on these intervals.

(d) The speed when $t = \frac{3}{2}$ equals $|v| = |-\frac{27}{2}| = \frac{27}{2}$.

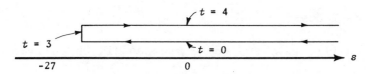

Figure N3-18

(e) The motion is shown in Figure N3-18. The particle moves to the left if $t < 3$ and to the right if $t > 3$, stopping instantaneously when $t = 0$ and $t = 3$, but reversing direction only when $t = 3$. Thus:

$$t: \quad 0 \quad\ \ 3 \quad\ \ 4$$
$$s: \quad 0 \ \ -27 \quad 0.$$

The particle travels a total of 54 units between $t = 0$ and $t = 4$.

(Compare example 18 above, where the function $f(x) = x^4 - 4x^3$ is investigated for maximum and minimum values, and also see Figure N3-10, where the curve is sketched.)

K. Motion Along a Curve.

Derivative of Arc Length. If the derivative of $y = f(x)$ is continuous, if Q is a fixed point on its curve and P any other point on it, and if s is the arc length from Q to P (see Figure N3-19), then the derivative of s is given by

$$\frac{ds}{dx} = \sqrt{1 + \left(\frac{dy}{dx}\right)^2} \tag{1}$$

or

$$\frac{ds}{dy} = \sqrt{1 + \left(\frac{dx}{dy}\right)^2} \tag{2}$$

where it is assumed that s is increasing with x in (1), with y in (2).

If the position of P is given parametrically by $x = f(t)$ and $y = g(t)$ then

$$\frac{ds}{dt} = \sqrt{\left(\frac{dx}{dt}\right)^2 + \left(\frac{dy}{dt}\right)^2} \qquad (3)$$

where s increases as t does.

The formulas in (1), (2), and (3) above can all be derived easily from the very simple formula

$$ds^2 = dx^2 + dy^2. \qquad (4)$$

If, for instance, x is expressed in terms of y, making it convenient to use formula (2), note that it follows from (4) that

$$\frac{ds^2}{dy^2} = \frac{dx^2}{dy^2} + 1,$$

$$\left(\frac{ds}{dy}\right)^2 = \left(\frac{dx}{dy}\right)^2 + 1,$$

and

$$\frac{ds}{dy} = \sqrt{1 + \left(\frac{dx}{dy}\right)^2},$$

which is (2).

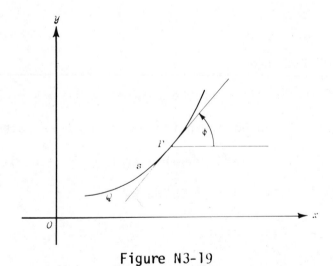

Figure N3-19

Curvature. If ϕ is the angle of inclination from the x-axis of the tangent line at point $P(x,y)$ on a curve, the *curvature* K at P

is defined as the rate of change of ϕ with respect to arc length s (see Figure N3-19). Thus,

$$K = \frac{d\phi}{ds},$$

where K is measured in radians per unit of arc length and is positive if ϕ increases as s does. The formulas for curvature are

$$K = \frac{\pm \frac{d^2y}{dx^2}}{\left[1 + \left(\frac{dy}{dx}\right)^2\right]^{3/2}}, \tag{5}$$

$$K = \frac{\pm \frac{d^2x}{dy^2}}{\left[1 + \left(\frac{dx}{dy}\right)^2\right]^{3/2}}, \tag{6}$$

or, if x and y are given parametrically in terms of t, then

$$K = \pm \frac{\frac{dx}{dt} \cdot \frac{d^2y}{dt^2} - \frac{dy}{dt} \cdot \frac{d^2x}{dt^2}}{\left[\left(\frac{dx}{dt}\right)^2 + \left(\frac{dy}{dt}\right)^2\right]^{3/2}} = \pm \frac{\dot{x}\ddot{y} - \dot{y}\ddot{x}}{(\dot{x}^2 + \dot{y}^2)^{3/2}}. \tag{7}$$

EXAMPLES:

26. Prove that the curvature of a circle is numerically equal to the reciprocal of the radius.

Let $x^2 + y^2 = a^2$ be the equation of the circle. Then differentiating twice yields $2x + 2y \cdot \frac{dy}{dx} = 0$, so that $\frac{dy}{dx} = -\frac{x}{y}$, and $\frac{d^2y}{dx^2} =$

$$-\frac{y(1) - x\left(-\frac{x}{y}\right)}{y^2} = -\frac{y^2 + x^2}{y^3} = -\frac{a^2}{y^3}.$$

If we use formula (5) for K then

$$K = \frac{\pm \frac{-a^2}{y^3}}{\left(1 + \frac{x^2}{y^2}\right)^{3/2}} = \frac{\pm a^2}{y^3 \left(\frac{y^2 + x^2}{y^2}\right)^{3/2}}$$

$$= \pm \frac{a^2}{y^3 \frac{a^3}{y^3}} = \pm \frac{1}{a}.$$

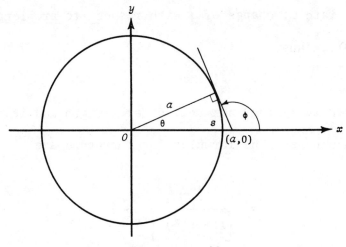

Figure N3-20

This result is obtainable almost immediately by using the definition

of curvature, $K = \frac{d\phi}{ds}$. See Figure N3-20. Since $s = a\theta$, $ds = a\,d\theta$; since

$\phi = \frac{\pi}{2} + \theta$, $d\phi = d\theta$. Thus $\frac{d\phi}{ds} = \frac{d\theta}{a\,d\theta} = \frac{1}{a}$.

27. For what t does the curve given parametrically by $x = t$,
$y = \ln t$ $(t > 0)$ have maximum curvature?

We can use formula (7) for curvature here. Note that

$$\dot{x} = 1 \qquad \ddot{x} = 0 \qquad \dot{y} = \frac{1}{t} \qquad \ddot{y} = -\frac{1}{t^2},$$

so

$$K = \pm \frac{-\frac{1}{t^2}}{\left(1 + \frac{1}{t^2}\right)^{3/2}} = -\frac{t}{(1 + t^2)^{3/2}}.$$

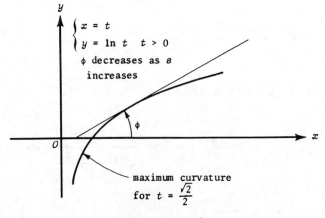

Figure N3-21

Here ϕ decreases as s increases (see Figure N3-21) so that K is negative.

$\dfrac{dK}{dt} = \dfrac{2t^2 - 1}{(1 + t^2)^{5/2}}$, and this derivative is zero when $t = \dfrac{1}{\sqrt{2}}$. The greatest

numerical curvature occurs for this t.

Circle and Radius of Curvature. The *circle of curvature* of a curve

at a point P is the circle tangent to the curve at P lying on the concave

side of the curve and whose radius is $\dfrac{1}{|K|}$, where K is the curvature at

P and is different from zero. The radius of this circle is called the

radius of curvature.

Velocity and Acceleration. If a point P moves along a curve in

accordance with the pair of parametric equations $x = f(t)$, $y = g(t)$,

where t represents time, then the vector from the origin to P is

called the *position vector*.

Vectors are symbolized either by boldface letters (thus: R, i, j)

or by italic letters with an arrow written over them (thus: $\vec{R}$, $\vec{i}$, $\vec{j}$).

When writing on a blackboard or with pencil and paper the arrow notation

is simpler, but in print the boldface notation is clearer, and will be

used here.

The position vector is denoted by R, and

$$R = x\mathbf{i} + y\mathbf{j},$$

where i is the (unit) vector from $(0,0)$ to $(1,0)$ and j is the (unit)

vector from $(0,0)$ to $(0,1)$, and x and y are respectively the horizontal

and vertical components of R.

The *velocity vector* is

$$\mathbf{v} = \frac{d\mathbf{R}}{dt} = \frac{dx}{dt}\mathbf{i} + \frac{dy}{dt}\mathbf{j}.$$

Alternative notations for $\dfrac{dx}{dt}$ and $\dfrac{dy}{dt}$ are respectively v_x and v_y or

$\dot{x}$ and $\dot{y}$; these are the components of v in the horizontal and vertical directions respectively. The slope of v is

$$\frac{\frac{dy}{dt}}{\frac{dx}{dt}} \; = \; \frac{dy}{dx},$$

which is the slope of the curve; the magnitude of v, denoted by $|v|$, is

$$\sqrt{\left(\frac{dx}{dt}\right)^2 + \left(\frac{dy}{dt}\right)^2} \; = \; \sqrt{v_x^{\,2} + v_y^{\,2}}$$

which equals $\frac{ds}{dt}$, the derivative of arc length. Thus, if the vector v is drawn initiating at P it will be tangent to the curve at P and its magnitude will be the speed of the particle at P.

The *acceleration vector* a is $\frac{dv}{dt}$ or $\frac{d^2R}{dt^2}$, and can be obtained by a second differentiation of the components of R. Thus

$$a \; = \; \frac{d^2x}{dt^2}i + \frac{d^2y}{dt^2}j;$$

the direction of a is

$$\tan^{-1} \frac{\frac{d^2y}{dt^2}}{\frac{d^2x}{dt^2}} \; ;$$

and its magnitude is

$$|a| \; = \; \sqrt{\left(\frac{d^2x}{dt^2}\right)^2 + \left(\frac{d^2y}{dt^2}\right)^2} \; = \; \sqrt{a_x^{\,2} + a_y^{\,2}}.$$

For both v and a the quadrant is determined by the signs of their components. i and j are shown in Figure N3-22a; R, v, and a, and their

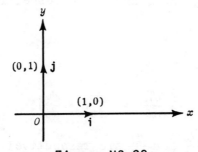

Figure N3-22a

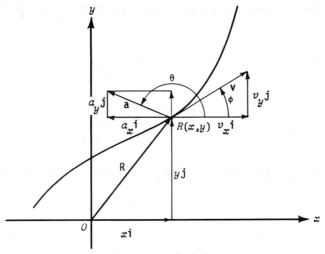

Figure N3-22b

components, are shown in Figure N3-22b. Note that v_x and v_y happen to be positive, so that ϕ is a first-quadrant angle, while $a_x < 0$ and $a_y > 0$ imply that θ is in the second quadrant.

EXAMPLES:

28. A point moves according to the equations $x = 3 \cos t$, $y = 2 \sin t$.

(a) Find a single equation in x and y for the path of the particle and sketch the curve.

(b) Find the velocity and acceleration vectors at any time t and show that $a = -R$ at all times.

(c) Find R, v, and a when (1) $t_1 = \frac{\pi}{6}$, (2) $t_2 = \pi$, and draw them on the sketch.

(d) Find the speed of the particle and the magnitude of its acceleration at each instant in (c).

(e) When is the speed a maximum? a minimum?

Solution:

(a) Since $\frac{x^2}{9} = \cos^2 t$ and $\frac{y^2}{4} = \sin^2 t$, therefore $\frac{x^2}{9} + \frac{y^2}{4} = 1$

and the particle moves in a counterclockwise direction along an ellipse, starting, when $t = 0$, at $(3,0)$ and returning to this point when $t = 2\pi$.

(b) We have

$$R = 3 \cos t \, i + 2 \sin t \, j,$$

$$v = -3 \sin t \, i + 2 \cos t \, j,$$

$$a = -3 \cos t \, i - 2 \sin t \, j = -R.$$

The acceleration, then, is always directed toward the center of the ellipse.

(c) At $t_1 = \dfrac{\pi}{6}$,

$$R_1 = \frac{3\sqrt{3}}{2} \, i + j,$$

$$v_1 = -\frac{3}{2} \, i + \sqrt{3} \, j,$$

$$a_1 = -\frac{3\sqrt{3}}{2} \, i - j.$$

At $t_2 = \pi$,

$$R_2 = -3 \, i,$$

$$v_2 = -2 \, j,$$

$$a_2 = 3 \, i.$$

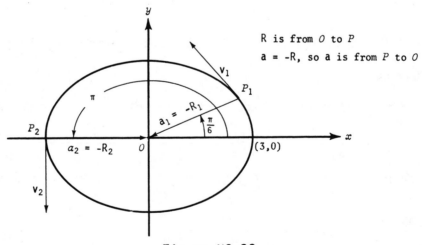

R is from O to P
a = -R, so a is from P to O

Figure N3-23

The curve, and v and a at those instants, are sketched in Figure N3-23.

(d) $t_1 = \dfrac{\pi}{6}$, $t_2 = \pi$,

$$|v_1| = \sqrt{\frac{9}{4} + 3} = \frac{\sqrt{21}}{2}, \qquad |v_2| = \sqrt{0 + 4} = 2,$$

$$|a_1| = \sqrt{\frac{27}{4} + 1} = \frac{\sqrt{31}}{2}; \qquad |a_2| = \sqrt{9 + 0} = 3.$$

(e)   The speed $|v|$ at any time equals $\sqrt{9 \sin^2 t + 4 \cos^2 t}$

$= \sqrt{4 \sin^2 t + 4 \cos^2 t + 5 \sin^2 t} = \sqrt{4 + 5 \sin^2 t}$. We see immediately

that the speed is a maximum when $t = \dfrac{\pi}{2}$ or $\dfrac{3\pi}{2}$ and a minimum when

$t = 0$ or π. The particle goes fastest at the ends of the minor

axis and most slowly at the ends of the major axis. Generally one

can determine maximum or minimum speed by finding $\dfrac{d}{dt}|v|$, setting it

equal to zero, and applying the usual tests to sort out values of t

that yield maximum or minimum speeds.

29.   A particle moves along the parabola $y = x^2 - x$ with

constant speed $\sqrt{10}$. Find v at $(2,2)$.

Since

$$v_y = \frac{dy}{dt} = (2x - 1)\frac{dx}{dt} = (2x - 1)v_x \qquad (1)$$

and

$$v_x^2 + v_y^2 = 10 \qquad (2)$$

we have

$$v_x^2 + (2x - 1)^2 v_x^2 = 10. \qquad (3)$$

Relation (3) holds at all times; specifically, at $(2,2)$, we get

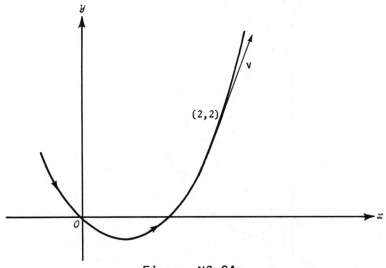

Figure N3-24a

$v_x{}^2 + 9v_x{}^2 = 10$ so that $v_x = \pm 1$. From (1), then, we see that $v_y = \pm 3$. Therefore $\mathbf{v}$ at (2,2) is either $\mathbf{i} + 3\mathbf{j}$ or $-\mathbf{i} - 3\mathbf{j}$. The former corresponds to counterclockwise motion along the parabola, as shown in Figure N3-24a, the latter to clockwise motion, indicated in Figure N3-24b.

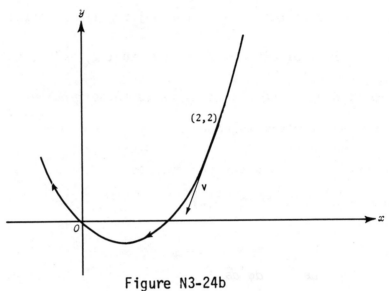

Figure N3-24b

Unit Tangent and Normal Vectors. The *unit vector, tangent* to the curve at P, is

$$\mathbf{T} = \frac{d\mathbf{R}}{ds} = \frac{dx}{ds}\mathbf{i} + \frac{dy}{ds}\mathbf{j}. \qquad (8)$$

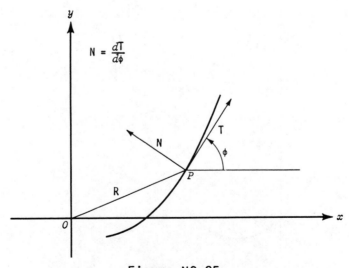

Figure N3-25

If ϕ is the angle of inclination from the x-axis to T (see Figure N3-25) then we see that

$$T = \cos \phi \; i + \sin \phi \; j \qquad (9)$$

and

$$\frac{dT}{d\phi} = -\sin \phi \; i + \cos \phi \; j. \qquad (10)$$

This derivative of T is also a unit vector, since $\left|\frac{dT}{d\phi}\right| =$ $\sqrt{\sin^2 \phi + \cos^2 \phi} = 1$. Furthermore, since the slope of $\frac{dT}{d\phi}$ is the negative reciprocal of that of T, T and $\frac{dT}{d\phi}$ are *perpendicular* unit vectors. If we replace ϕ in (9) by $\phi + 90°$, we get the right-hand member of (10). That is, $\frac{dT}{d\phi}$ is the unit vector obtained by rotating T counterclockwise through 90°. $\frac{dT}{d\phi}$ is, thus, the *unit normal vector*, and is denoted by N.

Note that

$$\frac{dT}{ds} = \frac{dT}{d\phi} \cdot \frac{d\phi}{ds} = N \cdot K \qquad (11)$$

where K is the curvature, defined earlier (p.48). The direction of $N \cdot K$ is always toward the concave side of the curve.

Tangent and Normal Components of Acceleration. Since

$$v = \frac{dR}{dt} = \frac{dR}{ds} \cdot \frac{ds}{dt} = T \cdot \frac{ds}{dt} \qquad (12)$$

we can obtain a, which is $\frac{dv}{dt}$, by differentiating the rightmost term in (12) with respect to t. So

$$a = T \cdot \frac{d^2s}{dt^2} + \frac{ds}{dt} \cdot \frac{dT}{dt}$$

$$= T \cdot \frac{d^2s}{dt^2} + \frac{ds}{dt} \cdot \frac{dT}{ds} \cdot \frac{ds}{dt}$$

$$= T \cdot \frac{d^2s}{dt^2} + \frac{dT}{ds} \cdot \left(\frac{ds}{dt}\right)^2,$$

where we can use (11) to get

$$a = T \cdot \frac{d^2s}{dt^2} + N \cdot K \cdot \left(\frac{ds}{dt}\right)^2. \qquad (13)$$

Equation (13) resolves the acceleration into components in the direction of the tangent and in that of the normal. These are often denoted respectively by a_T and a_N. We see from (13) that the *tangential component* $a_T = \frac{d^2s}{dt^2}$; this is the rate of change of the speed of the particle (and plays the same part in motion along a curve that acceleration does in motion along a line); and that the *normal component* $a_N = K \cdot \left(\frac{ds}{dt}\right)^2$ $= K \cdot |v|^2$; this measures the change in the direction of the velocity vector. (Recall that $N = \frac{dT}{d\phi}$, where ϕ is the angle of inclination of T, and that the directions of T and v are the same if $\frac{ds}{dt} > 0$.)

Since $a_x^2 + a_y^2 = |a|^2 = a_T^2 + a_N^2$, we can often find a_N by using

$$a_N = \sqrt{|a|^2 - a_T^2}. \tag{14}$$

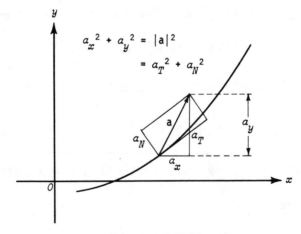

Figure N3-26

See Figure N3-26.

EXAMPLES:

30. A point's motion in a plane is given by $x = 3t - 3$, $y = t^2 + 1$. Find v, a, the speed, a_T, and a_N at any time; determine where on the curve the speed is a maximum or a minimum.

We have

$$R = (3t - 3)\, i + (t^2 + 1)\, j\, ;$$

$$v = 3\, i + 2t\, j\, ;$$

$$a = 2\, j\, .$$

Thus the speed $|v| = \sqrt{9 + 4t^2}$, which is clearly a minimum when $t = 0$; the speed increases with t so there is no maximum.

$$a_T = \frac{d^2 s}{dt^2} = \frac{d}{dt}|v| = \frac{4t}{\sqrt{9 + 4t^2}}. \quad \text{Since} \quad |a|^2 = 4 = a_T^2 + a_N^2,$$

from (14) we have $\quad 4 = \dfrac{16t^2}{9 + 4t^2} + a_N^2$, so that

$$a_N = \sqrt{\frac{36}{9 + 4t^2}} = \frac{6}{\sqrt{9 + 4t^2}}.$$

Note that $a_N \to 0$ as $|t| \to \infty$.

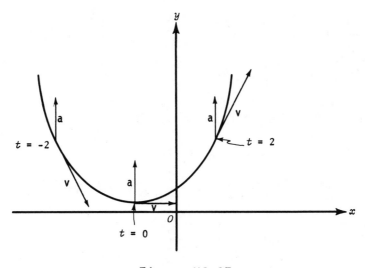

Figure N3-27

The point moves counterclockwise on the parabola $(x + 3)^2 = 9(y - 1)$. (This equation is obtained by eliminating t from the given pair of equations.) See Figure N3-27. The acceleration, in this example, is constant both in magnitude and in direction. The minimum speed occurs at the vertex, where all of the acceleration acts to change the direction of the particle and none of it to change the speed. As the point moves away from the vertex (that is, when t is large) more of the acceleration acts to change the speed and less to change the direction. $\mathbf{v}$ and $\mathbf{a}$ are shown in the figure at three different times, t = -2, 0, 2, to display the motion.

31.   If $x = e^t \cos t$ and $y = e^t \sin t$, (a) find $\mathbf{v}$ and $\mathbf{a}$ when $t = 0$, and (b) find a_T and a_N at any time.

(a)   We have

$$\mathbf{R} = e^t \cos t \, \mathbf{i} + e^t \sin t \, \mathbf{j};$$
$$\mathbf{v} = e^t(\cos t - \sin t) \, \mathbf{i} + e^t(\sin t + \cos t) \, \mathbf{j};$$
$$\mathbf{a} = -2e^t \sin t \, \mathbf{i} + 2e^t \cos t \, \mathbf{j}.$$

When $t = 0$, $\mathbf{R} = \mathbf{i}$, $\mathbf{v} = \mathbf{i} + \mathbf{j}$, $\mathbf{a} = 2\mathbf{j}$.

(b)   At any time, $|\mathbf{a}|^2 = 4e^{2t} \sin^2 t + 4e^{2t} \cos^2 t = 4e^{2t}$.

Since the speed $\frac{ds}{dt} = |\mathbf{v}| = \sqrt{2}e^t$, $a_T = \frac{d^2s}{dt^2} = \sqrt{2}e^t$, and, from

(14), $a_N = \sqrt{4e^{2t} - 2e^{2t}} = \sqrt{2}e^t$.

32.   In Example 29 above, a point moves along the parabola $y = x^2 - x$ with constant speed $\sqrt{10}$.   Find a_T and a_N at $(2,2)$.

Since $|\mathbf{v}| = \frac{ds}{dt} = \sqrt{10}$, $a_T = 0$.   Recall from (13) that $a_N = K(\frac{ds}{dt})^2$,

and use formula (5) for curvature to determine K.   Then, since $\frac{dy}{dx} = 2x - 1$

and $\frac{d^2y}{dx^2} = 2$, K at $(2,2)$ is $\dfrac{2}{(1 + 9)^{3/2}} = \dfrac{2}{10\sqrt{10}}$, and a_N is

$\dfrac{2}{10\sqrt{10}} \, 10 = \dfrac{2}{\sqrt{10}}$, or $\dfrac{\sqrt{10}}{5}$.

Multiple Choice Questions: Applications of Differential Calculus

1. The slope of the curve $y^3 - xy^2 = 4$ at the point where $y = 2$ is

    (A) -2   (B) ¼   (C) -½   (D) ½   (E) 2.

2. The slope of the curve $y^2 - xy - 3x = 1$ at the point $(0,-1)$ is

    (A) -1   (B) -2   (C) +1   (D) 2   (E) -3.

3. The equation of the tangent to the curve $y = x \sin x$ at the

    point $(\frac{\pi}{2}, \frac{\pi}{2})$ is

    (A) $y = x - \pi$ (B) $y = \frac{\pi}{2}$ (C) $y = \pi - x$

    (D) $y = x + \frac{\pi}{2}$ (E) $y = x$.

4. The tangent to the curve of $y = xe^{-x}$ is horizontal when x is equal to

    (A) 0   (B) 1   (C) -1   (D) $\frac{1}{e}$ (E) none of these.

5. The point on the curve $y = \sqrt{2x + 1}$ at which the normal is parallel

    to the line $y = -3x + 6$ is

    (A) $(4,3)$ (B) $(0,1)$ (C) $(1,\sqrt{3})$ (D) $(4,-3)$ (E) $(2,\sqrt{5})$.

6. The minimum value of the slope of the curve $y = x^5 + x^3 - 2x$ is

    (A) 0   (B) 2   (C) 6   (D) -2   (E) none of these.

7. The equation of the tangent to the curve $x^2 = 4ay$ $(a \neq 0)$ at any

    point (x_1, y_1) on the curve is

    (A) $x_1 x + 2ay = 2ay_1 + x^2$ (B) $y - y_1 = 2x_1(x - x_1)$

    (C) $y - y_1 = 2a(x - x_1)$ (D) $2ay - x_1 x = 0$

    (E) $xx_1 - 2ay = 2ay_1$.

8. The equation of the tangent to the hyperbola $x^2 - y^2 = 12$ at the

    point $(4,2)$ on the curve is

    (A) $x - 2y + 6 = 0$ (B) $y = 2x$ (C) $y = 2x - 6$

    (D) $y = \frac{x}{2}$ (E) $x + 2y = 6$.

9. The tangent to the curve $y^2 - xy + 9 = 0$ is vertical when

    (A) $y = 0$ (B) $y = \pm\sqrt{3}$ (C) $y = \frac{1}{2}$

    (D) $y = \pm 3$ (E) none of these.

*10. If differentials are used for computation, then the approximate value

    of $(1.98)^3 - (1.98)^2$ is

    (A) 3.84   (B) 3.92   (C) 4.16   (D) 4.08   (E) 3.94 .

*11. When $x = 3$, the equation $2x^2 - y^3 = 10$ has the solution $y = 2$.

    If differentials are used to compute, then when $x = 3.04$, y equals

    approximately

    (A) 1.6   (B) 1.96   (C) 2.04   (D) 2.14   (E) 2.4 .

*12. If the side e of a square is increased by 1% then the area is increased

    approximately by

    (A) $.02e$ (B) $.02e^2$ (C) $.01e^2$ (D) 1%   (E) $.01e$.

*13. The edge of a cube has length 10 inches with a possible error of 1%.

    The possible error, in cubic inches, in the volume of the cube is

    (A) 3   (B) 1%   (C) 10   (D) 30   (E) none of these.

14. The function $f(x) = x^4 - 4x^2$ has

    (A) one relative minimum and two relative maxima

    (B) one relative minimum and one relative maximum

    (C) two relative maxima and no relative minimum

    (D) two relative minima and no relative maximum

    (E) two relative minima and one relative maximum.

15. The number of inflection points of the curve in Problem 14 is

    (A) 0   (B) 1   (C) 2   (D) 3   (E) 4 .

16. The maximum value of the function $y = -4\sqrt{2 - x}$ is

    (A) 0   (B) -4   (C) 2   (D) -2   (E) none of these.

17. The total number of relative maximum and minimum points of the function whose derivative, for all x, is given by $f'(x) = x(x - 3)^2(x + 1)^4$ is

(A) 0   (B) 1   (C) 2   (D) 3   (E) none of these.

18. If $x \neq 0$, then the slope of $x \sin \frac{1}{x}$ equals zero whenever

(A) $\tan \frac{1}{x} = x$ (B) $\tan \frac{1}{x} = -x$ (C) $\cos \frac{1}{x} = 0$

(D) $\sin \frac{1}{x} = 0$ (E) $\tan \frac{1}{x} = \frac{1}{x}$.

19. On the closed interval $[0, 2\pi]$, the maximum value of the function $f(x) = 4 \sin x - 3 \cos x$ is

(A) 3   (B) 4   (C) $\frac{24}{5}$ (D) 5   (E) none of these.

20. If m_1 is the slope of the curve $xy = 2$ and m_2 is the slope of the curve $x^2 - y^2 = 4$, then at a point of intersection of the two curves

(A) $m_1 = -m_2$ (B) $m_1 m_2 = -1$ (C) $m_1 = m_2$

(D) $m_1 m_2 = 1$ (E) $m_1 m_2 = -2$.

21. The line $y = 3x + k$ is tangent to the curve $y = x^3$ when k is equal to

(A) 1 or -1   (B) 0   (C) 3 or -3

(D) 4 or -4   (E) 2 or -2 .

22. The two tangents that can be drawn from the point $(3,5)$ to the parabola $y = x^2$ have slopes

(A) 1 and 5   (B) 0 and 4   (C) 2 and 10

(D) 2 and -½   (E) 2 and 4.

In Problems 23-26, the motion of a particle on a straight line is given by $s = t^3 - 6t^2 + 12t - 8$.

23. s is increasing for

    (A) $t < 2$ (B) all t except $t = 2$ (C) $1 < t < 3$

    (D) $t < 1$ or $t > 3$ (E) $t > 2$.

24. The minimum value of the speed is

    (A) 1   (B) 2   (C) 3   (D) 0   (E) none of these.

25. The acceleration is positive

    (A) when $t > 2$ (B) for all t, $t \neq 2$ (C) when $t < 2$

    (D) for $1 < t < 3$ (E) for $1 < t < 2$.

26. The speed of the particle is decreasing for

    (A) $t > 2$ (B) $t < 3$ (C) all t (D) $t < 1$ or $t > 2$

    (E) none of these.

In Problems 27-29, a particle moves along a horizontal line according to the law $s = t^4 - 6t^3 + 12t^2 + 3$.

27. The particle is at rest when t is equal to

    (A) 1 or 2   (B) 0   (C) $\dfrac{9}{4}$ (D) 0, 2, or 3

    (E) none of these.

28. The velocity, v, is increasing when

    (A) $t > 1$ (B) $1 < t < 2$ (C) $t < 2$ (D) $t < 1$ or $t > 2$

    (E) $t > 0$.

29. The speed of the particle is increasing for

    (A) $0 < t < 1$ or $t > 2$ (B) $1 < t < 2$ (C) $t < 2$

    (D) $t < 0$ or $t > 2$ (E) $t < 0$.

30. The displacement from the origin of a particle moving on a line is given by $s = t^4 - 4t^3$. The maximum displacement during the time interval $-2 \leqq t \leqq 4$ is

    (A) 27   (B) 3   (C) $12\sqrt{3} + 3$ (D) 48   (E) none of these.

31. If a particle moves along a line according to the law $s = t^5 + 5t^4$, then the number of times it reverses direction is

(A) 0   (B) 1   (C) 2   (D) 3   (E) 4 .

In Problems 32-35, the motion of a particle in a plane is given by the pair of equations: $x = 2t$ $y = 4t - t^2$.

*32. The particle moves along

(A) an ellipse   (B) a circle   (C) a hyperbola

(D) a line   (E) a parabola.

*33. The speed of the particle at any time t is

(A) $\sqrt{6 - 2t}$ (B) $2\sqrt{t^2 - 4t + 5}$ (C) $2\sqrt{t^2 - 2t + 5}$

(D) $\sqrt{8}(|t - 2|)$ (E) $2(|3 - t|)$.

*34. The minimum speed of the particle is

(A) 2   (B) $2\sqrt{2}$ (C) 0   (D) 1   (E) 4 .

*35. The acceleration of the particle

(A) depends on t (B) is always directed upward
(C) is constant both in magnitude and in direction
(D) never exceeds 1 in magnitude   (E) is none of these.

In Problems 36-39, $R = 3 \cos \frac{\pi}{3}t\mathbf{i} + 2 \sin \frac{\pi}{3}t\mathbf{j}$ is the (position) vector $x\mathbf{i} + y\mathbf{j}$ from the origin to a moving point $P(x,y)$ at time t.

*36. A single equation in x and y for the path of the point is

(A) $x^2 + y^2 = 13$ (B) $9x^2 + 4y^2 = 36$ (C) $2x^2 + 3y^2 = 13$

(D) $4x^2 + 9y^2 = 1$ (E) $4x^2 + 9y^2 = 36$.

*37. When $t = 3$, the speed of the particle is

(A) $\frac{2\pi}{3}$ (B) 2   (C) 3   (D) π (E) $\frac{\sqrt{13}}{3}\pi$.

*38. The magnitude of the acceleration when $t = 3$ is

(A) 2   (B) $\dfrac{\pi^2}{3}$ (C) 3   (D) $\dfrac{2\pi^2}{9}$ (E) π .

*39. At the point where $t = \dfrac{1}{2}$, the slope of the curve along which the particle moves is

(A) $-\dfrac{2\sqrt{3}}{9}$ (B) $-\dfrac{\sqrt{3}}{2}$ (C) $\dfrac{2}{\sqrt{3}}$ (D) $-\dfrac{2\sqrt{3}}{3}$ (E) none of these.

*40. If a particle moves along a curve with constant speed, then

(A) the magnitude of its acceleration must equal 0

(B) the direction of acceleration must be constant

(C) the curve along which the particle moves must be a straight line

(D) its velocity and acceleration vectors must be perpendicular

(E) the curve along which the particle moves must be a circle.

*41. A particle is moving on the curve of $y = 2x - \ln x$ so that $\dfrac{dx}{dt} = -2$ at all time t. At the point $(1,2)$, $\dfrac{dy}{dt}$ is

(A) 4   (B) 2   (C) -4   (D) 1   (E) -2 .

42. A balloon is being filled with helium at the rate of 4 ft^3/min. The rate in ft^2/min at which the surface area is increasing when the volume is $\dfrac{32\pi}{3}$ ft^3 is

(A) 4π (B) 2   (C) 4   (D) 1   (E) 2π .

43. A circular conical reservoir, vertex down, has depth 20 ft and radius of the top 10 ft. Water is leaking out so that the surface is falling at the rate of ½ ft/hr. The rate in ft^3/hr at which the water is leaving the reservoir when the water is 8 ft deep is

(A) 4π (B) 8π (C) 16π (D) $\dfrac{1}{4\pi}$ (E) $\dfrac{1}{8\pi}$.

44. A vertical circular cylinder has radius r feet and height h feet. If

the height and radius both increase at the constant rate of 2 ft/sec, then the rate in ft^2/sec at which the lateral surface area increases is

(A) $4\pi r$ (B) $2\pi(r + h)$ (C) $4\pi(r + h)$

(D) $4\pi rh$ (E) $4\pi h$.

45. A relative minimum value of the function $y = \dfrac{e^x}{x}$ is

(A) $\dfrac{1}{e}$ (B) 1   (C) -1   (D) e (E) 0 .

46. The area of the largest rectangle that can be drawn with one side along the x-axis and two vertices on the curve of $y = e^{-x^2}$ is

(A) $\sqrt{\dfrac{2}{e}}$ (B) $\sqrt{2e}$ (C) $\dfrac{2}{e}$ (D) $\dfrac{1}{\sqrt{2e}}$ (E) $\dfrac{2}{e^2}$.

47. A tangent drawn to the parabola $y = 4 - x^2$ at the point $(1,3)$ forms a right triangle with the coordinate axes. The area of the triangle is

(A) $\dfrac{5}{4}$ (B) $\dfrac{5}{2}$ (C) $\dfrac{25}{2}$ (D) 1   (E) $\dfrac{25}{4}$.

48. If the cylinder of largest possible volume is inscribed in a given sphere, the ratio of the volume of the sphere to that of the cylinder is

(A) $\sqrt{3} : 1$ (B) $\sqrt{3} : 3$ (C) $3 : 1$

(D) $2\sqrt{3} : 3$ (E) $3\sqrt{3} : 4$.

49. A line is drawn through the point $(1,2)$ forming a right triangle with the positive x- and y-axes. The slope of the line forming the triangle of least area is

(A) -1   (B) -2   (C) -4   (D) $-\frac{1}{2}$ (E) -3 .

50. The point(s) on the curve $x^2 - y^2 = 4$ closest to the point $(6,0)$ is (are)

(A) $(2,0)$ (B) $(\sqrt{5}, \pm 1)$ (C) $(3, \pm\sqrt{5})$

(D) $(\sqrt{13}, \pm\sqrt{3})$ (E) none of these.

51. The sum of the squares of two positive numbers is 200; their minimum product is

    (A) 100   (B) $25\sqrt{7}$ (C) 28   (D) $24\sqrt{14}$ (E) none of these.

52. The first-quadrant point on the curve $y^2x = 18$ which is closest to the point (2,0) is

    (A) (2,3)   (B) $(6,\sqrt{3})$ (C) $(3,\sqrt{6})$ (D) $(1,3\sqrt{2})$

    (E) none of these.

53. Two cars are travelling along perpendicular roads, car A at 40 mi/hr, car B at 60 mi/hr. At noon when car A reaches the intersection, car B is 90 miles away, and moving toward it. At one P.M. the distance between the cars is changing (in mi/hr) at the rate of

    (A) -40   (B) 68   (C) 4   (D) -4   (E) 40 .

54. For Problem 53, if t is the number of hours of travel after noon, then the cars are closest together when t is

    (A) 0   (B) $\frac{27}{26}$ (C) $\frac{9}{5}$ (D) $\frac{3}{2}$ (E) $\frac{14}{13}$.

55. The function $f(x) = x^{2/3}$ on [-8, 8] does not satisfy the conditions of the Mean Value Theorem because

    (A) $f(0)$ is not defined   (B) $f(x)$ is not continuous on [-8, 8]

    (C) $f'(-1)$ does not exist   (D) $f(x)$ is not defined for $x < 0$

    (E) $f'(0)$ does not exist.

56. If $f(a) = f(b) = 0$ and $f(x)$ is continuous on $[a,b]$ then

    (A) $f(x)$ must be identically zero

    (B) $f'(x)$ may be different from zero for all x on $[a, b]$

    (C) there exists at least one number c, $a < c < b$, such that $f'(c) = 0$

    (D) $f'(x)$ must exist for every x on (a, b)

    (E) none of the preceding is true.

57. If c is the number defined by Rolle's Theorem, then for

$f(x) = 2x^3 - 6x$ on the interval $0 \leqq x \leqq \sqrt{3}$, c is

    (A)   1   (B)   -1   (C) $\sqrt{2}$ (D)   0   (E) $\sqrt{3}$.

58. The height of a rectangular box is 10 in. Its length increases at the rate of 2 in/sec; its width decreases at the rate of 4 in/sec. When the length is 8 in and the width is 6 in, the volume of the box is changing, in in^3/sec, at the rate of

    (A)   200   (B)   80   (C)   -80   (D)   -200   (E)   -20 .

59. A cube whose edge is x is contracting. When its surface area is changing at a rate which is equal to 6 times the rate of change of its edge, then the length of the edge is

    (A)   2   (B) $\frac{3}{4}$ (C)   1   (D) $\frac{4}{3}$ (E) $\frac{1}{2}$.

60. If $f(x) = ax^4 + bx^2$ and $ab > 0$ then

    (A)   the curve has no horizontal tangents

    (B)   the curve is concave up for all x

    (C)   the curve is concave down for all x

    (D)   the curve has no inflection point

    (E)   none of the preceding is necessary.

Section 4: Integration

Review of Definitions and Methods

A. **Antiderivative.** The *antiderivative* or *indefinite integral* of a function $f(x)$ is a function $F(x)$ whose derivative is $f(x)$. Since the derivative of a constant equals zero, the antiderivative of $f(x)$ is not unique; i.e., if $F(x)$ is an integral of $f(x)$ then so is $F(x) + C$, where C is any constant. The arbitrary constant C is called the *constant of integration*. The indefinite integral of $f(x)$ is written $\int f(x)\ dx$; thus $\int f(x)\ dx = F(x) + C$ if $\frac{dF(x)}{dx} = f(x)$. The function $f(x)$ is called the *integrand*. The Law of the Mean can be used to show that if two functions have the same derivative, on an interval, then they differ at most by a constant; i.e., if $\frac{dF(x)}{dx} = \frac{dG(x)}{dx}$ then $F(x) - G(x) = C$, C a constant.

B. **Basic Formulas.** Familiarity with the following fundamental integration formulas is essential.

$$\int k\ f(x)\ dx = k \int f(x)\ dx \qquad k \neq 0 \qquad (1)$$

$$\int [f(x) + g(x)]\ dx = \int f(x)\ dx + \int g(x)\ dx \qquad (2)$$

$$\int u^n\ du = \frac{u^{n+1}}{n+1} + C \qquad (n \neq -1) \qquad (3)$$

$$\int \frac{du}{u} = \ln |u| + C \qquad (4)$$

$$\int \cos u \; du \;=\; \sin u + C \tag{5}$$

$$\int \sin u \; du \;=\; -\cos u + C \tag{6}$$

$$\int \tan u \; du \;=\; \ln |\sec u| + C$$

$$\text{or} \;-\ln |\cos u| + C \tag{7}$$

$$\int \cot u \; du \;=\; \ln |\sin u| + C$$

$$\text{or} \;-\ln |\csc u| + C \tag{8}$$

$$\int \sec^2 u \; du \;=\; \tan u + C \tag{9}$$

$$\int \csc^2 u \; du \;=\; -\cot u + C \tag{10}$$

$$\int \sec u \tan u \; du \;=\; \sec u + C \tag{11}$$

$$\int \csc u \cot u \; du \;=\; -\csc u + C \tag{12}$$

$$\int \sec u \; du \;=\; \ln |\sec u + \tan u| + C \tag{13}$$

$$\int \csc u \; du \;=\; \ln |\csc u - \cot u| + C \tag{14}$$

$$\int e^u \; du \;=\; e^u + C \tag{15}$$

$$\int a^u \; du \;=\; \frac{a^u}{\ln a} + C \qquad (a > 0, \; a \neq 1) \tag{16}$$

$$\int \frac{du}{\sqrt{a^2 - u^2}} \;=\; \sin^{-1} \frac{u}{a} + C \tag{17}$$

$$\int \frac{du}{a^2 + u^2} \;=\; \frac{1}{a} \tan^{-1} \frac{u}{a} + C \tag{18}$$

$$\int \frac{du}{u\sqrt{u^2 - a^2}} \;=\; \frac{1}{a} \sec^{-1} \left| \frac{u}{a} \right| + C \tag{19}$$

Formulas (1) through (19) are used in the following illustrative

EXAMPLES:

1. $\int 5x \; dx \;=\; 5 \int x \; dx$ by (1), $=\; 5 \cdot \frac{x^2}{2} + C$ by (3).

2. $\int \left(x^4 + \sqrt[3]{x^2} - \frac{2}{x^2} - \frac{1}{3\sqrt[3]{x}} \right) dx \;=\; \int \left(x^4 + x^{2/3} - 2x^{-2} - \frac{1}{3} x^{-1/3} \right) dx$

$=\; \int x^4 \; dx \;+\; \int x^{2/3} \; dx \;-\; 2 \int x^{-2} \; dx \;-\; \frac{1}{3} \int x^{-1/3} \; dx$ by (1) and (2),

$$= \frac{x^5}{5} + \frac{x^{5/3}}{\frac{5}{3}} - \frac{2x^{-1}}{-1} - \frac{1}{3}\frac{x^{2/3}}{\frac{2}{3}} + C \quad \text{by (3),} \quad = \frac{x^5}{5} + \frac{3}{5}x^{5/3}$$

$$+ \frac{2}{x} - \frac{1}{2}x^{2/3} + C.$$

3. Similarly $\int (3 - 4x + 2x^3)\, dx = \int 3\, dx - 4\int x\, dx + 2\int x^3\, dx$

$$= 3x - \frac{4x^2}{2} + \frac{2x^4}{4} + C = 3x - 2x^2 + \frac{x^4}{2} + C.$$

4. $\int 2(1 - 3x)^2\, dx = 2\int (1 - 3x)^2\, dx = 2\int (1 - 6x + 9x^2)\, dx$

$$= 2(x - \frac{6x^2}{2} + \frac{9x^3}{3}) + C = 2x - 6x^2 + 6x^3 + C.$$ We have expanded

here, and used the fact that the integral of a sum is the sum of the

integrals ((2) above). Alternatively, we can let $u = 1 - 3x$; then

$du = -3\, dx$. Since $2\int (1 - 3x)^2\, dx = \frac{2}{-3}\int (1 - 3x)^2(-3)\, dx$, we

can now apply formula (3), getting $-\frac{2}{3}\int (1 - 3x)^2(-3)\, dx = -\frac{2}{3}\int u^2\, du$

$$= -\frac{2}{9}u^3 + C \quad \text{by (3),} \quad = -\frac{2}{9}(1 - 3x)^3 + C.$$ If this last function

is expanded, note that the two different answers to the given integral

differ only by a constant; in fact, the second function is precisely

the first function plus the constant $-\frac{2}{9}$.

5. $\int (2x^3 - 1)^5 \cdot x^2\, dx = \frac{1}{6}\int (2x^3 - 1)^5 \cdot 6x^2\, dx = \frac{1}{6}\int u^5\, du$

(where $u = 2x^3 - 1$), $= \frac{1}{6}\frac{u^6}{6} + C \quad \text{by (3),} \quad = \frac{1}{36}(2x^3 - 1)^6 + C.$

6. $\int \sqrt[3]{1 - x}\, dx = \int (1 - x)^{1/3}\, dx = -\int (1 - x)^{1/3}(-1)\, dx$

$$= -\int u^{1/3}\, du \quad \text{(where } u = 1 - x), \quad = -\frac{u^{4/3}}{\frac{4}{3}} + C \quad \text{by (3),}$$

$$= -\frac{3}{4}(1 - x)^{4/3} + C.$$

7. $\int \dfrac{x}{\sqrt{3 - 4x^2}} \, dx = \int (3 - 4x^2)^{-1/2} \cdot x \, dx = -\dfrac{1}{8} \int (3 - 4x^2)^{-1/2} (-8x) \, dx$

$= -\dfrac{1}{8} \int u^{-1/2} \, du$ (where $u = 3 - 4x^2$), $= -\dfrac{1}{8} \dfrac{u^{1/2}}{\frac{1}{2}} + C$ by (3),

$= -\dfrac{1}{4} \sqrt{3 - 4x^2} + C.$

8. $\int \dfrac{4x^2}{(x^3 - 1)^3} \, dx = 4 \int (x^3 - 1)^{-3} \cdot x^2 \, dx = \dfrac{4}{3} \int (x^3 - 1)^{-3} (3x^2) \, dx$

$= \dfrac{4}{3} \dfrac{(x^3 - 1)^{-2}}{-2} + C = -\dfrac{2}{3} \dfrac{1}{(x^3 - 1)^2} + C$ by (3).

9. $\int \dfrac{(1 + \sqrt{x})^4}{\sqrt{x}} \, dx = \int (1 + x^{1/2})^4 \cdot \dfrac{1}{x^{1/2}} \, dx.$ Now let $u = 1 + x^{1/2}$,

and note that $du = \dfrac{1}{2} x^{-1/2} \, dx$; this gives $2 \int (1 + x^{1/2})^4 \dfrac{1}{2x^{1/2}} \, dx$

$= \dfrac{2}{5} (1 + \sqrt{x})^5 + C$ by (3).

10. $\int (2 - y)^2 \cdot \sqrt{y} \, dy = \int (4 - 4y + y^2) \cdot y^{1/2} \, dy$

$= \int (4y^{1/2} - 4y^{3/2} + y^{5/2}) \, dy = 4 \cdot \dfrac{2}{3} y^{3/2} - 4 \cdot \dfrac{2}{5} y^{5/2} + \dfrac{2}{7} \cdot y^{7/2} + C$

by (2), $= \dfrac{8}{3} y^{3/2} - \dfrac{8}{5} y^{5/2} + \dfrac{2}{7} y^{7/2} + C.$

11. $\int \dfrac{x^3 - x - 4}{2x^2} \, dx = \dfrac{1}{2} \int (x - \dfrac{1}{x} - \dfrac{4}{x^2}) \, dx$

$= \dfrac{1}{2}(\dfrac{x^2}{2} - \ln |x| + \dfrac{4}{x}) + C.$ (1), (2), (3), and (4) have all been used.

12. $\int \dfrac{3x - 1}{\sqrt[3]{1 - 2x + 3x^2}} \, dx = \int (1 - 2x + 3x^2)^{-1/3} (3x - 1) \, dx$

$= \dfrac{1}{2} \int (1 - 2x + 3x^2)^{-1/3} (6x - 2) \, dx$ (where we have let $u = 1 - 2x + 3x^2$

and noted that $du = (-2 + 6x) \, dx$), $= \dfrac{1}{2} \cdot \dfrac{3}{2} (1 - 2x + 3x^2)^{2/3} + C$ by (3),

$= \dfrac{3}{4} (1 - 2x + 3x^2)^{2/3} + C.$

13. $\int \frac{2x^2 - 4x + 3}{(x - 1)^2} \, dx = \int \frac{2x^2 - 4x + 3}{x^2 - 2x + 1} \, dx = \int \left(2 + \frac{1}{(x - 1)^2}\right) \, dx$

$= \int 2 \, dx + \int \frac{dx}{(x - 1)^2} = 2x - \frac{1}{x - 1} + C.$ This example illustrates the

following principle: If the degree of the numerator of a rational

function is not less than that of the denominator, divide until a

remainder of lower degree is obtained.

14. $\int \frac{du}{u - 3} = \ln |u - 3| + C$ by (4).

15. $\int \frac{z \, dz}{1 - 4z^2} = -\frac{1}{8} \int \frac{-8z \, dz}{1 - 4z^2} = -\frac{1}{8} \ln |1 - 4z^2| + C$ by

formula (4) with $u = 1 - 4z^2.$

16. $\int \frac{\cos x}{5 + 2 \sin x} \, dx = \frac{1}{2} \int \frac{2 \cos x}{5 + 2 \sin x} \, dx = \frac{1}{2} \ln (5 + 2 \sin x) + C$

by (4) with $u = 5 + 2 \sin x.$ The absolute value sign is not necessary

here since $5 + 2 \sin x > 0$ for all $x.$

17. $\int \frac{e^x}{1 - 2e^x} \, dx = -\frac{1}{2} \int \frac{- 2e^x}{1 - 2e^x} \, dx = -\frac{1}{2} \ln |1 - 2e^x| + C$

by (4) with $u = 1 - 2e^x.$

18. $\int \frac{x}{1 - x} \, dx = \int \left(-1 + \frac{1}{1 - x}\right) \, dx$ by long division,

$= - x - \ln |1 - x| + C.$

19. $\int \sin (1 - 2y) \, dy = -\frac{1}{2} \int \sin (1 - 2y) (-2 \, dy)$

$= -\frac{1}{2} [- \cos (1 - 2y)] + C$ by (6), $= \frac{1}{2} \cos (1 - 2y) + C.$

20. $\int \sin^2 \frac{x}{2} \cos \frac{x}{2} \, dx = 2 \int \sin^2 \frac{x}{2} \cos \frac{x}{2} \frac{dx}{2} = \frac{2}{3} \sin^3 \frac{x}{2} + C$

by (3) with $u = \sin \frac{x}{2}$ so that $du = \cos \frac{x}{2} \left(\frac{1}{2} \, dx\right).$

21. $\displaystyle\int \frac{\sin x}{1 + 3\cos x}\, dx = -\frac{1}{3}\int \frac{-3\sin x}{1 + 3\cos x}\, dx$

$= -\frac{1}{3}\ln|1 + 3\cos x| + C$ by (4) with $u = 1 + 3\cos x$.

22. $\displaystyle\int e^{\tan y}\sec^2 y\, dy = e^{\tan y} + C$ by (15) with $u = \tan y$.

23. $\displaystyle\int e^x \tan e^x\, dx = -\ln|\cos e^x| + C$ by (7) with $u = e^x$.

24. $\displaystyle\int \frac{\cos z}{\sin^2 z}\, dz = \int \csc z \cot z\, dz = -\csc z + C$ by (12).

25. $\displaystyle\int \tan t \sec^2 t\, dt = \frac{\tan^2 t}{2} + C$ by (3) with $u = \tan t$ and

$du = \sec^2 t\, dt.$

26. $\displaystyle\int \sec^4 x\, dx = \int \sec^2 x \sec^2 x\, dx = \int (\tan^2 x + 1)\sec^2 x\, dx$

$= \displaystyle\int \tan^2 x \sec^2 x\, dx + \int \sec^2 x\, dx = \frac{\tan^3 x}{3} + \tan x + C$ by (3) and (9).

27. (a) $\displaystyle\int \frac{dz}{\sqrt{9 - z^2}} = \sin^{-1}\frac{z}{3} + C$ by (17) with $u = z$, $a = 3$.

(b) $\displaystyle\int \frac{z\, dz}{\sqrt{9 - z^2}} = -\frac{1}{2}\int (9 - z^2)^{-1/2}(-2z\, dz) = -\frac{1}{2}\frac{(9 - z^2)^{1/2}}{\frac{1}{2}} + C$

by (3) (with $u = 9 - z^2$, $n = -\frac{1}{2}$), $= -\sqrt{9 - z^2} + C.$

(c) $\displaystyle\int \frac{z\, dz}{9 - z^2} = -\frac{1}{2}\ln|9 - z^2| + C$ by (4) with $u = 9 - z^2$.

(d) $\displaystyle\int \frac{z\, dz}{(9 - z^2)^2} = \frac{1}{2(9 - z^2)} + C$ by (3).

(e) $\displaystyle\int \frac{dz}{9 + z^2} = \frac{1}{3}\tan^{-1}\frac{z}{3} + C$ by (18) with $u = z$, $a = 3$.

28. $\displaystyle\int \frac{dx}{\sqrt{x}(1 + 2\sqrt{x})} = \ln(1 + 2\sqrt{x}) + C$ by (4), with $u = 1 + 2\sqrt{x}$

and $du = \dfrac{dx}{\sqrt{x}}.$

29. $\int \sin x \cos x \, dx = \frac{1}{2} \sin^2 x + C$ by (3) with $u = \sin x$;

OR $= -\frac{1}{2} \cos^2 x + C$ by (3) with $u = \cos x$;   OR $= -\frac{1}{4} \cos 2x + C$ by

(6), where we use the trigonometric identity $\sin 2x = 2 \sin x \cos x$.

30. $\int \frac{\cos \sqrt{x}}{\sqrt{x}} \, dx = 2 \sin \sqrt{x} + C$ by (5) with $u = \sqrt{x}$.

31. $\int \sin^2 y \, dy = \int \left(\frac{1}{2} - \frac{\cos 2y}{2}\right) dy = \frac{y}{2} - \frac{\sin 2y}{4} + C.$

32. $\int \cos^2 z \sin^3 z \, dz = \int \cos^2 z \sin^2 z \sin z \, dz$

$= \int \cos^2 z \, (1 - \cos^2 z) \sin z \, dz = \int \cos^2 z \sin z \, dz - \int \cos^4 z \sin z \, dz$

$= -\frac{\cos^3 z}{3} + \frac{\cos^5 z}{5} + C,$ by repeated application of (3) with $u = \cos z$

and $du = -\sin z \, dz.$

33. $\int \frac{x \, dx}{x^4 + 1} = \frac{1}{2} \tan^{-1} x^2 + C$ by (18) with $u = x^2$, $a = 1.$

34. $\int \frac{dy}{\sqrt{6y - y^2}} = \int \frac{dy}{\sqrt{9 - (y^2 - 6y + 9)}} = \sin^{-1} \frac{y - 3}{3} + C$ by

(17), with $u = y - 3$, $a = 3.$

35. $\int \frac{e^x}{3 + e^{2x}} \, dx = \frac{1}{\sqrt{3}} \tan^{-1} \frac{e^x}{\sqrt{3}} + C$ by (18) with $u = e^x$, $a = \sqrt{3}.$

36. $\int \frac{e^x - e^{-x}}{e^x + e^{-x}} \, dx = \ln (e^x + e^{-x}) + C$ by (4) with $u = e^x + e^{-x}.$

37. To evaluate $\int \frac{x + 1}{x^2 + 4x + 13} \, dx$, we let $u = x^2 + 4x + 13,$

note that du is $(2x + 4) \, dx$, and rewrite the integral as

$\frac{1}{2} \int \frac{2x + 2}{x^2 + 4x + 13} \, dx = \frac{1}{2} \int \frac{2x + 2 + 2 - 2}{x^2 + 4x + 13} \, dx = \frac{1}{2} \int \frac{2x + 4}{x^2 + 4x + 13} \, dx$

$$-\int \frac{dx}{x^2 + 4x + 13} = \frac{1}{2} \ln (x^2 + 4x + 13) - \int \frac{dx}{(x + 2)^2 + 3^2}$$

$$= \frac{1}{2} \ln (x^2 + 4x + 13) - \frac{1}{3} \tan^{-1} \frac{x + 2}{3} + C, \quad \text{where we have used (4) for}$$

the first integral and (18) for the second.

38. $\displaystyle \int \frac{2x - 1}{\sqrt{8 - 2x - x^2}} \, dx = -\int \frac{-2x + 1}{\sqrt{8 - 2x - x^2}} \, dx = -\int \frac{-2x - 2 + 1 + 2}{\sqrt{8 - 2x - x^2}} \, dx$

$$= -\int \frac{-2x - 2}{\sqrt{8 - 2x - x^2}} \, dx - 3 \int \frac{dx}{\sqrt{8 - 2x - x^2}} = -\int (8 - 2x - x^2)^{-1/2}(-2x - 2) \, dx$$

$$- 3 \int \frac{dx}{\sqrt{9 - (x^2 + 2x + 1)}} = -2\sqrt{8 - 2x - x^2} \quad \text{(by (3))} \quad - 3 \sin^{-1} \frac{x + 1}{3}$$

(by (17)) $+ C$.

39. $\displaystyle \int \frac{dt}{\sin^2 2t} = \int \csc^2 2t \, dt = \frac{1}{2} \int \csc^2 2t \, (2 \, dt) = -\frac{1}{2} \cot 2t + C$

by (10).

40. $\displaystyle \int \cos^2 4z \, dz = \int (\frac{1}{2} + \frac{\cos 8z}{2}) \, dz \quad \text{by a trigonometric identity}$

$$= \frac{z}{2} + \frac{\sin 8z}{16} + C.$$

41. $\displaystyle \int \frac{\sin 2x}{1 + \sin^2 x} \, dx = \ln (1 + \sin^2 x) + C \quad \text{by (4) (with} \quad u = 1 + \sin^2 x$

and $du = 2 \sin x \cos x \, dx = \sin 2x \, dx)$.

42. $\displaystyle \int x^2 e^{-x^3} \, dx = -\frac{1}{3} e^{-x^3} + C \quad \text{by (15) with} \quad u = -x^3.$

43. $\displaystyle \int \frac{dy}{y\sqrt{1 + \ln y}} = 2\sqrt{1 + \ln y} + C \quad \text{by (3) with} \quad u = 1 + \ln y,$

$du = \frac{dy}{y}, \ n = -\frac{1}{2}.$

44. $\displaystyle \int \frac{\sqrt{x - 1}}{x} \, dx.$ We let $u = \sqrt{x - 1}, \quad u^2 = x - 1.$ Then $2u \, du = dx.$

Then $\int \dfrac{\sqrt{x-1}}{x}\, dx \;=\; 2\int \dfrac{u^2\, du}{u^2+1} \;=\; 2\int \dfrac{u^2+1-1}{u^2+1}\, du \;=\; 2\int \left(1-\dfrac{1}{u^2+1}\right)\, du$

$=\; 2(u-\tan^{-1} u) + C \;=\; 2(\sqrt{x-1} - \tan^{-1}\sqrt{x-1} \;+\; C.$

The examples above illustrate the technique of integration by substitution. Trigonometric substitutions are also effective for certain integrals, as indicated below.

C. Integrals involving $\sqrt{a^2-u^2}$, $\sqrt{a^2+u^2}$, $\sqrt{u^2-a^2}$. In $\sqrt{a^2-u^2}$, we let $u = a\sin\theta$ and replace a^2-u^2 by $a^2\cos^2\theta$. In $\sqrt{a^2+u^2}$, we let $u = a\tan\theta$ and replace a^2+u^2 by $a^2\sec^2\theta$. In $\sqrt{u^2-a^2}$, we let $u = a\sec\theta$ and replace u^2-a^2 by $a^2\tan^2\theta$. We thus obtain a new integrand, in each case involving trigonometric functions of θ. This technique is illustrated in the following EXAMPLES:

45. $\int \dfrac{x^2}{\sqrt{4-x^2}}\, dx.$ Let $x = 2\sin\theta$ $\left(-\dfrac{\pi}{2} < \theta < \dfrac{\pi}{2}\right)$. Then $dx = 2\cos\theta\, d\theta$ and $\sqrt{4-x^2} = 2\cos\theta$, where we have noted that $\cos\theta > 0$ on the prescribed interval. Then

$\int \dfrac{x^2\, dx}{\sqrt{4-x^2}} \;=\; \int \dfrac{4\sin^2\theta}{2\cos\theta}\, 2\cos\theta\, d\theta \;=\; 4\int \sin^2\theta\, d\theta$

$=\; 4\int \left(\dfrac{1}{2} - \dfrac{\cos 2\theta}{2}\right) d\theta \;=\; 4\left(\dfrac{\theta}{2} - \dfrac{\sin 2\theta}{4}\right) + C \;=\; 2\theta - \sin 2\theta + C$

or $2\theta - 2\sin\theta\cos\theta + C.$

If we draw an appropriate right triangle involving θ and x (see Figure N4-1) we can easily obtain the answer in terms of x. Thus

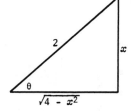

Figure N4-1

$\int \dfrac{x^2\, dx}{\sqrt{4-x^2}} \;=\; 2\sin^{-1}\dfrac{x}{2} - 2\dfrac{x}{2}\dfrac{\sqrt{4-x^2}}{2} + C \;=\; 2\sin^{-1}\dfrac{x}{2} - \dfrac{x\sqrt{4-x^2}}{2} + C.$

46. $\displaystyle\int \frac{dx}{x\sqrt{4x^2 + 9}}$.   Let $2x = 3 \tan \theta$ $\left(-\frac{\pi}{2} < \theta < \frac{\pi}{2}\right)$.

Then $2\ dx = 3 \sec^2 \theta\ d\theta$ and $\sqrt{4x^2 + 9} = 3 \sec \theta$, where $\sec \theta > 0$

on the above interval. So

$$\int \frac{dx}{x\sqrt{4x^2 + 9}} = \int \frac{3 \sec^2 \theta\ d\theta}{2\cdot\frac{3 \tan \theta}{2} \cdot 3 \sec \theta} = \frac{1}{3} \int \frac{\sec \theta}{\tan \theta} d\theta = \frac{1}{3} \int \csc \theta\ d\theta$$

$= \frac{1}{3} \ln |\csc \theta - \cot \theta| + C$ by (14) in B. We use Figure N4-2 to express

the answer in terms of x: $\displaystyle\int \frac{dx}{x\sqrt{4x^2 + 9}} = \frac{1}{3} \ln \left|\frac{\sqrt{4x^2 + 9}}{2x} - \frac{3}{2x}\right| + C$

$= \frac{1}{3} \ln \left|\frac{\sqrt{4x^2 + 9} - 3}{x}\right| + C'$, where we have

replaced $C - \frac{1}{3} \ln 2$ by C' in the final

answer.

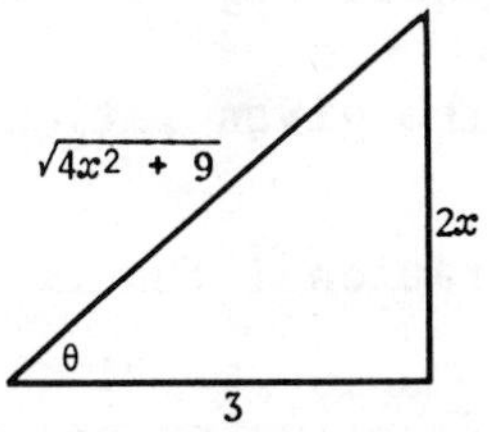

Figure N4-2

47. $\displaystyle\int \frac{du}{\sqrt{u^2 - 1}}$. Let $u = \sec \theta$; here $|u| > 1$. Then $du = \sec \theta \tan \theta\ d\theta$,

$\sqrt{u^2 - 1} = \tan \theta$ if $u > 1$, $= -\tan \theta$ if $u < -1$. Then $\displaystyle\int \frac{du}{\sqrt{u^2 - 1}}$

$= \pm \displaystyle\int \frac{\sec \theta \tan \theta\ d\theta}{\tan \theta} = \int \sec \theta\ d\theta$ if $u > 1$,

$= - \displaystyle\int \sec \theta\ d\theta$ if $u < -1$;

this yields $\ln |\sec \theta + \tan \theta| + C$ for $u > 1$,

$-\ln |\sec \theta - \tan \theta| + C$ for $u < -1$, by (13).

Note that $\sec \theta = u$, $\tan \theta = \pm\sqrt{u^2 - 1}$. Figure N4-3

enables us to write our answers as $\ln |u + \sqrt{u^2 - 1}| + C$

for $u > 1$, and as $-\ln |u - \sqrt{u^2 - 1}| + C$ for $u < -1$.

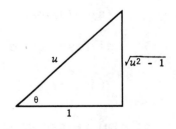

Figure N4-3

Since the latter can be rewritten $\ln \left| \dfrac{1}{u - \sqrt{u^2 - 1}} \cdot \dfrac{u + \sqrt{u^2 - 1}}{u + \sqrt{u^2 - 1}} \right| + C$

$= \ln |u + \sqrt{u^2 - 1}| + C$, we see that for all u, $|u| > 1$,

$$\int \frac{du}{\sqrt{u^2 - 1}} = \ln |u + \sqrt{u^2 - 1}| + C.$$

D. **Integration by Partial Fractions.** The method of partial fractions makes it possible to express a rational function $\dfrac{f(x)}{g(x)}$ as a sum of simpler fractions. Here $f(x)$ and $g(x)$ are real polynomials in x and it is assumed that $\dfrac{f(x)}{g(x)}$ is a proper fraction: that is, that $f(x)$ is of lower degree than $g(x)$. If not, we divide $f(x)$ by $g(x)$ to express the given rational function as the sum of a polynomial and a proper rational function. Thus $\dfrac{x^4 + x^2 - 4}{x(x^2 + 1)} = x - \dfrac{4}{x(x^2 + 1)}$, where the fraction on the right is proper.

Theoretically, every real polynomial can be expressed as a product of (powers of) real linear factors and (powers of) real quadratic factors. The particular form of the partial fractions depends both on the nature of these factors (i.e., linear versus quadratic) and on the power (i.e., the degree) to which each factor occurs. A real quadratic factor is irreducible if it cannot be decomposed into real linear factors.

In the following cases, all the capital letters denote constants to be determined.

(a) For each *distinct linear factor* $(x - a)$ of $g(x)$ we set up one partial fraction of the type $\dfrac{A}{x - a}$.

(b) For each *distinct irreducible quadratic factor* $(x^2 + bx + c)$ of $g(x)$ we set up one partial fraction of the form $\dfrac{Bx + C}{x^2 + bx + c}$. Note here that $b^2 - 4c$ is negative if $(x^2 + bx + c)$ is irreducible.

(c) If a linear factor $(x - a)$ of $g(x)$ occurs to the nth degree
(that is, is repeated n times), we set up n fractions for it as follows:

$$\frac{A_1}{(x - a)} + \frac{A_2}{(x - a)^2} + \frac{A_3}{(x - a)^3} + \ldots + \frac{A_n}{(x - a)^n} .$$

Note that (a) above is a special case of this where $n = 1$.

(d) If a quadratic factor $(x^2 + bx + c)$ is repeated m times,
we set up m fractions for it at follows:

$$\frac{B_1 x + C_1}{x^2 + bx + c} + \frac{B_2 x + C_2}{(x^2 + bx + c)^2} + \frac{B_3 x + C_3}{(x^2 + bx + c)^3} + \ldots + \frac{B_m x + C_m}{(x^2 + bx + c)^m} .$$

The techniques for determining the unknown constants above are illustrated
in the following EXAMPLES:

48. Find $\int \frac{x^2 - x + 4}{x^3 - 3x^2 + 2x} \, dx$. We factor the denominator and then set

$$\frac{x^2 - x + 4}{x(x - 1)(x - 2)} = \frac{A}{x} + \frac{B}{x - 1} + \frac{C}{x - 2} \qquad (1)$$

where the constants A, B, and C are to be determined. It follows that

$$x^2 - x + 4 = A(x - 1)(x - 2) + Bx(x - 2) + Cx(x - 1) . \qquad (2)$$

Since the polynomial on the right in (2) is to be identical to the one on
the left, we can find the constants by either of the following methods:

METHOD ONE. Expand and combine on the right in (2), getting

$$x^2 - x + 4 = (A + B + C)x^2 - (3A + 2B + C)x + 2A.$$

We then *equate coefficients of like powers in x* and solve simultaneously.
Thus

using the coefficients of x^2 we get $1 = A + B + C$

using the coefficients of x we get $-1 = -(3A + 2B + C)$

using the constant coefficient, $4 = 2A.$

These equations yield $A = 2$, $B = -4$, $C = 3$.

METHOD TWO.   Although equation (1) above is meaningless for $x = 0$, $x = 1$, or $x = 2$, it is still true that equation (2) must hold even for these special values. We see, in (2), that

if $x = 0$ then $4 = 2A$ and $A = 2$;

if $x = 1$ then $4 = -B$ and $B = -4$;

if $x = 2$ then $6 = 2C$ and $C = 3$.

The second method is shorter than the first and most convenient when the denominator of the given fraction can be decomposed into distinct linear factors. Sometimes a combination of these methods is effective.

Finally, then, the original integral equals $\displaystyle\int (\frac{2}{x} - \frac{4}{x-1} + \frac{3}{x-2})\, dx$

$= 2 \ln |x| - 4 \ln |x - 1| + 3 \ln |x - 2| + C' = \ln \dfrac{x^2 |x - 2|^3}{(x - 1)^4} + C'.$

[The symbol "C'" appears here for the constant of integration because "C" was used in simplifying the original rational function.]

49.   Integrate $\displaystyle\int \frac{12 - 8x}{x^2 (x^2 + 4)}\, dx$. Since the linear factor x occurs twice in the denominator and since $x^2 + 4$ is an irreducible quadratic factor, we write

$$\frac{12 - 8x}{x^2 (x^2 + 4)} = \frac{A}{x} + \frac{B}{x^2} + \frac{Cx + D}{x^2 + 4}.$$

Then

$$12 - 8x = Ax(x^2 + 4) + B(x^2 + 4) + (Cx + D)x^2.$$

We can let $x = 0$ and get $12 = 4B$, so that $B = 3$. We can then equate coefficients of like powers to determine the remaining constants A, C, and D. The following equations are obtained by using the coefficients of x^3, x^2, and x respectively:

$$0 = A + C$$

$$0 = B + D$$

$$-8 = 4A.$$

Thus, A = -2, B = 3, C = 2, and D = -3, and

$$\frac{12 - 8x}{x^2 (x^2 + 4)} = -\frac{2}{x} + \frac{3}{x^2} + \frac{2x - 3}{x^2 + 4}.$$

Therefore the original integral equals

$$\int \left(-\frac{2}{x} + \frac{3}{x^2} + \frac{2x - 3}{x^2 + 4}\right) dx = -2 \ln |x| - \frac{3}{x} + \ln (x^2 + 4) - \frac{3}{2} \tan^{-1}\frac{x}{2} + C'.$$

50. Integrate $\int \frac{2x^4 - 1}{(x^2 + 1)^2} dx$. Since the numerator is not of lower

degree than the denominator, we divide as indicated:

$$x^4 + 2x^2 + 1 \overline{\smash{\big)}\begin{array}{l} 2 \\ 2x^4 - 1 \\ \underline{2x^4 + 4x^2 + 2} \\ - 4x^2 - 3 \end{array}}.$$

So $\frac{2x^4 - 1}{(x^2 + 1)^2} = 2 - \frac{4x^2 + 3}{(x^2 + 1)^2}$. Since the (irreducible) quadratic factor

$x^2 + 1$ occurs twice in the denominator of the proper rational function on

the right, we set

$$\frac{4x^2 + 3}{(x^2 + 1)^2} = \frac{Ax + B}{x^2 + 1} + \frac{Cx + D}{(x^2 + 1)^2},$$

whence

$$4x^2 + 3 = (Ax + B)(x^2 + 1) + Cx + D.$$

We now equate coefficients of like powers, respectively those of x^3, x^2, x,

and x^0, to get

$$0 = A;$$
$$4 = B;$$
$$0 = A + C;$$
$$3 = B + D.$$

Thus A = C = 0, B = 4, and D = -1. So

$$\int \frac{2x^4 - 1}{(x^2 + 1)^2} dx = \int 2 \, dx - \left[\int \frac{4 \, dx}{x^2 + 1} - \int \frac{dx}{(x^2 + 1)^2} \right]$$

$$= 2x - 4 \tan^{-1} x + \int \frac{dx}{(x^2 + 1)^2}.$$

To evaluate the last integral, we let $x = \tan\theta$, so that $dx = \sec^2\theta\, d\theta$ and

$$\int \frac{dx}{(x^2 + 1)^2} = \int \frac{\sec^2\theta\, d\theta}{\sec^4\theta} = \int \cos^2\theta\, d\theta$$

$$= \frac{1}{2}\theta + \frac{\sin 2\theta}{4} + C'.$$

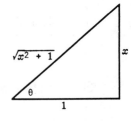

Figure N4-4 enables us to write this part of the

answer as $\quad \frac{1}{2}\tan^{-1}x + \frac{1}{4}\frac{2x}{(1 + x^2)} + C'.$

Figure N4-4

Finally, then,

$$\int \frac{2x^4 - 1}{(x^2 + 1)^2}\, dx = 2x - \frac{7}{2}\tan^{-1}x + \frac{x}{2(1 + x^2)} + C'.$$

E.   Integration by Parts.   The parts formula stems from that for the differential of a product: $d(uv) = u\, dv + v\, du$, or $u\, dv = d(uv) - v\, du$. Integrating, we get $\int u\, dv = uv - \int v\, du$, the parts formula.   Success in using this important technique depends on being able to separate a given integral into parts u and dv so that

(a) dv can be integrated, and

(b) $\int v\, du$ is no more difficult to calculate than the original integral (and hopefully simpler).

EXAMPLES:

51.   To integrate $\int x \cos x\, dx$, we let $u = x$ and $dv = \cos x\, dx$. Then $du = dx$ and $v = \sin x$.   Thus the parts formula yields

$$\int x \cos x\, dx = x \sin x - \int \sin x\, dx = x \sin x + \cos x + C.$$

52.   To integrate $\int x^4 \ln x\, dx$, we let $u = \ln x$ and $dv = x^4\, dx$. Then $du = \dfrac{dx}{x}$ and $v = \dfrac{x^5}{5}$.   Thus $\int x^4 \ln x\, dx = \dfrac{x^5}{5}\ln x - \dfrac{1}{5}\int x^4\, dx$

$$= \frac{x^5}{5}\ln x - \frac{x^5}{25} + C.$$

53. To integrate $\int x^2 e^x \, dx$ we let $u = x^2$ and $dv = e^x \, dx$. Then $du = 2x \, dx$ and $v = e^x$. So $\int x^2 e^x \, dx = x^2 e^x - 2 \int x e^x \, dx$. We use the parts formula again, letting $u = x$ and $dv = e^x \, dx$ so that $du = dx$ and $v = e^x$. Thus $\int x^2 e^x \, dx = x^2 e^x - 2 [x e^x - \int e^x \, dx]$ $= x^2 e^x - 2x e^x + 2 e^x + C$.

54. Let $I = \int e^x \cos x \, dx$. To integrate, we can let $u = e^x$ and $dv = \cos x \, dx$; then $du = e^x \, dx$, $v = \sin x$. So $I = e^x \sin x - \int e^x \sin x \, dx$.

To evaluate the integral on the right we again let $u = e^x$, $dv = \sin x \, dx$, so that $du = e^x \, dx$ and $v = -\cos x$. So

$$I = e^x \sin x - [-e^x \cos x + \int e^x \cos x \, dx]$$

$$I = e^x \sin x + e^x \cos x - I$$

$$2I = e^x (\sin x + \cos x)$$

$$I = \frac{1}{2} e^x (\sin x + \cos x) + C.$$

55. Let $I = \int x \tan^{-1} x \, dx$. To find I let $u = \tan^{-1} x$ and $dv = x \, dx$; then $du = \dfrac{dx}{1 + x^2}$ and $v = \dfrac{x^2}{2}$. We see that

$$I = \frac{1}{2} x^2 \tan^{-1} x - \frac{1}{2} \int \frac{x^2}{1 + x^2} \, dx$$

$$= \frac{1}{2} x^2 \tan^{-1} x - \frac{1}{2} \int \frac{1 + x^2 - 1}{1 + x^2} \, dx$$

$$= \frac{1}{2} x^2 \tan^{-1} x - \frac{1}{2} \int \left(1 - \frac{1}{1 + x^2}\right) \, dx$$

$$= \frac{1}{2} x^2 \tan^{-1} x - \frac{x}{2} + \frac{1}{2} \tan^{-1} x + C$$

$$= \frac{x^2 + 1}{2} \tan^{-1} x - \frac{x}{2} + C.$$

56. Integration by parts is frequently useful in obtaining reduction formulas.

Let $I_m = \int \sin^m x \, dx$; find a reduction formula for I_m. We let

$u = \sin^{m-1} x$ and $dv = \sin x\, dx$. Then $du = (m - 1)\sin^{m-2} x \cos x\, dx$ and $v = -\cos x$. So

$$I_m = -\sin^{m-1} x \cos x + (m - 1)\int \sin^{m-2} x \cos^2 x\, dx$$

$$= -\sin^{m-1} x \cos x + (m - 1)\int \sin^{m-2} x (1 - \sin^2 x)\, dx$$

$$= -\sin^{m-1} x \cos x + (m - 1)\int \sin^{m-2} x\, dx - (m - 1)\int \sin^m x\, dx.$$

$$I_m = -\sin^{m-1} x \cos x + (m - 1)I_{m-2} - (m - 1)I_m.$$

From this we get

$$mI_m = -\sin^{m-1} x \cos x + (m - 1)I_{m-2}\,;$$

$$I_m = -\frac{\sin^{m-1} x \cos x}{m} + \frac{m - 1}{m}\int \sin^{m-2} x\, dx.$$

The given integral has thus been expressed in terms of a simpler integral (i.e., with exponent reduced). The reduction formula can then be applied to the integral on the right.

Multiple Choice Questions: Integration

1. $\int (3x^2 - 2x + 3)\, dx =$

  (A) $x^3 - x^2 + C$

  (B) $3x^3 - x^2 + 3x + C$

  (C) $x^3 - x^2 + 3x + C$

  (D) $\frac{1}{2}(3x^2 - 2x + 3)^2 + C$

  (E) none of these.

2. $\int \left(x - \frac{1}{2x}\right)^2 dx =$

  (A) $\frac{1}{3}\left(x - \frac{1}{2x}\right)^3 + C$

  (B) $x^2 - 1 + \frac{1}{4x^2} + C$

  (C) $\frac{x^3}{3} - 2x - \frac{1}{4x} + C$

  (D) $\frac{x^3}{3} - x - \frac{4}{x} + C$

  (E) none of these.

3. $\int \sqrt{4 - 2t}\, dt =$

    (A) $-\frac{1}{3}(4 - 2t)^{3/2} + C$

    (B) $\frac{2}{3}(4 - 2t)^{3/2} + C$ (C) $-\frac{1}{6}(4 - 2t)^3 + C$

    (D) $+\frac{1}{2}(4 - 2t)^2 + C$ (E) $\frac{4}{3}(4 - 2t)^{3/2} + C$.

4. $\int (2 - 3x)^5\, dx =$

    (A) $\frac{1}{6}(2 - 3x)^6 + C$

    (B) $-\frac{1}{2}(2 - 3x)^6 + C$ (C) $\frac{1}{2}(2 - 3x)^6 + C$

    (D) $-\frac{1}{18}(2 - 3x)^6 + C$ (E) none of these.

5. $\int \dfrac{1 - 3y}{\sqrt{2y - 3y^2}}\, dy =$

    (A) $4\sqrt{2y - 3y^2} + C$

    (B) $\frac{1}{4}(2y - 3y^2)^2 + C$ (C) $\frac{1}{2}\ln\sqrt{2y - 3y^2} + C$

    (D) $\frac{1}{4}(2y - 3y^2)^{1/2} + C$ (E) $\sqrt{2y - 3y^2} + C$.

6. $\int \dfrac{dx}{3(2x - 1)^2} =$

    (A) $\dfrac{-3}{2x - 1} + C$

    (B) $\dfrac{1}{6 - 12x} + C$ (C) $+\dfrac{6}{2x - 1} + C$

    (D) $\dfrac{2}{3\sqrt{2x - 1}} + C$ (E) $\frac{1}{3}\ln |2x - 1| + C$.

7. $\int \dfrac{2\, du}{1 + 3u} =$

    (A) $\frac{2}{3}\ln |1 + 3u| + C$

    (B) $-\dfrac{1}{3(1 + 3u)^2} + C$ (C) $2\ln |1 + 3u| + C$

    (D) $\dfrac{3}{(1 + 3u)^2} + C$ (E) none of these.

8. $\displaystyle\int \frac{t}{\sqrt{2t^2 - 1}}\, dt$ =

(A) $\frac{1}{2} \ln \sqrt{2t^2 - 1} + C$

(B) $4 \ln \sqrt{2t^2 - 1} + C$

(C) $8\sqrt{2t^2 - 1} + C$

(D) $-\frac{1}{4(2t^2 - 1)} + C$

(E) $\frac{1}{2}\sqrt{2t^2 - 1} + C$.

9. $\displaystyle\int \cos 3x\, dx$ =

(A) $3 \sin 3x + C$

(B) $- \sin 3x + C$

(C) $- \frac{1}{3} \sin 3x + C$

(D) $\frac{1}{3} \sin 3x + C$

(E) $\frac{1}{2} \cos^2 3x + C$.

10. $\displaystyle\int \frac{x\,dx}{1 + 4x^2}$ =

(A) $\frac{1}{8} \ln (1 + 4x^2) + C$

(B) $\frac{1}{8(1 + 4x^2)^2} + C$

(C) $\frac{1}{4}\sqrt{1 + 4x^2} + C$

(D) $\frac{1}{2} \ln |1 + 4x^2| + C$

(E) $\frac{1}{2} \tan^{-1} 2x + C$.

11. $\displaystyle\int \frac{dx}{1 + 4x^2}$ =

(A) $\tan^{-1}(2x) + C$

(B) $\frac{1}{8} \ln (1 + 4x^2) + C$

(C) $\frac{1}{8(1 + 4x^2)^2} + C$

(D) $\frac{1}{2} \tan^{-1}(2x) + C$

(E) $\frac{1}{8x} \ln |1 + 4x^2| + C$.

12. $\displaystyle\int \frac{x}{(1 + 4x^2)^2}\, dx$ =

(A) $\frac{1}{8} \ln (1 + 4x^2)^2 + C$

(B) $\frac{1}{4}\sqrt{1 + 4x^2} + C$

(C) $- \frac{1}{8(1 + 4x^2)} + C$

(D) $- \frac{1}{3(1 + 4x^2)^3} + C$

(E) $- \frac{1}{(1 + 4x^2)} + C$.

13. $\displaystyle\int \frac{x\,dx}{\sqrt{1 + 4x^2}}$ =

(A) $\frac{1}{8}\sqrt{1 + 4x^2} + C$

(B) $\frac{\sqrt{1 + 4x^2}}{4} + C$

(C) $\frac{1}{2} \sin^{-1} 2x + C$

(D) $\frac{1}{2} \tan^{-1} 2x + C$

(E) $\frac{1}{8} \ln \sqrt{1 + 4x^2} + C$.

14. $\int \dfrac{dy}{\sqrt{4 - y^2}} =$

     (A) $\dfrac{1}{2} \sin^{-1} \dfrac{y}{2} + C$

     (B) $-\sqrt{4 - y^2} + C$

     (C) $\sin^{-1} \dfrac{y}{2} + C$

     (D) $-\dfrac{1}{2} \ln \sqrt{4 - y^2} + C$

     (E) $-\dfrac{1}{3(4 - y^2)^{3/2}} + C$.

15. $\int \dfrac{y\,dy}{\sqrt{4 - y^2}} =$

     (A) $\dfrac{1}{2} \sin^{-1} \dfrac{y}{2} + C$

     (B) $-\sqrt{4 - y^2} + C$

     (C) $\sin^{-1} \dfrac{y}{2} + C$

     (D) $-\dfrac{1}{2} \ln \sqrt{4 - y^2} + C$

     (E) $2\sqrt{4 - y^2} + C$.

16. $\int \dfrac{2x + 1}{2x}\,dx =$

     (A) $x + \dfrac{1}{2} \ln |x| + C$

     (B) $1 + \dfrac{1}{2} x^{-1} + C$

     (C) $x + 2 \ln |x| + C$

     (D) $x + \ln |2x| + C$

     (E) $\dfrac{1}{2}(2x - \dfrac{1}{x^2}) + C$.

17. $\int \dfrac{(x - 2)^3}{x^2}\,dx =$

     (A) $\dfrac{(x - 2)^4}{4x^2} + C$

     (B) $\dfrac{x^2}{2} - 6x + 6 \ln |x| - \dfrac{8}{x} + C$

     (C) $\dfrac{x^2}{2} - 3x + 6 \ln|x| + \dfrac{4}{x} + C$

     (D) $-\dfrac{(x - 2)^4}{4x} + C$

     (E) none of these.

18. $\int (\sqrt{t} - \dfrac{1}{\sqrt{t}})^2\,dt =$

     (A) $t - 2 + \dfrac{1}{t} + C$

     (B) $\dfrac{t^3}{3} - 2t - \dfrac{1}{t} + C$

     (C) $\dfrac{t^2}{2} + \ln |t| + C$

     (D) $\dfrac{t^2}{2} - 2t + \ln |t| + C$

     (E) $\dfrac{t^2}{2} - t - \dfrac{1}{t^2} + C$.

19. $\int (4x^{1/3} - 5x^{3/2} - x^{-1/2}) \, dx =$ (A) $3x^{4/3} - 2x^{5/2} - 2x^{1/2} + C$

   (B) $3x^{4/3} - 2x^{5/2} + 2x^{1/2} + C$

   (C) $6x^{2/3} - 2x^{5/2} - \frac{1}{2}x^2 + C$

   (D) $\frac{4}{3}x^{-2/3} - \frac{15}{2}x^{1/2} + \frac{1}{2}x^{-3/2} + C$

   (E)   none of these.

20. $\int \frac{x^3 - x - 1}{(x + 1)^2} \, dx =$

   (A) $(x - 2) + \frac{2x + 1}{(x + 1)^2} + C$

   (B) $x^2 - 2x + \frac{1}{2} \ln (x^2 + 2x + 1) + C$

   (C) $\frac{1}{2}x^2 - 2x + \ln |x + 1|^2 - \frac{1}{x + 1} + C$

   (D) $\frac{1}{2}(x - 2)^2 + 2 \ln |x + 1| + \frac{1}{x + 1} + C$

   (E)   none of these.

21. $\int \frac{dy}{\sqrt{y}(1 - \sqrt{y})} =$ (A) $4\sqrt{1 - \sqrt{y}} + C$

   (B) $\frac{1}{2} \ln |1 - \sqrt{y}| + C$ (C) $2 \ln (1 - \sqrt{y}) + C$

   (D) $2\sqrt{y} - \ln |y| + C$ (E) $-2 \ln |1 - \sqrt{y}| + C$.

22. $\int \frac{u \, du}{\sqrt{4 - 9u^2}} =$ (A) $\frac{1}{3} \sin^{-1} \frac{3u}{2} + C$

   (B) $-\frac{1}{18} \ln \sqrt{4 - 9u^2} + C$ (C) $2\sqrt{4 - 9u^2} + C$

   (D) $\frac{1}{6} \sin^{-1} \frac{3}{2}u + C$ (E) $-\frac{1}{9}\sqrt{4 - 9u^2} + C$.

23. $\int \sin \theta \cos \theta \, d\theta$ =

      (A) $- \dfrac{\sin^2 \theta}{2} + C$

      (B) $- \dfrac{1}{4} \cos 2\theta + C$

      (C) $\dfrac{\cos^2 \theta}{2} + C$

      (D) $\dfrac{1}{2} \sin 2\theta + C$

      (E) $\cos 2\theta + C$.

24. $\int \dfrac{\sin \sqrt{x}}{\sqrt{x}} \, dx$ =

      (A) $-2 \cos^{1/2} x + C$

      (B) $- \cos \sqrt{x} + C$

      (C) $-2 \cos \sqrt{x} + C$

      (D) $\dfrac{3}{2} \sin^{3/2} x + C$

      (E) $\dfrac{1}{2} \cos \sqrt{x} + C$.

25. $\int t \cos (2t)^2 \, dt$ =

      (A) $\dfrac{1}{8} \sin (4t^2) + C$

      (B) $\dfrac{1}{2} \cos^2 (2t) + C$

      (C) $- \dfrac{1}{8} \sin (4t^2) + C$

      (D) $\dfrac{1}{4} \sin (2t)^2 + C$

      (E) none of these.

26. $\int \cos^2 2x \, dx$ =

      (A) $\dfrac{x}{2} + \dfrac{\sin 4x}{8} + C$

      (B) $\dfrac{x}{2} - \dfrac{\sin 4x}{8} + C$

      (C) $\dfrac{x}{4} + \dfrac{\sin 4x}{4} + C$

      (D) $\dfrac{x}{4} + \dfrac{\sin 4x}{16} + C$

      (E) $\dfrac{1}{4}(x + \sin 4x) + C$.

27. $\int \sin 2\theta \, d\theta$ =

      (A) $\dfrac{1}{2} \cos 2\theta + C$

      (B) $-2 \cos 2\theta + C$

      (C) $- \sin^2 \theta + C$

      (D) $\cos^2 \theta + C$

      (E) $- \dfrac{1}{2} \cos 2\theta + C$.

*28. $\int x \cos x \, dx$ =

      (A) $x \sin x + C$

      (B) $x \sin x + \cos x + C$

      (C) $x \sin x - \cos x + C$

      (D) $\cos x - x \sin x + C$

      (E) $\dfrac{x^2}{2} \sin x + C$.

*29. $\displaystyle\int \frac{du}{\cos^2 3u} =$

(A) $-\dfrac{\sec 3u}{3} + C$

(B) $\tan 3u + C$

(C) $u + \dfrac{\sec 3u}{3} + C$

(D) $\dfrac{1}{3} \tan 3u + C$

(E) $\dfrac{1}{3 \cos 3u} + C$.

30. $\displaystyle\int \frac{\cos x \, dx}{\sqrt{1 + \sin x}} =$

(A) $-\dfrac{1}{2}(1 + \sin x)^{1/2} + C$

(B) $\ln \sqrt{1 + \sin x} + C$

(C) $2\sqrt{1 + \sin x} + C$

(D) $\ln |1 + \sin x| + C$

(E) $\dfrac{2}{3(1 + \sin x)^{3/2}} + C$.

31. $\displaystyle\int \frac{\cos (\theta - 1) \, d\theta}{\sin^2 (\theta - 1)}$

(A) $2 \ln \sin |\theta - 1| + C$

(B) $- \csc (\theta - 1) + C$

(C) $-\dfrac{1}{3} \sin^{-3} (\theta - 1) + C$

(D) $- \cot (\theta - 1) + C$

(E) $\csc (\theta - 1) + C$.

*32. $\displaystyle\int \sec \frac{t}{2} \, dt =$

(A) $\ln \left|\sec \dfrac{t}{2} + \tan \dfrac{t}{2}\right| + C$

(B) $2 \tan^2 \dfrac{t}{2} + C$

(C) $2 \ln \cos \dfrac{t}{2} + C$

(D) $\ln |\sec t + \tan t| + C$

(E) $2 \ln \left|\sec \dfrac{t}{2} + \tan \dfrac{t}{2}\right| + C$.

33. $\displaystyle\int \frac{\sin 2x \, dx}{\sqrt{1 + \cos^2 x}}$

(A) $-2\sqrt{1 + \cos^2 x} + C$

(B) $\dfrac{1}{2} \ln (1 + \cos^2 x) + C$

(C) $\sqrt{1 + \cos^2 x} + C$

(D) $- \ln \sqrt{1 + \cos^2 x} + C$

(E) $2 \ln |\sin x| + C$.

*34. $\int \sec^{3/2} x \tan x \, dx =$

(A) $\frac{2}{5} \sec^{5/2} x + C$

(B) $- \frac{2}{3} \cos^{-3/2} x + C$

(C) $\sec^{3/2} x + C$

(D) $\frac{2}{3} \sec^{3/2} x + C$

(E) none of these.

*35. $\int \tan \theta \, d\theta =$

(A) $- \ln |\sec \theta| + C$

(B) $\sec^2 \theta + C$

(C) $\ln |\sin \theta| + C$

(D) $\sec \theta + C$

(E) $- \ln |\cos \theta| + C$.

*36. $\int \frac{dx}{\sin^2 2x} =$

(A) $\frac{1}{2} \csc 2x \cot 2x + C$

(B) $- \frac{2}{\sin 2x} + C$

(C) $- \frac{1}{2} \cot 2x + C$

(D) $- \cot x + C$

(E) $- \csc 2x + C$.

*37. $\int \frac{\tan^{-1} y}{1 + y^2} \, dy =$

(A) $\sec^{-1} y + C$

(B) $(\tan^{-1} y)^2 + C$

(C) $\ln (1 + y^2) + C$

(D) $\ln (\tan^{-1} y) + C$

(E) none of these.

*38. $\int \sin^3 \theta \cos^3 \theta \, d\theta =$

(A) $\frac{\sin^4 \theta}{4} - \frac{\sin^6 \theta}{6} + C$

(B) $\frac{\cos^4 \theta}{4} - \frac{\cos^6 \theta}{6} + C$

(C) $\frac{\sin^4 \theta}{4} + C$

(D) $- \frac{\cos^4 \theta}{4} + C$

(E) $\frac{\sin^4 \theta \cos^4 \theta}{16} + C$.

*39. $\int \frac{\sin 2t}{1 - \cos 2t} \, dt =$

(A) $\frac{2}{(1 - \cos 2t)^2} + C$

(B) $- \ln |1 - \cos 2t| + C$

(C) $\ln \sqrt{1 - \cos 2t} + C$

(D) $\sqrt{1 - \cos 2t} + C$

(E) $2 \ln |1 - \cos 2t| + C$.

*40. $\int \cot 2u \ du \ =$ (A) $\ln |\sin u| + C$

      (B) $\frac{1}{2} \ln |\sin 2u| + C$ (C) $-\frac{1}{2} \csc^2 2u + C$

      (D) $-\sec 2u + C$ (E) $2 \ln |\sin 2u| + C$.

41. $\int \dfrac{e^x}{e^x - 1} \ dx \ =$ (A) $x + \ln |e^x - 1| + C$

      (B) $x - e^x + C$ (C) $x - \dfrac{1}{(e^x - 1)^2} + C$

      (D) $1 + \dfrac{1}{e^x - 1} + C$ (E) $\ln |e^x - 1| + C$.

*42. $\int \dfrac{x - 1}{x(x - 2)} \ dx \ =$ (A) $\frac{1}{2} \ln |x| + \ln |x - 2| + C$

      (B) $\frac{1}{2} \ln \left| \dfrac{x - 2}{x} \right| + C$ (C) $\ln |x - 2| + \ln |x| + C$

      (D) $\ln \sqrt{x^2 - 2x} + C$ (E) none of these.

43. $\int xe^{x^2} \ dx \ =$ (A) $\frac{1}{2} e^{x^2} + C$

      (B) $e^{x^2}(2x^2 + 1) + C$ (C) $2e^{x^2} + C$

      (D) $e^{x^2} + C$ (E) $\frac{1}{2} e^{x^2+1} + C$.

44. $\int \cos \theta \ e^{\sin \theta} \ d\theta \ =$ (A) $e^{\sin \theta + 1} + C$

      (B) $e^{\sin \theta} + C$ (C) $-e^{\sin \theta} + C$

      (D) $e^{\cos \theta} + C$ (E) $e^{\sin \theta}(\cos \theta - \sin \theta) + C$.

45. $\int e^{2\theta} \sin e^{2\theta} \ d\theta \ =$ (A) $\cos e^{2\theta} + C$

      (B) $2e^{4\theta}(\cos e^{2\theta} + \sin e^{2\theta}) + C$ (C) $-\frac{1}{2} \cos e^{2\theta} + C$

      (D) $-2 \cos e^{2\theta} + C$ (E) none of these.

46. $\int \dfrac{e^{\sqrt{x}}}{\sqrt{x}}\ dx\ =$

(A) $2\sqrt{x}(e^{\sqrt{x}} - 1) + C$

(B) $2e^{\sqrt{x}} + C$

(C) $\dfrac{e^{\sqrt{x}}}{2}(\dfrac{1}{x} + \dfrac{1}{x\sqrt{x}}) + C$

(D) $\dfrac{1}{2}\ e^{\sqrt{x}} + C$

(E) none of these.

*47. $\int xe^{-x}\ dx\ =$

(A) $e^{-x}(1 - x) + C$

(B) $\dfrac{e^{1-x}}{1 - x} + C$

(C) $-e^{-x}(x + 1) + C$

(D) $-\dfrac{x^2}{2}\ e^{-x} + C$

(E) $e^{-x}(x + 1) + C$.

*48. $\int x^2 e^x\ dx\ =$

(A) $e^x(x^2 + 2x) + C$

(B) $e^x(x^2 - 2x - 2) + C$

(C) $e^x(x^2 - 2x + 2) + C$

(D) $e^x(x - 1)^2 + C$

(E) $e^x(x + 1)^2 + C$.

49. $\int \dfrac{e^x + e^{-x}}{e^x - e^{-x}}\ dx\ =$

(A) $x - \ln |e^x - e^{-x}| + C$

(B) $x + 2 \ln |e^x - e^{-x}| + C$

(C) $-\dfrac{1}{2}(e^x - e^{-x})^{-2} + C$

(D) $\ln |e^x - e^{-x}| + C$

(E) $\ln (e^x + e^{-x}) + C$.

*50. $\int \dfrac{e^x}{1 + e^{2x}}\ dx\ =$

(A) $\tan^{-1} e^x + C$

(B) $\dfrac{1}{2} \ln (1 + e^{2x}) + C$

(C) $\ln (1 + e^{2x}) + C$

(D) $\dfrac{1}{2} \tan^{-1} e^x + C$

(E) $2 \tan^{-1} e^x + C$

51. $\int \dfrac{\ln v\ dv}{v}\ =$

(A) $\ln |\ln v| + C$

(B) $\ln \dfrac{v^2}{2} + C$

(C) $\dfrac{1}{2} (\ln v)^2 + C$

(D) $2 \ln v + C$

(E) $\dfrac{1}{2} \ln v^2 + C$.

52. $\int \dfrac{\ln \sqrt{x}}{x}\, dx\ =$

                                                    (A) $\dfrac{\ln^2 \sqrt{x}}{\sqrt{x}} + C$

(B) $\ln^2 x + C$

                                               (C) $\dfrac{1}{2} \ln |\ln x| + C$

(D) $\dfrac{(\ln \sqrt{x})^2}{2} + C$

                                             (E) $\dfrac{1}{4} \ln^2 x + C$.

*53. $\int \xi^3 \ln \xi\, d\xi\ =$

                                                  (A) $\xi^2 (3 \ln \xi + 1) + C$

(B) $\dfrac{\xi^4}{16} (4 \ln \xi - 1) + C$

                               (C) $\dfrac{\xi^4}{4} (\ln \xi - 1) + C$

(D) $3\xi^2 (\ln \xi - \dfrac{1}{2}) + C$

                                 (E) none of these.

*54. $\int \ln \eta\, d\eta\ =$

                                                  (A) $\dfrac{1}{2} \ln^2 \eta + C$

(B) $\eta(\ln \eta - 1) + C$

                                  (C) $\dfrac{1}{2} \ln \eta^2 + C$

(D) $\ln \eta\, (\eta - 1) + C$

                                  (E) $\eta \ln \eta + \eta + C$.

*55. $\int \ln x^3\, dx\ =$

                                                  (A) $\dfrac{3}{2} \ln^2 x + C$

(B) $3x(\ln x - 1) + C$

                                  (C) $3 \ln x\, (x - 1) + C$

(D) $\dfrac{3x \ln^2 x}{2} + C$

                                  (E) none of these.

*56. $\int \dfrac{\ln y}{y^2}\, dy\ =$

                                          (A) $\dfrac{1}{y} (1 - \ln y) + C$

(B) $\dfrac{1}{2y} \ln^2 y + C$

                                (C) $- \dfrac{1}{3y^3} (4 \ln y + 1) + C$

(D) $- \dfrac{1}{y} (\ln y + 1) + C$

                                (E) $\dfrac{\ln y}{y} - \dfrac{1}{y} + C$.

57. $\int \dfrac{dv}{v \ln v}\ =$

                                      (A) $\dfrac{1}{\ln v^2} + C$

(B) $- \dfrac{1}{\ln^2 v} + C$

                                (C) $- \ln |\ln v| + C$

(D) $\ln \dfrac{1}{v} + C$

                                (E) $\ln |\ln v| + C$.

58. $\int \frac{y-1}{y+1}\, dy =$ (A) $y - 2 \ln |y + 1| + C$

(B) $1 - \frac{2}{y+1} + C$ (C) $\ln \frac{|y|}{(y+1)^2} + C$

(D) $1 - 2 \ln |y + 1| + C$ (E) $\ln \left| \frac{e^y}{y+1} \right| + C$.

*59. $\int t\sqrt{t+1}\, dt =$ (A) $\frac{2}{3}(t+1)^{3/2} + C$

(B) $\frac{2}{15}(3t-2)(t+1)^{3/2} + C$ (C) $2\left[\frac{(t+1)^{5/2}}{5} + \frac{(t+1)^{3/2}}{5}\right] + C$

(D) $2t(t+1) + C$ (E) none of these.

60. $\int \sqrt{x}(\sqrt{x} - 1)\, dx =$ (A) $2(x^{3/2} - x) + C$

(B) $\frac{x^2}{2} - x + C$ (C) $\frac{1}{2}(\sqrt{x} - 1)^2 + C$

(D) $\frac{1}{2} x^2 - \frac{2}{3} x^{3/2} + C$ (E) $x - 2\sqrt{x} + C$.

*61. $\int e^\theta \cos \theta\, d\theta =$ (A) $e^\theta (\cos \theta - \sin \theta) + C$

(B) $e^\theta \sin \theta + C$ (C) $\frac{1}{2} e^\theta (\sin \theta + \cos \theta) + C$

(D) $2 e^\theta (\sin \theta + \cos \theta) + C$ (E) $\frac{1}{2} e^\theta (\sin \theta - \cos \theta) + C$.

62. $\int \frac{(1 - \ln t)^2}{t}\, dt =$ (A) $\frac{1}{3}(1 - \ln t)^3 + C$

(B) $\ln t - 2\ln^2 t + \ln^3 t + C$ (C) $-2(1 - \ln t) + C$

(D) $\ln t - \ln^2 t + \frac{\ln t^3}{3} + C$ (E) $-\frac{(1 - \ln t)^3}{3} + C$.

*63. $\int u \sec^2 u\, du =$ (A) $u \tan u + \ln |\cos u| + C$

(B) $\frac{u^2}{2} \tan u + C$ (C) $\frac{1}{2} \sec u \tan u + C$

(D) $u \tan u - \ln |\sin u| + C$ (E) $u \sec u - \ln |\sec u + \tan u| + C$.

*64. $\int \dfrac{2x + 1}{4 + x^2} \, dx \;=$

         (A) $\ln (x^2 + 4) + C$

         (B) $\ln (x^2 + 4) + \tan^{-1} \dfrac{x}{2} + C$ (C) $\dfrac{1}{2} \tan^{-1} \dfrac{x}{2} + C$

         (D) $\ln (x^2 + 4) + \dfrac{1}{2} \tan^{-1} \dfrac{x}{2} + C$ (E)   none of these.

*65. $\int \dfrac{x + 2}{x^2 + 2x + 10} \, dx \;=$

         (A) $\dfrac{1}{2} \ln (x^2 + 2x + 10) + C$

         (B) $\dfrac{1}{3} \tan^{-1} \dfrac{x + 1}{3} + C$

         (C) $\dfrac{1}{2} \ln (x^2 + 2x + 10) + \dfrac{1}{3} \tan^{-1} \dfrac{x + 1}{3} + C$

         (D) $\tan^{-1} \dfrac{x + 1}{3} + C$

         (E) $\dfrac{1}{2} \ln |x^2 + 2x + 10| - 2 \tan^{-1} \dfrac{x + 1}{3} + C \; .$

*66. $\int \dfrac{2x - 1}{\sqrt{4x - 4x^2}} \, dx \;=$

         (A) $4 \ln \sqrt{4x - 4x^2} + C$

         (B) $\sin^{-1} (1 - 2x) + C$ (C) $\dfrac{1}{2} \sqrt{4x - 4x^2} + C$

         (D) $-\dfrac{1}{4} \ln (4x - 4x^2) + C$ (E) $-\dfrac{1}{2} \sqrt{4x - 4x^2} + C \; .$

67. $\int \dfrac{e^{2x}}{1 + e^x} \, dx \;=$

         (A) $\tan^{-1} e^x + C$

         (B) $e^x - \ln (1 + e^x) + C$ (C) $e^x - x + \ln |1 + e^x| + C$

         (D) $e^x + \dfrac{1}{(e^x + 1)^2} + C$ (E)   none of these.

*68. $\int \dfrac{\cos \theta}{1 + \sin^2 \theta} \, d\theta \;=$

         (A) $\sec \theta \tan \theta + C$

         (B) $\sin \theta - \csc \theta + C$ (C) $\ln (1 + \sin^2 \theta) + C$

         (D) $\tan^{-1} (\sin \theta) + C$ (E) $-\dfrac{1}{(1 + \sin^2 \theta)^2} + C \; .$

*69. $\int x \tan^{-1} x \, dx =$

(A) $\frac{x^2}{2} \tan^{-1} x - \frac{x}{2} + C$

(B) $\frac{1}{2}[x^2 \tan^{-1} x + \ln (1 + x^2)] + C$

(C) $(\frac{x^2 + 1}{2}) \tan^{-1} x + C$

(D) $\frac{1}{2x}(\tan^{-1} x) + C$

(E) $\frac{1}{2}[(x^2 + 1) \tan^{-1} x - x] + C$.

*70. $\int \frac{dx}{1 - e^x} =$

(A) $- \ln |1 - e^x| + C$

(B) $x - \ln |1 - e^x| + C$

(C) $\frac{1}{(1 - e^x)^2} + C$

(D) $e^{-x} \ln |1 - e^x| + C$

(E) none of these.

*71. $\int \frac{(2 - y)^2}{4\sqrt{y}} \, dy =$

(A) $\frac{1}{6}(2 - y)^3 \sqrt{y} + C$

(B) $2\sqrt{y} - \frac{2}{3}y^{3/2} + \frac{8}{5}y^{5/2} + C$

(C) $\ln |y| - y + 2y^2 + C$

(D) $2y^{1/2} - \frac{2}{3}y^{3/2} + \frac{1}{10}y^{5/2} + C$

(E) none of these.

*72. $\int e^{2\ln u} \, du =$

(A) $\frac{1}{3} e^{u^3} + C$

(B) $e^{(1/3 \, u^3)} + C$

(C) $\frac{1}{3}u^3 + C$

(D) $\frac{2}{u}e^{2\ln u} + C$

(E) $e^{1+2\ln u} + C$.

*73. $\int \frac{dy}{y(1 + \ln y^2)} =$

(A) $\frac{1}{2} \ln |1 + \ln y^2| + C$

(B) $- \frac{1}{(1 + \ln y^2)^2} + C$

(C) $\ln |y| + \frac{1}{2} \ln |\ln y| + C$

(D) $\tan^{-1} (\ln |y|) + C$

(E) none of these.

*74. $\int (\tan \theta - 1)^2 \, d\theta =$ (A) $\sec \theta + \theta + 2 \ln |\cos \theta| + C$

(B) $\tan \theta + 2 \ln |\cos \theta| + C$ (C) $\tan \theta - 2 \sec^2 \theta + C$

(D) $\sec \theta + \theta - \tan^2 \theta + C$ (E) $\tan \theta - 2 \ln |\cos \theta| + C$.

*75. $\int \dfrac{d\theta}{1 + \sin \theta} =$ (A) $\sec \theta - \tan \theta + C$

(B) $\ln (1 + \sin \theta) + C$ (C) $\ln |\sec \theta + \tan \theta| + C$

(D) $\theta + \ln |\csc \theta - \cot \theta| + C$ (E)   none of these.

Section 5: Definite Integrals

Review of Definitions and Methods

A. **Definition of Definite Integral.** If f is continuous on the closed interval $[a,b]$ and $F' = f$, then according to the Fundamental Theorem of the Integral Calculus

$$\int_a^b f(x)\ dx\ =\ F(b) - F(a)\ .$$

$\int_a^b f(x)\ dx$ is the *definite integral of f from a to b*; $f(x)$ is called the *integrand*; and a and b are called respectively the *lower* and *upper limits of integration*.

B. **Properties of Definite Integrals.** The following theorems about definite integrals are important.

$$\frac{d}{dx} \int_a^x f(t)\ dt\ =\ f(x) \tag{1}$$

$$\int_a^b kf(x)\ dx\ =\ k \int_a^b f(x)\ dx \qquad k \text{ a constant} \tag{2}$$

$$\int_a^a f(x)\ dx\ =\ 0 \tag{3}$$

$$\int_a^b f(x)\ dx\ =\ -\int_b^a f(x)\ dx \tag{4}$$

$$\int_a^c f(x)\ dx\ +\ \int_c^b f(x)\ dx\ =\ \int_a^b f(x)\ dx \qquad a < c < b \tag{5}$$

If f and g are both integrable functions of x on $[a,b]$, then

$$\int_a^b [f(x) \pm g(x)]\ dx \ = \ \int_a^b f(x)\ dx \ \pm \ \int_a^b g(x)\ dx\ . \qquad (6)$$

The Mean Value Theorem for integrals: there exists at least one number c, $a < c < b$, such that

$$\int_a^b f(x)\ dx \ = \ f(c)(b - a) \qquad (7)$$

The evaluation of definite integrals is illustrated in the following EXAMPLES:

1. $\displaystyle\int_{-1}^{2} (3x^2 - 2x)\ dx \ = \ x^3 - x^2 \Big|_{-1}^{2} \ = \ (8 - 4) - (-1 - 1) \ = \ 6\ .$

2. $\displaystyle\int_{1}^{2} \frac{x^2 + x - 2}{2x^2}\ dx \ = \ \frac{1}{2}\int_{1}^{2} \left(1 + \frac{1}{x} - \frac{2}{x^2}\right)\ dx \ = \ \frac{1}{2}\left(x + \ln x + \frac{2}{x}\right)\Big|_{1}^{2}$

$= \ \frac{1}{2}\left[(2 + \ln 2 + 1) - (1 + 2)\right] \ = \ \frac{1}{2}\ln 2,\ \text{or}\ \ln \sqrt{2}\ .$

3. $\displaystyle\int_{5}^{8} \frac{dy}{\sqrt{9 - y}} \ = \ -\int_{5}^{8} (9 - y)^{-1/2}(-dy) \ = \ -2\sqrt{9 - y}\,\Big|_{5}^{8} \ = \ -2(1 - 2) \ = \ 2.$

4. $\displaystyle\int_{0}^{1} \frac{x\ dx}{(2 - x^2)^3} \ = \ -\frac{1}{2}\int_{0}^{1} (2 - x^2)^{-3}(-2x\ dx) \ = \ -\frac{1}{2}\frac{(2 - x^2)^{-2}}{-2}\Big|_{0}^{1}$

$= \ \frac{1}{4}\left(1 - \frac{1}{4}\right) \ = \ \frac{3}{16}\ .$

5. $\displaystyle\int_{0}^{3} \frac{dt}{9 + t^2} \ = \ \frac{1}{3}\tan^{-1}\frac{t}{3}\Big|_{0}^{3} \ = \ \frac{1}{3}(\tan^{-1} 1 - \tan^{-1} 0) \ = \ \frac{1}{3}\left(\frac{\pi}{4} - 0\right) \ = \ \frac{\pi}{12}\ .$

6. $\displaystyle\int_{0}^{1} (3x - 2)^3\ dx \ = \ \frac{1}{3}\int_{0}^{1} (3x - 2)^3(3\ dx) \ = \ \frac{(3x - 2)^4}{12}\Big|_{0}^{1}$

$= \ \frac{1}{12}(1 - 16) \ = \ -\frac{5}{4}\ .$

7. $\displaystyle\int_{0}^{1} xe^{-x^2}\ dx \ = \ -\frac{1}{2}e^{-x^2}\Big|_{0}^{1} \ = \ -\frac{1}{2}\left(\frac{1}{e} - 1\right) \ = \ \frac{e - 1}{2e}\ .$

8. $\displaystyle\int_{-\frac{\pi}{4}}^{\frac{\pi}{4}} \cos 2x\ dx \ = \ \frac{1}{2}\sin 2x\Big|_{-\frac{\pi}{4}}^{\frac{\pi}{4}} \ = \ \frac{1}{2}(1 + 1) \ = \ 1.$

9. $\displaystyle\int_{-1}^{1} x e^x \, dx = (x e^x - e^x)\Big|_{-1}^{1} = e - e - (-\frac{1}{e} - \frac{1}{e}) = \frac{2}{e}$.

10. $\displaystyle\int_{0}^{\frac{1}{2}} \frac{dx}{\sqrt{1 - x^2}} = \sin^{-1} x\Big|_{0}^{\frac{1}{2}} = \frac{\pi}{6}$.

11. $\displaystyle\int_{0}^{e-1} \ln(x + 1) \, dx = [(x + 1) \ln(x + 1) - x]_{0}^{e-1}$ (where the

parts formula has been used) $= e \ln e - (e - 1) - 0 = 1$.

12. To evaluate $\displaystyle\int_{-1}^{1} \frac{dy}{y^2 - 4}$ we use the method of partial fractions

and set $\displaystyle\frac{1}{y^2 - 4} = \frac{A}{y + 2} + \frac{B}{y - 2}$. Solving for A and B yields $A = -\frac{1}{4}$,

$B = \frac{1}{4}$. Thus $\displaystyle\int_{-1}^{1} \frac{dy}{y^2 - 4} = \frac{1}{4} \ln\left|\frac{y - 2}{y + 2}\right|_{-1}^{1} = \frac{1}{4}(\ln\frac{1}{3} - \ln 3) = -\frac{1}{2} \ln 3$.

13. $\displaystyle\int_{\frac{\pi}{3}}^{\frac{\pi}{2}} \tan\frac{\theta}{2} \sec^2\frac{\theta}{2} \, d\theta = \frac{2}{2} \tan^2\frac{\theta}{2}\Big|_{\frac{\pi}{3}}^{\frac{\pi}{2}} = 1 - \frac{1}{3} = \frac{2}{3}$.

14. $\displaystyle\int_{0}^{\frac{\pi}{2}} \sin^2\frac{1}{2} x \, dx = \int_{0}^{\frac{\pi}{2}} (\frac{1}{2} - \frac{\cos x}{2}) \, dx = \frac{x}{2} - \frac{\sin x}{2}\Big|_{0}^{\frac{\pi}{2}} = \frac{\pi}{4} - \frac{1}{2}$.

15. $\displaystyle\frac{d}{dx}\int_{-1}^{x} \sqrt{1 + \sin^2 t} \, dt = \sqrt{1 + \sin^2 x}$ by theorem (1).

16. $\displaystyle\frac{d}{dx}\int_{x}^{1} e^{-t^2} \, dt = \frac{d}{dx}(-\int_{1}^{x} e^{-t^2} \, dt)$ by theorem (4),

$= -\displaystyle\frac{d}{dx}\int_{1}^{x} e^{-t^2} \, dt = -e^{-x^2}$.

17. If $F(x) = \displaystyle\int_{1}^{x^2} \frac{dt}{3 + t}$, then $F'(x) = \frac{d}{dx}\int_{1}^{x^2} \frac{dt}{3 + t}$

$= \displaystyle\frac{d}{dx}\int_{1}^{u} \frac{dt}{3 + t}$ where $u = x^2$, $= \frac{d}{du}\int_{1}^{u} \frac{dt}{3 + t} \cdot \frac{du}{dx}$ by the chain rule,

$= (\displaystyle\frac{1}{3 + u})(2x) = \frac{2x}{3 + x^2}$.

18. If $F(x) = \int_0^{\cos x} \sqrt{1 - t^3}\, dt$, then to find $F'(x)$ we let $u = \cos x$.

Thus $\dfrac{dF}{dx} = \dfrac{dF}{du}\cdot\dfrac{du}{dx} = \sqrt{1 - u^3}(-\sin x) = -\sin x\sqrt{1 - \cos^3 x}$.

19. $\lim\limits_{h \to 0} \dfrac{1}{h} \int_x^{x+h} \sqrt{e^t - 1}\, dt = \sqrt{e^x - 1}$. Here we have let $f(t) = \sqrt{e^t - 1}$

and noted that $\lim\limits_{h \to 0} \dfrac{1}{h} \int_x^{x+h} f(t)\, dt = \lim\limits_{h \to 0} \dfrac{F(x+h) - F(x)}{h}$ where $\dfrac{dF(x)}{dx}$

$= f(x) = \sqrt{e^x - 1}$. The limit on the right, however, is, by definition,

the derivative of $F(x)$, i.e., $f(x)$.

20. Evaluate $\int_3^6 x\sqrt{x - 2}\, dx$. Here we let $u = \sqrt{x - 2}$, $u^2 = x - 2$

and $2u\, du = dx$. The limits of the given integral are values of x. When
we write the new integral in terms of the variable u, we can also write
the limits as the values of u which correspond to the given limits. Thus,
when $x = 3$, $u = 1$, and when $x = 6$, $u = 2$. So

$$\int_3^6 x\sqrt{x - 2}\, dx = 2\int_1^2 (u^2 + 2)u^2\, du = 2\int_1^2 (u^4 + 2u^2)\, du$$

$$= 2\left(\frac{u^5}{5} + \frac{2u^3}{3}\right)\Big|_1^2 = 2\left[\left(\frac{32}{5} + \frac{16}{3}\right) - \left(\frac{1}{5} + \frac{2}{3}\right)\right]$$

$$= \frac{326}{15} \ .$$

21. Evaluate $\int_1^{\sqrt{2}} \dfrac{x^2}{\sqrt{4 - x^2}}\, dx$. From problem 45, p. 78, we see that

if we let $x = 2 \sin \theta$ then $\int \dfrac{x^2\, dx}{\sqrt{4 - x^2}} = 2\int (1 - \cos 2\theta)\, d\theta$.

Since $\theta = \dfrac{\pi}{6}$ when $x = 1$ and $\theta = \dfrac{\pi}{4}$ when $x = \sqrt{2}$, we have

$$\int_{1}^{\sqrt{2}} \frac{x^2}{\sqrt{4 - x^2}} \, dx \; = \; 2 \int_{\frac{\pi}{6}}^{\frac{\pi}{4}} (1 - \cos 2\theta) \, d\theta \; = \; (2\theta - \sin 2\theta) \Big|_{\frac{\pi}{6}}^{\frac{\pi}{4}}$$

$$= \; (\tfrac{\pi}{2} - 1) - (\tfrac{\pi}{3} - \tfrac{\sqrt{3}}{2}) \; = \; \tfrac{\pi}{6} + \tfrac{\sqrt{3}}{2} - 1.$$

C. Integrals Involving Parametric Equations. The techniques are illustrated in the following two EXAMPLES:

22. To evaluate $\int_{-2}^{2} y \, dx$ when $\begin{cases} x = 2 \sin \theta \\ y = 2 \cos \theta \end{cases}$ we note that

$dx = 2 \cos \theta \, d\theta$ and that $\theta = -\frac{\pi}{2}$ when $x = -2$, $\theta = \frac{\pi}{2}$ when $x = 2$.

Then

$$\int_{-2}^{2} y \, dx \; = \; \int_{-\frac{\pi}{2}}^{\frac{\pi}{2}} 2 \cos \theta \, (2 \cos \theta) \, d\theta \; = \; 4 \int_{-\frac{\pi}{2}}^{\frac{\pi}{2}} \frac{1 + \cos 2\theta}{2} \, d\theta$$

$$= \; 2(\theta + \frac{\sin 2\theta}{2}) \Big|_{-\frac{\pi}{2}}^{\frac{\pi}{2}} \; = \; 2\pi \; .$$

When using parametric equations (as in the above integral) we must be sure to express all of the following in terms of the parameter: (1) the integrand; (2) the differential of the given variable; and (3) both limits. Note that the integral of Example 22 gives the area of the semicircle whose cartesian equation is $x^2 + y^2 = 4$.

23. Evaluate $\int_{0}^{2\pi} \sqrt{1 + (\frac{dy}{dx})^2} \, dx$ where $\begin{cases} x = t - \sin t \\ y = 1 - \cos t \end{cases}$.

We see that the integral can be rewritten $\int_{0}^{2\pi} \sqrt{dx^2 + dy^2}$. Since $dx = (1 - \cos t) \, dt$, $dy = \sin t \, dt$, $t = 0$ when $x = 0$ and $t = 2\pi$ when $x = 2\pi$, it follows that

$$\int_0^{2\pi} \sqrt{dx^2 + dy^2} = \int_0^{2\pi} \sqrt{(1 - \cos t)^2 + \sin^2 t} \; dt$$

$$= \sqrt{2} \int_0^{2\pi} \sqrt{1 - \cos t} \; dt = 2 \int_0^{2\pi} \sin \frac{t}{2} \; dt$$

$$= 4 \left(- \cos \frac{t}{2} \right) \Big|_0^{2\pi} = 8.$$

D. **Improper Integrals.** There are two classes of improper integrals: (1) those in which at least one of the limits of integration is infinite; and (2) those of the type $\int_a^b f(x) \; dx$ where $f(x)$ has a point of discontinuity (becoming infinite) at $x = c$, $a \leqq c \leqq b$.

Illustrations of improper integrals of class (1) are:

$$\int_0^\infty \frac{dx}{\sqrt[3]{x + 1}} \; ; \qquad \int_1^\infty \frac{dx}{x} \; ; \qquad \int_{-\infty}^\infty \frac{dx}{a^2 + x^2} \; ; \qquad \int_{-\infty}^0 e^{-x} \; dx \; ;$$

$$\int_{-\infty}^{-1} \frac{dx}{x^n} \; (n \text{ a real number}); \qquad \int_{-\infty}^\infty \frac{dx}{e^x + e^{-x}} \; ;$$

$$\int_0^\infty \frac{dx}{(4 + x)^2} \; ; \qquad \int_{-\infty}^\infty e^{-x^2} \; dx \; ; \qquad \int_1^\infty \frac{e^{-x^2}}{x^2} \; dx \; .$$

The following improper integrals of type $\int_a^b f(x) \; dx$ are of class (2):

$$\int_0^1 \frac{dx}{x} \; ; \qquad \int_1^2 \frac{dx}{(x - 1)^n} \; (n \text{ a real number}); \qquad \int_{-1}^1 \frac{dx}{1 - x^2} \; ;$$

$$\int_0^2 \frac{x}{\sqrt{4 - x^2}} \; dx \; ; \qquad \int_\pi^{2\pi} \frac{dx}{1 + \sin x} \; ; \qquad \int_{-1}^2 \frac{dx}{x(x - 1)^2} \; ;$$

$$\int_0^{2\pi} \frac{\sin x \; dx}{\cos x + 1} \; ; \qquad \int_a^b \frac{dx}{(x - c)^n} \; (n \text{ real; } a \leqq c \leqq b);$$

$$\int_0^1 \frac{dx}{\sqrt{x + x^4}} \; ; \qquad \int_{-2}^2 \sqrt{\frac{2 + x}{2 - x}} \; dx \; .$$

Sometimes an improper integral belongs to both classes. Consider, for example:

$$\int_0^\infty \frac{dx}{x} \;;\qquad \int_0^\infty \frac{dx}{\sqrt{x+x^4}} \;;\qquad \int_{-\infty}^1 \frac{dx}{\sqrt{1-x}} \;.$$

Each of the integrands in this set fails to exist at some point on the interval of integration.

Note, however, that each integral of the following set is *proper*:

$$\int_{-1}^3 \frac{dx}{\sqrt{x+2}} \;;\qquad \int_{-2}^2 \frac{dx}{x^2+4} \;;\qquad \int_0^{\frac{\pi}{6}} \frac{dx}{\cos x} \;;$$

$$\int_0^e \ln(x+1)\, dx \;;\qquad \int_{-3}^3 \frac{dx}{e^x+1} \;.$$

In each of the above the integrand is defined at each number on the interval of integration.

Improper integrals of class (1) are handled as follows:

$$\int_a^\infty f(x)\, dx \;=\; \lim_{b\to\infty} \int_a^b f(x)\, dx,$$

where f is continuous on $[a,b]$. If the limit on the right exists, the improper integral on the left is said to *converge* to this limit; if the limit on the right fails to exist, we say that the improper integral *diverges* (or is *meaningless*).

The evaluation of improper integrals of class (1) is illustrated in EXAMPLES 24 through 30:

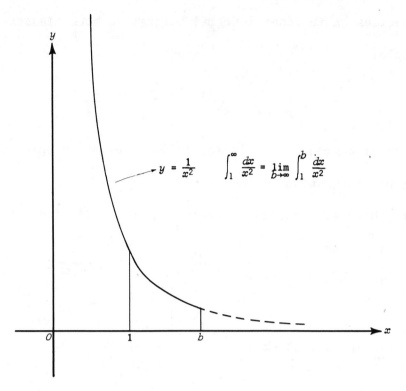

Figure   N5-1

24. $\displaystyle\int_1^\infty \frac{dx}{x^2} \;=\; \lim_{b\to\infty} \int_1^b x^{-2}\,dx \;=\; \lim_{b\to\infty} -\frac{1}{x}\Big|_1^b \;=\; \lim_{b\to\infty} -(\frac{1}{b} - 1) \;=\; 1.$

The given integral thus converges to 1. In Figure N5-1 we interpret

$\displaystyle\int_1^\infty \frac{dx}{x^2}$ as the area above the x-axis, under the curve of $y = \frac{1}{x^2}$, and

bounded at the left by the vertical line $x = 1$.

25. $\displaystyle\int_1^\infty \frac{dx}{\sqrt{x}} \;=\; \lim_{b\to\infty} \int_1^b x^{-1/2}\,dx \;=\; \lim_{b\to\infty} 2\sqrt{x}\Big|_1^b \;=\; \lim_{b\to\infty} 2(\sqrt{b} - 1) \;=\; +\infty.$

So $\displaystyle\int_1^\infty \frac{dx}{\sqrt{x}}$ diverges. It can be proved that $\displaystyle\int_1^\infty \frac{dx}{x^p}$ converges if $p > 1$ but

diverges if $p \leqq 1$. Figure N5-2 gives a geometric interpretation in terms

of area of $\displaystyle\int_1^\infty \frac{dx}{x^p}$ for $p = \frac{1}{2}$, 1, 2. Only the first quadrant area

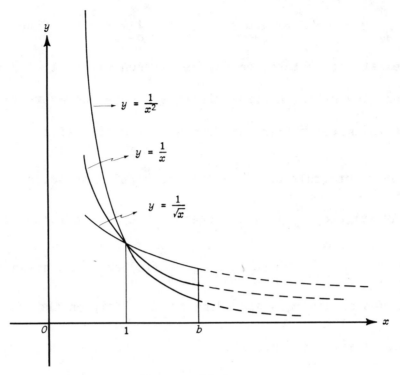

Figure   N5-2

under $y = \frac{1}{x^2}$ bounded at the left by $x = 1$ exists. Note that

$$\int_1^\infty \frac{dx}{x} = \lim_{b \to \infty} \ln x \Big|_1^b = +\infty.$$

26. $\displaystyle\int_0^\infty \frac{dx}{x^2 + 9} = \lim_{b \to \infty} \int_0^b \frac{dx}{x^2 + 9} = \lim_{b \to \infty} \frac{1}{3} \tan^{-1} \frac{x}{3} \Big|_0^b = \lim_{b \to \infty} \frac{1}{3} \tan^{-1} \frac{b}{3}$

$= \frac{1}{3} \cdot \frac{\pi}{2} = \frac{\pi}{6} .$

27. $\displaystyle\int_0^\infty \frac{dy}{e^y} = \lim_{b \to \infty} \int_0^b e^{-y} \, dy = \lim_{b \to \infty} -(e^{-b} - 1) = 1.$

28. $\displaystyle\int_{-\infty}^0 \frac{dz}{(z - 1)^2} = \lim_{b \to -\infty} \int_b^0 (z - 1)^{-2} \, dz = \lim_{b \to -\infty} - \frac{1}{z - 1} \Big|_b^0$

$= \lim_{b \to -\infty} -(-1 - \frac{1}{b - 1}) = 1.$

29. $\displaystyle\int_{-\infty}^0 e^{-x} \, dx = \lim_{b \to -\infty} -e^{-x} \Big|_b^0 = \lim_{b \to -\infty} -(1 - e^{-b}) = +\infty.$

Thus this improper integral diverges.

30. $\displaystyle\int_0^\infty \cos x \; dx \;=\; \lim_{b\to\infty} \sin x \Big|_0^b \;=\; \lim_{b\to\infty} \sin b.$ Since this limit

does not exist ($\sin b$ takes on values between -1 and 1 as $b \to \infty$) it

follows that the given integral diverges. Note, however, that it does

not become infinite; rather, it diverges by oscillation.

Improper integrals of class (2) are handled as follows.

To investigate $\displaystyle\int_a^b f(x) \; dx$ where f becomes infinite at $x = a$,

we define $\displaystyle\int_a^b f(x) \; dx$ to be $\displaystyle\lim_{h\to 0^+} \int_{a+h}^b f(x) \; dx.$ The given integral

then converges or diverges according as the limit on the right does

or does not exist. If f has its discontinuity at b, we define $\displaystyle\int_a^b f(x) \; dx$

to be $\displaystyle\lim_{h\to 0^+} \int_a^{b-h} f(x) \; dx;$ again, the given integral converges or

diverges as the limit does or does not exist. When, finally, the

integrand has a discontinuity at an interior point c on the interval

of integration ($a < c < b$), we let $\displaystyle\int_a^b f(x) \; dx \;=\; \lim_{h\to 0^+} \int_a^{c-h} f(x) \; dx$

$+ \displaystyle\lim_{h\to 0^+} \int_{c+h}^b f(x) \; dx.$ Now the improper integral converges only if

both of the limits exist. If *either* limit does not exist, the improper

integral diverges.

The evaluation of improper integrals of class (2) is illustrated

in EXAMPLES 31 through 38:

31. $\displaystyle\int_0^1 \frac{dx}{\sqrt[3]{x}} \;=\; \lim_{h\to 0^+} \int_h^1 x^{-1/3} \; dx \;=\; \lim_{h\to 0} \frac{3}{2} x^{2/3} \Big|_h^1 \;=\; \lim_{h\to 0^+} \frac{3}{2}(1 - h^{2/3}) = \frac{3}{2}.$

In Figure N5-3 we interpret this integral as the first quadrant area

under $y = \dfrac{1}{\sqrt[3]{x}}$ and to the left of $x = 1$.

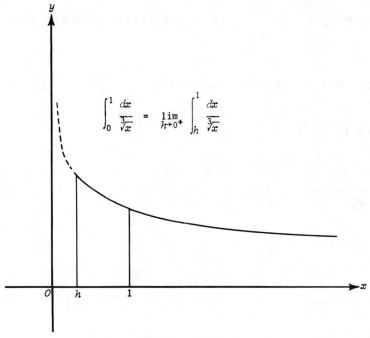

$$\int_0^1 \frac{dx}{\sqrt[3]{x}} \;=\; \lim_{h \to 0^+} \int_h^1 \frac{dx}{\sqrt[3]{x}}$$

Figure   N5-3

32. $$\int_0^1 \frac{dx}{x^3} \;=\; \lim_{h \to 0^+} \int_h^1 x^{-3}\, dx \;=\; \lim_{h \to 0^+} -\frac{1}{2x^2}\Big|_h^1 \;=\; \lim_{h \to 0^+} -\frac{1}{2}\Big(1 - \frac{1}{h^2}\Big) \;=\; \infty.$$

So this integral diverges.

It can be shown that $\displaystyle\int_0^a \frac{dx}{x^p}$ $(a > 0)$ converges if $p < 1$ but diverges
if $p \geqq 1$. Figure N5-4 shows an interpretation of $\displaystyle\int_0^1 \frac{dx}{x^p}$ in terms of

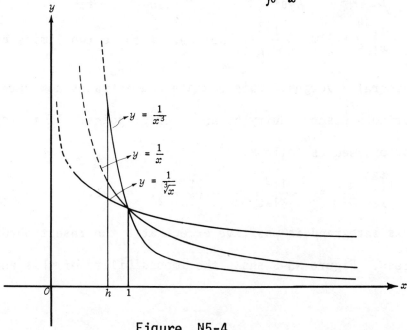

Figure   N5-4

areas where $p = \frac{1}{3}$, 1, and 3. Only the first quadrant area under $y = \dfrac{1}{\sqrt[3]{x}}$

to the left of $x = 1$ exists. Note that $\displaystyle\int_0^1 \frac{dx}{x} = \lim_{h \to 0^+} \ln x \Big|_h^1$

$= \displaystyle\lim_{h \to 0^+} \ln 1 - \ln h = +\infty.$

33. $\displaystyle\int_0^2 \frac{dy}{\sqrt{4 - y^2}} = \lim_{h \to 0^+} \int_0^{2-h} \frac{dy}{\sqrt{4 - y^2}} = \lim_{h \to 0^+} \sin^{-1} \frac{y}{2} \Big|_0^{2-h}$

$= \sin^{-1} 1 - \sin^{-1} 0 = \dfrac{\pi}{2}.$

34. $\displaystyle\int_2^3 \frac{dt}{(3 - t)^2} = \lim_{h \to 0^+} -\int_2^{3-h} (3 - t)^{-2}(-dt) = \lim_{h \to 0^+} \frac{1}{3 - t} \Big|_2^{3-h}$

$= +\infty.$ This integral diverges.

35. $\displaystyle\int_0^2 \frac{dx}{(x - 1)^{2/3}} = \lim_{h \to 0^+} \int_0^{1-h} (x - 1)^{-2/3} \, dx + \lim_{h \to 0^+} \int_{1+h}^2 (x - 1)^{-2/3} \, dx$

$= \displaystyle\lim_{h \to 0^+} 3(x - 1)^{1/3} \Big|_0^{1-h} + \lim_{h \to 0^+} 3(x - 1)^{1/3} \Big|_{1+h}^2 = 3(0 + 1) + 3(1 - 0) = 6.$

36. $\displaystyle\int_{-2}^2 \frac{dx}{x^2} = \lim_{h \to 0^+} \int_{-2}^{0-h} x^{-2} \, dx + \lim_{h \to 0^+} \int_{0+h}^2 x^{-2} \, dx$

$= \displaystyle\lim_{h \to 0^+} -\frac{1}{x} \Big|_{-2}^{-h} + \lim_{h \to 0^+} -\frac{1}{x} \Big|_h^2$. Neither of these two limits exists; the

given integral diverges. This example demonstrates how careful one must

be to notice a discontinuity at an interior point. If it is overlooked

one might proceed as follows:

$$\int_{-2}^2 \frac{dx}{x^2} = -\frac{1}{x} \Big|_{-2}^2 = -\left(\frac{1}{2} + \frac{1}{2}\right) = -1.$$

Since this integrand is positive except at 0 the result obtained is clearly

meaningless. Figure N5-5 shows the impossibility of this answer.

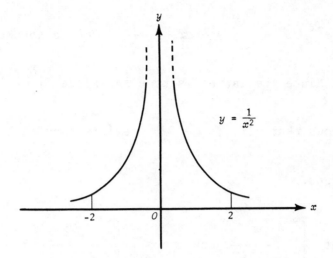

Figure N5-5

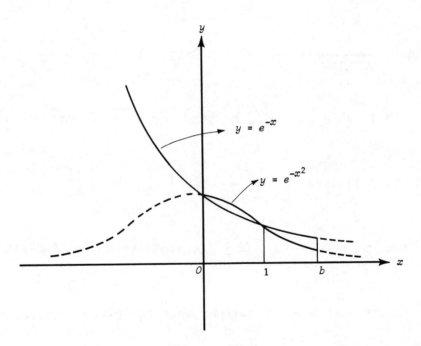

Figure N5-6

37. Determine whether or not $\int_1^\infty e^{-x^2}\,dx$ converges. Although

there is no elementary function whose derivative is e^{-x^2}, we can still

show that the given improper integral converges. Note, first, that if

$x \geqq 1$ then $x^2 \geqq x$, so that $-x^2 \leqq -x$ and $e^{-x^2} \leqq e^{-x}$. Figure N5-6

enables us to compare the areas under the curves of $y = e^{-x^2}$ and

$y = e^{-x}$ from $x = 1$ to $x = b$. Thus, if $b > 1$, then

$$\int_1^b e^{-x^2}\, dx \;\leq\; \int_1^b e^{-x}\, dx \;\leq\; \int_1^\infty e^{-x}\, dx \;=\; \frac{1}{e}\, .$$ Note also that $\int_1^b e^{-x^2} dx$

increases with b. Since the latter is true and since $\int_1^b e^{-x^2} dx$

is bounded it follows that $\displaystyle\lim_{b\to\infty} \int_1^b e^{-x^2}\, dx$ exists (and is $\leq \frac{1}{e}$). Therefore

$\int_1^\infty e^{-x^2}\, dx$ converges.

38. Show that $\displaystyle\int_0^\infty \frac{dx}{\sqrt{x + x^4}}$ converges. $\displaystyle\int_0^\infty \frac{dx}{\sqrt{x + x^4}} = \int_0^1 \frac{dx}{\sqrt{x + x^4}}$

$+ \displaystyle\int_1^\infty \frac{dx}{\sqrt{x + x^4}}$. Since if $0 < x \leq 1$ then $x + x^4 > x$ and $\sqrt{x + x^4} > \sqrt{x}$,

it follows that $\dfrac{1}{\sqrt{x + x^4}} < \dfrac{1}{\sqrt{x}}$ $(0 < x \leq 1)$. Thus $\displaystyle\int_0^1 \frac{dx}{\sqrt{x + x^4}} \leq \int_0^1 \frac{dx}{\sqrt{x}} = 2.$

Further, if $x \geq 1$ then $x + x^4 \geq x^4$ and $\sqrt{x + x^4} \geq \sqrt{x^4} = x^2$, so that

$\dfrac{1}{\sqrt{x + x^4}} \leq \dfrac{1}{x^2}$ $(x \geq 1)$, and $\displaystyle\int_1^\infty \frac{dx}{\sqrt{x + x^4}} \leq \int_1^\infty \frac{dx}{x^2} = -\frac{1}{x}\Big|_1^\infty = 1.$

Thus, since $\displaystyle\int_0^\infty \frac{dx}{\sqrt{x + x^4}} \leq (2 + 1)$, it is bounded. And since

$\int_0^b \dfrac{dx}{\sqrt{x + x^4}}$ increases with b, it follows that the given integral converges.

Further applications of improper integrals to area are considered in Multiple-Choice Questions, Set Six, problems 20-24 (p. 131); to volume in Multiple-Choice Questions, Set Seven, problems 21-25 (p. 139).

Multiple Choice Questions: Definite Integrals

1. $\int_{-1}^{1} (x^2 - x - 1)\, dx \;=\;$

      (A) $\frac{2}{3}$ (B) 0   (C) $-\frac{4}{3}$ (D) -2   (E) -1 .

2. $\int_{1}^{2} \frac{3x - 1}{3x}\, dx \;=\;$

      (A) $\frac{3}{4}$ (B) $1 - \frac{1}{3}\ln 2$ (C) $1 - \ln 2$ (D) $-\frac{1}{3}\ln 2$ (E) 1 .

3. $\int_{0}^{3} \frac{dt}{\sqrt{4 - t}} \;=\;$

      (A) 1   (B) -2   (C) 4   (D) -1   (E) 2 .

4. $\int_{-1}^{0} \sqrt{3u + 4}\, du \;=\;$

      (A) 2   (B) $\frac{14}{9}$ (C) $\frac{14}{3}$ (D) 6   (E) $\frac{7}{2}$.

5. $\int_{2}^{3} \frac{dy}{2y - 3} \;=\;$

      (A) $\ln 3$ (B) $\frac{1}{2}\ln \frac{3}{2}$ (C) $\frac{16}{9}$ (D) $\ln \sqrt{3}$ (E) $\sqrt{3} - 1$.

6. $\int_{0}^{\sqrt{3}} \frac{x}{\sqrt{4 - x^2}}\, dx \;=\;$

      (A) 1   (B) $\frac{\pi}{6}$ (C) $\frac{\pi}{3}$ (D) -1   (E) 2 .

7. $\int_{0}^{1} (2t - 1)^3\, dt \;=\;$

      (A) $\frac{1}{4}$ (B) 6   (C) $\frac{1}{2}$ (D) 0   (E) 4 .

8. $\int_{0}^{1} \frac{dx}{\sqrt{4 - x^2}} \;=\;$

      (A) $\frac{\pi}{3}$ (B) $2 - \sqrt{3}$ (C) $\frac{\pi}{12}$ (D) $2(\sqrt{3} - 2)$ (E) $\frac{\pi}{6}$.

9. $\displaystyle\int_4^9 \frac{2 + x}{2\sqrt{x}}\, dx\ =$

(A) $\dfrac{25}{3}$ (B) $\dfrac{41}{3}$ (C) $\dfrac{100}{3}$ (D) $\dfrac{5}{3}$ (E) $\dfrac{1}{3}$.

10. $\displaystyle\int_{-3}^3 \frac{dx}{9 + x^2}\ =$

(A) $\dfrac{\pi}{2}$ (B) 0 (C) $\dfrac{\pi}{6}$ (D) $-\dfrac{\pi}{2}$ (E) $\dfrac{\pi}{3}$.

11. $\displaystyle\int_0^1 e^{-x}\, dx\ =$

(A) $\dfrac{1}{e} - 1$ (B) $1 - e$ (C) $-\dfrac{1}{e}$ (D) $1 - \dfrac{1}{e}$ (E) $\dfrac{1}{e}$.

12. $\displaystyle\int_0^1 xe^{x^2}\, dx\ =$

(A) $e - 1$ (B) $\dfrac{1}{2}(e - 1)$ (C) $2(e - 1)$ (D) $\dfrac{e}{2}$ (E) $\dfrac{e}{2} - 1$.

13. $\displaystyle\int_0^{\frac{\pi}{4}} \sin 2\theta\, d\theta\ =$

(A) 2 (B) $\dfrac{1}{2}$ (C) -1 (D) $-\dfrac{1}{2}$ (E) -2 .

14. $\displaystyle\int_1^2 \frac{dz}{3 - z}\ =$

(A) $-\ln 2$ (B) $\dfrac{3}{4}$ (C) $2(\sqrt{2} - 1)$ (D) $\dfrac{1}{2}\ln 2$ (E) $\ln 2$.

*15. $\displaystyle\int_1^e \ln y\, dy\ =$

(A) $2e + 1$ (B) $\dfrac{1}{2}$ (C) 1 (D) $e - 1$ (E) -1 .

*16. $\displaystyle\int_{-4}^4 \sqrt{16 - x^2}\, dx\ =$

(A) 8π (B) 4π (C) 4 (D) 8 (E) none of these.

17. $\displaystyle\int_0^\pi \cos^2 \theta \sin \theta \, d\theta \ =$

    (A) $-\dfrac{2}{3}$ (B) $\dfrac{1}{3}$ (C) 1 (D) $\dfrac{2}{3}$ (E) 0 .

18. $\displaystyle\int_1^e \dfrac{\ln x}{x} \, dx \ =$

    (A) $\dfrac{1}{2}$ (B) $\dfrac{1}{2}(e^2 - 1)$ (C) 0 (D) 1 (E) $e - 1$.

*19. $\displaystyle\int_0^1 x e^x \, dx \ =$

    (A) -1 (B) $e + 1$ (C) 1 (D) $e - 1$ (E) $\dfrac{1}{2}(e - 1)$.

20. $\displaystyle\int_0^{\frac{\pi}{6}} \dfrac{\cos \theta}{1 + 2 \sin \theta} \, d\theta \ =$

    (A) $\ln 2$ (B) $\dfrac{3}{8}$ (C) $-\dfrac{1}{2} \ln 2$ (D) $\dfrac{3}{2}$ (E) $\ln \sqrt{2}$.

21. $\displaystyle\int_0^{\frac{\pi}{4}} \sqrt{1 - \cos 2\alpha} \, d\alpha \ =$

    (A) 1 (B) $\sqrt{2}$ (C) $\dfrac{1}{4}$ (D) $\sqrt{2} - 1$ (E) 2 .

22. $\displaystyle\int_{\sqrt{2}}^2 \dfrac{u}{u^2 - 1} \, du \ =$

    (A) $\ln \sqrt{3}$ (B) $\dfrac{8}{9}$ (C) $\ln \dfrac{3}{2}$ (D) $\ln 3$ (E) $1 - \sqrt{3}$.

23. $\displaystyle\int_{\sqrt{2}}^2 \dfrac{u \, du}{(u^2 - 1)^2} \ =$

    (A) $-\dfrac{1}{3}$ (B) $-\dfrac{2}{3}$ (C) $\dfrac{2}{3}$ (D) -1 (E) $\dfrac{1}{3}$.

24. $\displaystyle\int_0^{\frac{\pi}{4}} \cos^2 \theta \, d\theta \ =$

    (A) $\dfrac{1}{2}$ (B) $\dfrac{\pi}{8}$ (C) $\dfrac{\pi}{8} + \dfrac{1}{4}$ (D) $\dfrac{\pi}{8} + \dfrac{1}{2}$ (E) $\dfrac{\pi}{8} - \dfrac{1}{4}$.

25. $\displaystyle\int_{\frac{\pi}{12}}^{\frac{\pi}{4}} \frac{\cos 2x \, dx}{\sin^2 2x} =$

    (A) $-\dfrac{1}{4}$ (B) 1 (C) $\dfrac{1}{2}$ (D) $-\dfrac{1}{2}$ (E) -1 .

26. $\displaystyle\int_0^1 \frac{e^{-x} + 1}{e^{-x}} \, dx =$

    (A) e (B) $2 + e$ (C) $\dfrac{1}{e}$ (D) $1 + e$ (E) $e - 1$.

27. $\displaystyle\int_0^1 \frac{e^x}{e^x + 1} \, dx =$

    (A) $\ln 2$ (B) e (C) $1 + e$ (D) $-\ln 2$ (E) $\ln \dfrac{e + 1}{2}$.

*28. Which one of the following is an improper integral?

    (A) $\displaystyle\int_0^2 \frac{dx}{\sqrt{x + 1}}$ (B) $\displaystyle\int_{-1}^1 \frac{dx}{1 + x^2}$

    (C) $\displaystyle\int_0^2 \frac{x \, dx}{1 - x^2}$ (D) $\displaystyle\int_0^{\frac{\pi}{3}} \frac{\sin x \, dx}{\cos^2 x}$

    (E) none of these.

*29. $\displaystyle\int_0^{\infty} e^{-x} \, dx =$

    (A) 1 (B) $\dfrac{1}{e}$ (C) -1 (D) $-\dfrac{1}{e}$ (E) none of these.

*30. $\displaystyle\int_0^e \frac{du}{u} =$

    (A) 1 (B) $\dfrac{1}{e}$ (C) $-\dfrac{1}{e^2}$ (D) -1 (E) none of these.

*31. $\displaystyle\int_1^2 \frac{dt}{\sqrt[3]{t - 1}} =$

    (A) $\dfrac{2}{3}$ (B) $\dfrac{3}{2}$ (C) 3 (D) 1 (E) none of these.

*32. $\displaystyle\int_2^4 \frac{dx}{(x-3)^{2/3}}$ =

  (A) 6   (B) $\frac{6}{5}$ (C) $\frac{2}{3}$ (D) 0   (E) none of these.

*33. $\displaystyle\int_2^4 \frac{dx}{(x-3)^2}$ =

  (A) 2   (B) -2   (C) 0   (D) $\frac{2}{3}$ (E) none of these.

*34. $\displaystyle\int_0^{\frac{\pi}{2}} \frac{\sin x}{\sqrt{1-\cos x}}\, dx$ =

  (A) -2   (B) $\frac{2}{3}$ (C) 2   (D) $\frac{1}{2}$ (E) none of these.

*35. Which one of the following improper integrals diverges?

  (A) $\displaystyle\int_1^\infty \frac{dx}{x^2}$ (B) $\displaystyle\int_0^\infty \frac{dx}{e^x}$

  (C) $\displaystyle\int_{-1}^1 \frac{dx}{\sqrt[3]{x}}$ (D) $\displaystyle\int_{-1}^1 \frac{dx}{x^2}$

  (E) none of these.

*36. Which one of the following improper integrals diverges?

  (A) $\displaystyle\int_0^\infty \frac{dx}{1+x^2}$ (B) $\displaystyle\int_0^1 \frac{dx}{x^{1/3}}$

  (C) $\displaystyle\int_0^\infty \frac{dx}{x^3+1}$ (D) $\displaystyle\int_0^\infty \frac{dx}{e^x+2}$

  (E) $\displaystyle\int_1^\infty \frac{dx}{x^{1/3}}$.

37. If $f(x)$ is continuous on the interval $a \leqq x \leqq b$ and $a < c < b$, then

$\int_{c}^{b} f(x)\ dx$ is equal to

(A) $\int_{a}^{c} f(x)\ dx + \int_{c}^{b} f(x)\ dx$

(B) $\int_{a}^{c} f(x)\ dx - \int_{a}^{b} f(x)\ dx$

(C) $\int_{c}^{a} f(x)\ dx + \int_{b}^{a} f(x)\ dx$

(D) $\int_{a}^{b} f(x)\ dx - \int_{a}^{c} f(x)\ dx$

(E) $\int_{a}^{c} f(x)\ dx - \int_{b}^{c} f(x)\ dx$.

38. If $f(x)$ is continuous on $a \leqq x \leqq b$, then

(A) $\int_{a}^{b} f(x)\ dx = f(b) - f(a)$

(B) $\int_{a}^{b} f(x)\ dx = - \int_{b}^{a} f(x)\ dx$

(C) $\int_{a}^{b} f(x)\ dx \geqq 0$

(D) $\dfrac{d}{dx} \int_{a}^{x} f(t)\ dt = f'(x)$

(E) $\dfrac{d}{dx} \int_{a}^{x} f(t)\ dt = f(x) - f(a)$.

39. If $f(x)$ is continuous on the interval $a \leq x \leq b$, if this interval is partitioned into n equal subintervals of length Δx, and if x_k is a number in the kth subinterval, then $\lim\limits_{n \to \infty} \sum\limits_{1}^{n} f(x_k) \, \Delta x$ is equal to

   (A) $f(b) - f(a)$

   (B) $F(x) + C$, where $\dfrac{dF(x)}{dx} = f(x)$ and C is an arbitrary constant

   (C) $\displaystyle\int_a^b f(x) \, dx$

   (D) $F(b - a)$ where $\dfrac{dF(x)}{dx} = f(x)$

   (E) none of these.

40. If $F'(x) = G'(x)$ for all x, then

   (A) $\displaystyle\int_a^b F'(x) \, dx = \int_a^b G'(x) \, dx$

   (B) $\displaystyle\int F(x) \, dx = \int G(x) \, dx$

   (C) $\displaystyle\int_a^b F(x) \, dx = \int_a^b G(x) \, dx$

   (D) $\displaystyle\int F(x) \, dx = \int G(x) \, dx + C$

   (E) none of the preceding is necessary.

41. If $f(x)$ is continuous on the closed interval $[a, b]$ then there exists at least one number c, $a < c < b$, such that $\displaystyle\int_a^b f(x) \, dx$ is equal to

   (A) $\dfrac{f(c)}{b - a}$ (B) $f'(c)(b - a)$

   (C) $f(c)(b - a)$ (D) $\dfrac{f'(c)}{b - a}$

   (E) $f(c)[f(b) - f(a)]$.

42. If $f(x)$ is continuous on the closed interval $[a, b]$ and k is a constant,

then $\int_a^b k\, f(x)\, dx$ is equal to

   (A) $k(b - a)$

   (B) $k[f(b) - f(a)]$

   (C) $kF(b - a)$ where $\dfrac{dF(x)}{dx} = f(x)$

   (D) $k \int_a^b f(x)\, dx$

   (E) $\dfrac{[k\, f(x)]^2}{2} \Bigg]_a^b$.

43. $\dfrac{d}{dt} \int_0^t \sqrt{x^3 + 1}\, dx \;=\;$ (A) $\sqrt{t^3 + 1}$

   (B) $\dfrac{\sqrt{t^3 + 1}}{3t^2}$ (C) $\frac{2}{3}(t^3 + 1)(\sqrt{t^3 + 1} - 1)$

   (D) $3x^2\sqrt{x^3 + 1}$ (E) none of these.

44. If $F(u) \;=\; \int_1^u (2 - x^2)^3\, dx$ then $F'(u)$ is equal to

   (A) $- 6u(2 - u^2)^2$ (B) $\dfrac{(2 - u^2)^4}{4} - \dfrac{1}{4}$

   (C) $(2 - u^2)^3 - 1$ (D) $(2 - u^2)^3$

   (E) $- 2u(2 - u^2)^3$.

45. $\dfrac{d}{dx} \int_{\frac{\pi}{2}}^{x^2} \sqrt{\sin t}\, dt \;=\;$ (A) $\sqrt{\sin t^2}$

   (B) $2x\sqrt{\sin x^2} - 1$ (C) $\frac{2}{3}\left(\sin^{3/2} x^2 - 1\right)$

   (D) $\sqrt{\sin x^2} - 1$ (E) $2x\sqrt{\sin x^2}$.

46. If we let $x = \tan \theta$, then $\int_1^{\sqrt{3}} \sqrt{1 + x^2}\, dx$ is equivalent to

(A) $\displaystyle\int_{\frac{\pi}{4}}^{\frac{\pi}{3}} \sec \theta\, d\theta$ (B) $\displaystyle\int_1^{\sqrt{3}} \sec^3 \theta\, d\theta$

(C) $\displaystyle\int_{\frac{\pi}{4}}^{\frac{\pi}{3}} \sec^3 \theta\, d\theta$ (D) $\displaystyle\int_{\frac{\pi}{4}}^{\frac{\pi}{3}} \sec^2 \theta \tan \theta\, d\theta$

(E) $\displaystyle\int_1^{\sqrt{3}} \sec \theta\, d\theta$.

47. If the substitution $u = \sqrt{x + 1}$ is used, then $\int_0^3 \dfrac{dx}{x\sqrt{x + 1}}$ is equivalent to

(A) $\displaystyle\int_1^2 \dfrac{du}{u^2 - 1}$ (B) $\displaystyle\int_1^2 \dfrac{2\, du}{u^2 - 1}$

(C) $2\displaystyle\int_0^3 \dfrac{du}{(u - 1)(u + 1)}$ (D) $2\displaystyle\int_1^2 \dfrac{du}{u(u^2 - 1)}$

(E) $2\displaystyle\int_0^3 \dfrac{du}{u(u - 1)}$.

48. If $x = 4 \cos \theta$ and $y = 3 \sin \theta$ then $\int_2^4 xy\, dx$ is equivalent to

(A) $48\displaystyle\int_{\frac{\pi}{3}}^0 \sin \theta \cos^2 \theta\, d\theta$ (B) $48\displaystyle\int_2^4 \sin^2 \theta \cos \theta\, d\theta$

(C) $36\displaystyle\int_2^4 \sin \theta \cos^2 \theta\, d\theta$ (D) $-48\displaystyle\int_0^{\frac{\pi}{3}} \sin \theta \cos^2 \theta\, d\theta$

(E) $48\displaystyle\int_0^{\frac{\pi}{3}} \sin^2 \theta \cos \theta\, d\theta$.

49. A curve is defined by the parametric equations $y = 2a \cos^2 \theta$ and $x = 2a \tan \theta$, where $0 \leqq \theta \leqq \pi$. Then the definite integral

$$\pi \int_0^{2a} y^2 \, dx \text{ is equivalent to}$$

(A) $\quad 4\pi a^2 \displaystyle\int_0^{\frac{\pi}{4}} \cos^4 \theta \, d\theta$

(B) $\quad 8\pi a^3 \displaystyle\int_{\frac{\pi}{2}}^{\pi} \cos^2 \theta \, d\theta$

(C) $\quad 8\pi a^3 \displaystyle\int_0^{\frac{\pi}{4}} \cos^2 \theta \, d\theta$

(D) $\quad 8\pi a^3 \displaystyle\int_0^{2a} \cos^2 \theta \, d\theta$

(E) $\quad 8\pi a^3 \displaystyle\int_0^{\frac{\pi}{4}} \sin \theta \cos^2 \theta \, d\theta$.

50. A curve is given parametrically by $x = 1 - \cos t$ and $y = t - \sin t$, where $0 \leqq t \leqq \pi$. Then $\displaystyle\int_0^{\frac{3}{2}} y \, dx$ is equivalent to

(A) $\quad \displaystyle\int_0^{\frac{3}{2}} \sin t \, (t - \sin t) \, dt$

(B) $\quad \displaystyle\int_{\frac{2\pi}{3}}^{\pi} \sin t \, (t - \sin t) \, dt$

(C) $\quad \displaystyle\int_0^{\frac{2\pi}{3}} (t - \sin t) \, dt$

(D) $\quad \displaystyle\int_0^{\frac{2\pi}{3}} \sin t \, (t - \sin t) \, dt$

(E) $\quad \displaystyle\int_0^{\frac{3}{2}} (t - \sin t) \, dt$.

Section 6: Applications of Integration: Area

Review of Definitions and Methods

Most of the applications of integration involved in these questions are based on the Fundamental Theorem of the Integral Calculus. This theorem provides the tool for evaluating an infinite sum by means of a definite integral. Suppose that a function $f(x)$ is continuous on the closed interval $[a,b]$. Divide the interval into n equal* subintervals, of length $\Delta x = \dfrac{b - a}{n}$. Choose numbers, one in each subinterval, as follows: x_1 in the first, x_2 in the second, . . . , x_k in the kth, . . . , x_n in the nth. Then

$$\lim_{n \to \infty} \sum_{k=1}^{n} f(x_k)\ \Delta x = \int_a^b f(x)\ dx = F(b) - F(a) ,$$

$$\text{where} \quad \frac{dF(x)}{dx} = f(x) .$$

If $f(x)$ is nonnegative on $[a,b]$, we see (Figure N6-1) that $f(x_k)\ \Delta x$ can be regarded as the area of a typical approximating rectangle, and that the area bounded by the x-axis, the curve, and the vertical lines $x = a$ and $x = b$ is given exactly by

$$\lim_{n \to \infty} \sum_{k=1}^{n} f(x_k)\ \Delta x \quad \text{and hence by} \quad \int_a^b f(x)\ dx .$$

---

*It is not in fact necessary that the subintervals be of equal length, but the formulation is simpler if one assumes they are.

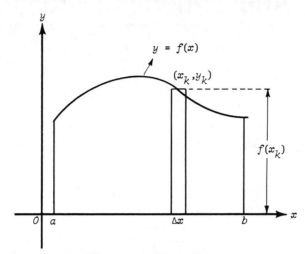

Figure N6-1

To find an area, we

(1) draw a sketch of the given region and of a typical element;

(2) write the expression for the area of a typical rectangle;

and

(3) set up the definite integral that is the limit of the sum of the n areas as $n \to \infty$.

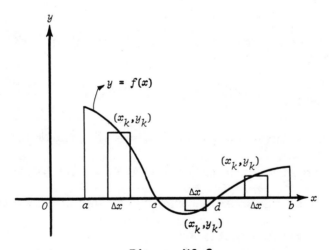

Figure N6-2

If $f(x)$ changes sign on the interval (**Figure N6-2**) we find the values of x for which $f(x) = 0$ and note where the function is positive, where it is negative. The total area bounded by the x-axis, the curve, $x = a$, and $x = b$ is here given exactly by

$$\int_a^c f(x) \; dx \quad - \quad \int_c^d f(x) \; dx \quad + \quad \int_d^b f(x) \; dx \; ,$$

where we have taken into account that $f(x_k)\Delta x$ is a negative number if $c < x < d$.

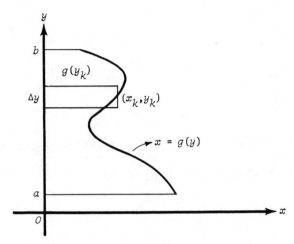

Figure N6-3

If x is given as a function of y , say $x = g(y)$, then (Figure N6-3) the subdivisions are made along the y-axis and the area bounded by the y-axis, the curve, and the horizontal lines $y = a$ and $y = b$ is given exactly by

$$\lim_{n \to \infty} \sum_{k=1}^n g(y_k) \; \Delta y \quad = \quad \int_a^b g(y) \; dy \; .$$

To find the area between curves (Figure N6-4) we first find where

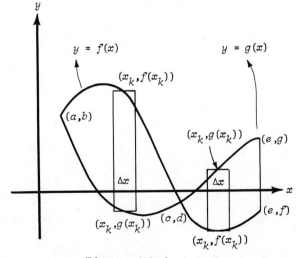

Figure N6-4

they intersect and then write the area of a typical element for each region between the points of intersection. To find the total area bounded by the curves $y = f(x)$ and $y = g(x)$ between $x = a$ and $x = e$, we see that, if they intersect at (c,d) , the total area is given **exactly** by

$$\int_a^c \left[f(x) - g(x) \right] \, dx \quad + \quad \int_c^e \left[g(x) - f(x) \right] dx \; .$$

In the key for this set of problems a sketch is given for each problem, and a typical element is indicated.

Multiple Choice Questions: Applications of Integration: Area

In Problems 1-12, choose the alternative that gives the area of the region whose boundaries are given.

1.   The curve of $y = x^2$, $y = 0$, $x = -1$, and $x = 2$ . .

   (A) $\frac{11}{3}$ (B) $\frac{7}{3}$ (C) 3 (D) 5 (E) none of these.

2.   The parabola $y = x^2 - 3$ and the line $y = 1$.

   (A) $\frac{8}{3}$ (B) 32 (C) $\frac{32}{3}$ (D) $\frac{16}{3}$ (E) none of these.

3.   The curve of $x = y^2 - 1$ and the y-axis.

   (A) $\frac{4}{3}$ (B) $\frac{2}{3}$ (C) $\frac{8}{3}$ (D) $\frac{1}{2}$ (E) none of these.

4.   The parabola $y^2 = x$ and the line $x + y = 2$.

   (A) $\frac{5}{2}$ (B) $\frac{3}{2}$ (C) $\frac{11}{6}$ (D) $\frac{9}{2}$ (E) $\frac{29}{6}$.

5.   The curve of $x^2 = y^2(4 - y^2)$.

   (A) $\frac{16}{3}$ (B) $\frac{32}{3}$ (C) $\frac{8}{3}$ (D) $\frac{64}{15}$ (E) 4 .

6.   The curve of $y = \frac{4}{x^2 + 4}$, the x-axis, and the vertical lines

   $x = -2$ and $x = 2$.

   (A) $\frac{\pi}{4}$ (B) $\frac{\pi}{2}$ (C) 2π (D) π (E) none of these.

7.   The parabolas $x = y^2 - 5y$ and $x = 3y - y^2$.

   (A) $\frac{32}{3}$ (B) $\frac{139}{6}$ (C) $\frac{64}{3}$ (D) $\frac{128}{3}$ (E) none of these.

8.   The curve of $y = \frac{2}{x}$ and $x + y = 3$.

   (A) $\frac{1}{2} - 2 \ln 2$ (B) $\frac{3}{2}$ (C) $\frac{1}{2} - \ln 4$

   (D) $\frac{5}{2}$ (E) $\frac{3}{2} - \ln 4$.

9. In the first quadrant, bounded below by the x-axis and above by the
    curves of $y = \sin x$ and $y = \cos x$.

    (A) $2 - \sqrt{2}$ (B) $2 + \sqrt{2}$ (C) 2   (D) $\sqrt{2}$ (E) $2\sqrt{2}$.

10. Above by the curve $y = \sin x$ and below by $y = \cos x$ from $x = \frac{\pi}{4}$
    to $x = \frac{5\pi}{4}$.

    (A) $2\sqrt{2}$ (B) $\frac{2}{\sqrt{2}}$ (C) $\frac{1}{2\sqrt{2}}$ (D) $2(\sqrt{2} - 1)$ (E) $2(\sqrt{2} + 1)$.

*11. The curve $y = \cot x$, the lines $x = \frac{\pi}{4}$ and $x = \frac{\pi}{2}$, and the x-axis.

    (A) $\ln 2$ (B) $+\ln \frac{1}{2}$ (C) 1   (D) $\frac{1}{2} \ln 2$ (E) 2 .

12. The curve of $y = x^3 - 2x^2 - 3x$ and the x-axis.

    (A) $\frac{28}{3}$ (B) $\frac{79}{6}$ (C) $\frac{45}{4}$ (D) $\frac{71}{6}$ (E) none of these.

13. The total area bounded by the cubic $x = y^3 - y$ and the line $x = 3y$
    is equal to

    (A) 4   (B) $\frac{16}{3}$ (C) 8   (D) $\frac{32}{3}$ (E) 16 .

14. The area bounded by $y = e^x$, $y = 1$, $y = 2$, and $x = 3$ is equal to

    (A) $3 + \ln 2$ (B) $3 - 3 \ln 3$ (C) $4 + \ln 2$

    (D) $3 - \frac{1}{2} \ln^2 2$ (E) $4 - \ln 4$.

*15. The area enclosed by the ellipse with parametric equations $x = 2 \cos \theta$
    and $y = 3 \sin \theta$ equals

    (A) 6π (B) $\frac{9}{2}\pi$ (C) 3π (D) $\frac{3}{2}\pi$ (E) none of these.

*16. The area enclosed by one loop of the cycloid with parametric equations
    $x = \theta - \sin \theta$ and $y = 1 - \cos \theta$ equals

    (A) $\frac{3\pi}{2}$ (B) 3π (C) 2π (D) 6π (E) none of these.

17. The area enclosed by the curve $y^2 = x(1 - x)$ is given by

    (A) $2 \int_0^1 x\sqrt{1 - x} \ dx$ (B) $2 \int_0^1 \sqrt{x - x^2} \ dx$

    (C) $4 \int_0^1 \sqrt{x - x^2} \ dx$ (D) π

    (E) 2π.

18. The area bounded by the parabola $y = 2 - x^2$ and the line $y = x - 4$ is given by

    (A) $\int_{-2}^{3} (6 - x - x^2) \ dx$ (B) $\int_{-2}^{1} (2 + x + x^2) \ dx$

    (C) $\int_{-3}^{2} (6 - x - x^2) \ dx$ (D) $2 \int_0^{\sqrt{2}} (2 - x^2) \ dx + \int_{-3}^{2} (4 - x) \ dx$

    (E) none of these.

*19. The area enclosed by the hypocycloid with parametric equations $x = \cos^3 t$ and $y = \sin^3 t$ is given by

    (A) $3 \int_{\frac{\pi}{2}}^{0} \sin^4 t \cos^2 t \ dt$ (B) $4 \int_0^1 \sin^3 t \ dt$

    (C) $-4 \int_{\frac{\pi}{2}}^{0} \sin^6 t \ dt$ (D) $12 \int_0^{\frac{\pi}{2}} \sin^4 t \cos^2 t \ dt$

    (E) none of these.

In Problems 20-24, choose the alternative which gives the area, if it exists, of the region described.

20. In the first quadrant under the curve of $y = e^{-x}$.

    (A) 1   (B) e (C) $\frac{1}{e}$ (D) 2   (E) none of these.

21. In the first quadrant under the curve of $y = xe^{-x^2}$.

    (A) 2   (B) $\frac{2}{e}$ (C) $\frac{1}{2}$ (D) $\frac{1}{2e}$ (E) none of these.

*22. In the first quadrant above $y = 1$ and bounded by the y-axis and

the curve $xy = 1$.

      (A) 1   (B) 2   (C) $\frac{1}{2}$ (D) 4   (E) none of these.

*23. Between the curve $y = \dfrac{4}{1 + x^2}$ and its asymptote.

      (A) 2π (B) 4π (C) 8π (D) π (E) none of these.

*24. Between the curve $y = \dfrac{4}{\sqrt{1 - x^2}}$ and its asymptotes.

      (A) $\dfrac{\pi}{2}$ (B) π (C) 2π (D) 4π (E) none of these.

25. The figure shows part of the curve
of $y = x^3$ and a rectangle with
two vertices at $(0,0)$ and $(c,0)$.
The ratio of the area of the rectangle to the shaded part of it above
the cubic is

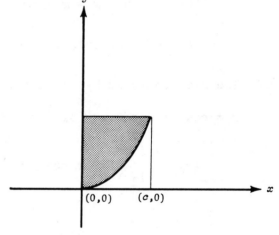

      (A) 4 : 3   (B) 4 : 1   (C) 3 : 2   (D) 3 : 1   (E) 5 : 4 .

Section 7: Applications of Integration: Volume

Review of Definitions

A second application of the Fundamental Theorem is in the determination of volumes. For *solids of revolution*, after a sketch is made of the area to be rotated, we decide whether to take the strips vertically or horizontally and then which type of element (disc, shell, or washer) is generated by the strip.

Note the following formulas for volume:

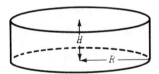

DISC:

$$V = \pi R^2 H \qquad \text{where}$$
$$R = \text{radius},$$
$$H = \text{height}.$$

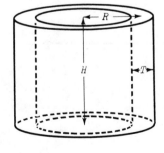

SHELL:

$$V = 2\pi RHT \qquad \text{where}$$
$$R = \text{mid-radius},$$
$$H = \text{height},$$
$$T = \text{thickness}.$$

WASHER: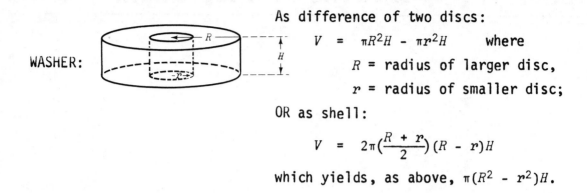

As difference of two discs:

$$V = \pi R^2 H - \pi r^2 H \quad \text{where}$$

R = radius of larger disc,

r = radius of smaller disc;

OR as shell:

$$V = 2\pi\left(\frac{R + r}{2}\right)(R - r)H$$

which yields, as above, $\pi(R^2 - r^2)H$.

Occasionally when more than one method is satisfactory we try to use the most efficient. In the key for Set Seven, a sketch is shown for each problem and for each the type and volume of a typical element are given. The required volume is then found by letting the number of elements become infinite and applying the Fundamental Theorem.

If the *area of a cross-section* of the solid *is known* and can be expressed in terms of x then the volume of a typical slice, ΔV, can be determined. The volume of the solid is obtained, as usual, by letting the number of slices increase indefinitely. In Figure N7-1, the slices

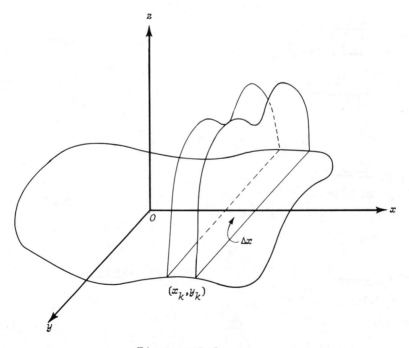

Figure N7-1

are taken perpendicular to the x-axis so that $\Delta V = A(x) \, \Delta x$, where $A(x)$ is the area of a cross-section and Δx is the thickness of the slice. When the cross-section is a circle, the solid can be generated by revolving a plane area.

Problems 26, 27, and 28 of this set illustrate solids with known cross-sections.

Multiple Choice Questions: Applications of Integration: Volume

In Problems 1-20, the region whose boundaries are given is rotated about the line indicated. Choose the alternative which gives the volume of the solid generated.

1. $y = x^2$, $x = 2$, and $y = 0$ about the x-axis.

(A) $\dfrac{64\pi}{3}$ (B) $\dfrac{32\pi}{5}$ (C) $\dfrac{8\pi}{3}$ (D) $\dfrac{128\pi}{5}$ (E) 8π.

2. $y = x^2$, $x = 2$, and $y = 0$ about the y-axis.

(A) $\dfrac{16\pi}{3}$ (B) 4π (C) $\dfrac{32\pi}{5}$ (D) 8π (E) $\dfrac{8\pi}{3}$.

3. $y = x^2$, $x = 2$, and $y = 0$ about the line $x = 2$.

(A) 4π (B) $\dfrac{4\pi}{3}$ (C) $\dfrac{8\pi}{3}$ (D) $\dfrac{16\pi}{3}$ (E) 8π.

4. The first quadrant region bounded by $y = x^2$, the y-axis, and $y = 4$; about the y-axis.

(A) 8π (B) 4π (C) $\dfrac{64\pi}{3}$ (D) $\dfrac{32\pi}{3}$ (E) $\dfrac{16\pi}{3}$.

5. $y = x^2$ and $y = 4$ about the x-axis.

(A) $\dfrac{64\pi}{5}$ (B) $\dfrac{512\pi}{15}$ (C) $\dfrac{256\pi}{5}$ (D) $\dfrac{128\pi}{5}$ (E) none of these.

6. $y = x^2$ and $y = 4$ about the line $x = 2$.

  (A) $2\pi \displaystyle\int_{-2}^{2} (2 - x)(4 - x^2)\, dx$ (B) $4\pi \displaystyle\int_{0}^{2} (2 - x)(4 - x^2)\, dx$

  (C) $4\pi \displaystyle\int_{0}^{2} (4 - x)(2 - x^2)\, dx$ (D) $4\pi \displaystyle\int_{0}^{4} \sqrt{y}\, dy$

  (E) $8\pi \displaystyle\int_{0}^{4} y\, dy$.

7. $y = x^2$ and $y = 4$ about the line $y = 4$.

  (A) $\dfrac{256\pi}{15}$ (B) $\dfrac{256\pi}{5}$ (C) $\dfrac{512\pi}{5}$ (D) $\dfrac{512\pi}{15}$ (E) $\dfrac{64\pi}{3}$.

8. $y = x^2$ and $y = 4$ about the line $y = -1$.

  (A) $4\pi \displaystyle\int_{-1}^{4} (y + 1)\sqrt{y}\, dy$ (B) $2\pi \displaystyle\int_{0}^{2} (4 - x^2)^2\, dx$

  (C) $\pi \displaystyle\int_{-2}^{2} (16 - x^4)\, dx$ (D) $4\pi \displaystyle\int_{0}^{4} (y + 1)\sqrt{y}\, dy$

  (E) none of these.

9. $y = 3x - x^2$ and $y = 0$ about the y-axis.

  (A) 27π (B) $\dfrac{81\pi}{10}$ (C) $\dfrac{648\pi}{15}$ (D) $\dfrac{27\pi}{4}$ (E) $\dfrac{27\pi}{2}$.

10. $y = 3x - x^2$ and $y = 0$ about the x-axis.

  (A) $\pi \displaystyle\int_{0}^{3} (9x^2 + x^4)\, dx$ (B) $\pi \displaystyle\int_{0}^{3} (3x - x^2)^2\, dx$

  (C) $\pi \displaystyle\int_{0}^{\sqrt{3}} (3x - x^2)\, dx$ (D) $2\pi \displaystyle\int_{0}^{3} y\sqrt{9 - 4y}\, dy$

  (E) $\pi \displaystyle\int_{0}^{\frac{9}{4}} y^2\, dy$.

11. $y = 3x - x^2$ and $y = x$ about the x-axis.

(A) $\pi \displaystyle\int_0^{\frac{3}{2}} [(3x - x^2)^2 - x^2]\, dx$ (B) $\pi \displaystyle\int_0^2 (9x^2 - 6x^3)\, dx$

(C) $\pi \displaystyle\int_0^2 [(3x - x^2)^2 - x^2]\, dx$ (D) $\pi \displaystyle\int_0^3 [(3x - x^2)^2 - x^4]\, dx$

(E) $\pi \displaystyle\int_0^3 (2x - x^2)^2\, dx$.

12. $y = 3x - x^2$ and $y = x$ about the y-axis.

(A) $\dfrac{8\pi}{3}$ (B) 4π (C) $\dfrac{40\pi}{3}$ (D) $\dfrac{32\pi}{3}$ (E) 8π .

13. An arch of $y = \sin x$ and the x-axis about the x-axis.

(A) $\dfrac{\pi}{2}(\pi - \dfrac{1}{2})$ (B) $\dfrac{\pi^2}{2}$ (C) $\dfrac{\pi^2}{4}$ (D) π^2 (E) $\pi(\pi - 1)$.

14. $y = \sin x$, $x = 0$, $x = \pi$, and $y = 0$ about the y-axis.

(A) $2\pi^2$ (B) $2\pi^2 - 2$ (C) 4π (D) π^2 (E) $\dfrac{\pi^2}{2}$.

15. The right branch of the hyperbola $x^2 - y^2 = 3$ and $x = 2$ about the y-axis.

(A) $\dfrac{8\pi}{3}$ (B) 4π (C) $\dfrac{4\pi}{3}$ (D) $\dfrac{2\pi}{3}(3\sqrt{3} - 5)$

(E) none of these.

16. The trapezoid with vertices at $(2,0)$, $(2,2)$, $(4,0)$, and $(4,4)$ about the y-axis.

(A) $\dfrac{56\pi}{3}$ (B) $\dfrac{128\pi}{3}$ (C) $\dfrac{92\pi}{3}$ (D) $\dfrac{112\pi}{3}$

(E) none of these.

17. $y = \ln x$, $y = 0$, $x = e$ about the line $x = e$.

$$\text{(A)} \quad 2\pi \int_1^e (e - x) \ln x \, dx \qquad \text{(B)} \quad \pi \int_0^1 (e - e^{2y}) \, dy$$

$$\text{(C)} \quad 2\pi \int_1^e (e - \ln x) \, dx \qquad \text{(D)} \quad \pi \int_0^e (e^2 - 2e^{y+1} + e^{2y}) \, dy$$

(E)   none of these.

18.   The circle $x^2 - 2x + y^2 = 0$ about the y-axis.

$$\text{(A)} \quad 8\pi \int_0^1 x\sqrt{2x - x^2} \, dx \qquad \text{(B)} \quad 4\pi \int_0^2 x\sqrt{2x - x^2} \, dx$$

$$\text{(C)} \quad 4\pi \int_{-2}^2 \sqrt{y^2 - 1} \, dy \qquad \text{(D)} \quad 2\pi \int_0^2 x\sqrt{2x - x^2} \, dx$$

(E)   none of these.

*19.   The circle with parametric equations $x = a \cos \theta$, $y = a \sin \theta$ $(a > 0)$, about the line $x = 2a$.

(A) $4\pi a^3 \displaystyle\int_0^\pi (2 \sin \theta - \sin^2 \theta) \cos \theta \, d\theta$

(B) $4\pi a^3 \displaystyle\int_\pi^0 (2 \sin \theta - \cos \theta) \, d\theta$

(C) $- 4\pi a^3 \displaystyle\int_\pi^0 (2 \sin \theta \cos \theta - \sin \theta \cos^2 \theta) \, d\theta$

(D) $16\pi a^3 \displaystyle\int_0^{\frac{\pi}{2}} \cos^2 \theta \, d\theta$

(E) $8\pi a^3 \displaystyle\int_0^{\frac{\pi}{2}} (2 \sin^2 \theta - \sin^2 \theta \cos \theta) \, d\theta$.

*20. The curve with parametric equations $x = \tan \theta$, $y = \cos^2 \theta$, and the
lines $x = 0$, $x = 1$, and $y = 0$ about the x-axis.

(A) $\pi \displaystyle\int_0^{\frac{\pi}{4}} \cos^4 \theta \; d\theta$

(B) $\pi \displaystyle\int_0^{\frac{\pi}{4}} \cos^2 \theta \; \sin \theta \; d\theta$

(C) $\pi \displaystyle\int_0^{\frac{\pi}{4}} \cos^2 \theta \; d\theta$

(D) $\pi \displaystyle\int_0^{1} \cos^2 \theta \; d\theta$

(E) $\pi \displaystyle\int_0^{1} \cos^4 \theta \; d\theta$.

In problems 21-25, choose the alternative which gives the volume, if
it exists, of the solid generated.

*21. $y = \dfrac{1}{x}$, $x = 1$, and $y = 0$ about the x-axis.

(A) $\dfrac{\pi}{2}$ (B) π (C) 2π (D) 4π (E) none of these.

*22. $y = \dfrac{1}{x}$, $x = 1$, and $y = 0$ about the y-axis.

(A) π (B) $\dfrac{\pi}{2}$ (C) 2π (D) 4π (E) none of these.

*23. The first quadrant region under $y = e^{-x}$ about the x-axis.

(A) π (B) 2π (C) 4π (D) $\dfrac{\pi}{2}$ (E) none of these.

*24. The first quadrant region under $y = e^{-x}$ about the y-axis.

(A) $\dfrac{\pi}{2}$ (B) π (C) 2π (D) 4π (E) none of these.

*25. The first quadrant region under $y = e^{-x^2}$ about the y-axis.

(A) π (B) $\dfrac{\pi}{2}$ (C) 2π (D) 4π (E) none of these.

26. A sphere of radius r is divided into two parts by a plane at distance h $(0 < h < r)$ from the center. The volume of the smaller part equals

(A) $\frac{\pi}{3}(2r^3 + h^3 - 3r^2h)$

(B) $\frac{\pi h}{3}(3r^2 - h^2)$

(C) $\frac{4}{3}\pi r^3 + \frac{h^3}{3} - r^2h$

(D) $\frac{\pi}{3}(2r^3 + 3r^2h - h^3)$

(E) none of these.

*27. The base of a solid is a circle of radius a and every plane section perpendicular to a diameter is a square. The solid has volume

(A) $\frac{8}{3}a^3$ (B) $2\pi a^3$ (C) $4\pi a^3$ (D) $\frac{16}{3}a^3$ (E) $\frac{8\pi}{3}a^3$.

*28. The base of a solid is the region bounded by the parabola $x^2 = 8y$ and the line $y = 4$ and each plane section perpendicular to the y-axis is an equilateral triangle. The volume of the solid is

(A) $\frac{64\sqrt{3}}{3}$ (B) $64\sqrt{3}$ (C) $32\sqrt{3}$ (D) 32 (E) none of these.

29. $f(x)$ is positive on $[a, b]$ where $0 < a < b$. If the region bounded by $y = 0$, $x = a$, $x = b$ and the curve of $y = f(x)$ is rotated about the y-axis, the volume generated is given by

(A) $2\pi \displaystyle\int_a^b (x - a)\, f(x)\, dx$

(B) $2\pi \displaystyle\int_0^b x\, f(x)\, dx$

(C) $2\pi \displaystyle\int_a^b x\, f(x)\, dx$

(D) $2\pi \displaystyle\int_0^b (x - a)\, f(x)\, dx$

(E) none of these.

30. If the curves of $f(x)$ and $g(x)$ intersect for $x = a$ and $x = b$ and if $f(x) > g(x) > 0$ for all x on (a, b), then the volume obtained when the region bounded by the curves is rotated about the x-axis is equal to

(A) $\pi \int_a^b f^2(x) \, dx - \int_a^b g^2(x) \, dx$

(B) $\pi \int_a^b [f(x) - g(x)]^2 \, dx$

(C) $2\pi \int_a^b x[f(x) - g(x)] \, dx$

(D) $\pi \int_a^b [f^2(x) - g^2(x)] \, dx$

(E) none of these.

Section 8: Further Applications of Integration

Review of Definitions and Methods

In Section Six we used definite integrals to find areas, and in Section Seven to find volumes. In this Section we review applications of integration to the following topics: length of a curve (arc length); surface area; average (mean) value of a function; motion in a straight line and along a curve; area and arc length in polar coordinates; and work.

A. Arc Length. If the derivative of a function $y = f(x)$ is continuous on the interval $a \leqq x \leqq b$, then the length s of the arc of the curve of $y = f(x)$ from the point where $x = a$ to the point where $x = b$ is given by

$$s = \int_a^b \sqrt{1 + (\tfrac{dy}{dx})^2}\, dx. \tag{1}$$

If the derivative of the function $x = g(y)$ is continuous on the interval $c \leqq y \leqq d$, then the length s of the arc from $y = c$ to $y = d$ is given by

$$s = \int_c^d \sqrt{1 + (\tfrac{dx}{dy})^2}\, dy. \tag{2}$$

If a curve is defined parametrically by the equations $x = x(t)$, $y = y(t)$, if the derivatives of the functions $x(t)$ and $y(t)$ are continuous on $[t_a, t_b]$, (and if the curve does not intersect itself), then the length of the arc from $t = t_a$ to $t = t_b$ is given by

$$s = \int_{t_a}^{t_b} \sqrt{(\tfrac{dx}{dt})^2 + (\tfrac{dy}{dt})^2} \; dt. \tag{3}$$

The parenthetical phrase above is equivalent to the requirement that the curve is traced out just once as t varies from t_a to t_b.

As indicated in Section Three K equation (4), p. 48, the formulas in (1), (2), and (3) above can all be derived easily from the very simply relation

$$ds^2 = dx^2 + dy^2. \tag{4}$$

EXAMPLES:

1. Find the length of the arc of $y = x^{3/2}$ from $x = 1$ to $x = 8$.

$\frac{dy}{dx} = \frac{3}{2} x^{1/2}$, so, by (1),

$$s = \int_1^8 \sqrt{1 + \frac{9}{4} x} \; dx = \frac{4}{9} \int_1^8 (1 + \frac{9}{4} x)^{1/2} \frac{9}{4} \; dx$$

$$= \frac{2}{3} \cdot \frac{4}{9} (1 + \frac{9}{4} x)^{3/2} \Big|_1^8 = \frac{8}{27} (19^{3/2} - \frac{13^{3/2}}{8}).$$

2. Find the length of the curve $(x - 2)^2 = 4y^3$ from $y = 0$ to $y = 1$.

Since

$$x - 2 = 2y^{3/2} \quad \text{and} \quad \frac{dx}{dy} = 3y^{1/2},$$

(2) yields

$$s = \int_0^1 \sqrt{1 + 9y} \; dy = \frac{2}{27} (1 + 9y)^{3/2} \Big|_0^1 = \frac{2}{27} (10^{3/2} - 1).$$

3. The position (x,y) of a particle at time t is given parametrically by $x = t^2$ and $y = \frac{t^3}{3} - t$. Find the distance it travels between $t = 1$ and $t = 2$.

We can use (4): $ds^2 = dx^2 + dy^2$, where $dx = 2t\ dt$ and $dy = (t^2 - 1)\ dt$. Thus $ds = \sqrt{4t^2 + t^4 - 2t^2 + 1}\ dt$, and

$$s = \int_1^2 \sqrt{(t^2 + 1)^2}\ dt = \int_1^2 (t^2 + 1)\ dt$$

$$= \left. \frac{t^3}{3} + t \right|_1^2 = \frac{10}{3}.$$

4. Find the length of the arc of $y = \ln \sec x$ from $x = 0$ to $x = \frac{\pi}{3}$.

$$\frac{dy}{dx} = \frac{\sec x \tan x}{\sec x}, \text{ so } s = \int_0^{\frac{\pi}{3}} \sqrt{1 + \tan^2 x}\ dx = \int_0^{\frac{\pi}{3}} \sec x\ dx$$

$$= \left. \ln (\sec x + \tan x) \right|_0^{\frac{\pi}{3}} = \ln (2 + \sqrt{3}).$$

B. Area of Surface of Revolution.   If (a,c) and (b,d) are two points on the curve of a differentiable function $y = f(x)$ and the arc between these points is rotated about the x-axis, then the area of the surface generated is given by either of these equations:

$$S = 2\pi \int_a^b y \sqrt{1 + \left(\frac{dy}{dx}\right)^2}\ dx; \tag{1}$$

$$S = 2\pi \int_c^d y \sqrt{1 + \left(\frac{dx}{dy}\right)^2}\ dy. \tag{2}$$

Either (1) or (2) may be used if the curve to be rotated about the x-axis is defined parametrically.

If the rotation is about the y-axis then we can use either of the following:

$$S = 2\pi \int_a^b x \sqrt{1 + \left(\frac{dy}{dx}\right)^2}\ dx; \tag{3}$$

$$S = 2\pi \int_c^d x \sqrt{1 + \left(\frac{dx}{dy}\right)^2}\ dy. \tag{4}$$

Equations (1) through (4) are all easily derived from the simple formula

$$S = 2\pi \int R \, ds, \qquad\qquad (5)$$

where ds is the element of arc length that satisfies the relation $ds^2 = dx^2 + dy^2$ and R is the distance from this element of arc to the axis of rotation. (Note that an element of surface area $dS = 2\pi R \, ds$ is the surface of a frustum of a cone of mid-radius R and slant height ds.) In a specific problem we must express R, ds, and the limits in terms of an appropriate variable, as indicated in the following

EXAMPLES:

5. Find the area of the surface generated by revolving about the y-axis the arc of $x = \frac{1}{3} y^3$ from $y = 0$ to $y = 2$.

We can use (4). $\frac{dx}{dy} = y^2$ and

$$S = 2\pi \int_0^2 x\sqrt{1 + y^4} \, dy = 2\pi \int_0^2 \frac{y^3}{3}\sqrt{1 + y^4} \, dy$$

$$= \frac{2\pi}{3}\cdot\frac{1}{4}\cdot\frac{2}{3}(1 + y^4)^{3/2}\Big|_0^2 = \frac{\pi}{9}(17^{3/2} - 1).$$

6. Find the surface of a sphere of radius a. The sphere can be generated by revolving a semicircle about the x-axis (see Figure N8-1). If we define the circle parametrically by $x = a \cos \theta$, $y = a \sin \theta$, and

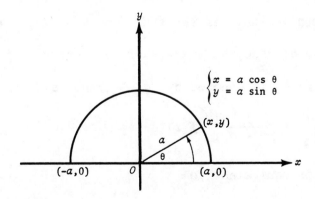

Figure N8-1

use equation (5), then we have $S = 2\pi \int R \, ds$. Since $dx = -a \sin \theta \, d\theta$, $dy = a \cos \theta \, d\theta$, and $R = y = a \sin \theta$, it follows that

$$S = 2\pi \int_0^\pi a \sin \theta \cdot a \, d\theta,$$

where the limits are obtained by noting that the sphere is generated as θ varies from 0 to π. Thus

$$S = 2\pi a^2 (-\cos \theta) \Big|_0^\pi = 4\pi a^2 .$$

7. Find the surface area obtained by rotating the arc of $y = \frac{1}{2}(e^x + e^{-x})$ about the x-axis from $x = -2$ to $x = 2$. We note that the curve is symmetric with respect to the y-axis. Since $\frac{dy}{dx} = \frac{1}{2}(e^x - e^{-x})$ and $(\frac{dy}{dx})^2 = \frac{1}{4}(e^{2x} - 2 + e^{-2x})$, we have (for use in equation (1))

$$1 + (\frac{dy}{dx})^2 = 1 + \frac{1}{4}e^{2x} - \frac{1}{2} + \frac{1}{4}e^{-2x} = \frac{1}{4}(e^{2x} + 2 + e^{-2x}) = \left[\frac{1}{2}(e^x + e^{-x})\right]^2.$$

(1) then yields

$$S = 2 \cdot 2\pi \int_0^2 y\left[\frac{1}{2}(e^x + e^{-x})\right] dx = 4\pi \int_0^2 \frac{1}{2}(e^x + e^{-x}) \frac{1}{2}(e^x + e^{-x}) \, dx$$

$$= 4\pi \cdot \frac{1}{4} \int_0^2 (e^{2x} + 2 + e^{-2x}) \, dx = \pi(\frac{e^{2x}}{2} + 2x - \frac{e^{-2x}}{2}) \Big|_0^2$$

$$= \pi\left[(\frac{e^4}{2} + 4 - \frac{e^{-4}}{2}) - (\frac{1}{2} - \frac{1}{2})\right] = \frac{\pi}{2}(e^4 + 8 - e^{-4}).$$

C. **Average (Mean) Value.** If the function $y = f(x)$ is continuous on the interval $a \le x \le b$, then the average or mean value of y with respect to x over the interval $[a,b]$ is denoted by $(y_{av})_x$ and is defined by

$$(y_{av})_x = \frac{1}{b-a} \int_a^b f(x) \, dx. \qquad (1)$$

If $a < b$ then (1) is equivalent to

$$(b - a)(y_{av})_x = \int_a^b f(x) \, dx. \qquad (2)$$

If $f(x) \geq 0$ for all x on $[a,b]$ we can interpret (2) in terms of areas as follows: The right-hand member represents the area under the curve of $y = f(x)$, above the x-axis, and bounded by the vertical lines $x = a$ and $x = b$. The left-hand member of (2) represents the area of a rectangle with base $(b - a)$ and height $(y_{av})_x$. See Figure N8-2.

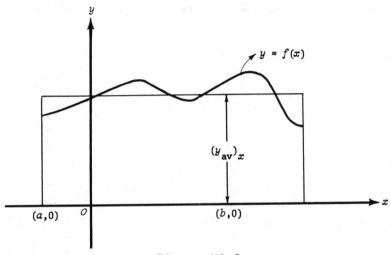

Figure N8-2

EXAMPLES:

8. The average (mean) value of $f(x) = \ln x$ with respect to x on the interval $[1,4]$ equals $\dfrac{1}{4-1}\displaystyle\int_1^4 \ln x\ dx = \dfrac{1}{3}(x \ln x - x)\Big|_1^4 = \dfrac{4 \ln 4 - 3}{3}$.

9. The mean value of ordinates of the semicircle $y = \sqrt{4 - x^2}$ with respect to x on $[-2,2]$ is given by

$$(y_{av})_x = \frac{1}{2 - (-2)} \int_{-2}^{2} \sqrt{4 - x^2}\ dx = \frac{1}{4}\frac{\pi(2^2)}{2} = \frac{\pi}{2}. \qquad (3)$$

In (3) we have used the fact that the definite integral equals exactly the area of a semicircle of radius 2.

10. Find the average ordinate of the semicircle $y = \sqrt{4 - x^2}$ over the arc of the semicircle. Whereas in Example 9 we may think of dividing the interval *along the x-axis* into equal subintervals, here we divide the

semicircle into arcs of equal length. We then seek the mean value of
the ordinates at these points of subdivision; i.e., we want $(y_{av})_s$, where
s denotes arc length. Thus,

$$(y_{av})_s \ = \ \frac{1}{2\pi} \int_{s_1}^{s_2} y \ ds, \tag{4}$$

where 2π is the length of the semicircle. Since $ds^2 = dx^2 + dy^2$

$$= dx^2 + \frac{x^2}{4 - x^2} \, dx^2 = \frac{4}{y^2} \, dx^2, \text{ (4) yields}$$

$$(y_{av})_s \ = \ \frac{1}{2\pi} \int_{-2}^{2} y \cdot \frac{2}{y} \, dx \ = \ \frac{1}{\pi} x \Big|_{-2}^{2} \ = \ \frac{4}{\pi}.$$

D. **Motion in a Straight Line.** If the motion of a particle P along
a straight line is given by the equation $s = F(t)$, where s is the distance
at time t of P from a fixed point on the line, then the velocity and
acceleration of P at time t are given respectively by

$$v \ = \ \frac{ds}{dt} \qquad \text{and} \qquad a \ = \ \frac{dv}{dt} \ = \ \frac{d^2s}{dt^2}.$$

This topic was discussed as an application of differentiation in Section 3 **J**
(p. 44). Here we shall apply integration.

If we know that the particle P has velocity $v = f(t)$, where v is a
continuous function, then the distance traveled by the particle during
the time interval from $t = a$ to $t = b$ is

$$s \ = \ \int_{a}^{b} |f(t)| \ dt. \tag{1}$$

If $f(t) \geqq 0$ for all t on $[a,b]$ (i.e., P moves only in the positive
direction), then (1) is equivalent to $s = \int_{a}^{b} f(t) \, dt$; similarly, if
$f(t) \leqq 0$ on $[a,b]$ (P moves only in the negative direction), then
$s = - \int_{a}^{b} f(t) \, dt$. If $f(t)$ changes sign on $[a,b]$ (i.e., the direction

of motion changes), then (1) gives the *total* distance traveled. Suppose, for example, that the situation is as follows:

$$a \leq t \leq c \qquad\qquad f(t) \geq 0$$

$$c \leq t \leq d \qquad\qquad f(t) \leq 0$$

$$d \leq t \leq b \qquad\qquad f(t) \geq 0.$$

Then the total distance s traveled during the time interval from $t = a$ to $t = b$ is exactly

$$s = \int_a^c f(t)\, dt - \int_c^d f(t)\, dt + \int_d^b f(t)\, dt.$$

EXAMPLES:

11. If a particle moves along a straight line with velocity $v = t^3 + 3t^2$, then the distance traveled between $t = 1$ and $t = 4$ is given by

$$s = \int_1^4 (t^3 + 3t^2)\, dt = \left.\left(\frac{t^4}{4} + t^3\right)\right|_1^4 = \frac{507}{4}.$$

Note that $v > 0$ for all t on $[1,4]$.

12. A particle moves along the x-axis so that its position at time t is given by $x(t) = 2t^3 - 9t^2 + 12t - 4$. Find the total distance covered between $t = 0$ and $t = 4$.

Since $v(t) = 6t^2 - 18t + 12 = 6(t - 1)(t - 2)$, we see that if

$$t < 1 \qquad\qquad v > 0$$

$$1 < t < 2 \qquad\qquad v < 0$$

$$2 < t \qquad\qquad v > 0.$$

Thus

$$s = \int_0^1 v(t)\, dt - \int_1^2 v(t)\, dt + \int_2^4 v(t)\, dt. \qquad (2)$$

If we substitute for $v(t)$ in (2), we get

$$s = x(t)\Big|_0^1 - x(t)\Big|_1^2 + x(t)\Big|_2^4 = x(1) - x(0) - x(2) + x(1)$$

$$+ x(4) - x(2) = x(4) - 2x(2) + 2x(1) - x(0)$$

$$= 28 - 2\cdot 0 + 2\cdot 1 - (-4) = 34.$$

This example is identical with Example 24(e) (p. 45), in which the required distance is computed by another method.

13. The acceleration of a particle moving on a line is given at time t by $a = \sin t$; when $t = 0$ the particle is at rest. Find the distance it travels from $t = 0$ to $t = \frac{5\pi}{6}$.

Since $a = \frac{d^2 s}{dt^2} = \frac{dv}{dt} = \sin t$, it follows that $v(t) = \frac{ds}{dt} = \int \sin t \, dt$;

$v(t) = -\cos t + C$. $v(0) = 0$ yields $C = 1$. Thus $v(t) = 1 - \cos t$, and since $\cos t \leq 1$ for all t we see that $v(t) \geq 0$ for all t. So

$$s = \int_0^{\frac{5\pi}{6}} (1 - \cos t) \, dt = (t - \sin t)\Big|_0^{\frac{5\pi}{6}} = \frac{5\pi}{6} - \frac{1}{2}.$$

14. Find k if a deceleration of k ft/sec² is needed to bring a particle moving with a velocity of 75 ft/sec to a stop in 5 sec.

Let $a = \frac{dv}{dt} = -k$; then

$$v = -kt + C. \tag{3}$$

Since $v = 0$ when $t = 5$, $C = 5k$ and (3) becomes $v = -kt + 5k$. Integrating (3) yields

$$s = -\frac{1}{2} kt^2 + 5kt + C'. \tag{4}$$

We let $s(0) = 0$, so C' in (4) is 0. We seek k so that $s(5) = 75$:

$$75 = -\frac{25k}{2} + 25k, \text{ or } 75 = \frac{25k}{2}; \text{ thus } k = 6.$$

E. Motion along a Plane Curve. Recall from Section 3 K (p. 47) that if the motion of a particle P along a curve is given parametrically by the equations $x = x(t)$ and $y = y(t)$, then at time t the position vector R, the velocity vector v, and the acceleration vector a have the following values:

$$R = x\mathbf{i} + y\mathbf{j};$$

$$v = \frac{dR}{dt} = \frac{dx}{dt}\mathbf{i} + \frac{dy}{dt}\mathbf{j} = \dot{x}\mathbf{i} + \dot{y}\mathbf{j} = v_x\mathbf{i} + v_y\mathbf{j};$$

$$a = \frac{d^2R}{dt^2} = \frac{dV}{dt} = \frac{d^2x}{dt^2}\mathbf{i} + \frac{d^2y}{dt^2}\mathbf{j} = \ddot{x}\mathbf{i} + \ddot{y}\mathbf{j} = a_x\mathbf{i} + a_y\mathbf{j}.$$

The components in the horizontal and vertical directions of R, v, and a are given respectively by the coefficients of i and j in the corresponding vector.

The slope of v is $\frac{dy}{dx}$; its magnitude, $|v| = \sqrt{\left(\frac{dx}{dt}\right)^2 + \left(\frac{dy}{dt}\right)^2} = \frac{ds}{dt}$, is the speed of the particle, and the velocity vector is tangent to the path.

The slope of a is $\frac{d^2y}{dt^2} \Big/ \frac{d^2x}{dt^2}$; its magnitude is $|a| = \sqrt{a_x^2 + a_y^2}$.

How integration may be used to solve problems of curvilinear motion is illustrated in the following

EXAMPLES:

15. The motion of a particle satisfied the equations $\frac{d^2x}{dt^2} = 0$, $\frac{d^2y}{dt^2} = -g$. Find parametric equations for the motion if the initial conditions are $x = y = 0$, $\frac{dx}{dt} = v_0 \cos \alpha$, and $\frac{dy}{dt} = v_0 \sin \alpha$, where v_0 and α are constants.

We integrate each of the given equations twice and determine the constants as indicated:

$$\frac{dx}{dt} \; = \; C_1 \; = \; v_0 \cos \alpha \qquad\qquad \frac{dy}{dt} \; = \; -gt + C_2$$

$$v_0 \sin \alpha \; = \; C_2$$

$$x \; = \; (v_0 \cos \alpha)t \; + C_3 \qquad\qquad y \; = -\frac{1}{2} gt^2 + (v_0 \sin \alpha)t + C_4$$

$$x(0) = 0 \text{ yields } C_3 = 0. \qquad\qquad y(0) = 0 \text{ yields } C_4 = 0.$$

Finally, then, we have

$$x \; = \; (v_0 \cos \alpha)t; \qquad\qquad y \; = \; -\frac{1}{2} gt^2 + (v_0 \sin \alpha)t.$$

These are the equations for the path of a projectile that starts at the origin with initial velocity v_0 and at an angle of elevation α.

If desired, t can be eliminated from this pair of equations to yield a parabola in rectangular coordinates.

16. A particle $P(x,y)$ moves along a curve so that $\dfrac{dx}{dt} \; = \; 2\sqrt{x}$ and

$\dfrac{dy}{dt} \; = \; \dfrac{1}{x}$ at any time $t \geq 0$. At $t = 0$, $x = 1$ and $y = 0$. Find the

parametric equations of motion.

Since $\dfrac{dx}{\sqrt{x}} \; = \; 2 \; dt$, we integrate to get $2\sqrt{x} \; = \; 2t + C$, and use

$x(0) = 1$ to find that $C = 2$. So $\sqrt{x} = t + 1$ and

$$x \; = \; (t + 1)^2. \tag{1}$$

Then $\dfrac{dy}{dt} \; = \; \dfrac{1}{x} \; = \; \dfrac{1}{(t + 1)^2}$ by (1), so $dy \; = \; \dfrac{dt}{(t + 1)^2}$ and

$$y \; = \; -\frac{1}{t + 1} + C'. \tag{2}$$

Since $y(0) = 0$, this yields $C' = 1$. So (2) becomes $y \; = \; 1 - \dfrac{1}{t + 1}$

$= \; \dfrac{t}{t + 1}$. Thus the parametric equations are

$$x \; = \; (t + 1)^2 \quad \text{and} \quad y \; = \; \frac{t}{t + 1}.$$

17. If a particle moves on a curve so that the acceleration vector is always perpendicular to the position vector, prove that the speed of the particle is constant.

The hypothesis is equivalent to the statement

$$\frac{\frac{d^2y}{dt^2}}{\frac{d^2x}{dt^2}} \cdot \frac{\frac{dy}{dt}}{\frac{dx}{dt}} = -1, \quad \text{or}$$

$$\frac{\ddot{y}}{\ddot{x}} \cdot \frac{\dot{y}}{\dot{x}} = -1. \tag{3}$$

(3) is equivalent to

$$\dot{y}\ddot{y} = -\dot{x}\ddot{x}, \tag{4}$$

and (4) is simply

$$\frac{d}{dt}(\frac{1}{2}\dot{y}^2) = \frac{d}{dt}(-\frac{1}{2}\dot{x}^2).$$

So $\frac{1}{2}\dot{y}^2 = -\frac{1}{2}\dot{x}^2 + C'$, or

$$\dot{y}^2 + \dot{x}^2 = C. \tag{5}$$

But since the left-hand member of (5) is precisely $(\frac{ds}{dt})^2$ or $|\mathbf{v}|^2$, (5) says that the square of the speed (and consequently the speed) is constant.

18. A particle $P(x,y)$ moves along a curve so that its acceleration

$\mathbf{a} = -4 \cos 2t\ \mathbf{i} - 2 \sin t\ \mathbf{j} \qquad (-\frac{\pi}{2} \leqq t \leqq \frac{\pi}{2})$; when $t = 0$ then $x = 1$,

$y = 0$, $\dot{x} = 0$, and $\dot{y} = 2$.

(a) Find the position vector $\mathbf{R}$ at any time t.

(b) Find a cartesian equation for the path of the particle and identify the conic on which P moves.

(a) $\mathbf{v} = (-2 \sin 2t + c_1)\mathbf{i} + (2 \cos t + c_2)\mathbf{j}$, and since $\mathbf{v} = 2\mathbf{j}$ when $t = 0$, it follows that $c_1 = c_2 = 0$. So $\mathbf{v} = -2 \sin 2t\ \mathbf{i} + 2 \cos t\ \mathbf{j}$.

Also $R = (\cos 2t + c_3)i + (2 \sin t + c_4)j$, and since $R = i$ when $t = 0$

we see that $c_3 = c_4 = 0$. Finally, then,

$$R = \cos 2t\ i + 2 \sin t\ j.$$

   (b) From (a) the parametric equations of motion are

$$x = \cos 2t \qquad\qquad y = 2 \sin t.$$

By a trigonometric identity,

$$x = 1 - 2 \sin^2 t = 1 - \frac{y^2}{2}.$$

P travels along *part* of a parabola with vertex at (1,0) and which opens
to the left. The path of the particle is sketched in Figure N8-3; note
that $-1 \leqq x \leqq 1$, $-2 \leqq y \leqq 2$.

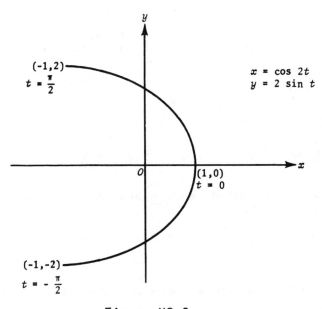

Figure N8-3

   F. **Work.** If the function F is continuous on the interval $a \leqq x \leqq b$,
then the work W done by the force F on an object as it moves along the
x-axis from a to b is given by

$$W = \int_b^a F(x)\ dx. \qquad\qquad (1)$$

In the special case that $F(x)$ is constant and equal to F, we see that

$$W = F \cdot (b - a), \qquad\qquad (2)$$

i.e., force times distance.

When the force is variable we use (2) to approximate an element of work, ΔW, done over a short distance Δx, by $\Delta W = F(x_k)\Delta x$, where $F(x_k)$ is the force acting at some point in the kth subinterval. We use the Fundamental Theorem to get

$$W = \lim_{n \to \infty} \sum_{k=0}^{n} F(x_k)\, \Delta x = \int_a^b F(x)\, dx.$$

If the force is given in pounds and the distance in feet then the work is given in foot-pounds (ft-lb). Problems typical of those involving computation of work are given in the following

EXAMPLES:

19. Find the work done by a force F (in lb) which moves a particle along the x-axis from $x = 4$ ft to $x = 9$ ft, if $F(x) = \frac{1}{2\sqrt{x}}$.

$$W = \int_4^9 \frac{dx}{2\sqrt{x}} = \sqrt{x}\,\Big|_4^9 = 3 - 2 = 1 \text{ ft-lb.}$$

20. If the natural length of a spring is 1 ft and it takes a force of 5 lb to extend it 3 in., how much work is done in stretching the spring

(a)   from its natural length to 16 in.?

(b)   from 14 in. to 18 in.?

By Hooke's law, the force $F(x)$ required to keep a spring extended (compressed) x units beyond (short of) its normal length is given by

$$F(x) = kx. \tag{3}$$

Since here $F(3)$ is 5, the "spring constant" k in (3) is determined by $5 = k \cdot 3$. Consequently $k = \frac{5}{3}$, and $F(x) = \frac{5}{3}x$.

(a) When the spring is 1 ft long, then $x = 0$; when it is 16 in. long, then $x = 4$. So

$$W = \int_0^4 \frac{5}{3}x\, dx = \frac{5}{6}x^2\,\Big|_0^4 = \frac{40}{3} \text{ in.-lb.}$$

(b) **When the spring is 14 in. long, then $x = 2$; when it is 18 in. long, then $x = 6$. So, here,**

$$W = \int_2^6 \frac{5}{3} x \, dx = \frac{5}{6} (36 - 4) = \frac{80}{3} \text{ in.-lb.}$$

21. **A conical cistern is full of water. If it has a radius of 6 ft and a height of 15 ft, find the work done**

(a) **in pumping all the water out of the cistern;**

(b) **in pumping the water to a height of 5 ft above the top of the cistern.**

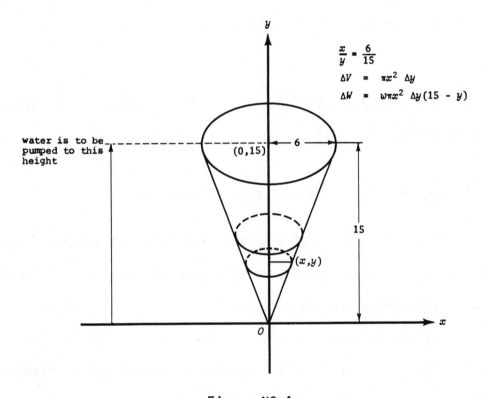

$$\frac{x}{y} = \frac{6}{15}$$
$$\Delta V = \pi x^2 \, \Delta y$$
$$\Delta W = w\pi x^2 \, \Delta y (15 - y)$$

water is to be pumped to this height

Figure N8-4a

(a) **See Figure N8-4a, where we have set up the coordinate axes so that the origin is at the bottom of the tank. We partition the interval along the y-axis from 0 to 15 and find the work ΔW done in lifting a typical slice (disc) of water. ΔW is the force (the weight of the slice) times the distance through which the force acts; the weight of the slice is its volume times w (the weight per cubic unit). We have, then,**

$$\Delta W = \Delta V \cdot w(15 - y) = \pi x^2 \Delta y \cdot w(15 - y);$$

and

$$W = \pi w \int_0^{15} x^2(15 - y)\, dy. \tag{4}$$

To express x in terms of y in (4), we use similar triangles and note that

$\dfrac{x}{y} = \dfrac{6}{15} = \dfrac{2}{5}$; so $x^2 = \dfrac{4}{25} y^2$, and (4) becomes

$$W = \frac{4}{25}\pi w \int_0^{15} y^2(15 - y)\, dy$$

$$= \frac{4}{25}\pi w \int_0^{15} (15y^2 - y^3)\, dy = 675\pi w \text{ ft-lb.}$$

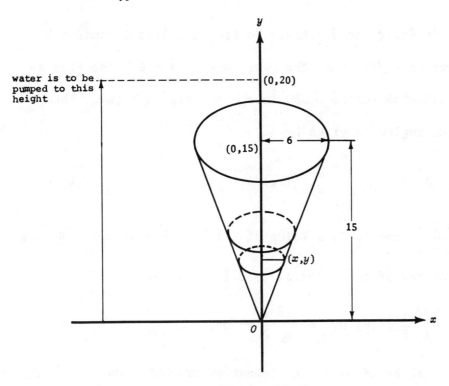

Figure N8-4b

(b)   See Figure N8-4b. This part differs from (a) only in the distance through which a slice moves. Here a slice is lifted $(20 - y)$ ft and

$$W = \frac{4}{25}\pi w \int_0^{15} y^2(20 - y)\, dy = 1575\pi w \text{ ft-lb.}$$

Note that the limits are the same as in part (a).

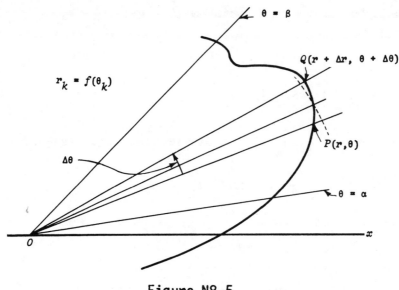

Figure N8-5

G. **Area in Polar Coordinates.** To find the area A bounded by the polar curve $r = f(\theta)$ and the rays $\theta = \alpha$, $\theta = \beta$ (see Figure N8-5). We divide the region AOB into n sectors as shown. Then the area of the region is given by

$$A = \lim_{n \to \infty} \sum_{k=1}^{n} \frac{1}{2} f^2(\theta_k) \, \Delta\theta \qquad (1)$$

where $\Delta\theta = \dfrac{\beta - \alpha}{n}$ and θ_k is a value of θ in the kth sector. By the Fundamental Theorem of the integral calculus, (1) equals

$$\int_{\alpha}^{\beta} \frac{1}{2} f^2(\theta) \, d\theta = \int_{\alpha}^{\beta} \frac{1}{2} r^2 \, d\theta. \qquad (2)$$

Note that if we think of dA as an element of area then $dA = \frac{1}{2} r^2 \, d\theta$, and this is the area of a circular sector of central angle θ and radius r.

We have assumed above that $f(\theta) \geqq 0$ on $[\alpha, \beta]$. We must be careful in determining the limits α and β in (2); often it helps to think of the required area as that "swept out" (or generated) as the radius vector (from the pole) rotates from $\theta = \alpha$ to $\theta = \beta$. It is also useful to exploit symmetry of the curve wherever possible.

Examples:

22. Find the area enclosed by the cardioid $r = 2(1 + \cos \theta)$.

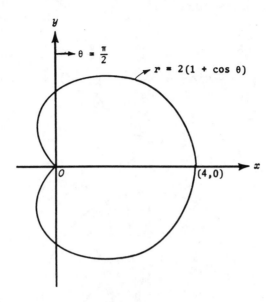

Figure N8-6

See Figure N8-6. We use the symmetry of the curve with respect to the polar axis and write

$$A = 2 \frac{1}{2} \int_0^\pi r^2 \, d\theta = 4 \int_0^\pi (1 + \cos \theta)^2 \, d\theta$$

$$= 4 \int_0^\pi (1 + 2 \cos \theta + \cos^2 \theta) \, d\theta$$

$$= 4 \int_0^\pi (1 + 2 \cos \theta + \frac{1}{2} + \frac{\cos 2\theta}{2}) \, d\theta$$

$$= 4 \left[\theta + 2 \sin \theta + \frac{\theta}{2} + \frac{\sin 2\theta}{4} \right]_0^\pi = 6\pi.$$

23. Find the area inside both the circle $r = 3 \sin \theta$ and the cardioid $r = 1 + \sin \theta$.

See Figure N8-7, where one half of the required area is shaded. Since $3 \sin \theta = 1 + \sin \theta$ when $\theta = \frac{\pi}{6}$ or $\frac{5\pi}{6}$, we see that the desired area is twice the sum of two parts: the area of the circle swept out by θ as it varies from 0 to $\frac{\pi}{6}$ plus the area of the cardioid swept out by a radius vector as

θ varies from $\frac{\pi}{6}$ to $\frac{\pi}{2}$.   Consequently

$$A = 2\left[\int_0^{\frac{\pi}{6}} \frac{9}{2} \sin^2 \theta \; d\theta \; + \; \int_{\frac{\pi}{6}}^{\frac{\pi}{2}} \frac{1}{2}(1 + \sin \theta)^2 \; d\theta\right] = \frac{5\pi}{4}.$$

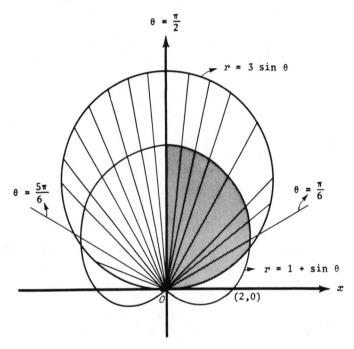

Figure N8-7

H.   Arc Length in Polar Coordinates.   The length s of the arc of the

continuous function $r = f(\theta)$ from $\theta = \alpha$ to $\theta = \beta$ can be obtained

from

$$s = \int ds \qquad\qquad (1)$$

(where $ds^2 = dx^2 + dy^2$); see Section 8 A, p. 142.   Since $x = r \cos \theta$ and

$y = r \sin \theta$ are the equations relating rectangular and polar coordinates,

it follows that

$$dx = -r \sin \theta \; d\theta + \cos \theta \; dr,$$

$$dy = r \cos \theta \; d\theta + \sin \theta \; dr.$$

If we substitute in (1) we get

$$ds^2 = r^2 \, d\theta^2 + dr^2 \qquad\qquad (2)$$

so $ds = \sqrt{r^2 + \left(\dfrac{dr}{d\theta}\right)^2} \, d\theta$, and

$$s = \int_\alpha^\beta \sqrt{r^2 + \left(\dfrac{dr}{d\theta}\right)^2} \, d\theta. \qquad\qquad (3)$$

Often (2) is as convenient to use as (3). We should avoid passing across a cusp, and take advantage of symmetry whenever possible.

EXAMPLES:

24. Find the length of the cardioid $r = 1 + \sin\theta$.

Half the cardioid is described as θ varies from $-\dfrac{\pi}{2}$ to $\dfrac{\pi}{2}$ (see Figure N8-7). Since $dr = \cos\theta \, d\theta$, (2) yields

$$ds^2 = (1 + \sin\theta)^2 \, d\theta^2 + \cos^2\theta \, d\theta^2$$

$$= (2 + 2\sin\theta) \, d\theta^2,$$

and

$$s = 2\sqrt{2} \int_{-\frac{\pi}{2}}^{\frac{\pi}{2}} \sqrt{1 + \sin\theta} \, d\theta$$

$$= 2\sqrt{2} \int_{-\frac{\pi}{2}}^{\frac{\pi}{2}} \frac{\sqrt{1 + \sin\theta} \, \sqrt{1 - \sin\theta}}{\sqrt{1 - \sin\theta}} \, d\theta$$

$$= 2\sqrt{2} \int_{-\frac{\pi}{2}}^{\frac{\pi}{2}} \frac{\cos\theta \, d\theta}{\sqrt{1 - \sin\theta}} = \left. -2\sqrt{2}\cdot 2(1 - \sin\theta)^{1/2} \right|_{-\frac{\pi}{2}}^{\frac{\pi}{2}}$$

$$= -4\sqrt{2}(0 - \sqrt{2}) = 8.$$

25. Find the length of the spiral $r = e^\theta$ from $\theta = 0$ to $\theta = 4$.

Since $dr = e^\theta \, d\theta$, we have from (2)

$$ds^2 = e^{2\theta} \, d\theta^2 + e^{2\theta} \, d\theta^2 = 2e^{2\theta} \, d\theta^2 .$$

Then $ds = \sqrt{2}e^{\theta} \, d\theta$ and

$$s = \sqrt{2} \int_0^4 e^{\theta} \, d\theta = \sqrt{2}(e^4 - 1).$$

I.   Recognition of Limits of Sums as Definite Integrals. In this section we use the Fundamental Theorem of the Integral Calculus to evaluate infinite sums by means of definite integrals. If f is a continuous function on $[a,b]$, if the interval $a \leq x \leq b$ has been partitioned into n equal subintervals of length $\Delta x = \dfrac{b-a}{n}$, and if $x_k = a + k\Delta x$, then

$$\lim_{n\to\infty} \sum_{k=1}^{n} f(x_k) \, \Delta x = \lim_{n\to\infty} \sum_{k=0}^{n-1} f(x_k) \, \Delta x = \int_a^b f(x) \, dx. \qquad (1)$$

For example,

$$\lim_{n\to\infty} \sum_{k=1}^{n} x_k^2 \, \Delta x = \int_a^b x^2 \, dx \;,$$

where the subdivisions are made on the interval $a \leq x \leq b$. Given an infinite sum, we need to identify Δx, x_k, $f(x_k)$, and the interval $[a,b]$. The technique is illustrated in the following

EXAMPLES:

26. To write

$$\lim_{n\to\infty} \left[f(\tfrac{1}{n})\tfrac{1}{n} + f(\tfrac{2}{n})\tfrac{1}{n} + \dots + f(\tfrac{n}{n})\tfrac{1}{n} \right] \qquad (2)$$

as a definite integral, we see that (2) is

$$\lim_{n\to\infty} \left[f(\tfrac{1}{n}) + f(\tfrac{2}{n}) + \dots + f(\tfrac{n}{n}) \right] \tfrac{1}{n}$$

$$\lim_{n\to\infty} \sum_{k=1}^{n} f(\tfrac{k}{n}) \, \Delta x = \lim_{n\to\infty} \sum_{k=1}^{n} f(x_k) \, \Delta x = \int_0^1 f(x) \, dx.$$

We have rewritten (2) precisely in the form of (1) with $\Delta x = \frac{1}{n}$; $x_k = 0 + \frac{k}{n}$

for $k = 1, 2, \ldots, n$; $a = 0$; and $b = 1$.

27. Evaluate

$$\lim_{n\to\infty} \frac{1}{n^4}(1^3 + 2^3 + \ldots + n^3) \tag{3}$$

by identifying it with an appropriate definite integral.

(3) is equivalent to

$$\lim_{n\to\infty} \left[(\tfrac{1}{n})^3 + (\tfrac{2}{n})^3 + \ldots + (\tfrac{n}{n})^3 \right]\frac{1}{n}$$

which equals

$$\lim_{n\to\infty} \sum_{k=1}^{n} (\tfrac{k}{n})^3 \frac{1}{n} = \lim_{n\to\infty} \sum_{k=1}^{n} x_k^3 \, \Delta x = \int_0^1 x^3 \, dx = \frac{1}{4}.$$

Here $\Delta x = \frac{1}{n}$; $x_k = 0 + \frac{k}{n}$ for $k = 1, 2, \ldots, n$; $f(x_k) = x_k$; and $a = 0$, $b = 1$.

28. Evaluate

$$\lim_{n\to\infty} (\tfrac{1}{n} + \frac{1}{n+1} + \ldots + \frac{1}{2n-1}). \tag{4}$$

(4) is equivalent to

$$\lim_{n\to\infty} \left[\frac{1}{1} + \frac{1}{1 + \frac{1}{n}} + \ldots + \frac{1}{2 - \frac{1}{n}} \right] \cdot \frac{1}{n} \tag{5}$$

where we have removed the factor $\frac{1}{n}$ to be identified as Δx. (5), then, equals

$$\lim_{n\to\infty} \sum_{k=0}^{n-1} \frac{1}{1 + \frac{k}{n}} \cdot \frac{1}{n} = \lim_{n\to\infty} \sum_{k=0}^{n-1} \frac{1}{1 + x_k} \, \Delta x$$

$$= \int_0^1 \frac{1}{1+x} \, dx = \ln(1 + x)\Big|_0^1 = \ln 2.$$

Note that $\Delta x = \frac{1}{n}$; $x_k = 0 + \frac{k}{n}$ for $k = 0, 1, 2, \ldots, n-1$; $f(x_k) = \frac{1}{1 + x_k}$;

and $a = 0$, $b = 1$.

We can arrive at the same answer by rewriting

$$\lim_{n \to \infty} \sum_{k=0}^{n-1} \frac{1}{1 + \frac{k}{n}} \cdot \frac{1}{n} \;=\; \lim_{n \to \infty} \sum_{k=0}^{n-1} \frac{1}{x_k} \, \Delta x$$

$$=\; \int_1^2 \frac{1}{x} \, dx \;=\; \ln 2 .$$

Again, $\Delta x = \frac{1}{n}$; **but now** $x_k = 1 + \frac{k}{n}$, $k = 0, 1, \ldots, n-1$; $f(x_k) = \frac{1}{x_k}$; $a = 1$, $b = 2$.

In Figures N8-8a and N8-8b the two equivalent definite integrals are interpreted as areas.

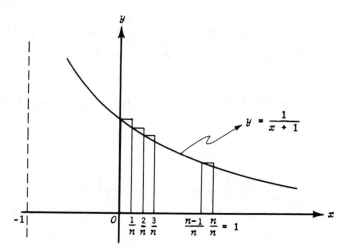

Figure N8-8a

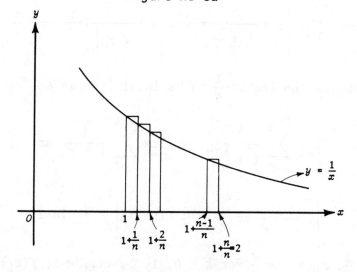

Figure N8-8b

29.

$$\lim_{n\to\infty} \sum_{k=0}^{n-1} \frac{\cos \frac{k\pi}{n}}{n} \;=\; \lim_{n\to\infty} \sum_{k=0}^{n-1} (\cos \pi \frac{k}{n}) \cdot \frac{1}{n}$$

$$=\; \int_0^1 \cos \pi x \; dx \;=\; \frac{1}{\pi} \sin \pi x \Big|_0^1 \;=\; 0,$$

where $\Delta x = \frac{1}{n}$; $x_k = \frac{k}{n}$; $f(x_k) = \cos \pi x_k$; $a = 0$, $b = 1$. **Alternatively**

$$\lim_{n\to\infty} \sum_{k=0}^{n-1} (\cos \frac{k\pi}{n}) \cdot \frac{1}{n} \;=\; \lim_{n\to\infty} \frac{1}{\pi} \sum_{k=0}^{n-1} (\cos k \frac{\pi}{n}) \cdot \frac{\pi}{n}$$

$$=\; \frac{1}{\pi} \int_0^\pi \cos x \; dx \;=\; \frac{1}{\pi} \sin x \Big|_0^\pi \;=\; 0.$$

We see here that we can let $\Delta x = \frac{\pi}{n}$; $x_k = \frac{k\pi}{n}$, $k = 0, 1, \ldots, n-1$; $f(x_k) = \cos x_k$; $a = 0$, $b = \pi$.

30. **Evaluate**

$$\lim_{n\to\infty} \sum_{k=1}^{n} \frac{1}{\sqrt{n^2 + kn}} \;. \tag{6}$$

(6) equals

$$\lim_{n\to\infty} \sum_{k=1}^{n} \frac{1}{\sqrt{1 + \frac{k}{n}}} \cdot \frac{1}{n}$$

$$=\; \int_0^1 \frac{dx}{\sqrt{1 + x}} \quad \text{or} \quad \int_1^2 \frac{dx}{\sqrt{x}}$$

$$=\; 2(\sqrt{2} - 1) \text{ in either case.}$$

Multiple Choice Questions: Further Applications of Integration

*1.   The length of the arc of the curve $y^2 = x^3$ cut off by the line

$x = 4$ is

(A) $\frac{4}{3}(10\sqrt{10} - 1)$ (B) $\frac{8}{27}(10^{3/2} - 1)$ (C) $\frac{16}{27}(10^{3/2} - 1)$

(D) $\frac{16}{27} 10\sqrt{10}$ (E) none of these.

*2.   The length of the arc of $y = \ln \cos x$ from $x = \frac{\pi}{4}$ to $x = \frac{\pi}{3}$ equals

(A) $\ln \frac{\sqrt{3} + 2}{\sqrt{2} + 1}$ (B) 2   (C) $\ln (1 + \sqrt{3} - \sqrt{2})$

(D) $\sqrt{3} - 2$ (E) $\frac{\ln (\sqrt{3} + 2)}{\ln (\sqrt{2} + 1)}$.

*3.   The length of one arch of the cycloid $\begin{array}{l} x = t - \sin t \\ y = 1 - \cos t \end{array}$ equals

(A) 3π (B) 4   (C) 16   (D) 8   (E) 2π.

*4.   The length of the arc of the parabola $4x = y^2$ cut off by the

line $x = 2$ is given by the integral

(A) $\int_{-1}^{1} \sqrt{x^2 + 1} \, dx$ (B) $\frac{1}{2} \int_{0}^{2} \sqrt{4 + y^2} \, dy$ (C) $\int_{-1}^{1} \sqrt{1 + x} \, dx$

(D) $\int_{0}^{2\sqrt{2}} \sqrt{4 + y^2} \, dy$ (E) none of these.

*5.   The length of $x = e^t \cos t$, $y = e^t \sin t$ from $t = 2$ to $t = 3$

is equal to

(A) $\sqrt{2}e^2\sqrt{e^2 - 1}$ (B) $\sqrt{2}(e^3 - e^2)$ (C) $2(e^3 - e^2)$

(D) $e^3(\cos 3 + \sin 3) - e^2(\cos 2 + \sin 2)$ (E) none of these.

*6.   The area of the surface of revolution generated by revolving the arc

of $y = x^3$ from $x = 0$ to $x = 1$ about the x-axis is

(A) $\frac{\pi}{18}(10\sqrt{10} - 1)$ (B) $\frac{\pi}{27}10^{3/2}$ (C) $\frac{4\pi}{3}(10\sqrt{10} - 1)$

(D) $\frac{40\pi}{3}\sqrt{10}$ (E) $\frac{\pi}{27}(10\sqrt{10} - 1)$.

*7.   The area of the surface of revolution obtained by rotating about

the y-axis the hypocycloid $x^{2/3} + y^{2/3} = 1$ equals

(A) $\frac{12\pi}{5}$ (B) 3π (C) 2π (D) $\frac{6\pi}{5}$ (E) none of these.

*8.   The area of the surface generated by revolving about the x-axis the

arc of $4x = y^2$ from $x = 0$ to $x = 3$ equals

(A) $\frac{56\pi}{3}$ (B) 4π (C) $\frac{64\pi}{3}$ (D) $\frac{28\pi}{3}$ (E) none of these.

*9.   The area of the surface generated by rotating the arc of the

curve $x = t^2$, $y = t$ about the x-axis from $t = 0$ to $t = \sqrt{2}$ is

(A) $\frac{13\pi}{2}$ (B) $\frac{104\pi}{3}$ (C) $\frac{\pi}{6}(17^{3/2} - 1)$

(D) $\frac{13\pi}{3}$ (E) none of these.

10.   The average (mean) value of $\cos x$ over the interval $\frac{\pi}{3} \leqq x \leqq \frac{\pi}{2}$

is

(A) $\frac{3}{\pi}$ (B) $\frac{1}{2}$ (C) $\frac{3(2 - \sqrt{3})}{\pi}$ (D) $\frac{3}{2\pi}$ (E) $\frac{2}{3\pi}$.

11.   The average (mean) value of $\csc^2 x$ over the interval from

$x = \frac{\pi}{6}$ to $x = \frac{\pi}{4}$ is

(A) $\frac{3\sqrt{3}}{\pi}$ (B) $\frac{\sqrt{3}}{\pi}$ (C) $\frac{12}{\pi}(\sqrt{3} - 1)$ (D) $3\sqrt{3}$ (E) $3(\sqrt{3} - 1)$.

12. Let the motion of a freely falling body be given by $s(t) = 16t^2$ (where s is the distance in feet that the body has fallen in t seconds). The average velocity with respect to s of the body from $t = 0$ to $t = 1$ is equal (in feet per second) to

(A) $\dfrac{32}{3}$ (B) 16   (C) $\dfrac{64}{3}$ (D) 32   (E) none of these.

*13. If the force F, in pounds, acting on a particle on the x-axis is given by $F = \dfrac{1}{x^2}$, then the work done (in ft-lbs) in moving it from $x = 1$ to $x = 3$ (in feet) is equal to

(A) 2   (B) $\dfrac{2}{3}$ (C) $\dfrac{26}{27}$ (D) 1   (E) $\dfrac{3}{2}$.

*14. A force of 40 lbs is required to stretch a spring from its natural length, 10 ft, to 11 ft. The work done in stretching it from a length of 12 ft to a length of 14 ft is equal (in ft-lbs) to

(A) 360   (B) 80   (C) 320   (D) 160   (E) 240.

*15. A cylindrical reservoir of diameter 4 ft and height 6 ft is half full of water weighing w lb/ft^3. The work done (in ft-lbs) in emptying it over the top is equal to

(A) $216\pi w$ (B) $18\pi w$ (C) $72\pi w$ (D) $54\pi w$ (E) $108\pi w$.

16. A body moves along a straight line so that its velocity v at time t is given by $v = 4t^3 + 3t^2 + 5$. The distance it covers from $t = 0$ to $t = 2$ equals

(A) 34   (B) 55   (C) 24   (D) 44   (E) none of these.

17. A particle moves along a line with velocity $v = 3t^2 - 6t$. The total distance travelled from $t = 0$ to $t = 3$ equals

(A) 9   (B) 4   (C) 2   (D) 16   (E) none of these.

18. The acceleration of a particle moving on a straight line is given by $a = \cos t$ and when $t = 0$ the particle is at rest. The distance it covers from $t = 0$ to $t = 2$ equals

   (A) $\sin 2$ (B) $1 - \cos 2$ (C) $\cos 2$

   (D) $\sin 2 - 1$ (E) $- \cos 2$.

*19. The area enclosed by the four-leaved rose $r = \cos 2\theta$ equals

   (A) $\frac{\pi}{4}$ (B) $\frac{\pi}{2}$ (C) π (D) 2π (E) $\frac{\pi}{2} + \frac{1}{2}$.

*20. The area bounded by the small loop of the limaçon $r = 1 - 2 \sin \theta$ is given by the definite integral

   (A) $\displaystyle\int_{\frac{\pi}{3}}^{\frac{5\pi}{3}} \left[\frac{1}{2}(1 - 2 \sin \theta)\right]^2 d\theta$ (B) $\displaystyle\int_{\frac{7\pi}{6}}^{\frac{3\pi}{2}} (1 - 2 \sin \theta)^2 d\theta$

   (C) $\displaystyle\int_{\frac{\pi}{6}}^{\frac{\pi}{2}} (1 - 2 \sin \theta)^2 d\theta$

   (D) $\displaystyle\int_{0}^{\frac{\pi}{6}} \left[\frac{1}{2}(1 - 2 \sin \theta)\right]^2 d\theta + \int_{\frac{5\pi}{6}}^{\pi} \left[\frac{1}{2}(1 - 2 \sin \theta)\right]^2 d\theta$

   (E) $\displaystyle\int_{0}^{\frac{\pi}{3}} (1 - 2 \sin \theta)^2 d\theta$.

*21. The length of the spiral whose polar equation is $r = e^{\theta/2}$ from $\theta = 0$ to $\theta = \ln 16$ equals

   (A) $\frac{\sqrt{5}}{2}(e^4 - 1)$ (B) 2 (C) $\frac{3}{2}\sqrt{5}$ (D) $\frac{1}{2}(e^4 - 1)$ (E) $3\sqrt{5}$.

*22. The length of the polar graph of $r = 3 \csc \theta$ from $\theta = \frac{\pi}{4}$ to $\theta = \frac{3\pi}{4}$ is

   (A) 6 (B) $6\sqrt{2}$ (C) π (D) $\frac{\pi}{2}$ (E) none of these.

*23. $\lim\limits_{n\to\infty} \left[\dfrac{1}{n} \left[\dfrac{1}{1} + \dfrac{1}{1 + \dfrac{1}{n}} + \dfrac{1}{1 + \dfrac{2}{n}} + \ldots + \dfrac{1}{1 + \dfrac{n-1}{n}} \right] \right]$ is equal to

the definite integral

(A) $\displaystyle\int_1^2 \ln x \; dx$ 　　　　 (B) $\displaystyle\int_1^2 \dfrac{1}{x} \; dx$ 　　　　 (C) $\displaystyle\int_1^2 \dfrac{1}{1+x} \; dx$

(D) $\displaystyle\int_1^2 x \; dx$ 　　　　 (E) none of these.

*24. $\lim\limits_{n\to\infty} \left(\dfrac{1}{n+1} + \dfrac{1}{n+2} + \ldots + \dfrac{1}{n+n} \right)$ is equal to

(A) $\ln 2$ 　　 (B) $\dfrac{3}{8}$ 　　 (C) $\ln \dfrac{3}{2}$ 　　 (D) $\dfrac{3}{2}$ 　　 (E) none of these.

*25. $\lim\limits_{n\to\infty} \displaystyle\sum_{k=0}^{n-1} \dfrac{e^{k/n}}{n}$ is equal to the definite integral

(A) $\displaystyle\int_0^1 \dfrac{e^x}{x} \; dx$ 　　　　 (B) $\displaystyle\int_1^2 e^x \; dx$ 　　　　 (C) $\displaystyle\int_0^1 e^x \; dx$

(D) $\dfrac{1}{x} \displaystyle\int_0^1 e^x \; dx$ 　　　　 (E) none of these.

*26. $\lim\limits_{n\to\infty} \displaystyle\sum_{k=1}^{n} \dfrac{1}{\sqrt{kn}}$ is equal to

(A) 2 　　 (B) $\dfrac{2}{3}$ 　　 (C) $\dfrac{3}{2}$ 　　 (D) 1 　　 (E) none of these.

*27. $\lim\limits_{n\to\infty} \displaystyle\sum_{k=0}^{n-1} \left(\sin \dfrac{\pi k}{n} \right) \dfrac{1}{n}$ is equal to the definite integral

(A) $\dfrac{1}{\pi} \displaystyle\int_0^\pi \sin x \; dx$ 　　 (B) $\displaystyle\int_0^\pi \sin x \; dx$ 　　 (C) $\displaystyle\int_0^\pi \sin \pi x \; dx$

(D) $\displaystyle\int_0^1 \sin \pi x \; dx$ 　　 (E) $\dfrac{1}{\pi} \displaystyle\int_0^1 \sin \pi x \; dx$.

Section 9: Sequences and Series

Review of Principles

   A.   Sequences of Real Numbers.

   A1.   Definitions.   An *infinite sequence* is a function whose domain
is the set of positive integers.   The sequence $\{n, f(n) \mid n = 1, 2, 3, \ldots\}$
is often denoted simply by $\{f(n)\}$.   The sequence defined, for example,

by $f(n) = \frac{1}{n}$ is the set of numbers $1, \frac{1}{2}, \frac{1}{3}, \ldots, \frac{1}{n}, \ldots$.   The elements

in this set are called the *terms* of the sequence, and the *nth* or *general*

term of this sequence is $\frac{1}{n}$. Frequently the sequence is denoted by its

*n*th term: $\{s_n\}$ is the sequence whose *n*th term is s_n.   Thus

$$\{\frac{n}{n^2 + 1}\} \ = \ \frac{1}{2}, \frac{2}{5}, \frac{3}{10}, \ldots;$$

$$\{\frac{2^n}{n!}\} \ = \ \frac{2}{1}, \frac{2^2}{2!}, \frac{2^3}{3!}, \ldots .$$

[Recall that for every nonnegative integer the definition of *n*! (read
"*n* factorial") is given by $0! = 1$, $(n + 1)! = (n + 1)n!$.   So, for
example, $1! = 1$, $2! = 2 \cdot 1$, $7! = 7 \cdot 6 \cdot 5 \cdot 4 \cdot 3 \cdot 2 \cdot 1$.]

$$\{1 + (-1)^n\} \ = \ 0, 2, 0, 2, \ldots;$$

$$\{1 + \frac{(-1)^n}{n}\} \ = \ 0, \frac{3}{2}, \frac{2}{3}, \frac{5}{4}, \frac{4}{5}, \frac{7}{6}, \frac{6}{7}, \ldots .$$

   A sequence $\{s_n\}$ is said to have the *limit L* if, given any positive ϵ,
we can find an integer N such that all terms beyond the Nth in the sequence

171

differ from L by less than ε. If $\{s_n\}$ has the limit L, we say it *converges to* L, and write

$$\lim_{n \to \infty} s_n \;=\; L.$$

If $\lim_{n \to \infty} s_n = L$ then for every $\varepsilon > 0$ there exists an integer N such that $|s_n - L| < \varepsilon$ for all $n > N$. The sequence is said to be *convergent* in this case. If a sequence fails to have a (finite) limit it is said to be *divergent*.

A2. **Theorems.** Several theorems follow from the definition of convergence:

THEOREM 2a. The limit of a convergent sequence is unique.

THEOREM 2b. $\lim_{n \to \infty} (c \cdot s_n) \;=\; c \lim_{n \to \infty} s_n$ (c a number).

THEOREM 2c. If two sequences converge, so do their sum, product, and quotient (with division by zero to be avoided).

EXAMPLES:

1. $\lim_{n \to \infty} \dfrac{1}{n} \;=\; 0.$

2. $\lim_{n \to \infty} 1 + \dfrac{(-1)^n}{n} \;=\; 1.$

3. $\lim_{n \to \infty} \dfrac{2n^2}{3n^3 - 1} \;=\; 0$ (see Section 1 C, p. 5).

4. $\lim_{n \to \infty} \dfrac{3n^4 + 5}{4n^4 - 7n^2 + 9} \;=\; \dfrac{3}{4}.$

5. $\{\dfrac{n^2 - 1}{n}\}$ diverges (to infinity), since $\lim_{n \to \infty} \dfrac{n^2 - 1}{n} \;=\; \infty.$

6. $\{\sin n\}$ diverges since the sequence fails to have a limit, but note that it does not diverge to infinity.

7. $\{(-1)^{n+1}\}$ = 1, -1, 1, -1, ... diverges because it oscillates.

8. $\lim\limits_{n\to\infty} \dfrac{\ln n}{n}$ = $\lim\limits_{n\to\infty} \dfrac{\frac{1}{n}}{1}$ = 0 by L'Hôpital's Rule (see section 1 E).

9. $\lim\limits_{n\to\infty} \dfrac{e^n}{n^2}$ = $\lim\limits_{n\to\infty} \dfrac{e^n}{2n}$ = $\lim\limits_{n\to\infty} \dfrac{e^n}{2}$ = ∞ by repeated application

of L'Hôpital's Rule; the sequence diverges.

DEFINITIONS. The sequence $\{s_n\}$ is said to be *increasing* if, for all n, $s_n \leqq s_{n+1}$, and to be *decreasing* if, for all n, $s_{n+1} \leqq s_n$; a *monotonic* sequence is either increasing or decreasing. If $|s_n| \leqq M$ for all n, then $\{s_n\}$ is said to be *bounded*. The following theorem is the basic one on sequences:

THEOREM 2d. A monotonic sequence converges if and only if it is bounded.

In particular, if $\{s_n\}$ is increasing and $s_n \leqq M$ for all n, then $\{s_n\}$ converges to a limit which is less than or equal to M.

THEOREM 2e. Every unbounded sequence diverges.
(Of course, a bounded sequence may also diverge; for example 1, -1, 1, -1, ... , or $\{\cos n\}$.)

EXAMPLES:

10. Use Theorem 2d to prove that $\{1 - \frac{2}{n}\}$ converges. If $s_n = 1 - \frac{2}{n}$ then $-1 \leqq s_n < 1$ for all n; also $s_{n+1} > s_n$, since

$$s_{n+1} - s_n = (1 - \frac{2}{n+1}) - (1 - \frac{2}{n}) = \frac{2}{n} - \frac{2}{n+1} = \frac{2}{n(n+1)},$$

which is positive for all n. Note that $\{s_n\}$ converges to 1.

11. For what r's does $\{r^n\}$ converge?

If $|r| > 1$, then $\{r^n\}$ is unbounded, so diverges by Theorem 2e.

If $|r| < 1$, then $\lim\limits_{n \to \infty} r^n = 0$.

If $r = 1$, then $\{r^n\}$ converges to 1.

If $r = -1$, then $\{r^n\}$ diverges by oscillation.

Finally, then, $\{r^n\}$ converges if $-1 < r \leq 1$.

B. Series of Constants.

B1. **Definitions.** If $\{u_n\}$ is a sequence of real numbers, then an *infinite series* is an expression of the form

$$\sum_{k=1}^{\infty} u_k = u_1 + u_2 + u_3 + \ldots + u_n + \ldots \qquad (1)$$

The elements in the sum (1) are called *terms*; u_n is the *nth* or *general* term of the series (1). Associated with the series (1) is the sequence $\{s_n\}$ where

$$s_n = u_1 + u_2 + u_3 + \ldots + u_n; \qquad (2)$$

that is,

$$s_n = \sum_{k=1}^{n} u_k.$$

The sequence $\{s_n\}$ is called the *sequence of partial sums* of the series (1). Note that

$$\{s_n\} = s_1, s_2, s_3, \ldots, s_n, \ldots \qquad (3)$$

$$= u_1, u_1 + u_2, u_1 + u_2 + u_3, \ldots,$$

$$u_1 + u_2 + \ldots + u_n, \ldots .$$

If there is a finite number S such that

$$\lim_{n \to \infty} s_n \; = \; S,$$

then we say that the series (1) is *convergent*, or *converges to S*, or *has the sum S*. We write, in this case,

$$\sum_{k=1}^{\infty} u_k \; = \; S, \; \text{where} \; \sum_{k=1}^{\infty} u_k \; = \; \lim_{n \to \infty} \sum_{k=1}^{n} u_k.$$

When there is no source of confusion, the infinite series (1) may be indicated simply by

$$\sum u_k.$$

Note that if the sequence $\{s_n\}$ of partial sums given by (3) converges then so does the series (1); if the sequence $\{s_n\}$ diverges then so does the series.

EXAMPLES:

12. Show that the series

$$\frac{1}{2} + \frac{1}{4} + \ldots + \frac{1}{2^n} + \ldots \tag{4}$$

converges to 1. The series can be rewritten

$$\left(1 - \frac{1}{2}\right) + \left(\frac{1}{2} - \frac{1}{4}\right) + \ldots + \left(\frac{1}{2^{n-1}} - \frac{1}{2^n}\right) + \ldots; \tag{5}$$

hence

$$s_n \; = \; \left(1 - \frac{1}{2}\right) + \left(\frac{1}{2} - \frac{1}{4}\right) + \ldots + \left(\frac{1}{2^{n-1}} - \frac{1}{2^n}\right)$$

$$= \; 1 - \frac{1}{2^n}.$$

$$\lim_{n \to \infty} s_n \; = \; 1; \; \text{therefore} \; \sum_{k=1}^{\infty} \frac{1}{2^k} \; = \; 1.$$

The trick above is equivalent to the following:

$$s_n = \frac{1}{2} + \frac{1}{4} + \frac{1}{8} + \ldots + \frac{1}{2^n} ; \qquad (6)$$

$$\frac{1}{2} s_n = \frac{1}{4} + \frac{1}{8} + \ldots + \frac{1}{2^n} + \frac{1}{2^{n+1}} . \qquad (7)$$

Subtracting (7) from (6) yields

$$\frac{1}{2} s_n = \frac{1}{2} - \frac{1}{2^{n+1}} \quad \text{or} \quad s_n = 1 - \frac{1}{2^n} .$$

So, as before, $\lim\limits_{n \to \infty} s_n = 1$.

13. Show that the *harmonic series*

$$1 + \frac{1}{2} + \frac{1}{3} + \frac{1}{4} + \ldots + \frac{1}{n} + \ldots \qquad (8)$$

diverges.

The terms in (8) can be grouped as follows:

$$1 + \frac{1}{2} + \left(\frac{1}{3} + \frac{1}{4}\right) + \left(\frac{1}{5} + \frac{1}{6} + \frac{1}{7} + \frac{1}{8}\right) + \left(\frac{1}{9} + \frac{1}{10} + \ldots + \frac{1}{16}\right)$$

$$+ \left(\frac{1}{17} + \ldots + \frac{1}{32}\right) + \ldots \qquad (9)$$

The sum in (9) clearly exceeds

$$1 + \frac{1}{2} + 2\left(\frac{1}{4}\right) + 4\left(\frac{1}{8}\right) + 8\left(\frac{1}{16}\right) + 16\left(\frac{1}{32}\right) + \ldots$$

which equals

$$1 + \frac{1}{2} + \frac{1}{2} + \frac{1}{2} + \frac{1}{2} + \frac{1}{2} + \ldots \ldots \qquad (10)$$

Since the sum in (10) can be made arbitrarily large it follows that $\sum \frac{1}{n}$ diverges.

14. Show that the *geometric series*

$$\sum_{k=1}^{\infty} ar^{k-1} = a + ar + ar^2 + \ldots + ar^{n-1} + \ldots \quad (a \neq 0) \qquad (11)$$

converges if $|r| < 1$ but diverges if $|r| \geqq 1$.

The series (4) in Example 12 is a special case of (11); the technique applied there is used here. For (11),

$$s_n = a + ar + ar^2 + \ldots + ar^{n-1};$$

$$rs_n = \qquad ar + ar^2 + \ldots + ar^{n-1} + ar^n;$$

$$s_n(1 - r) = a - ar^n = a(1 - r^n);$$

and

$$s_n = \begin{cases} \dfrac{a(1 - r^n)}{1 - r} & \text{if } r \neq 1 \\ a + a + \ldots + a = na & \text{if } r = 1. \end{cases} \qquad (12)$$

We now investigate $\lim\limits_{n \to \infty} s_n$ to determine the behavior of series (11).

We see from (12) that there are four cases, respectively for $|r| < 1$, $|r| > 1$, $r = 1$, and $r = -1$.

If $|r| < 1$, then since $\lim\limits_{n \to \infty} r^n = 0$, $\lim\limits_{n \to \infty} s_n = \dfrac{a}{1 - r}$; thus

$$\sum ar^{k-1} = \frac{a}{1 - r} . \qquad (13)$$

If $|r| > 1$, then $\lim\limits_{n \to \infty} s_n$ does not exist, because $\lim\limits_{n \to \infty} r^n = \infty$.

If $r = 1$ then the given series diverges.

If $r = -1$, then $\sum ar^{k-1} = a - a + a - a + \ldots$; thus $s_1 = a$, $s_2 = 0$, $s_3 = a$, $s_4 = 0$. $\{s_n\}$ oscillates and thus diverges; and so does the series.

B2. Theorems about Convergence or Divergence of Series of Constants. The following theorems are important.

THEOREM 2a. If $\sum u_k$ converges then $\lim\limits_{n \to \infty} u_n = 0$.

This provides a convenient and useful test for divergence, since it is equivalent to the statement: If u_n does not approach zero, then the series $\sum u_n$ diverges. Note, however, particularly that the converse of Theorem 2a is *not* true. The condition that u_n approach zero is *necessary but not sufficient* for the convergence of the series. The harmonic series $\sum \frac{1}{n}$ is an excellent example of a series whose nth term goes to zero but which diverges (see Example 13 above). The series $\sum \frac{n}{n+1}$ diverges because $\lim\limits_{n \to \infty} u_n = 1$, not zero; the series $\sum \frac{n}{n^2+1}$ does not converge even though $\lim\limits_{n \to \infty} u_n = 0$.

THEOREM 2b. A finite number of terms may be added to or deleted from a series without affecting its convergence or divergence; thus

$$\sum_{k=1}^{\infty} u_k \quad \text{and} \quad \sum_{k=m}^{\infty} u_k$$

(where m is any positive integer) both converge or both diverge. (Of course, the sums may differ.)

THEOREM 2c. The terms of a series may be multiplied by a nonzero constant without affecting the convergence or divergence; thus

$$\sum_{k=1}^{\infty} a_k \quad \text{and} \quad \sum_{k=1}^{\infty} ca_k \qquad (c \neq 0)$$

both converge or both diverge. (Again, the sums may differ.)

THEOREM 2d. If $\sum a_n$ and $\sum b_n$ both converge so does $\sum (a_n + b_n)$.

THEOREM 2e. If the terms of a convergent series are regrouped, the new series converges.

B3. **Tests for Convergence of Positive Series.** The series $\sum u_n$ is called a *positive* series if $u_n > 0$ for all n. Note for such a series that the associated sequence of partial sums $\{s_n\}$ is increasing. It then follows from Theorem 2d (Section A2) that a positive series converges if and only if $\{s_n\}$ has an upper bound.

EXAMPLES:

15. $\sum \frac{1}{k!} = 1 + \frac{1}{2!} + \frac{1}{3!} + \ldots + \frac{1}{n!} + \ldots$ converges, since

$$s_n = 1 + \frac{1}{2!} + \frac{1}{3!} + \frac{1}{4!} + \ldots + \frac{1}{n!}$$

$$< 1 + \frac{1}{2} + \frac{1}{2 \cdot 2} + \frac{1}{2 \cdot 2 \cdot 2} + \ldots + \frac{1}{2^n}$$

$$< 2$$

(see equation (13) in Section B1). Thus $\{s_n\}$ has an upper bound and the given series converges.

16. $\sum \frac{1}{n}$ diverges since the sequence of sums $\{s_n\}$ is unbounded (see Example 13).

TESTS TO APPLY TO $\{u_n\}$ IF $u_n > 0$.

TEST 3a. If $\lim_{n \to \infty} u_n \neq 0$, then $\sum u_n$ diverges. This is Theorem 2a of Section B2 above.

TEST 3b. THE INTEGRAL TEST. If $f(x)$ is a continuous, positive, decreasing function for which $f(n)$ is the nth term u_n of the series, then $\sum u_n$ converges if and only if the improper integral $\int_1^\infty f(x)\, dx$ converges.

EXAMPLES:

17. Does $\sum \dfrac{n}{n^2 + 1}$ converge?

The associated improper integral is

$$\int_1^\infty \frac{x \; dx}{x^2 + 1}$$

which equals

$$\lim_{b \to \infty} \frac{1}{2} \ln (x^2 + 1)\Big|_1^b \; = \; \infty.$$

The improper integral and the infinite series both diverge.

18. Test the series $\sum \dfrac{n}{e^n}$ for convergence.

$$\int_1^\infty \frac{x}{e^x} \; dx \;=\; \lim_{b \to \infty} \int_1^b xe^{-x} \; dx \;=\; \lim_{b \to \infty} -e^{-x}(1 + x)\Big|_1^b$$

$$=\; -\lim_{b \to \infty} \left| \frac{1 + b}{e^b} - \frac{2}{e} \right| \;=\; \frac{2}{e}$$

by an application of L'Hôpital's Rule. Thus $\sum \dfrac{n}{e^n}$ converges.

19. Show that the *p-series* $\sum \dfrac{1}{n^p}$ converges if $p > 1$ but diverges
if $p \leqq 1$.

Let $f(x) \;=\; \dfrac{1}{x^p}$ and investigate $\displaystyle\int_1^\infty \dfrac{dx}{x^p}$.

(a) If $p > 1$, then

$$\int_1^\infty x^{-p} \; dx \;=\; \lim_{b \to \infty} \frac{1}{1 - p} \cdot x^{1-p}\Big|_1^b \;=\; \lim_{b \to \infty} \frac{1}{1 - p}(b^{1-p} - 1)$$

$$=\; \frac{1}{p - 1} \lim_{b \to \infty}(1 - \frac{1}{b^{p-1}}) \;=\; \frac{1}{p - 1} \; .$$

Consequently, $\sum \dfrac{1}{n^p}$ converges if $p > 1$.

(b) If $p = 1$, the improper integral is $\displaystyle\int_1^\infty \dfrac{dx}{x} \;=\; \lim_{b \to \infty} \ln b \;=\; \infty$,

so $\sum \dfrac{1}{n}$ diverges, a result previously well-established.

(c) If $p < 1$, then $\int_1^\infty x^{-p}\,dx = \lim_{b\to\infty} \frac{1}{1-p}(b^{1-p} - 1) = \infty$,

so $\sum \frac{1}{n^p}$ diverges.

TEST 3c. THE COMPARISON TEST. We compare the general term of $\sum u_n$, the positive series we are investigating, with the general term of a series known to converge or diverge.

(1) If $\sum a_n$ converges and $u_n \leqq a_n$, then $\sum u_n$ converges,

(2) If $\sum b_n$ diverges and $u_n \geqq b_n$, then $\sum u_n$ diverges.

Any known series can be used for comparison; particularly useful are the p-series, which converges if $p > 1$ but diverges if $p \leqq 1$ (see Example 19), and the geometric series, which converges if $|r| < 1$ but diverges if $|r| \geqq 1$ (see Example 14).

EXAMPLES:

20. $1 + \frac{1}{2!} + \frac{1}{3!} + \ldots + \frac{1}{n!} + \ldots$ converges, since $\frac{1}{n!} < \frac{1}{2^{n-1}}$,

and the latter is the general term of the geometric series $\sum_1^\infty r^{n-1}$ with $r = \frac{1}{2}$.

21. $\frac{1}{\sqrt{2}} + \frac{1}{\sqrt{5}} + \frac{1}{\sqrt{8}} + \ldots + \frac{1}{\sqrt{3n-1}} + \ldots$ diverges, since

$\frac{1}{\sqrt{3n-1}} > \frac{1}{\sqrt{3n}} = \frac{1}{\sqrt{3}\cdot n^{1/2}}$; the latter is the general term of the

divergent p-series $\sum \frac{c}{n^p}$ where $c = \frac{1}{\sqrt{3}}$ and $p = \frac{1}{2}$.

Remember in using this test that we may discard a finite number of terms of the series we are testing without affecting its convergence.

22. $\sum \dfrac{1}{n^n} = 1 + \dfrac{1}{2^2} + \dfrac{1}{3^3} + \ldots + \dfrac{1}{n^n} + \ldots$ converges, since

$\dfrac{1}{n^n} < \dfrac{1}{2^{n-1}}$ and $\sum \dfrac{1}{2^{n-1}}$ converges.

TEST 3d. THE RATIO TEST. Let $\displaystyle\lim_{n\to\infty} \dfrac{u_{n+1}}{u_n} = L$, if it exists. Then

$\sum u_n$ converges if $L < 1$ and diverges if $L > 1$. If $L = 1$, this test

fails and we must apply one of the other tests.

EXAMPLES:

23. For $\sum \dfrac{1}{n!}$, $\displaystyle\lim_{n\to\infty} \dfrac{u_{n+1}}{u_n} = \lim_{n\to\infty} \dfrac{\dfrac{1}{(n+1)!}}{\dfrac{1}{n!}} = \lim_{n\to\infty} \dfrac{n!}{(n+1)!}$

$= \displaystyle\lim_{n\to\infty} \dfrac{1}{n+1} = 0$. Therefore this series converges. (Compare Examples

15, 20.)

24. For $\sum \dfrac{n^n}{n!}$, $\dfrac{u_{n+1}}{u_n} = \dfrac{(n+1)^{n+1}}{(n+1)!} \cdot \dfrac{n!}{n^n} = \dfrac{(n+1)^n}{n^n}$, and

$\displaystyle\lim_{n\to\infty} \left(\dfrac{n+1}{n}\right)^n = \lim_{n\to\infty} \left(1 + \dfrac{1}{n}\right)^n = e$. (See Section 1, Example 22, p. 8.)

25. If the Ratio Test is applied to the p-series, $\sum \dfrac{1}{n^p}$, then

$\dfrac{u_{n+1}}{u_n} = \dfrac{\dfrac{1}{(n+1)^p}}{\dfrac{1}{n^p}} = \left(\dfrac{n}{n+1}\right)^p$; and $\displaystyle\lim_{n\to\infty} \left(\dfrac{n}{n+1}\right)^p = 1$ for all p.

But if $p > 1$ then $\sum \dfrac{1}{n^p}$ converges, while if $p \leq 1$ then $\sum \dfrac{1}{n^p}$ diverges.

This illustrates the failure of the ratio test to resolve the question of

convergence when the limit of the ratio is 1.

B4. Alternating Series and Absolute Convergence. Any test that

can be applied to a positive series can be used for a series all of

whose terms are negative. We consider here only one type of series
with mixed signs, the so-called *alternating series*. This has the
form:

$$\sum_{k=1}^{\infty} (-1)^{k+1} u_k = u_1 - u_2 + u_3 - u_4 + \ldots + (-1)^{k+1} u_k + \ldots, \qquad (1)$$

where each $u_k > 0$. The series

$$1 - \frac{1}{2} + \frac{1}{3} - \frac{1}{4} + \ldots + (-1)^{n+1} \cdot \frac{1}{n} + \ldots \qquad (2)$$

is the *alternating harmonic* series.

THEOREM 4a. The alternating series (1) converges if $u_{n+1} < u_n$ for
all n and if $\lim\limits_{n \to \infty} u_n = 0$.

EXAMPLES:

26. The alternating harmonic series (2) converges, since $\frac{1}{n+1} < \frac{1}{n}$
for all n and since $\lim\limits_{n \to \infty} \frac{1}{n} = 0$.

27. The series $\frac{1}{2} - \frac{2}{3} + \frac{3}{4} - \ldots$ diverges since $\lim\limits_{n \to \infty} u_n = \lim\limits_{n \to \infty} \frac{n}{n+1}$
is 1, not zero.

THEOREM 4b. If $u_{n+1} < u_n$ and $\lim\limits_{n \to \infty} u_n = 0$ for the alternating series,
then the numerical difference between the sum of the first n terms and the
sum of the series is less than u_{n+1}; that is,

$$\left| \sum_{k=1}^{\infty} u_k - \sum_{k=1}^{n} u_k \right| < u_{n+1}.$$

Theorem 4b is exceedingly useful in computing the maximum possible
error if a finite number of terms of a convergent series is used to

approximate the sum of the series. If we stop with the nth term, the error is less than u_{n+1}, the first term omitted.

EXAMPLE:

28. The sum $\displaystyle\sum_{k=1}^{\infty} \frac{(-1)^{k+1}}{k}$ differs from the sum

$(1 - \frac{1}{2} + \frac{1}{3} - \frac{1}{4} + \frac{1}{5} - \frac{1}{6})$ by less than $\frac{1}{7}$.

A series with mixed signs is said to *converge absolutely* (or to be *absolutely convergent*) if the series obtained by taking the absolute values of its terms converges; that is, $\sum u_n$ converges absolutely if $\sum |u_n| = |u_1| + |u_2| + \ldots + |u_n| + \ldots$ converges. A series which converges but not absolutely is said to converge *conditionally* (or to be *conditionally convergent*). The alternating harmonic series (2) converges conditionally since it converges, but does not converge absolutely. (The harmonic series diverges.)

THEOREM 4c. If a series converges absolutely, then it converges.

EXAMPLES:

29. Determine whether $\displaystyle\sum \frac{\sin \frac{n\pi}{3}}{n^2}$ converges absolutely, conditionally, or diverges. Note that, since $\left| \sin n\frac{\pi}{3} \right| \leqq 1$,

$$\left| \frac{\sin n \frac{\pi}{3}}{n^2} \right| \leqq \frac{1}{n^2} \text{ for all } n.$$

But $\frac{1}{n^2}$ is the general term of a convergent p-series, so by the Comparison Test the given series converges absolutely (therefore, by Theorem 4c, it converges).

30. The series $1 + \frac{1}{2} - \frac{1}{4} - \frac{1}{8} + \frac{1}{16} + \frac{1}{32} - \ldots (\pm)\frac{1}{2^n} \pm \ldots$,   (3)

whose signs are + + - - + + - - . . . ., converges absolutely, since $\sum \frac{1}{2^n}$

is a convergent geometric series. Consequently, (3) converges.

C. Power Series.

C1. Definitions; Convergence. An expression of the form

$$\sum_{k=0}^{\infty} a_k x^k = a_0 + a_1 x + a_2 x^2 + \ldots + a_n x^n + \ldots,$$ (1)

where the a's are constants, is called a *power series in* x; and

$$\sum_{k=0}^{\infty} a_k (x - a)^k = a_0 + a_1 (x - a) + a_2 (x - a)^2$$ (2)

$$+ \ldots + a_n (x - a)^n + \ldots$$

is called a *power series in* $(x - a)$.

If in (1) or (2) x is replaced by a specific real number then the power series becomes a series of constants that either converges or diverges. Note that series (1) converges if $x = 0$ and series (2) converges if $x = a$.

The set of values of x for which a power series converges is called its *interval of convergence*. If the interval of convergence of the power series (1) contains values of x other than 0, then 0 will be the midpoint of this interval; similarly, a is the midpoint of the interval of convergence of series (2).

The interval of convergence of a power series may be found by applying the Ratio Test to the series of absolute values.

EXAMPLES:

31. Find the interval of convergence of

$$1 + x + x^2 + \ldots + x^n + \ldots \ldots \qquad (3)$$

We find

$$\lim_{n \to \infty} \left| \frac{u_{n+1}}{u_n} \right| = \lim_{n \to \infty} \left| \frac{x^{n+1}}{x^n} \right| = \lim_{n \to \infty} |x| = |x|.$$

The series clearly converges absolutely (and therefore converges) if $|x| < 1$; it diverges if $|x| > 1$. The endpoints must be tested separately since the Ratio Test fails when the limit equals 1. When $x = 1$, (3) becomes $1 + 1 + 1 + \ldots$ and diverges; when $x = -1$, (3) becomes $1 - 1 + 1 - 1 + \ldots$ and diverges. So the interval of convergence of (3) is $-1 < x < 1$.

32. For what x's does $\displaystyle\sum_{n=1}^{\infty} \frac{(-1)^{n-1} x^{n-1}}{n+1}$ converge?

$$\lim_{n \to \infty} \left| \frac{u_{n+1}}{u_n} \right| = \lim_{n \to \infty} \left| \frac{x^n}{n+2} \cdot \frac{n+1}{x^{n-1}} \right| = \lim_{n \to \infty} |x| = |x|.$$

The series converges if $|x| < 1$ and diverges if $|x| > 1$. When $x = 1$ we have $\frac{1}{2} - \frac{1}{3} + \frac{1}{4} - \frac{1}{5} + \ldots$, an alternating convergent series; when $x = -1$ the series is $\frac{1}{2} + \frac{1}{3} + \frac{1}{4} + \ldots$, which diverges. So the series converges if $-1 < x \leqq 1$.

33. $\displaystyle\sum_{n=1}^{\infty} \frac{x^n}{n!}$ converges for all x, since

$$\lim_{n\to\infty} \left| \frac{u_{n+1}}{u_n} \right| \; = \; \lim_{n\to\infty} \left| \frac{x^{n+1}}{(n+1)!} \cdot \frac{n!}{x^n} \right| \; = \; \lim_{n\to\infty} \frac{|x|}{n+1} \; = \; 0,$$

if $x \neq 0$. Thus the interval of convergence is $-\infty < x < \infty$.

34. Find the interval of convergence of

$$1 + \frac{x-2}{2^1} + \frac{(x-2)^2}{2^2} + \ldots + \frac{(x-2)^{n-1}}{2^{n-1}} + \ldots \qquad (4)$$

$$\lim_{n\to\infty} \left| \frac{u_{n+1}}{u_n} \right| \; = \; \lim_{n\to\infty} \left| \frac{(x-2)^n}{2^n} \cdot \frac{2^{n-1}}{(x-2)^{n-1}} \right| \; = \; \lim_{n\to\infty} \frac{|x-2|}{2} \; = \; \frac{|x-2|}{2},$$

which is less than 1 if $|x-2| < 2$, i.e., if $0 < x < 4$. Series (4) converges on this interval and diverges if $|x-2| > 2$, i.e., if $x < 0$ or $x > 4$.

When $x = 0$, (4) is $1 - 1 + 1 - 1 + \ldots$ and diverges. When $x = 4$, (4) is $1 + 1 + 1 + \ldots$ and diverges. So (4) converges if $0 < x < 4$.

35. $\displaystyle\sum_{n=1}^{\infty} n!x^n$ converges only at $x = 0$, since

$$\lim_{n\to\infty} \frac{u_{n+1}}{u_n} \; = \; \lim_{n\to\infty} (n+1)x \; = \; \infty$$

unless $x = 0$.

RADIUS OF CONVERGENCE. If the power series (1) converges when $|x| < r$ and diverges when $|x| > r$, then r is called the *radius of convergence*. Similarly, r is the radius of convergence of series (2) when (2) converges if $|x-a| < r$ but diverges if $|x-a| > r$. Note the radii of convergence for the series investigated in Examples 31-35:

EXAMPLE	INTERVAL OF CONVERGENCE	RADIUS OF CONVERGENCE
31	$-1 < x < 1$	1
32	$-1 < x \leqq 1$	1
33	$-\infty < x < \infty$	∞
34	$0 < x < 4$	2
35	$x = 0$ only	0.

THEOREMS ABOUT CONVERGENCE. The following theorems about convergence of power series are useful:

THEOREM 1a. If $\sum a_n x^n$ converges for a nonzero number c then it converges absolutely for all x such that $|x| < |c|$.

THEOREM 1b. If $\sum a_n x^n$ diverges for $x = d$ then it diverges for all x such that $|x| > |d|$.

C2. Functions Defined by Power Series. If $x = x_0$ is a number within the interval of convergence of the power series $\sum_{k=0}^{\infty} a_k (x - a)^k$, then the sum at $x = x_0$ is unique. We let the function f be defined by

$$f(x) = \sum_{k=0}^{\infty} a_k (x - a)^k = a_0 + a_1 (x - a) + \ldots \qquad (1)$$

$$+ a_n (x - a)^n + \ldots;$$

its domain is the interval of convergence of the series; and it follows that

$$f(x_0) = \sum_{k=0}^{\infty} a_k (x_0 - a)^k.$$

Functions defined by power series behave very much like polynomials, as indicated by the following *properties*:

PROPERTY 2a.   The function defined by (1) is continuous for each x in the interval of convergence of the series.

PROPERTY 2b.   The series formed by differentiating the terms of series (1) converges to $f'(x)$ for each x within the interval of convergence of (1); i.e.,

$$f'(x) \; = \; \sum_{1}^{\infty} k a_k (x - a)^{k-1} \; = \; a_1 + 2a_2 (x - a) + \ldots \qquad (2)$$
$$+ \, n a_n (x - a)^{n-1} + \ldots .$$

Note that we can conclude from 2b that the power series (1) and its derived series (2) have the same radius of convergence but not necessarily the same interval of convergence.

EXAMPLE:

36.   Let

$$f(x) \; = \; \sum_{k=1}^{\infty} \frac{x^k}{k(k + 1)} \; = \; \frac{x}{1 \cdot 2} + \frac{x^2}{2 \cdot 3} + \ldots + \frac{x^n}{n(n + 1)} + \ldots; \qquad (3)$$

then

$$f'(x) \; = \; \sum_{k=1}^{\infty} \frac{x^{k-1}}{k + 1} \; = \; \frac{1}{2} + \frac{x}{3} + \frac{x^2}{4} + \ldots + \frac{x^{n-1}}{n + 1} + \ldots . \qquad (4)$$

From (3) we see that

$$\lim_{n \to \infty} \left| \frac{x^{n+1}}{(n + 1)(n + 2)} \cdot \frac{n(n + 1)}{x^n} \right| \; = \; |x|;$$

that

$$f(1) \; = \; \frac{1}{1 \cdot 2} + \frac{1}{2 \cdot 3} + \ldots + \frac{1}{n(n + 1)} + \ldots;$$

and that

$$f(-1) = -\frac{1}{1\cdot2} + \frac{1}{2\cdot3} - \cdots + \frac{(-1)^n}{n(n+1)} + \cdots;$$

and conclude that (3) converges if $-1 \leqq x \leqq 1$.

From (4) we see that

$$\lim_{n\to\infty} \left| \frac{x^n}{n+2} \cdot \frac{n+1}{x^{n-1}} \right| = |x|;$$

that

$$f'(1) = \frac{1}{2} + \frac{1}{3} + \frac{1}{4} + \cdots;$$

and that

$$f'(-1) = \frac{1}{2} - \frac{1}{3} + \frac{1}{4} - \cdots;$$

and conclude that series (4) converges if $-1 \leqq x < 1$.

So the series given for $f(x)$ and $f'(x)$ do have the same radius of convergence but not the same interval.

PROPERTY 2c. The series obtained by integrating the terms of the given series (1) converges to $\int_a^x f(t)\ dt$ for each x within the interval of convergence of (1); i.e.,

$$\int_a^x f(t)\ dt = a_0(x-a) + \frac{a_1(x-a)^2}{2} + \frac{a_2(x-a)^3}{3}$$

$$+ \cdots + \frac{a_n(x-a)^{n+1}}{n+1} + \cdots \tag{5}$$

$$= \sum_{k=0}^{\infty} \frac{a_k(x-a)^{k+1}}{k+1}.$$

EXAMPLE:

37.   Obtain a series for $\dfrac{1}{(1 - x)^2}$ by long division.

$$
\begin{array}{r}
1 + 2x + 3x^2 + 4x^3 + \ldots \\
1 - 2x + x^2 \overline{\big)\; 1 } \\
1 - 2x + x^2 \\
\hline
2x - x^2 \\
2x - 4x^2 + 2x^3 \\
\hline
+\, 3x^2 - 2x^3 \\
3x^2 - 6x^3 + 3x^4 \\
\hline
4x^3 - 3x^4
\end{array}
$$

So

$$
\frac{1}{(1 - x)^2} \;=\; 1 + 2x + 3x^2 + \ldots + (n + 1)x^n + \ldots \qquad (6)
$$

Let us assume that the power series on the right in (6) converges to

$$
f(x) = \frac{1}{(1 - x)^2} \quad \text{if } -1 < x < 1. \quad \text{Then by property 2c}
$$

$$
\int_0^x \frac{1}{(1 - t)^2}\, dt \;=\; \int_0^x \left[1 + 2t + 3t^2 + \ldots + (n + 1)t^n + \ldots \right] dt
$$

$$
=\; \left. \frac{1}{1 - t} \right|_0^x \;=\; \frac{1}{1 - x} - 1
$$

$$
=\; x + x^2 + x^3 + \ldots + x^{n+1} + \ldots
$$

So

$$
\frac{1}{1 - x} \;=\; 1 + x + x^2 + x^3 + \ldots + x^n + \ldots \qquad (7)
$$

Note that the series on the right in (7) is exactly the one obtained for

the function $\dfrac{1}{1 - x}$ by long division:

$$
\begin{array}{r}
1 + x + x^2 + x^3 + \ldots \\
1 - x \overline{\big)\; 1 } \\
1 - x \\
\hline
+\, x \\
x - x^2 \\
\hline
x^2 \\
x^2 - x^3 \\
\hline
+\, x^3
\end{array}
$$

Furthermore, the right-hand member of (7) is a geometric series with ratio $r = x$ and with $a = 1$; if $|x| < 1$, its sum is $\frac{a}{1 - r} = \frac{1}{1 - x}$.

PROPERTY 2d.   Two series may be added, subtracted, multiplied, or divided (with division by zero to be avoided) for x's which lie within the intervals of convergence of both.

EXAMPLE:

38.   If

$$\frac{1}{1 - x} = 1 + x + x^2 + \ldots + x^n + \ldots$$

$$(|x| < 1)$$

(8)

then $\frac{1}{(1 - x)^2}$ can be obtained by multiplying (8) by itself.

$$
\begin{array}{l}
1 + x + x^2 + x^3 + \ldots \\
1 + x + x^2 + x^3 + \ldots \\
\hline
1 + x + x^2 + x^3 + \ldots \\
 + x + x^2 + x^3 + \ldots \\
 + x^2 + x^3 + \ldots \\
 + x^3 + \ldots \\
\hline
\end{array}
$$

$$\frac{1}{(1 - x)^2} = 1 + 2x + 3x^2 + 4x^3 + \ldots \quad (|x| < 1)$$

(9)

The series on the right in (9) is precisely the one obtained for

$\frac{1}{(1 - x)^2}$ by long division in Example 37.

C3.   Finding a Power Series for a Function; Taylor Series.   If a function $f(x)$ is representable by a power series of the form

$$a_0 + a_1(x - a) + a_2(x - a)^2 + \ldots + a_n(x - a)^n + \ldots$$

on an interval $|x - a| < r$, then

$$a_0 = f(a), \; a_1 = f'(a), \; a_2 = \frac{f''(a)}{2!}, \; \ldots, \; a_n = \frac{f^{(n)}(a)}{n!}, \; \ldots, \tag{1}$$

so that

$$f(x) \;=\; f(a) + f'(a)(x - a) + \frac{f''(a)}{2!}(x - a)^2 + \frac{f^{(n)}(a)}{n!}(x - a)^n + \ldots \tag{2}$$

(2) is called the *Taylor series* of the function f about the number a.   There
is never more than one power series in $(x - a)$ for $f(x)$.   Implicit in (2)
is the requirement that the function and all its derivatives exist at $x = a$
if the function $f(x)$ is to generate a Taylor series expansion.

When $a = 0$ we have a special case of (2) given by

$$f(x) \;=\; f(0) + f'(0)x + \frac{f''(0)}{2!}x^2 + \ldots + \frac{f^{(n)}(0)}{n!}x^n + \ldots \tag{3}$$

(3) is called the *Maclaurin series* of the function f; this is the expansion
of f about $x = 0$.

EXAMPLES:

39.   If $f(x)$ and all its derivatives exist at $x = 0$ and if $f(x)$
is representable by a power series in x, show that it will have precisely
the form given by (3).

Let $f(x) \;=\; a_0 + a_1 x + a_2 x^2 + a_3 x^3 + \ldots + a_n x^n + \ldots$ for all
x in the interval of convergence.   Then

$f'(x) = a_1 + 2a_2 x + 3a_3 x^2 + \ldots \qquad\qquad + na_n x^{n-1} + \ldots$

$f''(x) = \qquad\quad 2a_2 + 3\cdot 2a_3 x + \ldots \qquad\qquad + n(n - 1)a_n x^{n-2} + \ldots$

$f'''(x) = \qquad\qquad\qquad 3\cdot 2a_3 + 4\cdot 3\cdot 2a_4 x + \ldots + n(n - 1)(n - 2)a_n x^{n-3} + \ldots$

$f^{iv}(x) = \qquad\qquad\qquad\qquad 4\cdot 3\cdot 2a_4 + \ldots + n(n - 1)(n - 2)(n - 3)a_n x^{n-4} + \ldots$

$$\vdots$$

$f^{(n)}(x) = \qquad\qquad\qquad\qquad\qquad\qquad\qquad n!a_n + \ldots$

If we let $x = 0$ in each of the above equations, we get

$$f(0) = a_0 \qquad \text{so that} \qquad a_0 = f(0)$$

$$f'(0) = a_1 \qquad\qquad\qquad a_1 = f'(0)$$

$$f''(0) = 2a_2 \qquad\qquad\qquad a_2 = \frac{f''(0)}{2}$$

$$f'''(0) = 3!a_3 \qquad\qquad\qquad a_3 = \frac{f'''(0)}{3!}$$

$$f^{iv}(0) = 4!a_4 \qquad\qquad\qquad a_4 = \frac{f^{iv}(0)}{4!}$$

$$\vdots \qquad\qquad\qquad\qquad \vdots$$

$$f^{(n)}(0) = n!a_n \qquad\qquad\qquad a_n = \frac{f^{(n)}(0)}{n!} \, .$$

40. Find the Maclaurin series for $f(x) = e^x$.

Here $f'(x) = e^x, \ldots, f^{(n)}(x) = e^x, \ldots,$ for all n. So $f'(0) = 1, \ldots, f^{(n)}(0) = 1, \ldots,$ for all n. By (3), then,

$$e^x = 1 + x + \frac{x^2}{2!} + \frac{x^3}{3!} + \ldots + \frac{x^n}{n!} + \ldots$$

41. Find the Maclaurin expansion for $f(x) = \sin x$.

$$f(x) = \sin x \qquad\qquad f(0) = 0$$

$$f'(x) = \cos x \qquad\qquad f'(0) = 1$$

$$f''(x) = -\sin x \qquad\qquad f''(0) = 0$$

$$f'''(x) = -\cos x \qquad\qquad f'''(0) = -1$$

$$f^{iv}(x) = \sin x \qquad\qquad f^{iv}(0) = 0.$$

Thus

$$\sin x = x - \frac{x^3}{3!} + \frac{x^5}{5!} - \ldots + (-1)^{n-1} \frac{x^{2n-1}}{(2n-1)!} + \ldots$$

42. Find the Maclaurin series for $f(x) = \dfrac{1}{1-x}$.

$$f(x) = (1-x)^{-1} \qquad f(0) = 1$$

$$f'(x) = (1-x)^{-2} \qquad f'(0) = 1$$

$$f''(x) = 2(1-x)^{-3} \qquad f''(0) = 2$$

$$f'''(x) = 3!(1-x)^{-4} \qquad f'''(0) = 3!$$

$$\vdots \qquad\qquad \vdots$$

$$f^{(n)}(x) = n!(1-x)^{-(n+1)} \qquad f^{(n)}(0) = n!.$$

So

$$\frac{1}{1-x} = 1 + x + x^2 + x^3 + \ldots + x^n + \ldots.$$

Note that this agrees exactly with the power series in x obtained previously by two different methods in Example 37.

43. Find the Taylor series for the function $f(x) = \ln x$ about $x = 1$.

$$f(x) = \ln x \qquad\qquad f(1) = \ln 1 = 0$$

$$f'(x) = \frac{1}{x} \qquad\qquad f'(1) = 1$$

$$f''(x) = -\frac{1}{x^2} \qquad\qquad f''(1) = -1$$

$$f'''(x) = \frac{2}{x^3} \qquad\qquad f'''(1) = 2$$

$$f^{iv}(x) = \frac{-3!}{x^4} \qquad\qquad f^{iv}(1) = -3!$$

$$\vdots \qquad\qquad\qquad \vdots$$

$$f^{(n)}(x) = \frac{(-1)^{n-1}(n-1)!}{x^n} \qquad f^{(n)}(1) = (-1)^{n-1}(n-1)!.$$

So

$$\ln x = (x-1) - \frac{(x-1)^2}{2} + \frac{(x-1)^3}{3} - \frac{(x-1)^4}{4}$$

$$+ \ldots + \frac{(-1)^{n-1}(x-1)^n}{n} + \ldots.$$

FUNCTIONS THAT GENERATE NO SERIES. Note that the following functions are among those that fail to generate a specific series in $(x - a)$ because the function and/or one or more derivatives do not exist at $x = a$:

FUNCTION	SERIES IT FAILS TO GENERATE
$\ln x$	about 0
$\ln (x - 1)$	about 1
$\sqrt{x - 2}$	about 2
$\sqrt{x - 2}$	about 0
$\tan x$	about $\frac{\pi}{2}$
$\sqrt{1 + x}$	about -1.

C4. **Taylor's Formula with Remainder.** The following theorems resolve the problem of determining *when* a function is representable by a power series.

THEOREM 4a (TAYLOR'S THEOREM). If a function f and its first $(n + 1)$ derivatives are continuous on the interval $|x - a| < r$ then for each x in this interval

$$f(x) = f(a) + f'(a)(x - a) + \frac{f''(a)}{2!}(x - a)^2 + \ldots \qquad (1)$$

$$+ \frac{f^{(n)}(a)}{n!}(x - a)^n + R_n(x),$$

where

$$R_n(x) = \frac{1}{n!} \int_a^x (x - t)^n f^{(n+1)}(t) \, dt.$$

Note that $R_n(x)$ is the remainder after $(n + 1)$ terms of the Taylor series for $f(x)$.

Two forms of the remainder other than the integral form (1) are given here because they are usually easier to use:

LAGRANGE'S FORM OF THE REMAINDER is

$$R_n(x) \ = \ \frac{f^{(n+1)}(\xi)(x - a)^{n+1}}{(n + 1)!} \ , \tag{2}$$

where ξ is some number between a and x.

CAUCHY'S FORM OF THE REMAINDER is

$$R_n(x) \ = \ \frac{f^{(n+1)}(\xi^*)(x - \xi^*) \ (x - a)}{n!} \tag{3}$$

where ξ^* is some number between a and x.

When we truncate a series after the $(n + 1)$st term we can compute R_n, according to Lagrange, for example, if we know what to substitute for ξ. In practice we do not find R_n exactly but only an upper bound for it by assigning to ξ the value between a and x which makes R_n as large as possible.

THEOREM 4b. If the function f has derivatives of all orders in some interval about $x = a$ then the power series

$$f(a) \ + \ f'(a)(x - a) \ + \ \frac{f''(a)}{2!}(x - a)^2 \ + \ . \ . \ . \ + \ \frac{f^{(n)}(a)(x - a)^n}{n!} \ + \ . \ . \ .$$

represents the function f for those x's, and only those, for which $\lim_{n \to \infty} R_n(x) = 0$; here $R_n(x)$ is the remainder given above by (1), (2), or (3).

EXAMPLES:

44. Prove that the Maclaurin Series generated by e^x represents the function e^x for all real numbers.

From Example 40 we know that $f(x) = e^x$ generates the Maclaurin Series

$$e^x = 1 + x + \frac{x^2}{2!} + \ldots + \frac{x^n}{n!} + \ldots . \qquad (4)$$

The Lagrange remainder, by (2), is

$$R_n(x) = \frac{e^{\xi}(x)^{n+1}}{(n+1)!} \qquad (0 < \xi < x).$$

If x is a positive fixed number, then $0 < e^{\xi} < e^x = C$, where C is a constant, and

$$\left| R_n(x) \right| < \frac{Cx^{n+1}}{(n+1)!} .$$

We showed in Example 33 that $\sum_1^\infty \frac{x^k}{k!}$ converges for all x; consequently, by Theorem 2a of B2 it follows that the general term must approach zero. So, if $x > 0$ then $R_n(x) \to 0$. By Theorem 4b, then, (4) represents e^x if $x > 0$.

If $x = 0$, then (4) reduces to 1.

If $x < 0$, then $x < \xi < 0$ and $e^{\xi} < 1$. So

$$\left| R_n(x) \right| < \frac{|x|^{n+1}}{(n+1)!} ,$$

which approaches 0.

Consequently, (4) represents e^x for all real x.

45. Find the Maclaurin expansion for $\ln(1 + x)$ with the integral form of the remainder.

$$f(x) = \ln (1 + x) \qquad\qquad f(0) = 0$$

$$f'(x) = \frac{1}{1 + x} \qquad\qquad f'(0) = 1$$

$$f''(x) = - \frac{1}{(1 + x)^2} \qquad\qquad f''(0) = -1$$

$$f'''(x) = \frac{2}{(1 + x)^3} \qquad\qquad f'''(0) = 2!$$

$$\vdots \qquad\qquad\qquad\qquad \vdots$$

$$f^{(n)}(x) = \frac{(-1)^{n-1}(n - 1)!}{(1 + x)^n} \qquad\qquad f^{(n)}(0) = (-1)^{n-1}(n - 1)!$$

$$f^{(n+1)}(x) = \frac{(-1)^n \cdot n!}{(1 + x)^{n+1}} \; .$$

So

$$\ln (1 + x) = x - \frac{x^2}{2} + \frac{x^3}{3} - \frac{x^4}{4} + \ldots + (-1)^{n-1} \cdot \frac{x^n}{n} + R_n(x),$$

where

$$R_n(x) = \int_0^x \frac{(-1)^n (x - t)^n}{(1 + t)^{n+1}} \, dt \; .$$

46. For what x may $\cos x$ be represented by its power series in $(x - \frac{\pi}{3})$?

$$f(x) = \cos x \qquad\qquad f(\tfrac{\pi}{3}) = \frac{1}{2}$$

$$f'(x) = - \sin x \qquad\qquad f'(\tfrac{\pi}{3}) = - \frac{\sqrt{3}}{2}$$

$$f''(x) = - \cos x \qquad\qquad f''(\tfrac{\pi}{3}) = - \frac{1}{2}$$

$$f'''(x) = \sin x \qquad\qquad f'''(\tfrac{\pi}{3}) = \frac{\sqrt{3}}{2}$$

$$f^{iv}(x) = \cos x \qquad\qquad f^{iv}(\tfrac{\pi}{3}) = \frac{1}{2} \; .$$

Note that $f^{(n)}(x) = \pm \sin x$ or $\pm \cos x$.

$$\cos x = \frac{1}{2} - \frac{\sqrt{3}}{2}(x - \frac{\pi}{3}) - \frac{1}{2} \cdot \frac{(x - \frac{\pi}{3})^2}{2} + \frac{\sqrt{3}}{2} \cdot \frac{(x - \frac{\pi}{3})^3}{3!} + \ldots .$$

The Lagrange remainder (2) is

$$R_n(x) = \frac{f^{(n+1)}(\xi)\left(x - \frac{\pi}{3}\right)^{n+1}}{(n+1)!} \qquad \left(x < \xi < \frac{\pi}{3}\right).$$

Although we do not know exactly what ξ equals, we do know that

$$\left| f^{(n+1)}(\xi) \right| \leqq 1,$$

so that

$$\left| R_n(x) \right| \leq \frac{\left| x - \frac{\pi}{3} \right|^{n+1}}{(n+1)!} \quad \text{and} \quad \lim_{n \to \infty} R_n(x) = 0$$

for all x.

C5. **Computations with Power Series.** We list here for reference some frequently used series expansions together with their intervals of convergence:

FUNCTION	SERIES EXPANSION	INTERVAL OF CONVERGENCE	
$\sin x$	$x - \dfrac{x^3}{3!} + \dfrac{x^5}{5!} - \ldots + \dfrac{(-1)^{n-1} x^{2n-1}}{(2n-1)!} + \ldots$	$-\infty < x < \infty$	(1)
$\sin x$	$\sin a + (x - a)\cos a - \dfrac{(x-a)^2}{2!}\sin a$ $-\dfrac{(x-a)^3}{3!}\cos a + \ldots$	$-\infty < x < \infty$	(2)
$\cos x$	$1 - \dfrac{x^2}{2!} + \dfrac{x^4}{4!} - \ldots + \dfrac{(-1)^{n-1} x^{2n-2}}{(2n-2)!} + \ldots$	$-\infty < x < \infty$	(3)
$\cos x$	$\cos a - (x - a)\sin a - \dfrac{(x-a)^2}{2!}\cos a$ $+ \dfrac{(x-a)^3}{3!}\sin a + \ldots$	$-\infty < x < \infty$	(4)
e^x	$1 + x + \dfrac{x^2}{2!} + \dfrac{x^3}{3!} + \ldots + \dfrac{x^n}{n!} + \ldots$	$-\infty < x < \infty$	(5)
$\ln(x+1)$	$x - \dfrac{x^2}{2} + \dfrac{x^3}{3} - \dfrac{x^4}{4} + \ldots + \dfrac{(-1)^{n-1} x^n}{n} + \ldots$	$-1 < x \leqq 1$	(6)

FUNCTION	SERIES EXPANSION	INTERVAL OF CONVERGENCE

$\ln x$ $\qquad (x - 1) - \dfrac{(x - 1)^2}{2} + \dfrac{(x - 1)^3}{3} - \ldots$ $\qquad\qquad 0 < x \leqq 2 \qquad$ (7)

$$+ \frac{(-1)^{n-1}(x - 1)^n}{n} + \ldots$$

$\tan^{-1} x \qquad x - \dfrac{x^3}{3} + \dfrac{x^5}{5} - \dfrac{x^7}{7} + \ldots + \dfrac{(-1)^{n-1}x^{2n-1}}{2n - 1} + \ldots \quad -1 \leqq x \leqq 1 \quad$ (8)

If we use the nth partial sum of a convergent power series for $f(x_0)$ as an approximation to $f(x_0)$, we need information about the magnitude of the error involved. We know that, if the first $(n + 1)$ terms of the Taylor series are used for $f(x_0)$, the error is $R_n(x_0)$ as given by (1), (2), or (3) in section B4. We have also indicated that it is not necessary that we know exactly how large the error is but only that we find an upper bound for it. If a convergent geometric series is involved, then

$$\sum_{n=1}^{\infty} ar^n = a + ar + \ldots + ar^{n-1} + R_n,$$

where

$$|R_n| = \left| \frac{ar^n}{1 - r} \right|.$$

Recall,also, that for a convergent alternating series the error is less absolutely than the first term dropped; i.e., if

$$S = a_1 - a_2 + a_3 - \ldots + (-1)^{n-1}a_n + R_n$$

then

$$|R_n| < a_{n+1} ;$$

in fact, R_n has the same sign as the $(n + 1)$st term.

EXAMPLES:

47.   Compute $\dfrac{1}{\sqrt{e}}$ to four decimal places.

We can use the Maclaurin Series (5),

$$e^x \;=\; 1 + x + \dfrac{x^2}{2!} + \dfrac{x^3}{3!} + \dfrac{x^4}{4!} + \;\cdot\;\cdot\;\cdot\;,$$

and let $x = -\dfrac{1}{2}$ to get

$$e^{-1/2} \;=\; 1 - \dfrac{1}{2} + \dfrac{1}{4\cdot 2} - \dfrac{1}{8\cdot 3!} + \dfrac{1}{16\cdot 24} - \dfrac{1}{32\cdot 5!} + R_5;$$

$$e^{-1/2} \;=\; 1 - .50000 + .12500 - .02083 + .00260 - .00026 + R_5$$

$$\;=\; 0.60651 + R_5.$$

Note that, since we have a convergent alternating series, R_5 is less than the first term dropped:

$$R_5 \;<\; \dfrac{1}{64\cdot 6!} \;<\; 0.00003.$$

So $\dfrac{1}{\sqrt{e}} = 0.6065$, correct to four decimal places.

48.   Compute $\cos 32°$ correct to four decimal places.

The Taylor series in powers of $\left(x - \dfrac{\pi}{6}\right)$ is obtained immediately from

(4) with $a = \dfrac{\pi}{6}$.

$$\cos x = \cos \dfrac{\pi}{6} - \left(x - \dfrac{\pi}{6}\right)\sin \dfrac{\pi}{6} - \dfrac{\left(x - \dfrac{\pi}{6}\right)^2}{2!}\cos \dfrac{\pi}{6} + \dfrac{\left(x - \dfrac{\pi}{6}\right)^3}{3!}\sin \dfrac{\pi}{6} + \;\cdot\;\cdot\;\cdot\;\cdot$$

Since $x = 32°$, $\left(x - \dfrac{\pi}{6}\right) = 2° = 2(.01745) = 0.03490$, and

$$\cos 32° \;=\; \dfrac{\sqrt{3}}{2} - (0.03490)\dfrac{1}{2} - \dfrac{(0.03490)^2}{2}\cdot\dfrac{\sqrt{3}}{2} + R_2$$

$$\;=\; 0.86602 - 0.01745 - 0.00053 + R_2$$

$$\;=\; 0.84804 + R_2.$$

If we use the Lagrange remainder here, then

$$R_2 = \frac{f'''(\xi)(x - \frac{\pi}{3})^3}{3!} = \frac{(\sin \xi)(0.03490)^3}{6},$$

where $30° < \xi < 32°$. Although we do not know exactly what ξ is we do know that $\sin \xi < 1$; so $R_2 < 0.00001$ and $\cos 32° = 0.8480$ to four decimal places.

49. For what values of x is the approximate formula

$$\ln (1 + x) = x - \frac{x^2}{2} \tag{9}$$

correct to three decimal places?

We can use series (6):

$$\ln (1 + x) = x - \frac{x^2}{2} + \frac{x^3}{3} - \ldots$$

Since this is a convergent alternating series, the error committed by using the first two terms is less than $\frac{|x|^3}{3}$. If $\frac{|x|^3}{3} < .0005$ then the approximate formula (9) will yield accuracy to three decimal places. We therefore require that $|x|^3 < 0.0015$ or that $|x| < 0.115$.

50. Estimate the error if the approximate formula

$$\sqrt{1 + x} = 1 + \frac{x}{2} \tag{10}$$

is used and $|x| < 0.02$.

We obtain the first few terms of the Maclaurin Series generated by $f(x) = \sqrt{1 + x}$:

$$f(x) = \sqrt{1 + x} \qquad\qquad f(0) = 1$$

$$f'(x) = \frac{1}{2}(1 + x)^{-1/2} \qquad\qquad f'(0) = \frac{1}{2}$$

$$f''(x) = -\frac{1}{4}(1 + x)^{-3/2} \qquad\qquad f''(0) = -\frac{1}{4}$$

$$f'''(x) = \frac{3}{8}(1 + x)^{-5/2} \qquad\qquad f'''(0) = \frac{3}{8} ;$$

So

$$\sqrt{1 + x} = 1 + \frac{x}{2} - \frac{1}{4} \cdot \frac{x^2}{2} + \frac{3}{8} \cdot \frac{x^3}{6} - \ldots$$

If the first term is omitted the series is strictly alternating; so if formula (10) is used then $|R_1| < \frac{1}{4} \cdot \frac{x^2}{2}$. With $|x| < 0.02$, $|R_1| < 0.00005$.

Notice that the Lagrange remainder $|R_1|$ here is $\left| \frac{f''(\xi)x^2}{2!} \right|$, where $0 < \xi < 0.02$. Since $|\xi| < 0.02$ we see that $|R_1| < \dfrac{(0.02)^2}{8(1 + 0.02)^{3/2}} < 0.00005$.

INDETERMINATE FORMS. Series may also be used to evaluate indeterminate forms, as indicated in Examples 51, 52, and 53.

51. Use series to evaluate $\displaystyle\lim_{x\to 0} \frac{\sin x}{x}$.

From (1),

$$\sin x = x - \frac{x^3}{3!} + \frac{x^5}{5!} - \cdots$$

$$\lim_{x\to 0} \frac{\sin x}{x} = \lim_{x\to 0}\left(1 - \frac{x^2}{3!} + \frac{x^4}{5!} - \cdots\right) = 1,$$

a well-established result obtained previously.

52. Use series to evaluate $\displaystyle\lim_{x\to 0} \frac{\ln(x + 1)}{3x}$.

We can use (6) and write

$$\lim_{x\to 0} \frac{x - \frac{x^2}{2} + \frac{x^3}{3} - \frac{x^4}{4} + \cdots}{3x} = \lim_{x\to 0} \frac{1}{3} - \frac{x}{6} + \frac{x^2}{9} - \cdots$$

$$= \frac{1}{3}.$$

53. $\displaystyle\lim_{x\to 0} \frac{e^{-x^2} - 1}{x^2} = \lim_{x\to 0} \frac{\left(1 - x^2 + \frac{x^4}{2!} - \frac{x^6}{3!} + \cdots\right) - 1}{x^2}$

$$= \lim_{x\to 0} \frac{-x^2 + \frac{x^4}{2!} - \cdots}{x^2} = \lim_{x\to 0} -1 + \frac{x^2}{2!} - \frac{x^4}{4!} + \cdots$$

$$= -1.$$

54. Show how series may be used to evaluate π.

Since $\frac{\pi}{4}$ = $\tan^{-1} 1$, a series for $\tan^{-1} x$ may prove helpful. Note that $\tan^{-1} x$ = $\int_0^x \frac{dt}{1 + t^2}$ and that a series for $\frac{1}{1 + t^2}$ is obtainable easily by long division to yield

$$\frac{1}{1 + t^2} = 1 - t^2 + t^4 - t^6 + \ldots \tag{11}$$

If we integrate (11) term by term and then evaluate the definite integral we get

$$\tan^{-1} x = x - \frac{x^3}{3} + \frac{x^5}{5} - \frac{x^7}{7} + \ldots + \frac{(-1)^{n-1} x^{2n-1}}{2n - 1} + \ldots \tag{12}$$

Compare with series (8) above, and note especially that (12) converges on $-1 \leqq x \leqq 1$. We replace x by 1 in (12) to get

$$\tan^{-1} 1 = 1 - \frac{1}{3} + \frac{1}{5} - \frac{1}{7} + \ldots$$

So

$$\frac{\pi}{4} = 1 - \frac{1}{3} + \frac{1}{5} - \frac{1}{7} + \ldots \tag{13}$$

and

$$\pi = 4(1 - \frac{1}{3} + \frac{1}{5} - \frac{1}{7} + \ldots).$$

It must be pointed out that it would take several hundred terms of (13) to get even two-place accuracy; there are series expressions for π that converge more rapidly than (13).

55. Use series to evaluate $\int_0^{0.1} e^{-x^2} \, dx$ to four decimal places.

Although $\int e^{-x^2} \, dx$ cannot be expressed in terms of elementary functions we can write a series for e^u, replace u by $(-x^2)$, and integrate term by term. Thus

$$e^{-x^2} = 1 - x^2 + \frac{x^4}{2!} - \frac{x^6}{3!} + \ldots,$$

so

$$\int_0^{0.1} e^{-x^2}\, dx = x - \frac{x^3}{3} + \frac{x^5}{5 \cdot 2!} - \frac{x^7}{7 \cdot 3!} + \cdots \Big|_0^{0.1}$$

$$= 0.1 - \frac{0.001}{3} + \frac{0.00001}{10} - \frac{0.0000001}{42} + \cdots \qquad (14)$$

$$= 0.1 - 0.00033 + 0.000001 + R_6$$

$$= 0.09967 + R_6.$$

Since (14) is a convergent alternating series, $|R_6| < \frac{10^{-7}}{42}$, which will not affect the fourth decimal place. So, correct to four decimal places,

$$\int_0^{0.1} e^{-x^2}\, dx = 0.997 .$$

C6. **Power Series over the Complex Numbers.** A *complex number* is one of the form $a + bi$, where a and b are real and $i^2 = -1$. If we allow complex numbers as replacements for x in power series we obtain some interesting results.

Consider, for instance, the series

$$e^x = 1 + x + \frac{x^2}{2!} + \frac{x^3}{3!} + \frac{x^4}{4!} + \cdots + \frac{x^n}{n!} \cdots \qquad (1)$$

When $x = yi$ then (1) becomes

$$e^{yi} = 1 + yi + \frac{(yi)^2}{2!} + \frac{(yi)^3}{3!} + \frac{(yi)^4}{4!} + \cdots$$

$$= 1 + yi - \frac{y^2}{2!} - \frac{y^3 i}{3!} + \frac{y^4}{4!} + \cdots$$

$$= \left(1 - \frac{y^2}{2!} + \frac{y^4}{4!} + \cdots\right) + i\left(y - \frac{y^3}{3!} + \frac{y^5}{5!} - \cdots\right), \qquad (2)$$

So

$$e^{yi} = \cos y + i \sin y, \qquad (3)$$

since the series within the parentheses of equation (2) converge respectively to $\cos y$ and $\sin y$. (3) is called *Euler's formula*. It follows from

(3) that

$$e^{\pi i} = -1 \qquad \text{and} \qquad e^{2\pi i} = 1;$$

the latter is sometimes referred to as *Euler's magic formula*.

*Multiple Choice Questions: Sequences and Series

(The asterisk applies to all the questions in this set. See the Introduction.)

1. If a sequence $\{s_n\}$ converges to L then

 (A) L equals zero.   (B) $|s_n - L| < \varepsilon$ for all n.

 (C) the difference between s_n and L may be made arbitrarily small.

 (D) if $\varepsilon > 0$, there is a number N such that $|s_n - L| < \varepsilon$ when

 $n > N$.

 (E) $s_n \leqq L$ for all n.

2. If $\{s_n\} = \{1 + \dfrac{(-1)^n}{n}\}$ then

 (A) $\{s_n\}$ diverges by oscillation.   (B) $\{s_n\}$ converges to 0.

 (C) $\lim\limits_{n\to\infty} s_n = 1$.   (D) $\{s_n\}$ diverges to infinity.

 (E) none of the above is true.

3. The sequence $\{\sin \dfrac{n\pi}{6}\}$

 (A) is unbounded.   (B) is monotonic.

 (C) converges to a number less than 1.

 (D) is bounded.   (E) diverges to infinity.

4. Which of the following sequences diverges?

 (A) $\{\dfrac{1}{n}\}$ (B) $\{\dfrac{(-1)^{n+1}}{n}\}$ (C) $\{\dfrac{2^n}{e^n}\}$

 (D) $\{\dfrac{n^2}{e^n}\}$ (E) $\{\dfrac{n}{\ln n}\}$.

5. Which of the following statements about sequences is false?

    (A) If $\{s_n\}$ is bounded then it is convergent.

    (B) If $\lim_{n\to\infty} s_n = L$ then $|s_n - L| < 0.001$ except for at most

         a finite number of n's.

    (C) If $\{s_n\}$ converges then $\{s_n\}$ is bounded.

    (D) If $\{s_n\}$ is unbounded then it diverges.

    (E) None of the above.

6. The sequence $\{r^n\}$ converges if and only if

    (A) $|r| < 1$ (B) $|r| \leqq 1$ (C) $-1 < r \leqq 1$

    (D) $0 < r < 1$ (E) $|r| > 1$.

7. $\{s_n\}$ where $s_n = \dfrac{n}{n + 1}$ converges to 1. It follows then, if $\varepsilon > 0$,

    that there exists a positive integer N such that $|s_n - 1| < \varepsilon$ when

    $n > N$. Let $\varepsilon = 0.01$; then the least such N is

         (A) 10   (B) 90   (C) 99   (D) 100   (E) 101.

8. $\sum u_n$ is a series of constants for which $\lim_{n\to\infty} u_n = 0$. Which of the

    following statements is always true?

    (A) $\sum u_n$ converges to a finite sum.   (B) $\sum u_n$ equals zero.

    (C) $\sum u_n$ does not diverge to infinity.   (D) $\sum u_n$ is a positive series.

    (E) None of the preceding.

9. Note that $\dfrac{1}{n(n + 1)} = \dfrac{1}{n} - \dfrac{1}{n + 1}$ $(n \geqq 1)$. $\displaystyle\sum_{n=1}^{\infty} \dfrac{1}{n(n + 1)}$ equals

    (A) $\dfrac{4}{3}$ (B) 1   (C) $\dfrac{3}{2}$ (D) $\dfrac{3}{4}$ (E) ∞.

10. The sum of the geometric series $(2 - 1 + \dfrac{1}{2} - \dfrac{1}{4} + \dfrac{1}{8} - \ldots)$ is

         (A) $\dfrac{4}{3}$ (B) $\dfrac{5}{4}$ (C) 1   (D) $\dfrac{3}{2}$ (E) $\dfrac{3}{4}$.

11. Which of the following statements about series is true?

(A) If $\lim\limits_{n \to \infty} u_n = 0$, then $\sum u_n$ converges.

(B) If $\lim\limits_{n \to \infty} u_n \neq 0$, then $\sum u_n$ diverges.

(C) If $\sum u_n$ diverges then $\lim\limits_{n \to \infty} u_n \neq 0$.

(D) $\sum u_n$ converges if and only if $\lim\limits_{n \to \infty} u_n = 0$.

(E) None of the preceding.

12. Which of the following statements about series is false?

(A) $\displaystyle\sum_{k=1}^{\infty} u_k = \sum_{k=m}^{\infty} u_k$, where m is any positive integer.

(B) If $\sum u_n$ converges so does $\sum c u_n$ if $c \neq 0$.

(C) If $\sum a_n$ and $\sum b_n$ converge so does $\sum (c a_n + b_n)$ where $c \neq 0$.

(D) If 1000 terms are added to a convergent series, the new series also converges.

(E) Rearranging the terms of a positive convergent series will not affect its convergence or its sum.

13. Which of the following series converges?

(A) $\displaystyle\sum \frac{1}{\sqrt[3]{n}}$

(B) $\displaystyle\sum \frac{1}{\sqrt{n}}$

(C) $\displaystyle\sum \frac{1}{n}$

(D) $\displaystyle\sum \frac{1}{10n - 1}$

(E) $\displaystyle\sum \frac{2}{n^2 - 5}$.

14. Which of the following series diverges?

(A) $\displaystyle\sum_{n=1}^{\infty} \frac{1}{n(n+1)}$ (B) $\displaystyle\sum_{n=1}^{\infty} \frac{n+1}{n!}$ (C) $\displaystyle\sum_{n=2}^{\infty} \frac{1}{n \ln n}$

(D) $\displaystyle\sum_{n=1}^{\infty} \frac{\ln n}{2^n}$ (E) $\displaystyle\sum_{n=1}^{\infty} \frac{n}{2^n}$.

15. Which of the following series diverges?

(A) $\sum \frac{1}{n^2}$ (B) $\sum \frac{1}{n^2+n}$ (C) $\sum \frac{n}{n^3+1}$ (D) $\sum \frac{n}{\sqrt{4n^2-1}}$

(E)   none of the preceding.

16. For which of the following series does the Ratio Test fail?

(A) $\sum \frac{1}{n!}$ (B) $\sum \frac{n}{2^n}$ (C) $1 + \frac{1}{2^{3/2}} + \frac{1}{3^{3/2}} + \frac{1}{4^{3/2}} + \ldots$

(D) $\frac{\ln 2}{2^2} + \frac{\ln 3}{2^3} + \frac{\ln 4}{2^4} + \ldots$ (E) $\sum \frac{n^n}{n!}$.

17. Which of the following alternating series diverges?

(A) $\sum \frac{(-1)^{n-1}}{n}$ (B) $\sum \frac{(-1)^{n+1}(n-1)}{n+1}$ (C) $\sum \frac{(-1)^{n+1}}{\ln (n+1)}$

(D) $\sum \frac{(-1)^{n-1}}{\sqrt{n}}$ (E) $\sum \frac{(-1)^{n-1}(n)}{n^2+1}$.

18. Which of the following series converges conditionally?

(A) $3 - 1 + \frac{1}{9} - \frac{1}{27} + \ldots$

(B) $\frac{1}{\sqrt{2}} - \frac{1}{\sqrt{3}} + \frac{1}{\sqrt{4}} - \ldots$

(C) $\frac{1}{2^2} - \frac{1}{3^2} + \frac{1}{4^2} - \ldots$

(D) $1 - 1.1 + 1.21 - 1.331 + \ldots$

(E) $\frac{1}{1 \cdot 2} - \frac{1}{2 \cdot 3} + \frac{1}{3 \cdot 4} - \frac{1}{4 \cdot 5} + \ldots$

19. Let $S = \sum_{n=1}^{\infty} \left(\frac{2}{3}\right)^n$; then S equals

(A) 1   (B) $\frac{3}{2}$ (C) $\frac{4}{3}$ (D) 2   (E) 3.

20. Which of the following statements is true?

(A) If a series converges, then it converges absolutely.

(B) If a series is truncated after the nth term, then the error is less than the first term omitted.

(C) If the terms of an alternating series decrease then the series converges.

(D) If $r < 1$ then the series $\sum r^n$ converges.

(E) None of the preceding.

21. Which of the following expansions is impossible?

(A) $\sqrt{x - 1}$ in powers of x

(B) $\sqrt{x + 1}$ in powers of x

(C) $\ln x$ in powers of $(x - 1)$

(D) $\tan x$ in powers of $(x - \frac{\pi}{4})$

(E) $\ln (1 - x)$ in powers of x.

22. The power series $x + \frac{x^2}{2} + \frac{x^3}{3} + \ldots + \frac{x^n}{n} + \ldots$ converges if and only if

(A) $-1 < x < 1$

(B) $-1 \leq x \leq 1$

(C) $-1 \leq x < 1$

(D) $-1 < x \leq 1$

(E) $x = 0$.

23. The power series

$$(x + 1) - \frac{(x + 1)^2}{2!} + \frac{(x + 1)^3}{3!} - \frac{(x + 1)^4}{4!} + \ldots$$

diverges

    (A) for no real x (B) if $-2 < x \leqq 0$

    (C) if $x < -2$ or $x > 0$ (D) if $-2 \leqq x < 0$

    (E) if $x \neq -1$.

24. The series $\displaystyle\sum_{n=0}^{\infty} n!(x - 3)^n$ converges if and only if

    (A) $x = 0$ (B) $2 < x < 4$ (C) $x = 3$

    (D) $2 \leqq x \leqq 4$ (E) $x < 2$ or $x > 4$.

25. The interval of convergence of the series obtained by differentiating term by term the series

$$(x - 2) + \frac{(x - 2)^2}{4} + \frac{(x - 2)^3}{9} + \frac{(x - 2)^4}{16} + \ldots$$

is

    (A) $1 \leqq x \leqq 3$ (B) $1 \leqq x < 3$ (C) $1 < x \leqq 3$

    (D) $0 \leqq x \leqq 4$ (E) none of the preceding.

26. Let $f(x) = \displaystyle\sum_{n=0}^{\infty} x^n$. The interval of convergence of $\displaystyle\int_0^x f(t)\, dt$ is

    (A) $x = 0$ only   (B) $|x| \leqq 1$ (C) $-\infty < x < \infty$

    (D) $-1 \leqq x < 1$ (E) $-1 < x < 1$.

27. The coefficient of x^4 in the Maclaurin series for $f(x) = e^{-x/2}$ is

    (A) $-\dfrac{1}{24}$ (B) $\dfrac{1}{24}$ (C) $\dfrac{1}{96}$ (D) $-\dfrac{1}{384}$ (E) $\dfrac{1}{384}$.

28. The first four terms of the power series in x for $f(x) = \sqrt{1 + x}$ are

(A) $1 + \dfrac{x}{2} - \dfrac{x^2}{4} + \dfrac{3x^3}{8}$.

(B) $1 + \dfrac{x}{2} - \dfrac{x^2}{8} + \dfrac{x^3}{16}$.

(C) $1 - \dfrac{x}{2} + \dfrac{x^2}{8} - \dfrac{x^3}{16}$.

(D) $1 + \dfrac{x}{2} - \dfrac{x^2}{8} + \dfrac{x^3}{8}$.

(E) $1 - \dfrac{x}{2} + \dfrac{x^2}{4} - \dfrac{3x^3}{8}$.

29. The Taylor series expansion for e^x about $x = 1$ is

(A) $\displaystyle\sum_{n=1}^{\infty} \dfrac{(x - 1)^{n-1}}{(n - 1)!}$

(B) $e\left[1 + (x - 1) + \dfrac{(x - 1)^2}{2} + \dfrac{(x - 1)^3}{3} + \ldots\right]$

(C) $e\left[1 + (x + 1) + \dfrac{(x + 1)^2}{2!} + \dfrac{(x + 1)^3}{3!} + \ldots\right]$

(D) $e\displaystyle\sum_{n=0}^{\infty} \dfrac{(x - 1)^n}{n!}$

(E) $e\left[1 - (x - 1) + \dfrac{(x - 1)^2}{2!} - \dfrac{(x - 1)^3}{3!} + \ldots\right]$.

30. The coefficient of $\left(x - \dfrac{\pi}{4}\right)^3$ in the Taylor series about $\dfrac{\pi}{4}$ of $f(x) = \cos x$ is

(A) $\dfrac{\sqrt{3}}{12}$ (B) $-\dfrac{1}{12}$ (C) $\dfrac{1}{12}$ (D) $\dfrac{1}{6\sqrt{2}}$ (E) $-\dfrac{1}{3\sqrt{2}}$.

31. Which of the following series can be used to compute $\ln 0.8$?

(A) $\ln (x - 1)$ expanded about $x = 0$.

(B) $\ln x$ about $x = 0$.   (C) $\ln x$ in powers of $(x - 1)$.

(D) $\ln (x - 1)$ in powers of $(x - 1)$.

(E) none of the preceding.

32. If $e^{-0.1}$ is computed using series, then, correct to three decimal places, it equals

(A) 0.905   (B) 0.950   (C) 0.904   (D) 0.900   (E) 0.949.

33. The coefficient of x^2 in the Maclaurin series for $e^{\sin x}$ is

(A) 0   (B) 1   (C) $\frac{1}{2!}$ (D) -1   (E) $\frac{1}{4}$.

34. Let $f(x) = \sum_{n=0}^{\infty} a_n x^n$, $g(x) = \sum_{n=0}^{\infty} b_n x^n$, and let x_0 be a number for which both these series converge. Which of the following statements is false?

(A) $\sum_{n=0}^{\infty} (a_n + b_n)(x_0)^n$ converges to $f(x_0) + g(x_0)$.

(B) $\left[\sum_{n=0}^{\infty} a_n (x_0)^n\right]\left[\sum_{n=0}^{\infty} b_n (x_0)^n\right]$ converges to $f(x_0) g(x_0)$.

(C) $f(x) = \sum_{n=0}^{\infty} a_n x^n$ is continuous at $x = x_0$.

(D) $\sum_{n=1}^{\infty} n a_n x^{n-1}$ converges to $f'(x_0)$.

(E) None of the preceding.

35. The coefficient of $(x - 1)^5$ in the Taylor series for $x \ln x$ about $x = 1$ is

(A) $-\frac{1}{20}$ (B) $\frac{1}{5!}$ (C) $-\frac{1}{5!}$ (D) $\frac{1}{4!}$ (E) $-\frac{1}{4!}$.

36. If the approximation $1° = 0.01745$ (radians) is used then the value of $\sin 2°$ correct to four decimal places is

(A) 0.0340   (B) 0.0345   (C) 0.0349

(D) 0.0350   (E) 0.0352.

37. If the approximate formula $\sin x = x - \dfrac{x^3}{3!}$ is used and $|x| < 1$ (radian), then the error is numerically less than

(A) 0.001   (B) 0.003   (C) 0.005   (D) 0.008   (E) 0.009.

38. If an appropriate series is used to evaluate $\displaystyle\int_0^{0.3} x^2 e^{-x^2}\, dx$, then, correct to three decimal places, the definite integral equals

(A) 0.009   (B) 0.082   (C) 0.098   (D) 0.008   (E) 0.090.

39. If a suitable series is used then $\displaystyle\int_0^{0.2} \dfrac{e^{-x} - 1}{x}\, dx$, correct to three decimal places, is

(A) - 0.200   (B) 0.180   (C) 0.190

(D) - 0.190   (E) - 0.990.

40. $f(x) = \displaystyle\sum_{n=0}^{\infty} a_n x^n$ and $f'(x) = - f(x)$ for all x. If $f(0) = 1$ then $f(0.2)$, correct to three decimal places, is

(A) 0.905   (B) 1.221   (C) 0.819

(D) 0.820   (E) 1.220.

Section 10: Differential Equations

Review of Principles and Methods

A. **Introduction and Definitions.** An equation containing derivatives or differentials is called a *differential equation*. We consider here only ordinary differential equations, i.e., those involving only one independent variable. (If the equation involves several independent variables, and partial derivatives occur, it is called a *partial* differential equation.)

The *order* of a differential equation is that of the derivative of highest order that appears in it. If an nth order differential equation is expressible as a polynomial equation in the dependent variable and its derivatives, then the highest power of the nth derivative is the *degree* of the equation.

Thus, $\frac{dy}{dx} = e^x + x - 1$, $x\, dy = y\, dx$, $y' = 2y$, and $xy' + y^2 = 0$ are all of the first order and first degree; $\frac{d^2y}{dx^2} + (\frac{dy}{dx})^2 = x^3$ is of order two and degree one; $y = xy' + yy'^3$ is of the first order and of degree three.

A *solution* (or integral) of a differential equation is a relation between the variables containing no derivatives or differentials which satisfies the differential equation identically. The equation

$$f(x, y, y', y'', \ldots, y^{(n)}) = 0 \tag{1}$$

has the solution $y = F(x)$ if

$$f(x,\ F(x),\ F'(x),\ \dots,\ F^{(n)}(x)) \ = \ 0 \tag{2}$$

for each x in the domain of F.

Most nth order differential equations have not only one solution but a family of solutions which depend, in general, on n arbitrary constants. Such a family of solutions for (1) is often indicated by $y \ = \ F(x,\ C_1,\ C_2,\ \dots,\ C_n)$, and is called the *general solution* of (1).

A *particular* solution is one obtained from the general solution by assigning specific values to the arbitrary constants. For example, if

$$\frac{dy}{dx} \ = \ 3x^2 + 2x \tag{3}$$

then the general solution is

$$y \ = \ x^3 + x^2 + C. \tag{4}$$

Note that (4) satisfies (3) for every real C and that any particular solution of (3) is obtainable from (4) by choosing C appropriately. $y \ = \ x^3 + x^2 - 5$ is a particular solution of (3).

A differential equation of the first order, then, that has a (particular) solution $y = F(x)$ has a general solution $y = F(x,\ C)$, C an arbitrary constant or *parameter*. Similarly, one of the second order has a general solution $y = F(x,\ C_1,\ C_2)$, C_1 and C_2 arbitrary constants. We shall consider here various types of first- and second-order differential equations.

B. Differential Equations of the First Order and First Degree.

B1. Variables Separable. A differential equation of the first order and first degree **has variables separable if it is of the form**

$$\frac{dy}{dx} = \frac{f(x)}{g(y)} \quad \text{or} \quad g(y) \, dy - f(x) \, dx = 0 \qquad (1)$$

The general solution is

$$\int g(y) \, dy - \int f(x) \, dx = C \qquad C \text{ arbitrary.} \qquad (2)$$

EXAMPLES:

1. $\frac{dy}{dx} = \frac{x}{y}$. We can separate variables to get $y \, dy = x \, dx$;

then $\int y \, dy = \int x \, dx$, or $\frac{1}{2} y^2 = \frac{1}{2} x^2 + C$. The general solution is

defined implicitly by $y^2 = x^2 + C'$, where we have replaced the

arbitrary constant $2C$ by C'.

2. $\frac{ds}{dt} = \sqrt{st}$. We separate: $\frac{ds}{\sqrt{s}} = \sqrt{t} \, dt$; and integrate:

$2\sqrt{s} = \frac{2}{3} t^{3/2} + C$. The general solution can be given as $6\sqrt{s} = 2t\sqrt{t} + C'$.

3. $(\ln y) \frac{dy}{dx} = \frac{y}{x}$. Separate to get $\frac{(\ln y) \, dy}{y} = \frac{dx}{x}$; integrate

obtaining $\frac{\ln^2 y}{2} = \ln |x| + C$, or $\frac{1}{2} \ln^2 y = \ln k|x|$ where we have

replaced the arbitrary constant C by the equally **arbitrary** constant $\ln k$.

4. $\frac{du}{dv} = e^{v-u}$. We rewrite as $\frac{du}{dv} = \frac{e^v}{e^u}$, so that $e^u \, du = e^v \, dv$,

and then integrate to get $e^u = e^v + C$.

B2. **Homogeneous Differential Equations.** A first-order differential equation of the first degree

$$M\ dx\ +\ N\ dy\ =\ 0, \tag{1}$$

is said to be *homogeneous* if M and N are homogeneous of the same degree in x and y.

Recall that a function $f(x, y)$ is homogeneous, of degree n, if $f(tx, ty) = t^n f(x, y)$. For example, $f(x, y) = x^2 - 5xy + \dfrac{3x^3}{y}$ is

homogeneous of degree two, since $f(tx, ty) = t^2 x^2 - 5(tx)(ty) + \dfrac{3t^3 x^3}{ty}$

$= t^2 \left(x^2 - 5xy + \dfrac{3x^3}{y}\right) = t^2 f(x, y)$. Similarly, $3x - 2y \cos \dfrac{x}{y}$ is

homogeneous of degree one.

The differential equations $(2x - y)\ dx + (x + 3y)\ dy = 0$ and $(xe^{y/x} + y)\ dx = x\ dy$ are both homogeneous.

A homogeneous differential equation of the form (1) can be transformed into an equation in v and x with variables separable by letting

$$y\ =\ vx,\quad dy\ =\ v\ dx + x\ dv. \tag{2}$$

EXAMPLES:

5. The following equation

$$(y^2 - xy)\ dx + x^2\ dy\ =\ 0 \tag{3}$$

is transformed by means of (2) into

$$(v^2 x^2 - vx^2)\ dx + x^2 (v\ dx + x\ dv)\ =\ 0. \tag{4}$$

Since $x = 0$ does not satisfy (3) for all y, we may divide (4) by x^2 and get $(v^2 - v)\ dx + (v\ dx + x\ dv) = 0$. Collecting terms and

separating yields $\dfrac{dx}{x} + \dfrac{dv}{v^2} = 0$, whose solution is $\ln |x| - \dfrac{1}{v} = C_1$,

or $\ln |x| - \frac{x}{y} = \ln C_2$, or $\ln \frac{x}{C_2} = \frac{x}{y}$, or, finally, $x = Ce^{x/y}$.
The substitution $x = vy$ also leads to a new equation with variables separable.

6. Solve the equation $(xe^{y/x} + y)\ dx = x\ dy$ if $y = 0$ when $x = 1$.
By (2) we have $(xe^{v} + vx)\ dx = x(v\ dx + x\ dv)$. Division by x $(\neq 0)$ yields $(e^{v} + v)\ dx = v\ dx + x\ dv$ or $e^{v}\ dx = x\ dv$. Separating results in $\frac{dx}{x} = \frac{dv}{e^{v}}$. So the general solution is $\ln |x| = -e^{-v} + C$.

Since $y = 0$ when $x = 1$, therefore $v = 0$. Using these values in the general solution, we get $0 = -1 + C$, or $C = 1$. The particular solution in this case is then $\ln |x| = -e^{-y/x} + 1$.

B3. Homogeneous Linear Differential Equations of the First Order.
The first order *linear* equation is of the form

$$\frac{dy}{dx} + Py = Q \qquad (1)$$

with P and Q functions of x. The word "linear" is used because y and $\frac{dy}{dx}$ occur only to the first power.

We consider first a special case of (1), that in which $Q = 0$:

$$\frac{dy}{dx} + P(x)y = 0. \qquad (2)$$

Equation (2) is said to be *homogeneous* (in y and y'); but it must be pointed out that the meaning of "homogeneous" here is different from its meaning in section B2 above. The variables in any equation of type (2) are always separable, yielding

$$\frac{dy}{y} + P(x)\ dx = 0. \qquad (3)$$

Integrating yields $\ln |y| + \int P(x)\, dx = \ln C'$. Since C' is arbitrary, the general solution of (2) is

$$y = Ce^{\int P(x)\, dx} \tag{4}$$

An interesting special case of (2) with wide applications is that in which $P(x)$ is constant; namely,

$$y' = ky \qquad k \text{ constant.} \tag{5}$$

We have $\dfrac{dy}{y} = k\, dx$ with general solution $\ln |y| = kx + \ln C$, or

$$y = Ce^{kx}. \tag{6}$$

If a quantity increases or decreases at any time t at a rate proportional to the amount s present at that time then it satisfies the differential equation

$$\frac{ds}{dt} = kt, \tag{7}$$

which is of the form (5). If the quantity grows with time then $k > 0$; if it decays or diminishes, then $k < 0$. Thus (7) is sometimes referred to as the *law of natural growth and decay*.

EXAMPLES:

7. The bacteria in a certain culture increase continuously at a rate proportional to the number present. (a) If the number triples in 6 hr, how many are there in 12 hr? (b) In how many hours will the original number quadruple?

We let N be the number at time t and N_0 the number initially. Then

$\dfrac{dN}{dt} = kN$, $\dfrac{dN}{N} = k\, dt$, $\ln N = kt + C$, and $\ln N_0 = 0 + C$, so that

C = $\ln N_0$. The general solution is then N = $N_0 e^{kt}$, with k still to be determined.

Since N = $3N_0$ when $t = 6$, we see that $3N_0$ = $N_0 e^{6k}$ and that k = $\frac{1}{6} \ln 3$. Thus

$$N = N_0 e^{(t\ln 3)/6} . \tag{8}$$

(a)   When $t = 12$, $N = N_0 e^{2\ln 3} = N_0 e^{\ln 3^2} = N_0 e^{\ln 9} = 9N_0$.

(b)   We let $N = 4N_0$ in (8), and get $4 = e^{(t\ln 3)/6}$, $\ln 4 = \frac{t}{6} \ln 3$, and $t = \dfrac{6 \ln 4}{\ln 3}$.

B4.   Nonhomogeneous Linear Equations of the First Order.   The standard form of the nonhomogeneous equation is

$$\frac{dy}{dx} + Py = Q. \tag{1}$$

Theoretically, (1) can always be solved by multiplying the equation by the factor $e^{\int P dx}$. It then becomes

$$e^{\int P dx} \cdot \frac{dy}{dx} + e^{\int P dx} \cdot Py = e^{\int P dx} \cdot Q. \tag{2}$$

The left-hand member of (2) is simply $\dfrac{d}{dx}\left[e^{\int P dx} \cdot y\right]$, the derivative of a product. The function $e^{\int P dx}$ is called an *integrating factor* since multiplying by it makes integration possible.

EXAMPLES:

8.   To solve $xy' + 2y = x^2$, we rewrite it in standard form: $\frac{dy}{dx} + \frac{2y}{x} = x$. So $P = \frac{2}{x}$ and $Q = x$. An integrating factor is

$e^{\int P dx} = e^{\int 2/x \, dx} = e^{2 \ln x} = x^2$. Multiplying by x^2 yields

$x^2 \cdot \frac{dy}{dx} + 2xy = x^3$, or $\frac{d}{dx}(x^2 y) = x^3$. So the general solution

is $x^2 y = \frac{x^4}{4} + C$ or $y = \frac{x^2}{4} + \frac{C}{x^2}$.

Note that $x = 0$ does not satisfy the given equation identically (that is, for all y).

9. To find the general solution of

$$\frac{dy}{dx} + y = \cos x \qquad (3)$$

we note that $P = 1$ and $Q = \cos x$, and multiply by $e^{\int dx} = e^x$.

(3) becomes $e^x \cdot \frac{dy}{dx} + e^x y = e^x \cos x$, or $\frac{d}{dx}(e^x y) = e^x \cos x$.

The general solution of (3) is thus $e^x y = \frac{1}{2} e^x (\cos x + \sin x) + C$,

where the right-hand member has been obtained by integrating by parts twice; or

$$y = \frac{1}{2}(\cos x + \sin x) + Ce^{-x}. \qquad (4)$$

Note that the first term of (4) is a particular solution of (3),

while Ce^{-x} is the general solution of $\frac{dy}{dx} + y = 0$, the homogeneous

equation *associated with* (3).

C. Linear Second-Order Differential Equations with Constant Coefficients. The only second-order differential equations with which we will be concerned are those of the type

$$\frac{d^2 y}{dx^2} + a_1 \cdot \frac{dy}{dx} + a_2 y = Q(x) \qquad (1)$$

where the a's are constant. Since this equation is of the first degree in y and its derivatives, it is called *linear*.

C1. Homogeneous Linear Equations with Constant Coefficients. If, in (1), $Q(x) = 0$, then the equation

$$\frac{d^2y}{dx^2} + a_1 \cdot \frac{dy}{dx} + a_2 y = 0 \qquad (2)$$

is said to be *homogeneous*. This equation has the following important property: If y_1 and y_2 are two (particular) solutions, and c_1 and c_2 are real numbers, then $c_1 y_1 + c_2 y_2$ is also a solution.

The proof is easy. Since y_1 and y_1 are solutions of (2), it follows that

$$\frac{d^2y_1}{dx^2} + a_1 \cdot \frac{dy_1}{dx} + a_2 y_1 = 0 \qquad \text{identically}$$

and that

$$\frac{d^2y_2}{dx^2} + a_1 \cdot \frac{dy_2}{dx} + a_2 y_2 = 0 \qquad \text{identically.}$$

Then also

$$c_1 \left(\frac{d^2y_1}{dx^2} + a_1 \cdot \frac{dy_1}{dx} + a_2 y_1 \right) + c_2 \left(\frac{d^2y_2}{dx^2} + a_1 \cdot \frac{dy_2}{dx} + a_2 y_2 \right) = 0, \qquad (3)$$

also identically. But (3) can be rewritten

$$\frac{d^2}{dx^2}(c_1 y_1 + c_2 y_2) + a_1 \cdot \frac{d}{dx}(c_1 y_1 + c_2 y_2) + a_2(c_1 y_1 + c_2 y_2) = 0.$$

So we see that $c_1 y_1 + c_2 y_2$ is a solution of (2). We will use this property below to solve equation (2).

C2. Differential Operators and Their Use in Solving Linear Differential Equations. If D denotes the operation of differentiation with respect to x, then

$$Dy = \frac{dy}{dx}, \qquad D^2y = D(Dy) = \frac{d^2y}{dx^2},$$

$$D^3y = D(D^2y) = \frac{d^3y}{dx^3},$$

and, generally,

$$D^ky = D(D^{k-1}y) = \frac{d^ky}{dx^k} \qquad k \text{ any natural number.}$$

"D" is referred to here as an *operator*. If in any polynomial

$$f(w) = w^n + a_1w^{n-1} + a_2w^{n-2} + \ldots + a_{n-1}w + a_n$$

we replace w by D, then the resulting polynomial $f(D)$ is called a *linear differential operator*.

If L_1 and L_2 are linear differential operators, we define their sum by $(L_1 + L_2)y = L_1y + L_2y$, and their product by $L_1L_2y = L_1(L_2y)$. It can be shown that linear operators behave like ordinary polynomials with respect to the laws of algebra for addition, multiplication, and factoring.

Note that the differential equation $\frac{d^2y}{dx^2} + 5\frac{dy}{dx} + 6y = 0$ can be rewritten as $(D^2 + 5D + 6)y = 0$. Similarly, $(D^2 - D - 2)f(x) = D^2f(x) - Df(x) - 2f(x) = \frac{d^2f(x)}{dx^2} - \frac{df(x)}{dx} - 2f(x)$. And $(D + 2)(D - 3)y = D[(D - 3)y] + 2[(D - 3)y] = D(Dy - 3y) + 2(Dy - 3y) = D^2y - 3Dy + 2Dy - 6y = D^2y - Dy - 6y = (D^2 - D - 6)y$; so $(D + 2)(D - 3) = D^2 - D - 6$.

We now use operator notation to rewrite the second-order linear homogeneous equation (C1 above),

$$\frac{d^2y}{dx^2} + a_1 \cdot \frac{dy}{dx} + a_2y = 0$$

as

$$(D^2 + a_1D + a_2)y = 0. \tag{1}$$

We have already seen that the corresponding first-order linear equation

$$\frac{dy}{dx} = ky \qquad \text{or} \qquad (D - k)y = 0 \qquad k \text{ constant}$$

has the general solution

$$y = Ce^{kx} \qquad (C \text{ arbitrary}).$$

We now investigate the possibility that $y = e^{mx}$ is a solution of (1) for some constant m. If this is the case, then

$$(D^2 + a_1D + a_2)e^{mx} = 0;$$

that is,

$$m^2e^{mx} + a_1me^{mx} + a_2e^{mx} = 0$$

or

$$e^{mx}(m^2 + a_1m + a_2) = 0.$$

Since $e^{mx} \neq 0$, we see that the left-hand member is zero if and only if

$$m^2 + a_1m + a_2 = 0 \tag{2}$$

Equation (2) is called the *characteristic* or *auxiliary* equation of (1). It follows, then, that $y = e^{m_1x}$ is a solution of (1) if m_1 is a solution of the auxiliary equation (2).

EXAMPLE:

10. Solve

$$\frac{d^2y}{dx^2} - 3\frac{dy}{dx} - 4y = 0. \tag{3}$$

We can rewrite (3) as $(D^2 - 3D - 4)y = 0$. Its characteristic equation, $m^2 - 3m - 4 = 0$, has roots $m_1 = -1$ and $m_2 = 4$. Thus both e^{-x} and e^{4x} are solutions of (3), and from the property stated in the preceding section (C1) it follows that the general solution of (3) is $y = c_1e^{-x} + c_2e^{4x}$, where c_1 and c_2 are arbitrary constants.

THE GENERAL CASE, CONTINUED. The form of the general solution of equation (1) above depends on the nature of the roots m_1 and m_2 of equation (2). There are three cases.

CASE ONE: m_1 and m_2 real and distinct. Here we see, from Example 10, that the general solution is $y = c_1e^{m_1x} + c_2e^{m_2x}$.

CASE TWO: $m_1 = m_2$. Equation (1) here takes the form

$$(D^2 - 2m_1D + m_1^2)y = 0 \tag{4}$$

with characteristic equation $m^2 - 2m_1m + m_1^2 = 0$, or

$$(m - m_1)^2 = 0.$$

One solution of (4) is $y = e^{m_1x}$; another is $y = xe^{m_1x}$. To verify the second part of this statement, note that

$$Dy = D(xe^{m_1x}) = m_1xe^{m_1x} + e^{m_1x}$$

and

$$D^2y = D^2(xe^{m_1x}) = m_1^2xe^{m_1x} + 2m_1e^{m_1x},$$

and substitute these into (4). But

$$(m_1{}^2x + 2m_1 - 2m_1{}^2x - 2m_1 + m_1{}^2x)e^{m_1x} = 0$$

identically in x since the left-hand factor equals zero identically. The general solution of (4) is then

$$y = c_1e^{m_1x} + c_2xe^{m_1x}.$$

CASE THREE: m_1 and m_2 are complex conjugates. Let $m_1 = \alpha + i\beta$ and $m_2 = \alpha - i\beta$ (α, β real, and $\beta \neq 0$). Since $m_1 \neq m_2$ the general solution of (1) is

$$y = C_1e^{(\alpha+i\beta)x} + C_2e^{(\alpha-i\beta)x}. \qquad (5)$$

By Euler's formula (p. 206),

$$e^{i\beta x} = \cos \beta x + i \sin \beta x$$

and

$$e^{-i\beta x} = \cos \beta x - i \sin \beta x;$$

so (5) becomes

$$y = e^{\alpha x}[(C_1 + C_2) \cos \beta x + i(C_1 - C_2) \sin \beta x].$$

If we let $c_1 = C_1 + C_2$ and $c_2 = i(C_1 - C_2)$, then the general solution of (1) in this case is

$$y = e^{\alpha x}(c_1 \cos \beta x + c_2 \sin \beta x). \qquad (6)$$

SUMMARY: If the second-order linear homogeneous equation

$$(D^2 + a_1D + a_2)y = 0 \qquad (1)$$

has constant coefficients, and if its characteristic equation

$$m^2 + a_1m + a_2 = 0 \qquad (2)$$

has roots m_1 and m_2, then the situation is as indicated below (c_1 and c_2 arbitrary constants; α and β real, $\beta \neq 0$):

NATURE OF THE ROOTS OF (2)	GENERAL SOLUTION OF (1)
m_1 and m_2 real and distinct	$y = c_1 e^{m_1 x} + c_2 e^{m_2 x}$;
$m_1 = m_2$	$y = c_1 e^{m_1 x} + c_2 x e^{m_1 x}$;
$m_1 = \alpha + i\beta,\ m_2 = \alpha - i\beta$	$y = e^{\alpha x}(c_1 \cos \beta x + c_2 \sin \beta x)$.

EXAMPLES:

11. Solve $\dfrac{d^2 y}{dx^2} - 2\dfrac{dy}{dx} = 0$. The characteristic equation $m^2 - 2m = 0$ has distinct roots $m_1 = 0$ and $m_2 = 2$. The general solution is

$$y = c_1 + c_2 e^{2x}.$$

12. Solve $\dfrac{d^2 y}{dx^2} + 4\dfrac{dy}{dx} + 4y = 0$. The equation $m^2 + 4m + 4 = 0$ has one (double) root, $m = -2$. The general solution is

$$y = c_1 e^{-2x} + c_2 x e^{-2x}.$$

13. $y'' - 6y' + 10y = 0$ has the characteristic equation $m^2 - 6m + 10 = 0$ with roots $\dfrac{6 \pm \sqrt{-4}}{2}$. Thus $m_1 = 3 + i$, $m_2 = 3 - i$, and $\alpha = 3$, $\beta = 1$. The general solution is $y = e^{3x}(c_1 \cos x + c_2 \sin x)$.

C3. Nonhomogeneous Linear Differential Equations with Constant Coefficients. To solve the *nonhomogeneous* equation

$$\frac{d^2 y}{dx^2} + a_1 \cdot \frac{dy}{dx} + a_2 y = Q(x) \quad \text{or} \quad (D^2 + a_1 D + a_2)y = Q(x) \qquad (1)$$

we make use of the fact that the general solution of the associated *homogeneous* equation

$$\frac{d^2y}{dx^2} + a_1 \cdot \frac{dy}{dx} + a_2y = 0 \qquad \text{or} \qquad (D^2 + a_1D + a_2)y = 0 \qquad (2)$$

is known.

Let $y_c = c_1u_1 + c_2u_2$ (where u_1 and u_2 are functions of x) be the general solution of (2). The subscript "c" of "y_c" is used here because y_c is called the *complementary* function in connection with the general solution of (1). If we can find a *particular* solution, y_p, of (1), by discovery, inspection, or any other means, then the general solution of (1) is

$$y = y_c + y_p. \qquad (3)$$

For note, first, that

$$(D^2 + a_1D + a_2)y_c + (D^2 + a_1D + a_2)y_p = 0 + Q(x) = Q(x),$$

so that y given by (3) is indeed a solution of (1). Secondly: since y_c involves two arbitrary constants it follows that y does too, and is thus the general solution of (1).

EXAMPLE:

14. Find the general solution of $y'' - y = 3$. The associated homogeneous equation $y'' - y = 0$ has auxiliary equation $m^2 - 1 = 0$ with roots $m = \pm 1$; so here $y_c = c_1e^x + c_2e^{-x}$. By trial we see that $y_p = -3$ is a particular integral of the original equation. Thus, by (3), the general solution of the given equation is $y = c_1e^x + c_2e^{-x} - 3$.

THE METHOD OF UNDETERMINED COEFFICIENTS. This method for finding a particular solution of (1) is usable when $Q(x)$ is a function all of whose derivatives are linear combinations of only a finite number of different forms. For example, $Q(x)$ may contain terms of the type x^n (n a natural number), e^{kx}, $\sin kx$, $\cos kx$, or products of these. Functions like $\sec x$, $\frac{1}{x}$, e^{x^2} do not qualify. A particular solution is obtained by assuming a solution which is a sum of appropriate forms with undetermined constant coefficients. The method is illustrated in the following

EXAMPLES:

15. Find the general solution of

$$y'' - 4y' + 3y = 3x^2 + x + 2. \qquad (4)$$

Since the auxiliary equation of the associated homogeneous equation is $m^2 - 4m + 3 = 0$, with roots $m_1 = 1$ and $m_2 = 3$, we know that $y_c = c_1 e^x + c_2 e^{3x}$.

Now we assume that $y_p = ax^2 + bx + c$, with a, b, c to be determined, is a solution of (4). So $y_p' = 2ax + b$, $y_p'' = 2a$, and it follows upon substituting in (4) that $2a - 4(2ax + b) + 3(ax^2 + bx + c)$ must equal $3x^2 + x + 2$ identically. It is necessary, then, that $3ax^2 + (3b - 8a)x + 2a - 4b + 3c = 3x^2 + x + 2$. We equate coefficients of like powers as follows:

$$\text{coefficient of } x^2: \qquad 3a = 3$$
$$\text{coefficient of } x: \qquad 3b - 8a = 1$$
$$\text{constant coefficient: } 2a - 4b + 3c = 2.$$

So $a = 1$, $b = 3$, $c = 4$; $y_p = x^2 + 3x + 4$; and the general solution of (4) is thus

$$y = c_1 e^x + c_2 e^{3x} + x^2 + 3x + 4.$$

16. Solve

$$(D^2 + 2D + 1)y = e^x + \sin x. \qquad (5)$$

We see that $y_c = c_1e^{-x} + c_2xe^{-x}$; we let $y_p = ae^x + b \sin x + c \cos x$.

Since $Dy_p = ae^x + b \cos x - c \sin x$ and $D^2y_p = ae^x - b \sin x - c \cos x$, (5) becomes, on substitution,

$$ae^x - b \sin x - c \cos x + 2ae^x + 2 b \cos x - 2 c \sin x$$

$$+ ae^x + b \sin x + c \cos x = e^x + \sin x.$$

We equate coefficients of corresponding terms as follows:

for e^x: $4a = 1$

for $\sin x$: $-2c = 1$

for $\cos x$: $2b = 0.$

Then $a = \frac{1}{4}$, $b = 0$, and $c = -\frac{1}{2}$. The general solution of (5) is

$$y = c_1e^{-x} + c_2xe^{-x} + \frac{1}{4} e^x - \frac{1}{2} \cos x.$$

It can be easily verified that this solution satisfies (5).

THE METHOD OF UNDETERMINED COEFFICIENTS, CONTINUED. In using this method to solve (1), the form of y_p to be assumed is as indicated below:

FORM OF $Q(x)$	ASSUMPTION FOR y_p
a polynomial of degree n	a polynomial of degree n with undetermined coefficients
e^{kx}	ae^{kx}, a to be determined
$\cos kx$, $\sin kx$, or a linear combination of these	$a \cos kx + b \sin kx$, a, b to be determined
any linear combination of the above	a linear combination of the corresponding forms above
$e^{kx} \cos Ax$ or $e^{kx} \sin Ax$	$e^{kx}(a \cos Ax + b \sin Ax)$, a, b to be determined.

The procedure has to be modified, however, if u is a term in y_c and

$Q(x)$ contains a multiple of u or of $x^m u$. This is illustrated in the following

EXAMPLES:

17. Solve

$$y'' - y' = 3e^x - \cos 2x. \qquad (6)$$

The characteristic equation of the corresponding homogeneous equation is $m^2 - m = 0$; so $y_c = c_1 + c_2 e^x$. Since $Q(x)$, the right-hand member of (6), contains a multiple of e^x, $y = ae^x$ cannot be a particular solution of (6) (its substitution into the left-hand member of (6) reduces it to zero). Here, then, we let

$$y_p = axe^x + b \cos 2x + c \sin 2x;$$

$$y_p' = axe^x + ae^x - 2b \sin 2x + 2c \cos 2x;$$

$$y_p'' = axe^x + 2ae^x - 4b \cos 2x - 4c \sin 2x.$$

Substitution into (6) shows that $ae^x - (4b + 2c) \cos 2x + (2b - 4c) \sin 2x$ must equal $3e^x - \cos 2x$. Thus

$$a = 3 - 4b - 2c = -1,$$

$$2b - 4c = 0.$$

We find that $a = 3$, $b = \frac{1}{5}$, and $c = \frac{1}{10}$. The general solution of (6) is

$$y = c_1 + c_2 e^x + 3e^x + \frac{1}{5} \cos 2x + \frac{1}{10} \sin 2x.$$

A check insures against careless errors.

18. For the equation

$$y'' + 3y' = 4x^2, \qquad (7)$$

with $y_c = c_1 + c_2 e^{-3x}$, it is clear that no quadratic will serve. We try a cubic: $y_p = ax^3 + bx^2 + cx$. Then $y_p' = 3ax^2 + 2bx + c$ and

$y_p'' = 6ax + 2b$. The following must be an identity:

$$9ax^2 + (6a + 6b)x + 2b + 3c = 4x^2.$$

Thus $a = \frac{4}{9}$, $b = -\frac{4}{9}$, and $c = \frac{8}{27}$. The general solution of (7) is

$$y = c_1 + c_2 e^{-3x} + \frac{4}{9} x^3 - \frac{4}{9} x^2 + \frac{8}{27} x.$$

19.   To solve

$$y'' + y = \sin x, \tag{8}$$

we note that the characteristic equation is $m^2 + 1 = 0$ with roots i and $-i$. So, by (6) in C2 above, $y_c = c_1 \cos x + c_2 \sin x$. Since any function of type y_c reduces the left-hand member of (8) to zero, we set

$$y_p = ax \cos x + bx \sin x.$$

Now

$$y_p' = -ax \sin x + a \cos x + bx \cos x + b \sin x,$$

and

$$y_p'' = -ax \cos x - 2a \sin x - bx \sin x + 2b \cos x.$$

For our y_p, $y'' + y$ simplifies to $2b \cos x - 2a \sin x$, and this must equal $\sin x$.

Thus $a = -\frac{1}{2}$ and $b = 0$, and $y_p = -\frac{1}{2} x \cos x$. The general solution of (8) is, finally,

$$y = c_1 \cos x + c_2 \sin x - \frac{1}{2} x \cos x.$$

C4.   **Simple Harmonic Motion.**   One special case of the homogeneous linear equation of second order with constant coefficients merits special consideration here: that of the type

$$y'' = -k^2 y. \tag{1}$$

A motion that leads to a differential equation of the form (1) is called a *simple harmonic motion*. Since (1) can be rewritten

$$(D^2 + k^2)y = 0,$$

its characteristic equation is $m^2 + k^2 = 0$, with complex roots $\pm ki$. The general solution of (1) is

$$y = c_1 \cos kx + c_2 \sin kx. \tag{2}$$

If we multiply the right-hand member of (2) by 1 in the form $\dfrac{\sqrt{c_1^2 + c_2^2}}{\sqrt{c_1^2 + c_2^2}}$, we get

$$y = \sqrt{c_1^2 + c_2^2}\left(\frac{c_1}{\sqrt{c_1^2 + c_2^2}} \cos kx + \frac{c_2}{\sqrt{c_1^2 + c_2^2}} \sin kx\right). \tag{3}$$

If we now let α be the angle for which

$$\cos \alpha = \frac{c_1}{\sqrt{c_1^2 + c_2^2}}, \qquad \sin \alpha = \frac{c_2}{\sqrt{c_1^2 + c_2^2}},$$

then (3) becomes

$$y = A(\cos \alpha \cos kx + \sin \alpha \sin kx)$$

$$= A \cos (kx - \alpha) \tag{4}$$

where we have used a trigonometric identity and have replaced the arbitrary constant $\sqrt{c_1^2 + c_2^2}$ by the equally arbitrary constant A.

Equation (4) is a very convenient form for the general solution of (1) since it reveals the periodicity of the motion. The arbitrary constants A and α are determined for a particular motion to satisfy (given) physical conditions. A is called the *amplitude* of the motion, and the *period* is $\dfrac{2\pi}{k}$.

In the following examples we assume there is no air resistance or other friction.

EXAMPLES:

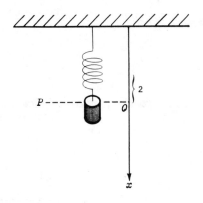

Spring has come to equi-
librium after weight is
hung.

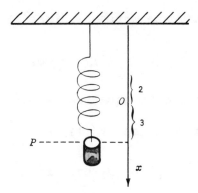

Weight has been pulled down
3 ft; this is time $t = 0$.

Figure N10-1   Figure N10-2

20.   A 20-lb weight when hung at the very bottom P of a spring

stretches the spring 2 ft.   The weight is then pulled down another 3 ft

and released.   Find an equation which describes the motion of P.

Let O be the point at which the weight hangs at rest before being

pulled down.   See Figure N10-1 where the positive direction is taken

downwards.   Figure N10-2 shows the weight pulled down another three ft.

(At this instant, $t = 0$.)   We let y be the directed distance of P at

any time t.   When the weight is released, the bottom of the spring, P,

is subject to a force (upward) which tends to restore it to a position

of equilibrium and which equals, by Hooke's Law (see p. 155) $-ky$.

Hooke's Law says that the force F (in lb) needed to stretch a spring

is proportional to the elongation s (in ft) of the spring; i.e.,

$F = ks$.   By Newton's second law, $F = ma$, where m is the mass and a

the acceleration of P.   Also, $m = \frac{w}{g}$, w the weight and g the acceleration

due to gravity (approximately 32 ft/sec^2).   Since the acceleration of P

at time t is $\frac{d^2y}{dt^2}$ it follows that

$$m \cdot \frac{d^2y}{dt^2} = -ky \qquad \text{or} \qquad \frac{w}{g} \cdot \frac{d^2y}{dt^2} = -ky. \qquad (5)$$

$F = ks$ in this case yields $20 = k \cdot 2$, so the "spring constant" is

$k = 10$ and (5) becomes

$$\frac{20}{32} \cdot y'' = -10y \qquad \text{or} \qquad y'' + 16y = 0. \qquad (6)$$

Equation (6) has precisely the form of (1), and its general solution

is $y = c_1 \cos 4t + c_2 \sin 4t$, or

$$y = A \cos (4t - \alpha). \qquad (7)$$

To find the constants here, note that

$$v = \frac{dy}{dt} = -4A \sin (4t - \alpha) \qquad (8)$$

and that when $t = 0$, $v = 0$ and $y = 3$. So we get

from (7) $\qquad\qquad 3 = A \cos \alpha,$

from (8) $\qquad\qquad 0 = 4A \sin \alpha.$

These yield $\alpha = 0$ and $A = 3$. The equation of motion of P is thus

$$y = 3 \cos 4t.$$

The weight oscillates up and down with O as center of motion. The

amplitude is 3 and the period $\frac{\pi}{2}$.

21. A particle moving along a line is attracted toward a fixed point

O on the line with a force which varies directly as its distance from O.

It starts from rest 4 ft from O; when it is 2 ft from O its acceleration

is 8 ft/sec^2 directed toward O. Find an equation which describes the

motion of the particle.

Let O be the origin of a horizontal line and let P, with coordinate

x, be the position on it of the particle at any time t. Then the

velocity of P is $\frac{dx}{dt}$ and its acceleration is $\frac{d^2x}{dt^2}$.

Since the particle is attracted towards O, we see that $F = -kx$ if $k > 0$, so that when $x > 0$ the force is directed negatively (towards the left) while if $x < 0$ the force is directed positively (towards the right). By Newton's Law, then,

$$ma = -kx \quad \text{or} \quad m \cdot \frac{d^2x}{dt^2} = -kx, \quad \text{and} \quad \frac{d^2x}{dt^2} = -\frac{k}{m}x.$$

Since the acceleration equals -8 when $x = 2$, it follows that $x'' = -4x$ or

$$x'' + 4x = 0. \tag{9}$$

Equation (9) has precisely the form (1), and its general solution is $x = c_1 \cos 2t + c_2 \sin 2t$, or

$$x = A \cos (2t - \alpha). \tag{10}$$

To find the constants A and α we note that

$$v = \frac{dx}{dt} = -2A \sin (2t - \alpha) \tag{11}$$

and that when $t = 0$, $x = 4$ and $v = 0$. We get

$$\text{from (10)} \qquad 4 = A \cos \alpha,$$
$$\text{from (11)} \qquad 0 = 2A \sin \alpha,$$

so that $\alpha = 0$ and $A = 4$. Finally, then, the equation of motion of is

$$x = 4 \cos 2t.$$

The particle moves back and forth on the line with O as center of motion. The amplitude is 4 and the period is π seconds.

*Multiple Choice Questions: Differential Equations

(The asterisk applies to all the questions in this set. See the Introduction.)

1. A solution of the differential equation $y \, dy \; = \; x \, dx$ is

    (A) $x^2 - y^2 = 4$ (B) $x^2 + y^2 = 4$ (C) $y^2 = 4x^2$

    (D) $x^2 - 4y^2 = 0$ (E) $x^2 = 9 - y^2$.

2. If $\dfrac{dy}{dx} \; = \; \dfrac{y}{2\sqrt{x}}$ and $y = 1$ when $x = 4$ then

    (A) $y^2 = 4\sqrt{x} - 7$ (B) $\ln y \; = \; 4\sqrt{x} - 8$ (C) $\ln y \; = \; \sqrt{x} - 2$

    (D) $y \; = \; e^{\sqrt{x}}$ (E) $y \; = \; e^{\sqrt{x} - 2}$.

3. If $\dfrac{dy}{dx} \; = \; e^y$ and $y = 0$ when $x = 1$, then

    (A) $y \; = \; \ln |x|$ (B) $y \; = \; \ln |2 - x|$ (C) $e^{-y} \; = \; 2 - x$

    (D) $y \; = \; -\ln |x|$ (E) $e^{-y} \; = \; x - 2$.

4. If $\dfrac{dy}{dx} \; = \; \dfrac{x}{\sqrt{9 + x^2}}$ and $y = 5$ when $x = 4$, then

    (A) $y \; = \; \sqrt{9 + x^2} - 5$ (B) $y \; = \; \sqrt{9 + x^2}$

    (C) $y \; = \; 2\sqrt{9 + x^2} - 5$ (D) $y \; = \; \dfrac{\sqrt{9 + x^2} + 5}{2}$

    (E) none of these.

5. If $\dfrac{ds}{dt} \; = \; \sin^2 \dfrac{\pi}{2} s$ and if when $t = 0$, $s = 1$, then when $s = \dfrac{3}{2}$,

    t is equal to

    (A) $\dfrac{1}{2}$ (B) $\dfrac{\pi}{2}$ (C) 1 (D) $\dfrac{2}{\pi}$ (E) $-\dfrac{2}{\pi}$.

6. The general solution of the differential equation $x \, dy \; = \; y \, dx$

    is a family of

    (A) circles   (B) hyperbolas   (C) parallel lines

    (D) parabolas   (E) lines passing through the origin.

7. The general solution of the differential equation $\frac{dy}{dx} = y$ is a

    family of

    (A) parabolas   (B) straight lines (C) hyperbolas

    (D) ellipses   (E) none of these.

8. A function $f(x)$ which satisfies the equations $f(x)f'(x) = x$

    and $f(0) = 1$ is

    (A) $f(x) = \sqrt{x^2 + 1}$ (B) $f(x) = \sqrt{1 - x^2}$

    (C) $f(x) = x$ (D) $f(x) = e^x$ (E) none of these.

9. The curve that passes through the point $(1,1)$ and whose slope at

    any point (x,y) is equal to $\frac{3y}{x}$ has the equation

    (A) $3x - 2 = y$ (B) $y^3 = x$ (C) $y = x^3$

    (D) $3y^2 = x^2 + 2$ (E) $3y^2 - 2x = 1$.

10. If radium decomposes at a rate proportional to the amount present,

    then the amount R left after t years, if R_0 is present initially

    and c is the negative constant of proportionality, is given by

    (A) $R = R_0 ct$ (B) $R = R_0 e^{ct}$ (C) $R = R_0 + \frac{1}{2}ct^2$

    (D) $R = e^{R_0 ct}$ (E) $R = e^{R_0 + ct}$.

11. The population of a city increases continuously at a rate proportional,

    at any time, to the population at that time. The population doubles

    in 50 years. After 75 years the ratio of the population P to the

    initial population P_0 is

    (A) $\frac{9}{4}$ (B) $\frac{5}{2}$ (C) $\frac{4}{1}$ (D) $\frac{2\sqrt{2}}{1}$ (E) none of these.

12. If a substance decomposes at a rate proportional to the amount of the

    substance present, and if the amount decreases from 40 gm to 10 gm in 2 hr, then the constant of proportionality is

(A) $- \ln 2$ (B) $- \frac{1}{2}$ (C) $- \frac{1}{4}$ (D) $\ln \frac{1}{4}$ (E) $\ln \frac{1}{8}$.

13. If $\frac{dy}{dx} = \frac{k}{x}$, k a constant, and if $y = 2$ when $x = 1$ and $y = 4$

when $x = e$, then when $x = 2$, $y =$

(A) 2   (B) 4   (C) $\ln 8$ (D) $\ln 2 + 2$ (E) $\ln 4 + 2$.

14. The general solution of the differential equation $(2x + y) \, dx - x \, dy = 0$

is

(A) $y = Ce^{y/2x}$ (B) $x^3 = Cy$ (C) $x^3 = y + Cx$

(D) $x^2 + y^2 = C$ (E) none of these.

15. The general solution of $2xy \, dy - (y^2 + 2x^2) \, dx = 0$ is

(A) $3xy^2 = 2x^3 + C$ (B) $y^2 + x^2 = C$ (C) $y^2 = 2x^2 + Ce^{-x}$

(D) $y^2 - 2x^2 = Cx$ (E) $y^2 = 2x^2 + C$.

16. The general solution of the nonhomogeneous linear equation

$y' + y = e^{-x}$ is

(A) $y(e^x - 1) = C$ (B) $y = Ce^x + x$ (C) $y = xe^{-x} + Ce^{-x}$

(D) $x(e^y - 1) = C$ (E) $y = cxe^{-x}$.

17. If $y = 0$ when $x = 0$ then a particular solution of the equation

$(x^2 + 1) \frac{dy}{dx} + 2xy = x^2$ is

(A) $3xy^2 + 3x = y^3$ (B) $3y(x^2 + 1) = x^3$

(C) $(x^2 + 1)y = x^3$ (D) $y(x^2 + 1) = x - \tan^{-1} x$

(E) none of these.

18. The general solution of $\cos y \, dx + 2x \sin y \, dy = \sin 2y \, dy$ is

(A) $2x \sin y - \sin 2y = C$ (B) $x \cos y + \cos 2y = C$

(C) $2x \cos y - \sin 2y = C$ (D) $x = \sec y + C \sec^2 y$

(E) $x = 2 \cos y + C \cos^2 y$.

19. If $(g'(x))^2 = g(x)$ for all real x and $g(0) = 0$, $g(4) = 4$, then $g(1)$ equals

  (A) $\frac{1}{4}$ (B) $\frac{1}{2}$ (C) 1   (D) 2   (E) 4.

20. The general solution of $y'' - 4y' - 5y = 0$ is

  (A) $y = c_1 e^x + c_2 e^{5x}$ (B) $y = c_1 e^x + c_2 e^{-5x}$

  (C) $y = e^{2x}(c_1 \cos x + c_2 \sin x)$ (D) $y = c_1 e^{-x} + c_2 e^{5x}$

  (E) $y = e^{2x}(c_1 \cos 2x + c_2 \sin 2x)$.

21. The general solution of $y'' + 4y' = 0$ is

  (A) $y = C_1(\cos 2x + C_2)$ (B) $y = c_1 e^{2x} + c_2 x e^{2x}$

  (C) $y = c_1 \cos 2x + c_2 \sin 2x$ (D) $y = c_1 e^{-4x} + c_2$

  (E) $y = c_1 e^{2x} + c_2 e^{-2x}$.

22. A particular solution of the nonhomogeneous linear differential equation $y'' + 3y' + 2y = 2x^2 + 4x$ is

  (A) $y = x^2 - x$ (B) $y = 2x^2 + x + \frac{1}{2}$ (C) $y = x^2 - x + \frac{1}{2}$

  (D) $y = e^{-x} + e^{-2x}$ (E) $y = e^{-x} + x^2 - x$.

23. A solution of the equation $y'' + 6y' + 9y = e^{-3x}$ is

  (A) $y = e^{-3x}$ (B) $y = \frac{1}{2} x^2 e^{-3x}$ (C) $y = x^2 e^{-3x}$

  (D) $y = x^2 e^{3x}$ (E) $y = x e^{3x}$.

24. A particular solution of $y'' - 4y = 3 \cos x$ is $-\frac{3}{5} \cos x$. The general solution of the equation is

  (A) $y = c_1 e^{2x} + c_2 x e^{2x} - \frac{3}{5} \cos x$ (B) $y = c_1 + c_2 e^{2x} - \frac{3}{5} \cos x$

  (C) $y = c_1 e^{2x} + c_2 e^{-2x} - \frac{3}{5} \cos x$

  (D) $y = c_1 \cos 2x + c_2 \sin 2x - \frac{3}{5} \cos x$

  (E) none of these.

25. If $\frac{d^2x}{dt^2} = -9x$ and if $x = 10$ and $\frac{dx}{dt} = 0$ when $t = 0$, then

    (A) $x = 10 \cos 3t$ (B) $x = 10 \cos (3t + \frac{\pi}{2})$

    (C) $x = 10 \cos 3t + 10 \sin 3t$ (D) $x = 10 \sin 3t$

    (E) $x = 10 \cos 3(t + \frac{\pi}{6})$.

26. The general solution of $y'' - 2y' = 4$ is

    (A) $y = -2x + C$ (B) $y = -2x + c_1 e^{2x} + c_2$

    (C) $y = c_1 e^{2x} + c_2$ (D) $y = 2x^2 + c_1 e^{2x} + c_2$

    (E) none of these.

27. A 10-1b weight stretches a spring 6 in. If the weight is drawn down a foot below the equilibrium position and then released, then $\frac{\pi}{8}$ sec after it has been released it is

    (A) 6 in. below the equilibrium position

    (B) 1 ft below the equilibrium position

    (C) at the equilibrium position

    (D) 6 in. above the equilibrium position

    (E) 1 ft above the equilibrium position.

28. A particle moving along a line is attracted towards a fixed point O with a force which is proportional to its distance from O. If it starts from rest 2 ft from O and its acceleration is 4 ft/sec^2 directed toward O when it is 1 ft from O, then its velocity after $\frac{\pi}{12}$ sec is

    (A) 1 ft/sec towards O (B) $2\sqrt{3}$ ft/sec towards O

    (C) 2 ft/sec towards O (D) 2 ft/sec away from O

    (E) 1 ft/sec away from O.

Multiple Choice Questions: Miscellaneous

1. The line through the point (2,-1) and perpendicular to the line

    $3x - y = 4$ has y-intercept

    (A) $\frac{1}{3}$ (B) $-\frac{5}{2}$ (C) 5   (D) $-\frac{1}{3}$ (E) $-\frac{5}{3}$.

2. The equation of the line with x-intercept $-\frac{1}{3}$ and slope $\frac{1}{2}$ is

    (A) $3x - 6y - 1 = 0$ (B) $3x - 6y + 2 = 0$

    (C) $3x - 6y - 2 = 0$ (D) $6x - 3y + 2 = 0$

                (E) $3x - 6y + 1 = 0$.

3. If the lines $ax + by = 3$ and $a'x + b'y = 4$ are perpendicular,

    then it follows that

    (A) $\frac{a}{b'} = \frac{b}{a'}$ (B) $ab' = -a'b$ (C) $aa' = -bb'$

    (D) $\frac{a}{a'} = \frac{b}{b'}$ (E)   none of these is true.

4. The distance between the point (3,0) and the line $x - 2y + 2 = 0$

    equals

        (A) $\sqrt{5}$ (B) $5\sqrt{5}$ (C) 1   (D) $\sqrt{2}$ (E)   none of these.

5. The equation of the circle with center (2,-3) and radius $\sqrt{13}$ is

    (A) $x^2 + y^2 - 4x + 6y = 0$ (B) $(x + 2)^2 + (y - 3)^2 = 13$

    (C) $x^2 + y^2 + 4x - 6y = 0$ (D) $x^2 + y^2 + 4x - 6y = 26$

                (E) $(x - 2)^2 + (y + 3)^2 = \sqrt{13}$.

6. The graph of the equation $x^2 - 2x + 4y - 7 = 0$ is a

    (A) hyperbola   (B) pair of straight lines

    (C) circle   (D) ellipse   (E) parabola.

7. The equation of the parabola with vertex at (2,1) and focus
    at (2,5) is

    (A) $(x - 2)^2 = 16(y - 1)$ (B) $(y - 2)^2 = 8(x - 1)$

    (C) $(x - 1)^2 = 2(y - 2)$ (D) $(y - 1)^2 = 16(x - 2)$

                    (E) $x^2 - 4x - y = 0$.

8. The graph of $y^2 = 1 + 4x + x^2$ is symmetric to

    (A) the x-axis   (B) the x-axis and the y-axis

    (C) the origin   (D) the x- and y-axes and the origin

                    (E) the y-axis.

9. The rectangular equation of the curve given parametrically by
    $x = 1 - \sin t$ and $y = 4 - 2 \cos t$ is

    (A) $4(x - 1)^2 + (y - 4)^2 = 1$ (B) $4(x - 1)^2 + (y - 4)^2 = 4$

    (C) $(x - 1)^2 + 4(y - 4)^2 = 1$ (D) $(x - 1)^2 + (y - 4)^2 = 4$

                    (E) none of these.

10. The graph of the pair of parametric equations $x = \sin t - 2$,
    $y = \cos^2 t$ is

    (A) part of a circle   (B) part of a parabola

    (C) a hyperbola   (D) a line   (E) a cycloid.

11. The distance between the centers of the two circles
    $x^2 - 4x + y^2 + 2y = 4$ and $x^2 + y^2 - 6y = 0$ is

    (A) $\sqrt{5}$ (B) $2\sqrt{5}$ (C) $2\sqrt{2}$ (D) $\sqrt{2}$ (E) 1 .

12. The set of x for which $|x - 3| \leq 2$ and for which $|x| > 4$ is

    (A) $4 < x \leq 5$ (B) $-4 < x \leq 1$ (C) $x < -4$ or $x \geq 1$

    (D) $1 \leq x < 3$ (E) none of these.

13. If $x = 2 \sin u$ and $y = \cos 2u$, then a single equation in x and y is

    (A) $x^2 + y^2 = 1$ (B) $x^2 + 4y^2 = 4$ (C) $x^2 + 2y = 2$

    (D) $x^2 + y^2 = 4$ (E) $x^2 - 2y = 2$.

14. If $f(x) = \begin{cases} x^2 & x \leq 1 \\ 2x - 1 & x > 1 \end{cases}$ then

    (A) $f(x)$ is not continuous at $x = 1$

    (B) $f(x)$ is continuous at $x = 1$ but $f'(1)$ does not exist

    (C) $f'(1)$ exists and equals 1

    (D) $f'(1) = 2$

    (E) $\lim\limits_{x \to 1} f(x)$ does not exist.

15. The curve of the pair of parametric equations $x = 2e^t$, $y = e^{-t}$ is

    (A) a straight line   (B) a parabola   (C) a hyperbola

    (D) an ellipse   (E) none of these.

16. The number of points in the set for which the inequalities $x^2 + y^2 < 9$ and $x + y \geq 5$ both hold is

    (A) 0   (B) 1   (C) 2   (D) infinite   (E) none of these.

17. The curve of $y = \dfrac{2x^2}{4 - x^2}$ has

    (A) 2 horizontal asymptotes   (B) 2 horizontal asymptotes and one vertical asymptote   (C) 2 vertical but no horizontal asymptotes   (D) 1 horizontal and 1 vertical asymptote   (E) 1 horizontal and 2 vertical asymptotes.

18. The curve of $f(x) = x \sin \dfrac{1}{x}$ is symmetric to

    (A) the y-axis   (B) the x-axis   (C) the origin

    (D) the line $y = x$ (E) none of these.

19. Which of the following sets does not define a function of x ?

      (A) $\{(0,1), (1,3), (2,3)\}$

      (B) $\{(x,y) \mid -\infty \leqq x \leqq \infty , y = x^2\}$

      (C) $\{(1,2), (2,1), (4,3), (5,4)\}$

      (D) $\{(x,y) \mid -1 \leqq x , y^2 = (x + 1)\}$

      (E) $\{(x,y) \mid x \text{ is real and } y = \pi\}$.

20. The locus of the polar equation $r = 2 \sin \theta$ is

      (A) a circle with center on the x-axis

      (B) a circle with center on the y-axis

      (C) the line $y = 2$ (D) the line $x = 2$

      (E) a circle with radius 2.

21. Which one of the following functions has a derivative at $x = 0$?

      (A) $f(x) = \sin \dfrac{1}{x}$ (B) $f(x) = |x|$

      (C) $f(x) = x|x|$ (D) $f(x) = x \sin \dfrac{1}{x}$

      (E) $f(x) = [x]$ (greatest integer function).

22. If x and y are real numbers, then the domain of the function
$f(x) = \sqrt{x^2 - 4}$ is

      (A) $|x| \geqq 2$ (B) $|x| \leqq 2$ (C) $x > 2$ or $x < -2$

      (D) all x except $x = 2$ or -2 (E) all x .

*23. The area bounded by the lemniscate with polar equation $r^2 = 2 \cos 2\theta$
is equal to

      (A) 4   (B) 1   (C) $\dfrac{1}{2}$ (D) 2   (E) none of these.

*24. The area inside the circle $r = 3 \sin \theta$ and outside the cardioid

$r = 1 + \sin \theta$ is given by

(A) $\displaystyle \int_{\frac{\pi}{6}}^{\frac{\pi}{2}} \left[9 \sin^2 \theta - (1 + \sin \theta)^2 \right] d\theta$

(B) $\displaystyle \int_{\frac{\pi}{6}}^{\frac{\pi}{2}} (2 \sin \theta - 1)^2 \, d\theta$ (C) $\displaystyle \frac{1}{2} \int_{\frac{\pi}{6}}^{\frac{5\pi}{6}} (8 \sin^2 \theta - 1) \, d\theta$

(D) $\displaystyle \frac{9\pi}{4} - \frac{1}{2} \int_{\frac{\pi}{6}}^{\frac{5\pi}{6}} (1 + \sin \theta)^2 \, d\theta$ (E) none of these.

25. The graph of the polar equation $r = \theta$, where θ is a real number, is

(A) a circle   (B) a hyperbolic spiral asymptotic to the

line $y = 1$ (C) a straight line of slope 1   (D) a

pair of straight lines passing through the origin

(E) a double spiral which passes through the origin.

26. The graphs of $y = x^2 + 1$ and $x^2 - y^2 = 1$ have the following

points in common:

(A) (1,2) and (-1,2)   (B) (1,0)   (C) (0,1)

(D) (1,0), (-1,0), (0,1), and (0,-1)   (E) none of these.

27. Which of the following functions is continuous at $x = 0$?

(A) $f(x) \begin{cases} = \sin \dfrac{1}{x} & x \neq 0 \\ \\ = 0 & x = 0 \end{cases}$

(B) $f(x) = [x]$ (greatest integer function)

(C) $f(x) \begin{cases} = \dfrac{x}{x} & x \neq 0 \\ \\ = 0 & x = 0 \end{cases}$

(D) $f(x) \begin{cases} = x \sin \dfrac{1}{x} & x \neq 0 \\ \\ = 0 & x = 0 \end{cases}$

(E) $f(x) = \dfrac{x + 1}{x}$.

28.   If the curve of the function $y = f(x)$ is symmetric to the origin then it follows that

   (A) $f(0) = 0$ (B) $f(-x) = -f(x)$ (C) $f(-x) = f(x)$

   (D) the curve is also symmetric to both the x- and y-axes

   (E) none of the preceding is necessary.

29.   The locus of points whose distance from the line $x = 1$ is twice that from the point $(-1,0)$ is

   (A) a parabola   (B) a circle   (C) an ellipse

   (D) a hyperbola   (E) a straight line.

30.   If the graph of a function is as shown, then the function $f(x)$ could be given by

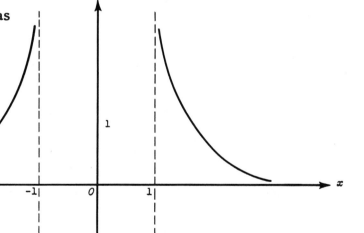

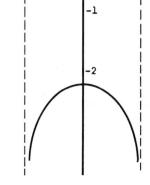

   (A) $f(x) = \dfrac{x + 2}{x^2 - 1}$

   (B) $f(x) = \dfrac{1}{1 - x^2}$

   (C) $f(x) = \dfrac{x^2 - 1}{x^2 + 1}$

   (D) $f(x) = \dfrac{2}{x^2 - 1}$

   (E) $f(x) = \dfrac{2}{1 - x^2}$.

31. If the graph of a function is as shown, then the function $f(x)$ could be given by

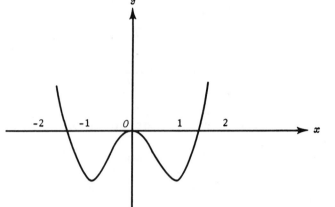

(A) $f(x) = x^4 - 2x^2$

(B) $f(x) = x^3 - 2x^2$

(C) $f(x) = x^3 - 2x$

(D) $f(x) = x(x - 2)^2$

(E) $f(x) = 2x^2 - x^4$.

32. If $\lim\limits_{x \to c} f(x) = L$ (L a finite number) then it follows that

(A) $f'(c)$ exists   (B) $f(x)$ is continuous at $x = c$

(C) $f(c) = L$ (D) $f(c)$ is defined

(E)   none of the preceding is necessary.

33. A function $f(x)$ equals $\dfrac{x^2 - x}{x - 1}$ for all x except $x = 1$. In order that the function be continuous at $x = 1$, the value of $f(1)$ must be

(A) 0   (B) 1   (C) 2   (D) ∞ (E) none of these.

34. If $f(u) = e^u$ and $g(u) = \ln u$ then $f(g(u))$ equals

(A) $(\ln u)\, e$ (B)   1   (C) u (D) e^{-u} (E) e .

*35. The graph of the polar equation $r = \dfrac{1}{\sin \theta - 2 \cos \theta}$ is

(A)   a line with slope 2   (B)   a line with slope 1

(C)   a circle   (D)   a parabola   (E)   a semicircle.

36. If the tangent to the curve $ky^2 + xy = 2 - k$ at the point (-2,1) passes through the origin, then k equals

(A) 0   (B) -2   (C) 1   (D) -1   (E) 2 .

37. Which of the following statements about the graph of $y = \dfrac{x^2 + 1}{x^2 - 1}$

is not true?

    (A) the graph is symmetric to the y-axis

    (B) the graph has two vertical asymptotes

    (C) there is no y-intercept

    (D) the graph has one horizontal asymptote

    (E) there is no x-intercept.

38. A circle has center at $(2,-1)$ and is tangent to the line $x + 2y + 5 = 0$.
Its equation is

    (A) $x^2 + y^2 - 4x + 2y = 10$ (B) $x^2 + y^2 - 4x + 2y = 0$

    (C) $(x - 2)^2 + (y + 1)^2 = 25$

    (D) $x^2 + y^2 + 4x - 2y = 0$ (E) none of these.

39. The equation of the locus of a point $P(x,y)$, which moves so that the
product of the slopes of the lines joining it to $(2,0)$ and to $(-3,1)$
is 1, is

    (A) $y^2 - x^2 - x - y + 6 = 0$ (B) $y = x^2 + x - 5$

    (C) $x^2 + y^2 + x + y - 6 = 0$ (D) $x^2 - y^2 - x - y + 6 = 0$

    (E) $y^2 - x^2 + y - 6 = 0$.

40. If $f(x) = 2x - \dfrac{2}{x}$, then $f(\tfrac{1}{x})$ equals

    (A) $f(x)$ (B) $f(-\tfrac{1}{x})$ (C) $-f(-x)$

    (D) $-f(x)$ (E) none of these.

Practice Examinations

1. $\lim\limits_{x\to\infty} \dfrac{3x^2 - 4}{2 - 7x - x^2}$ is

   (A) 3   (B) 1   (C) -3   (D) ∞ (E) 0 .

2. The value of k for which the line $3x + ky - 5 = 0$ is perpendicular to the line $x - 2y + 7 = 0$ is

   (A) $\dfrac{3}{2}$ (B) $-\dfrac{3}{2}$ (C) 6   (D) -6   (E) $\dfrac{2}{3}$.

3. $\lim\limits_{h\to 0} \dfrac{\cos\left(\frac{\pi}{2} + h\right)}{h}$ is

   (A) 1   (B) nonexistent   (C) 0   (D) -1   (E) none of these.

4. The distance between the point $(1,-2)$ and the line $4x - 3y - 5 = 0$ is

   (A) $\sqrt{10}$ (B) 2   (C) 1   (D) $\dfrac{16}{5}$ (E) none of these.

5. The equation of the parabola with vertex at $(2,1)$ and focus at $(2,0)$ is

   (A) $x^2 - 4x - 4y + 8 = 0$ (B) $4y^2 - 8y + x + 2 = 0$

   (C) $y^2 - 4x - 2y + 9 = 0$ (D) $x^2 - 2x + 4y - 7 = 0$

   (E) $x^2 - 4x + 4y = 0$.

6. The graph of $(x + 1)^2 - (y - 3)^2 = 0$ consists of

   (A) a hyperbola   (B) a point   (C) an ellipse

   (D) two intersecting lines   (E) two parallel lines.

7. The maximum value of the function $f(x) = x^4 - 4x^3 + 6$ on the closed interval $[1,4]$ is

    (A) 1   (B) 0   (C) 3   (D) 6   (E) none of these.

8. The equation of the cubic with a relative maximum at $(0,0)$ and a point of inflection at $(1,-2)$ is

    (A) $y = x^3 - 3x^2$ (B) $y = -x^3 + 3x^2$

    (C) $y = 4x^3 - 6x^2$ (D) $y = x^3 - 3x$

    (E) $y = 3x - x^3$.

9. If $f(x)$ is continuous at the point where $x = a$, which of the following statements may be false?

    (A) $\lim\limits_{x \to a} f(x)$ exists   (B) $\lim\limits_{x \to a} f(x) = f(a)$

    (C) $f'(a)$ exists   (D) $f(a)$ is defined

    (E) $\lim\limits_{x \to a^-} f(x) = \lim\limits_{x \to a^+} f(x)$.

10. Which of the following functions is not everywhere continuous?

    (A) $y = |x|$ (B) $y = \dfrac{x}{x^2 + 1}$ (C) $y = \sqrt{x^2 + 8}$

    (D) $y = x^{2/3}$ (E) $y = \dfrac{4}{(x + 1)^2}$.

11. The equation of the tangent to the curve of $y = x^2 - 4x$ at the point where the curve crosses the y-axis is

    (A) $y = 8x - 4$ (B) $y = -4x$ (C) $y = -4$

    (D) $y = 4x$ (E) $y = 4x - 8$.

12. If y is a differentiable function of x, then the slope of the curve of $xy^2 - 2y + 4y^3 = 6$ at the point where $y = 1$ is

    (A) $-\dfrac{1}{18}$ (B) $-\dfrac{1}{26}$ (C) $\dfrac{5}{18}$ (D) $-\dfrac{11}{18}$ (E) 2 .

13. If $x = 2t - 1$ and $y = 3 - 4t^2$ then $\frac{dy}{dx}$ is

    (A) $4t$ (B) $-4t$ (C) $-\dfrac{1}{4t}$ (D) $2(x + 1)$

    (E) $-4(x + 1)$.

*14. A curve is given parametrically by $x = e^t$ and $y = 2e^{-t}$. The equation of the tangent to the curve at $t = 0$ is

    (A) $2x + y = 0$ (B) $x + 2y = 5$ (C) $y = -2x + 5$

    (D) $2x + y = 4$ (E) $y = 2x$.

15. If, for all x, $f'(x) = (x - 2)^4 (x - 1)^3$, it follows that the function f has

    (A) a relative minimum at $x = 1$

    (B) a relative maximum at $x = 1$

    (C) both a relative minimum at $x = 1$ and a relative maximum at $x = 2$

    (D) neither a relative maximum nor a relative minimum

    (E) relative minima at $x = 1$ and at $x = 2$.

16. If a particle's motion along a straight line is given by

    $s = t^3 - 6t^2 + 9t + 2$, then s is increasing

    (A) when $1 < t < 3$ (B) when $-1 < t < 3$

    (C) for all t (D) when $|t| > 3$

    (E) when $t < 1$ or $t > 3$.

17. Which of the following statements is *not* true of the graph of $y^2 = x^3 - x$?

    (A) It is symmetric to the x-axis.

    (B) It intersects the x-axis at 0, 1, and -1.

    (C) It exists only for $|x| \leqq 1$.

    (D) It has no horizontal asymptotes.

    (E) It has no vertical asymptotes.

18. The area in the first quadrant bounded by the curve $y = x^2$ and the

line $y - x - 2 = 0$ is equal to

(A) $\frac{3}{2}$ (B) $\frac{2}{3}$ (C) $\frac{7}{6}$ (D) $\frac{10}{3}$ (E) $\frac{9}{2}$.

*19. If differentials are used for the evaluation, then $\sqrt[4]{15}$ is approximately

equal to

(A) 2.97   (B) 1.97   (C) 2.03   (D) 1.99   (E) 1.94 .

20. The curve of the equation $(x^2 - 1)y = x^2 - 4$ has

(A) one horizontal and one vertical asymptote

(B) two vertical but no horizontal asymptotes

(C) one horizontal and two vertical asymptotes

(D) two horizontal and two vertical asymptotes

(E) neither a horizontal nor a vertical asymptote.

*21. If $\frac{dy}{dx} = \cos x \cos^2 y$ and $y = \frac{\pi}{4}$ when $x = 0$, then

(A) $\tan y = \sin x + 1$ (B) $\tan y = -\sin x + 1$

(C) $\sec^2 y = \sin x + 2$ (D) $\tan y = \frac{1}{2}(\cos^2 x + 1)$

(E) $\tan y = \sin x - \frac{\sqrt{2}}{2}$.

22. If $f(x) = \cos x \sin 3x$, then $f'(\frac{\pi}{6})$ is equal to

(A) $\frac{1}{2}$ (B) $-\frac{\sqrt{3}}{2}$ (C) 0   (D) 1   (E) $-\frac{1}{2}$.

*23. The region in the first quadrant bounded by the x-axis, the y-axis,

and the curve of $y = e^{-x}$ is rotated about the x-axis. The volume

of the solid obtained is equal to

(A) π (B) 2π (C) $\frac{1}{2}$ (D) $\frac{\pi}{2}$ (E) none of these.

24. If $y = x^2 \ln x$, $(x > 0)$, then y'' is equal to

(A) $3 + \ln x$ (B) $3 + 2 \ln x$ (C) $3 \ln x$

(D) $3 + 3 \ln x$ (E) $2 + x + \ln x$.

25. $\int_0^1 \dfrac{x\ dx}{x^2 + 1}$ is equal to

   (A) $\dfrac{\pi}{4}$ (B) $\ln \sqrt{2}$ (C) $\frac{1}{2}(\ln 2 - 1)$ (D) $\dfrac{3}{2}$ (E) $\ln 2$.

26. $\int_0^{\pi/2} \sin^2 x\ dx$ is equal to

   (A) $\dfrac{1}{3}$ (B) $\dfrac{\pi}{4} - \dfrac{1}{4}$ (C) $\dfrac{\pi}{2}$ (D) $\dfrac{\pi}{2} - \dfrac{1}{3}$ (E) $\dfrac{\pi}{4}$.

27. The acceleration of a particle moving along a straight line is given
   by $a = 6t$. If, when $t = 0$, its velocity, v, is 1 and its distance, s,
   is 3, then at any time t

   (A) $s = t^3 + 3$ (B) $s = t^3 + 3t + 1$ (C) $s = t^3 + t + 3$

   (D) $s = \dfrac{t^3}{3} + t + 3$ (E) $s = \dfrac{t^3}{3} + \dfrac{t^2}{2} + 3$.

28. If $y = f(x^2)$ and $f'(x) = \sqrt{5x - 1}$, then $\dfrac{dy}{dx}$ is equal to

   (A) $2x\sqrt{5x^2 - 1}$ (B) $\sqrt{5x - 1}$ (C) $2x\sqrt{5x - 1}$

   (D) $\dfrac{\sqrt{5x - 1}}{2x}$ (E) none of these.

29. The equation of the ellipse with center at the origin and with a focus
   and a vertex respectively at (2,0) and (3,0) is

   (A) $13x^2 + 9y^2 = 117$ (B) $9x^2 + 5y^2 = 45$

   (C) $5x^2 - 9y^2 = 45$ (D) $5x^2 + 9y^2 = 45$

   (E) $5x^2 + 4y^2 = 20$.

*30. $\int_0^1 xe^x\ dx$ equals

   (A) 1   (B) -1   (C) $2 - e$ (D) $\dfrac{e^2}{2} - e$ (E) $e - 1$.

31. A 26-foot ladder leans against a building so that its foot moves away
   from the building at the rate of 3 feet per second. When the foot of
   the ladder is 10 feet from the building, then the top is moving down
   at the rate of r ft/sec, where r is

(A) $\dfrac{46}{3}$ (B) $\dfrac{3}{4}$ (C) $\dfrac{5}{4}$ (D) $\dfrac{5}{2}$ (E) $\dfrac{4}{5}$.

*32. If the arc of the curve $y^2 = x$ between $(0,0)$ and $(2,\sqrt{2})$ is rotated about the x-axis, then the area of the surface generated is equal to

(A) $\dfrac{104\pi}{3}$ (B) $\dfrac{13\pi}{3}$ (C) $\dfrac{\pi}{6}(17\sqrt{17} - 1)$

(D) 5π (E) none of these.

33. If $\dfrac{dx}{dt} = kx$ and if $x = 2$ when $t = 0$ and $x = 6$ when $t = 1$, then k equals

(A) $\ln 4$ (B) 8 (C) e^3 (D) 3 (E) none of these.

34. The locus of the polar equation $r = 2 \sec \theta$ is

(A) a circle   (B) a vertical line

(C) a horizontal line   (D) a parabola

(E) an oblique line through the pole.

35. If $f(x) = \sqrt{1 - \dfrac{2}{x}}$ and $g(x) = \dfrac{1}{x}$, $(x \neq 0)$, then the derivative of $f(g(x))$ is equal to

(A) 0 (B) $\dfrac{1}{x^2\sqrt{1 - \dfrac{2}{x}}}$ (C) does not exist

(D) $-\dfrac{1}{\sqrt{1 - 2x}}$ (E) $\dfrac{-2}{(x^2 - 2)^{3/2}}$.

*36. A hemispherical tank of radius 4 ft is filled with a liquid weighing w lb/ft^3. The work done in pumping all the liquid just to the top of the tank, expressed in foot-pounds, is

(A) $128\pi w$ (B) $\dfrac{256}{3}\pi w$ (C) $\dfrac{320}{3}\pi w$ (D) $96\pi w$ (E) $64\pi w$.

37. Which one of the following functions does not satisfy the hypotheses of Rolles' Theorem?

(A) $f(x) = \dfrac{x^2 - 9x}{x - 2}$

(B) $f(x) = x^2 - 3x$

(C) $f(x) = \dfrac{x^2 - 1}{x^2 + 1}$

(D) $f(x) = (x - 1)(e^x - 1)$

(E) $f(x) = \dfrac{x^2 - x}{x + 1}$.

*38. $\displaystyle\lim_{n\to\infty} \dfrac{1}{n}\left[\dfrac{1}{n^2} + \left(\dfrac{2}{n}\right)^2 + \left(\dfrac{3}{n}\right)^2 + \dots + \left(\dfrac{n}{n}\right)^2\right]$ is

(A) ln 2   (B) ¼   (C) $\dfrac{1}{3}$ (D) 0   (E) ∞ .

39. The first quadrant area under the curve $y = \dfrac{1}{\sqrt{1 - x^2}}$ and bounded at the right by $x = 1$ is

(A) ∞   (B) $\dfrac{\pi}{2}$ (C) $\dfrac{\pi}{4}$ (D) 2   (E) none of these.

40. The curve of $y = \dfrac{1 - x}{x - 3}$ is concave up when

(A) $x > 3$ (B) $1 < x < 3$ (C) $x > 1$

(D) $x < 1$ (E) $x < 3$.

41. The area of the largest isosceles triangle that can be drawn with one vertex at the origin and with the others on a line parallel to the x-axis and on the curve $y = 27 - x^2$ is

(A) 108   (B) 27   (C) $12\sqrt{3}$ (D) 54   (E) $24\sqrt{3}$.

42. The average (mean) value of $\tan x$ on the interval from $x = 0$ to $x = \dfrac{\pi}{3}$ is

(A) ln 2   (B) $\dfrac{3}{\pi}$ ln 2   (C) ln ½   (D) $\dfrac{9}{\pi}$ (E) $\dfrac{\sqrt{3}}{2}$.

*43. A particle moves along the curve given parametrically by $x = \tan t$ and $y = \sec t$. At the instant when $t = \frac{\pi}{6}$, its speed equals

     (A) $\sqrt{2}$ (B) $2\sqrt{7}$ (C) $\frac{2\sqrt{5}}{3}$ (D) $\frac{2\sqrt{13}}{3}$ (E) none of these.

44. If $y = \sin(x^2 - 1)$ and $x = \sqrt{u^2 + 1}$, then $\frac{dy}{du}$ equals

     (A) $\frac{u \cos u^2}{\sqrt{1 + u^2}}$ (B) $\cos u^2$ (C) $\frac{\cos u^2}{2\sqrt{1 + u^2}}$

     (D) $2u \cos u^2$ (E) $\frac{u \cos(x^2 - 1)}{\sqrt{1 + u^2}}$.

45. If $f(x) = x^n$, n a positive integer, the first derivative of $f(x)$ which is identically zero is

     (A) the nth   (B) the $(n-1)$st   (C) the $(n+2)$nd

     (D) the first   (E) the $(n+1)$st .

Practice Examination: 2

---

1. $\lim\limits_{x \to \infty} \frac{20x^2 - 13x + 5}{5 - 4x^3}$ is

     (A) -5   (B) ∞ (C) 0   (D) 5   (E) 1 .

2. $\lim\limits_{x \to \frac{\pi}{2}} \frac{\cos x}{x - \frac{\pi}{2}}$ is

     (A) -1   (B) 1   (C) 0   (D) ∞ (E) none of these.

3. $\lim\limits_{x \to 0} x \sin \frac{1}{x}$ is

     (A) 1   (B) 0   (C) ∞ (D) -1   (E) none of these.

4. $\lim\limits_{h \to 0} \frac{\ln(2 + h) - \ln 2}{h}$ is

     (A) 0   (B) $\ln 2$ (C) $\frac{1}{2}$ (D) $\frac{1}{\ln 2}$ (E) ∞ .

5. If $y = \dfrac{x - 3}{2 - 5x}$ then $\dfrac{dy}{dx}$ equals

   (A) $\dfrac{17 - 10x}{(2 - 5x)^2}$ (B) $\dfrac{13}{(2 - 5x)^2}$ (C) $\dfrac{x - 3}{(2 - 5x)^2}$

   (D) $\dfrac{17}{(2 - 5x)^2}$ (E) $\dfrac{-13}{(2 - 5x)^2}$.

6. If $y = e^{-x^2}$ then $y''(0)$ equals

   (A) 2   (B) -2   (C) $\dfrac{2}{e}$ (D) 0   (E) -4 .

7. If $f(x) = x \cos \dfrac{1}{x}$, then $f'(\dfrac{2}{\pi})$ equals

   (A) $\dfrac{\pi}{2}$ (B) $-\dfrac{2}{\pi}$ (C) -1   (D) $-\dfrac{\pi}{2}$ (E) 1 .

8. If $xy^2 - 3x + 4y - 2 = 0$ and y is a differentiable function of x , then $\dfrac{dy}{dx}$ equals

   (A) $-\dfrac{1 + y^2}{2xy}$ (B) $\dfrac{3}{2y + 4}$ (C) $\dfrac{3}{2xy + 4}$

   (D) $\dfrac{3 - y^2}{2xy + 4}$ (E) $\dfrac{5 - y^2}{2xy + 4}$.

9. If $x = \sqrt{1 - t^2}$ and $y = \sin^{-1} t$ then $\dfrac{dy}{dx}$ equals

   (A) $-\dfrac{\sqrt{1 - t^2}}{t}$ (B) $-t$ (C) $\dfrac{t}{1 - t^2}$

   (D) 2   (E) $-\dfrac{1}{t}$.

10. If y is a differentiable function of x , then the derivative of $\sin^2 (x + y)$ with respect to x is

   (A) $2[\sin (x + y)] \dfrac{dy}{dx}$ (B) $[\cos^2 (x + y)](1 + \dfrac{dy}{dx})$

   (C) $[\sin 2(x + y)](1 + \dfrac{dy}{dx})$ (D) $\cos^2 (x + y)$

   (E) $2 \sin (x + y)$.

11. The equation of the tangent to the curve $y = e^x \ln x$ where $x = 1$ is

    (A) $y = ex$ (B) $y = e^x + 1$ (C) $y = e(x - 1)$

    (D) $y = ex + 1$ (E) $y = x - 1$.

*12. If differentials are used for computation, then $\sqrt[3]{63}$ is approximately equal, to the nearest hundredth, to

    (A) 4.00   (B) 3.98   (C) 3.93   (D) 3.80   (E) 3.88 .

13. The hypotenuse AB of a right triangle ABC is 5 ft and one leg AC is decreasing at the rate of 2 ft/sec. The rate in ft^2/sec at which the area is changing when $AC = 3$ is

    (A) $\frac{25}{4}$ (B) $\frac{7}{4}$ (C) $-\frac{3}{2}$ (D) $-\frac{7}{4}$ (E) $-\frac{7}{2}$.

14. The derivative of a function f is given for all x by $f'(x) = x^2(x + 1)^3(x - 4)^2$. The set of x for which f is a relative maximum is

    (A) $\{0, -1, 4\}$ (B) $\{-1\}$ (C) $\{0, 4\}$

    (D) $\{1\}$ (E) none of these.

15. The position of a point P on a line at time t is given by $s = t^3 + t^2 - t - 3$. P is moving to the right for

    (A) $t > -1$ (B) $t < -\frac{1}{3}$ or $t > 1$

    (C) $t < -1$ or $t > \frac{1}{3}$ (D) $-1 < t < \frac{1}{3}$

    (E) $t < \frac{1}{3}$.

16. If the displacement from the origin of a particle on a line is given by $s = 3 + (t - 2)^4$, then the number of times the particle reverses direction is

    (A) 0   (B) 1   (C) 2   (D) 3   (E) none of these.

*17. If a particle moves in a plane so that $x = 2 \cos 3t$ and $y = \sin 3t$, then its speed on the interval $0 \leq t < \frac{\pi}{2}$ is a maximum when t equals

(A) 0   (B) $\frac{\pi}{6}$ (C) $\frac{\pi}{4}$ (D) $\frac{\pi}{3}$ (E) $\frac{\pi}{2}$.

18. The maximum value of the function $f(x) = xe^{-x}$ is

(A) $\frac{1}{e}$ (B) e (C) 1   (D) -1   (E) none of these.

19. A rectangle of perimeter 18 inches is rotated about one of its sides to generate a right circular cylinder. The rectangle which generates the cylinder of largest volume has area (in in.^{2}) of

(A) 14   (B) 20   (C) $\frac{81}{4}$ (D) 18   (E) $\frac{77}{4}$.

20. If $f'(x)$ exists on the closed interval $[a, b]$, then it follows that

(A) $f(x)$ is constant on $[a, b]$

(B) there exists a number c, $a < c < b$, such that $f'(c) = 0$

(C) the function has a maximum value on the open interval (a, b)

(D) the function has a minimum value on the open interval (a, b)

(E) the mean value theorem applies.

21. $\int_1^2 (3x - 2)^3 \, dx$ is equal to

(A) $\frac{16}{3}$ (B) $\frac{63}{4}$ (C) $\frac{13}{3}$ (D) $\frac{85}{4}$ (E) none of these.

22. $\int_{\frac{\pi}{4}}^{\frac{\pi}{2}} \sin^3 \alpha \cos \alpha \, d\alpha$ is equal to

(A) $\frac{3}{16}$ (B) $\frac{1}{8}$ (C) $-\frac{1}{8}$ (D) $-\frac{3}{16}$ (E) $\frac{3}{4}$.

23. $\int x \cos x^2 \, dx$ equals

    (A) $\sin x^2 + C$ (B) $2 \sin x^2 + C$

    (C) $-\frac{1}{2} \sin x^2 + C$ (D) $\frac{1}{4} \cos^2 x^2 + C$

    (E) $\frac{1}{2} \sin x^2 + C$.

24. $\int_0^1 \dfrac{e^x}{(2 - e^x)^2} \, dx$ equals

    (A) $2 \ln (e - 2)$ (B) 1 (C) $\dfrac{1}{2 - e}$

    (D) $\dfrac{e - 1}{2 - e}$ (E) none of these.

*25. If we let $x = 2 \sin \theta$, then $\displaystyle\int_0^2 \dfrac{x^2 \, dx}{\sqrt{4 - x^2}}$ is equivalent to

    (A) $4 \displaystyle\int_0^1 \sin^2 \theta \, d\theta$ (B) $\displaystyle\int_0^{\frac{\pi}{2}} 4 \sin^2 \theta \, d\theta$

    (C) $\displaystyle\int_0^{\frac{\pi}{2}} 2 \sin \theta \tan \theta \, d\theta$ (D) $\displaystyle\int_0^2 \dfrac{2 \sin^2 \theta}{\cos^2 \theta} \, d\theta$

                (E) $4 \displaystyle\int_{\frac{\pi}{2}}^0 \sin^2 \theta \, d\theta$.

26. $\int \dfrac{x^2 + x - 1}{x^2 - x} \, dx$ equals

    (A) $x + 2 \ln |x^2 - x| + C$ (B) $\ln |x| + \ln |x - 1| + C$

    (C) $1 + \ln |x^2 - x| + C$ (D) $x + \ln |x^2 - x| + C$

        (E) $x - \ln |x| - \ln |x - 1| + C$.

27. $\int_{-1}^1 (1 - |x|) \, dx$ equals

    (A) 0 (B) $\frac{1}{2}$ (C) 1 (D) 2 (E) none of these.

28. $\displaystyle\int_{-1}^{0} e^{-x}\, dx$ equals

    (A)　$1 - e$　　(B)　$\dfrac{1 - e}{e}$　　(C)　$e - 1$

    (D)　$1 - \dfrac{1}{e}$　　(E)　$e + 1$.

29. The general solution of the differential equation $\dfrac{dy}{dx} = \dfrac{1 - 2x}{y}$

is a family of

    (A)　straight lines　　(B)　circles　　(C)　hyperbolas

    (D)　parabolas　　(E)　ellipses.

30. If $F'(x) = G'(x)$ for all x and k is a constant, then it is necessary that

    (A)　$F(x) = G(x) + k$　　　　(B)　$F(x) = G(x)$

    (C)　$F(k) = G(k)$　　　　　　(D)　$F(x) = kG(x)$

              (E)　$F(x) = G(x + k)$.

31. The area enclosed by the curve of $y^2 = x^3$ and the line segment joining $(1,1)$ and $(4,-8)$ is given by

    (A)　$2\displaystyle\int_{0}^{1} x^{3/2}\, dx + \int_{1}^{4} (-3x + 4 - x^{3/2})\, dx$

    (B)　$2\displaystyle\int_{0}^{1} x^{3/2}\, dx + \int_{1}^{4} (4 - 3x + x^{3/2})\, dx$

    (C)　$\displaystyle\int_{0}^{4} (4 - 3x - x^{3/2})\, dx$

    (D)　$2\displaystyle\int_{0}^{1} x^{3/2}\, dx + \int_{-8}^{1} \left(\dfrac{4 - y}{3} - y^{2/3}\right) dy$

    (E)　$\displaystyle\int_{1}^{4} (x^{3/2} + 3x - 4)\, dx$.

32. The first quadrant area bounded below by the x-axis and laterally

by the curves of $y = x^2$ and $y = 4 - x^2$ equals

(A) $6 - 2\sqrt{3}$ (B) $\frac{10}{3}$ (C) $\frac{8}{3}(2 - \sqrt{2})$

(D) $\frac{4\sqrt{2}}{3}$ (E) none of these.

33. The equation of the curve shown is

$y = \dfrac{4}{1 + x^2}$. The area of the

shaded region of the rectangle

equals

(A) $4 - \dfrac{\pi}{4}$ (B) $8 - 2\pi$

(C) $8 - \pi$ (D) $8 - \dfrac{\pi}{2}$

(E) $2\pi - 4$.

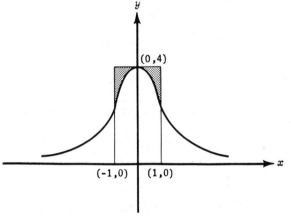

*34. A curve is given parametrically by the equations $x = t$, $y = 1 - \cos t$.
The area bounded by the curve and the x-axis on the interval $0 \leq t \leq 2\pi$
is equal to

(A) $2(\pi + 1)$ (B) π (C) 4π (D) $\pi + 1$ (E) 2π .

*35. The volume of an "inner tube" with inner diameter 4 ft and outer
diameter 8 ft is, in ft^3,

(A) $4\pi^2$ (B) $12\pi^2$ (C) $8\pi^2$ (D) $24\pi^2$ (E) $6\pi^2$.

36. The volume generated by rotating the region bounded by $y = \dfrac{1}{\sqrt{x}}$,

$x = 1$, $x = 4$, and $y = 0$ about the y-axis is

(A) $\dfrac{28\pi}{3}$ (B) $\pi \ln 4$ (C) $\dfrac{64\pi}{3}$ (D) $\dfrac{14\pi}{3}$ (E) $\dfrac{16\pi}{3}$.

37. If $f(x)$ and $g(x)$ are both continuous functions on the closed

interval $[a,b]$, if $f(a) = g(a)$ and $f(b) = g(b)$, and if, further, $f(x) > g(x)$ for all x , $a < x < b$, then it follows

that

(A) $\displaystyle\int_a^b f(x)\ dx \geqq 0$

(B) $\displaystyle\int_a^b |g(x)|\ dx \ > \ \int_a^b |f(x)|\ dx$

(C) $\displaystyle\int_a^b |f(x)|\ dx \ > \ \int_a^b |g(x)|\ dx$

(D) $\displaystyle\int_a^b f(x)\ dx \ > \ \int_a^b g(x)\ dx$

(E)   none of the preceding is necessary.

*38.   The length of the arc of $y = \frac{1}{2}(e^x + e^{-x})$ from $x = 0$ to $x = 1$ equals

(A) $\frac{1}{2}(e + e^{-1})$ (B) $\frac{1}{2}(e - e^{-1})$ (C) $e - \frac{1}{e}$

(D) $e + \frac{1}{e} - 2$ (E) $\frac{1}{2}(e + \frac{1}{e}) - 1$.

*39.   The area of the surface of revolution generated if one arch of the

cycloid $x = \theta - \sin \theta$, $y = 1 - \cos \theta$ is rotated about the x-axis

is given by the integral

(A) $\displaystyle 4\pi \int_0^{2\pi} \sin \frac{\theta}{2}\ d\theta$ (B) $\displaystyle 2\sqrt{2}\pi \int_0^{\pi} (1 - \cos \theta)^{1/2}\ d\theta$

(C) $\displaystyle 2\sqrt{2}\pi \int_0^{2\pi} (1 - \cos \theta)^{3/2}\ d\theta$ (D) $\displaystyle 2\sqrt{2}\pi \int_0^{2\pi} (\theta - \sin \theta)\sqrt{1 - \cos \theta}\ d\theta$

(E)   none of these.

40.   A particle moves along a line with velocity (in ft/sec) $v = t^2 - t$.

The total distance (in ft) travelled from $t = 0$ to $t = 2$ equals

(A) $\frac{1}{3}$ (B) $\frac{2}{3}$ (C) 2   (D) 1   (E) $\frac{4}{3}$.

*41. $\displaystyle\lim_{n\to\infty} \frac{\sqrt{1} + \sqrt{2} + \ldots + \sqrt{n}}{n^{3/2}}$ is equal to the definite integral

(A) $\displaystyle\int_0^1 \sqrt{x}\, dx$ (B) $\displaystyle\int_0^1 \frac{1}{\sqrt{x}}\, dx$ (C) $\displaystyle\int_1^2 \sqrt{x}\, dx$

(D) $\displaystyle\int_0^1 \frac{1}{x}\, dx$ (E) none of these.

*42. A force of 20 lb compresses a spring from its natural length of 30 inches to 26 inches. The work done (in inch-lb) in compressing it from 26 inches to 22 inches is equal to

(A) 20   (B) 40   (C) 80   (D) 120   (E) 240 .

43. The lines $x - ky = 3$ and $kx + y = 4$ are perpendicular for

(A) no real k (B) $k = 0$ only   (C) $k = 1$ only

(D) $k = -1$ only   (E) all real k .

44. The cartesian equation of the polar curve $r = 2 \sin\theta + 2 \cos\theta$ is

(A) $(x - 1)^2 + (y - 1)^2 = 2$ (B) $x^2 + y^2 = 2$

(C) $x + y = 2$ (D) $x^2 + y^2 = 4$ (E) $y^2 - x^2 = 4$.

45. If x and y are real numbers, the domain of the function

$f(x) = \dfrac{\sqrt{x^2 + 1}}{4 - x}$ is

(A) all x except $x = 2$ or $x = -2$ (B) all x except $x = 4$

(C) $|x| \le 1$ (D) $x > 1$ or $x < -1$ (E) all x .

Practice Examination: 3

1. $\displaystyle\lim_{x\to 2} \frac{x^2 - 2}{4 - x^2}$ is

(A) -2   (B) -1   (C) $-\dfrac{1}{2}$ (D) 0   (E) nonexistent.

2. $\lim\limits_{x\to\infty} \dfrac{\sqrt{x} - 4}{4 - 3\sqrt{x}}$ is

   (A) $-\dfrac{1}{3}$ (B) -1 (C) ∞ (D) 0 (E) $\dfrac{1}{3}$.

3. $\lim\limits_{x\to 0} \dfrac{\sin^2 \frac{x}{2}}{x^2}$ is

   (A) 4 (B) 0 (C) $\dfrac{1}{4}$ (D) 2 (E) nonexistent.

4. $\lim\limits_{x\to 0} \dfrac{e^x - 1}{x}$ is

   (A) 1 (B) e (C) $\dfrac{1}{e}$ (D) 0 (E) nonexistent.

5. The slope of $y = |x|$ at the point where $x = \dfrac{1}{2}$ is

   (A) -1 (B) 0 (C) $\dfrac{1}{2}$ (D) 1 (E) nonexistent.

6. If $y = \dfrac{e^{\ln u}}{u}$ then $\dfrac{dy}{du}$ equals

   (A) $\dfrac{e^{\ln u}}{u^2}$ (B) $e^{\ln u}$ (C) $\dfrac{2e^{\ln u}}{u^2}$ (D) 1 (E) 0 .

7. If $y = \sin^3 (1 - 2x)$ then $\dfrac{dy}{dx}$ is

   (A) $3 \sin^2 (1 - 2x)$ (B) $-2 \cos^3 (1 - 2x)$

   (C) $-6 \sin^2 (1 - 2x)$ (D) $-6 \sin^2 (1 - 2x) \cos (1 - 2x)$

   (E) $-6 \cos^2 (1 - 2x)$.

8. If $f(u) = \tan^{-1} u^2$ and $g(u) = e^u$ then the derivative of $f(g(u))$ is

   (A) $\dfrac{2ue^u}{1 + u^4}$ (B) $\dfrac{2ue^{u^2}}{1 + u^4}$ (C) $\dfrac{2e^u}{1 + 4e^{2u}}$

   (D) $\dfrac{2e^{2u}}{1 + e^{4u}}$ (E) $\dfrac{2e^{2u}}{\sqrt{1 - e^{4u}}}$.

9. The equation of the tangent to the curve of $xy - x + y = 2$ at the point where $x = 0$ is

(A) $y = -x$ (B) $y = \frac{1}{2}x + 2$ (C) $y = x + 2$

(D) $y = 2$ (E) $y = 2 - x$.

10. If $y = \frac{1}{x}$ then $y^{iv}(1)$ equals

(A) $-4!$ (B) $-3!$ (C) $4!$ (D) $5!$ (E) $3!$.

11. If $y = x^2 e^{1/x}$ $(x \neq 0)$, then $\frac{dy}{dx}$ is

(A) $xe^{1/x}(x + 2)$ (B) $e^{1/x}(2x - 1)$ (C) $\frac{-2e^{1/x}}{x}$

(D) $e^{-x}(2x - x^2)$ (E) none of these.

*12. If differentials are used for computation, then $\sqrt[3]{127}$ is approximately equal to

(A) 5.27 (B) 5.01 (C) 5.03 (D) 5.10 (E) 5.07 .

13. A point moves along the curve $y = x^2 + 1$ so that the x-coordinate is increasing at the constant rate of $\frac{3}{2}$ units per second. The rate in units per second at which the distance from the origin is changing when the point has coordinates $(1,2)$ is equal to

(A) $\frac{7\sqrt{5}}{10}$ (B) $\frac{3\sqrt{5}}{2}$ (C) $3\sqrt{5}$ (D) $\frac{15}{2}$ (E) $\sqrt{5}$.

14. The set of x for which the curve of $y = 1 - 6x^2 - x^4$ has inflection points is

(A) $\{0\}$ (B) $\{\pm\sqrt{3}\}$ (C) $\{1\}$ (D) $\{\pm 1\}$

(E) none of these.

15. If the position of a particle on a line at time t is given by $s = t^3 + 3t$, then the speed of the particle is decreasing when

(A) $-1 < t < 1$ (B) $-1 < t < 0$ (C) $t < 0$

(D) $t > 0$ (E) $|t| > 1$.

*16. A particle moves along the parabola $x = 3y - y^2$ so that $\frac{dy}{dt} = 3$ at all time t. The speed of the particle when it is at position (2,1) is equal to

   (A) 0   (B) 3   (C) $\sqrt{13}$ (D) $3\sqrt{2}$ (E) none of these.

*17. The motion of a particle in a plane is given by the pair of equations $x = e^t \cos t$, $y = e^t \sin t$. The magnitude of its acceleration at any time t equals

   (A) $\sqrt{x^2 + y^2}$ (B) $2e^t\sqrt{\cos 2t}$ (C) $2e^t$

   (D) e^t (E) $2e^{2t}$.

18. A rectangle with one side on the x-axis is inscribed in the triangle formed by the lines $y = x$, $y = 0$, and $2x + y = 12$. The area of the largest such rectangle is

   (A) 6   (B) 3   (C) $\frac{5}{2}$ (D) 5   (E) 7 .

19. The abscissa of the first-quadrant point which is on the curve of $x^2 - y^2 = 1$ and closest to the point (3,0) is

   (A) 1   (B) $\frac{3}{2}$ (C) 2   (D) 3   (E) none of these.

20. If c represents the number defined by Rolle's Theorem, then for the function $f(x) = x^3 - 3x^2$ on the interval $0 \le x \le 3$, c is equal to

   (A) 2   (B) 1   (C) 0   (D) $\sqrt{2}$ (E) none of these.

21. $\int \frac{x\,dx}{\sqrt{9 - x^2}}$ equals

   (A) $-\frac{1}{2} \ln \sqrt{9 - x^2} + C$ (B) $\sin^{-1} \frac{x}{3} + C$

   (C) $-- \sqrt{9 - x^2} + C$ (D) $-\frac{1}{4}\sqrt{9 - x^2} + C$

   (E) $2\sqrt{9 - x^2} + C$.

*22. $\int_{\frac{\pi}{4}}^{\frac{\pi}{3}} \sec^2 x \tan^2 x \ dx$ equals

(A) 5   (B) $\sqrt{3} - 1$ (C) $\frac{8}{3} - \frac{2\sqrt{2}}{3}$ (D) $\sqrt{3}$ (E) $\sqrt{3} - \frac{1}{3}$.

23. $\int \frac{(y - 1)^2}{2y} \ dy$ equals

(A) $\frac{y^2}{4} - y + \frac{1}{2} \ln \ |y| + C$ (B) $y^2 - y + \ln \ |2y| + C$

(C) $y^2 - 4y + \frac{1}{2} \ln \ |2y| + C$ (D) $\frac{(y - 1)^3}{3y^2} + C$

(E) $\frac{1}{2} - \frac{1}{2y^2} + C$.

*24. $\int_{\frac{\pi}{6}}^{\frac{\pi}{2}} \cot x \ dx$ equals

(A) $\ln \frac{1}{2}$ (B) $\ln 2$ (C) $- \ln (2 - \sqrt{3})$

(D) $\ln (\sqrt{3} - 1)$ (E) none of these.

*25. $\int_1^e \ln x \ dx$ equals

(A) $\frac{1}{2}$ (B) $e - 1$ (C) $e + 1$ (D) 1   (E) -1 .

26. If $F(x) = \int_1^x \sqrt{t^2 + 3t} \ dt$ then $F'(x)$ equals

(A) $\frac{2}{3}[(x^2 + 3x)^{3/2} - 8]$ (B) $\sqrt{x^2 + 3x}$

(C) $\sqrt{x^2 + 3x} - 2$ (D) $\frac{1}{2} \frac{(2x + 3)}{\sqrt{x^2 + 3x}}$ (E) none of these.

*27. Which one of the following improper integrals converges?

(A) $\int_{-1}^1 \frac{dx}{(x + 1)^2}$ (B) $\int_1^\infty \frac{dx}{\sqrt{x}}$ (C) $\int_0^\infty \frac{dx}{(x^2 + 1)}$

(D) $\int_1^3 \frac{dx}{(2 - x)^3}$ (E) none of these.

28. If $f(x)$ is continuous on the interval $-a \leq x \leq a$ then it

    follows that $\displaystyle\int_{-a}^{a} f(x)\ dx$

       (A) equals $2\displaystyle\int_{0}^{a} f(x)\ dx$ (B) equals 0

       (C) equals $f(a) - f(-a)$ (D) represents the total
       area bounded by the curve $y = f(x)$, the x-axis, and
       the vertical lines $x = -a$ and $x = a$

       (E) is not necessarily any of these.

29. If $\dfrac{dy}{dx} = \dfrac{y}{x}$ $(x > 0,\ y > 0)$ and $y = 3$ when $x = 1$, then

       (A) $x^2 + y^2 = 10$ (B) $y = x + \ln 3$ (C) $y^2 - x^2 = 8$
       (D) $y = 3x$ (E) $y^2 - 3x^2 = 6$.

30. The area bounded by the cubic $y = x^3 - 3x^2$ and the line $y = -4$
    is given by the integral

       (A) $\displaystyle\int_{-1}^{2} (x^3 - 3x^2 + 4)\ dx$ (B) $\displaystyle\int_{-1}^{2} (x^3 - 3x^2 - 4)\ dx$

       (C) $2\displaystyle\int_{0}^{2} (x^3 - 3x^2 - 4)\ dx$ (D) $\displaystyle\int_{-1}^{2} (4 - x^3 + 3x^2)\ dx$

              (E) $\displaystyle\int_{0}^{3} (3x^2 + x^3)\ dx$.

31. The area bounded by the curve $y = \dfrac{1}{x + 1}$, the axes, and the
    line $x = e - 1$ equals

       (A) $1 - \dfrac{1}{e^2}$ (B) $\ln (e - 1)$ (C) 1   (D) 2

       (E) $2\sqrt{e + 1} - 2$.

32. The area bounded by the curve $x = 3y - y^2$ and the line $x = -y$
    is represented by

(A) $\int_0^4 (2y - y^2)\, dy$ (B) $\int_0^4 (4y - y^2)\, dy$

(C) $\int_0^3 (3y - y^2)\, dy + \int_0^4 y\, dy$ (D) $\int_0^3 (y^2 - 4y)\, dy$

(E) $\int_0^3 (2y - y^2)\, dy$.

*33. The area bounded by the curve with parametric equations $x = 2a \tan \theta$,
$y = 2a \cos^2 \theta$, and the lines $x = 0$ and $x = 2a$ is equal to

(A) πa^2 (B) $2\pi a^2$ (C) $\dfrac{\pi a}{4}$ (D) $\dfrac{\pi a}{2}$ (E) none of these.

34. A solid is cut out of a sphere of radius 2 by two parallel planes
each 1 unit from the center. The volume of this solid is

(A) 8π (C) $\dfrac{32\pi}{3}$ (C) $\dfrac{25\pi}{3}$ (D) $\dfrac{22\pi}{3}$ (E) $\dfrac{20\pi}{3}$.

35. The volume generated by rotating the region bounded by

$y = \dfrac{1}{\sqrt{1 + x^2}}$, $y = 0$, $x = 0$, and $x = 1$ about the y-axis is

(A) $\dfrac{\pi^2}{4}$ (B) $\pi\sqrt{2}$ (C) $2\pi(\sqrt{2} - 1)$ (D) $\dfrac{2\pi}{3}(2\sqrt{2} - 1)$

(E) $1 + \dfrac{\pi^2}{4}$.

36. The region bounded by $y = e^x$, $y = 1$, and $x = 2$ is rotated about
the x-axis. The volume of the solid generated is given by the integral:

(A) $\pi \int_0^2 e^{2x}\, dx$ (B) $2\pi \int_1^{e^2} (2 - \ln y)(y - 1)\, dy$

(C) $\pi \int_0^2 (e^{2x} - 1)\, dx$ (D) $2\pi \int_0^{e^2} y(2 - \ln y)\, dy$

(E) $\pi \int_0^2 (e^x - 1)^2\, dx$.

37. A particle moves on a straight line so that its velocity at time t is given by $v = 4s$, where s is its distance from the origin. If $s = 3$ when $t = 0$, then when $t = \frac{1}{2}$, s equals

    (A) $1 + e^2$ (B) $2e^3$ (C) e^2 (D) $2 + e^2$ (E) $3e^2$.

*38. The length of the arc of $y = \frac{1}{2}x^2 - \frac{1}{4} \ln x$ from $x = 1$ to $x = 4$ is

    (A) $\frac{15}{2} + \ln 2$ (B) $\frac{1}{2}(15 + \ln 2)$ (C) $\frac{1}{2}(17 + \ln 2)$

    (D) $3\frac{15}{64}$ (E) $\frac{45}{16}$.

39. The average (mean) value of $y = (x - 3)^2$ over the interval from $x = 1$ to $x = 3$ equals

    (A) 2 (B) $\frac{2}{3}$ (C) $\frac{4}{3}$ (D) $\frac{8}{3}$ (E) none of these.

*40. $\lim\limits_{n \to \infty} \left[\ln \left(1 + \frac{1}{n}\right) + \ln \left(1 + \frac{2}{n}\right) + \ldots + \ln \left(1 + \frac{n}{n}\right) \right] \cdot \frac{1}{n}$ is equal to the definite integral

    (A) $\int_0^1 \ln x \, dx$ (B) $\int_1^2 \ln \frac{1}{x} \, dx$ (C) $\int_1^2 \ln (1 + x) \, dx$

    (D) $\int_1^2 \ln x \, dx$ (E) none of these.

41. A particle moves along a line so that its acceleration, a, at time t is $a = - t^2$. If the particle is at the origin when $t = 0$ and 3 units to the right of the origin when $t = 1$, then its velocity at $t = 0$ is

    (A) 0 (B) $\frac{1}{12}$ (C) $2\frac{11}{12}$ (D) $\frac{37}{12}$ (E) none of these.

42. The curve with parametric equations $x = \sqrt{t - 2}$ and $y = \sqrt{6 - t}$ is

    (A) part of a circle   (B) a parabola   (C) a straight line

    (D) part of a hyperbola   (E) none of these.

43. The distance from (-4,5) to the line $3y + 2x - 7 = 0$ is

     (A) $\frac{9}{5}$ (B) $\frac{9}{\sqrt{13}}$ (C) 1   (D) $\sqrt{13}$ (E) none of these.

44. The set of x for which $|x + 1| > 2$ and $|x - 1| \leqq 2$ is

     (A) the null set   (B) $x < -3$ or $x > -1$

     (D) $x < -3$ or $x \geqq -1$ (D) $1 < x \leqq 3$

               (E) none of these.

45. Which of the following functions could have the graph sketched below?

     (A) $f(x) = xe^{x}$ (B) $f(x) = xe^{-x}$ (C) $f(x) = \frac{e^{x}}{x}$

     (D) $f(x) = \frac{x}{x^{2} + 1}$ (E) $f(x) = \frac{x^{2}}{x^{3} + 1}$.

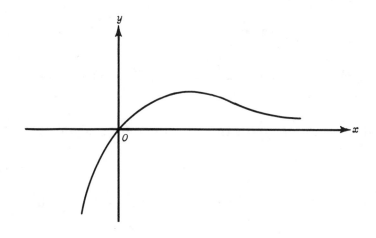

Practice Examination:4

1. $\lim\limits_{x \to 0} \dfrac{x^{3} - 3x^{2}}{x}$ is

     (A) 0   (B) ∞ (C) -3   (D) 1   (E) 3 .

2. $\lim\limits_{h \to 0} \dfrac{\sin \left(\frac{\pi}{2} + h\right) - 1}{h}$ is

     (A) 1   (B) -1   (C) 0   (D) ∞ (E) none of these.

3. $\lim\limits_{x \to 2} [x]$ (where $[x]$ is the greatest integer in x)   is

      (A) 1   (B) 2   (C) 3   (D) ∞ (E) nonexistent.

4. $\lim\limits_{x \to \infty} x \tan \dfrac{\pi}{x}$ is

      (A) 0   (B) 1   (C) $\dfrac{1}{\pi}$ (D) π (E) ∞ .

5. If $y = \ln \dfrac{x}{\sqrt{x^2 + 1}}$ then $\dfrac{dy}{dx}$ is

      (A) $\dfrac{1}{x^2 + 1}$ (B) $\dfrac{1}{x(x^2 + 1)}$ (C) $\dfrac{2x^2 + 1}{x(x^2 + 1)}$

      (D) $\dfrac{1}{x\sqrt{x^2 + 1}}$ (E) $\dfrac{1 - x^2}{x(x^2 + 1)}$.

6. If $y = \sqrt{x^2 + 16}$, then $\dfrac{d^2y}{dx^2}$ is

      (A) $-\dfrac{1}{4(x^2 + 16)^{3/2}}$ (B) $4(3x^2 + 16)$

      (C) $\dfrac{16}{\sqrt{x^2 + 16}}$ (D) $\dfrac{2x^2 + 16}{(x^2 + 16)^{3/2}}$ (E) $\dfrac{16}{(x^2 + 16)^{3/2}}$.

7. If $x = a \cot \theta$ and $y = a \sin^2 \theta$, then $\dfrac{dy}{dx}$, when $\theta = \dfrac{\pi}{4}$, is

    equal to

      (A) $\dfrac{1}{2}$ (B) -1   (C) 2   (D) $-\dfrac{1}{2}$ (E) $-\dfrac{1}{4}$.

8. The equation of the tangent to the curve $2x^2 - y^4 = 1$ at the

    point (-1,1) is

      (A) $y = -x$ (B) $y = 2 - x$ (C) $4y + 5x + 1 = 0$

      (D) $x - 2y + 3 = 0$ (E) $x - 4y + 5 = 0$.

9. If $f(x) = x \ln x$ then $f'''(e)$ equals

      (A) $\dfrac{1}{e}$ (B) 0   (C) $-\dfrac{1}{e^2}$ (D) $\dfrac{1}{e^2}$ (E) $\dfrac{2}{e^3}$.

10. If $y = \sqrt{\ln (x^2 + 1)}$ $(x > 0)$, then the derivative of y^2 with

respect to $\ln x$ is equal to

(A) $\dfrac{2x}{x^2 + 1}$ (B) $\dfrac{2}{x^2 + 1}$ (C) $\dfrac{2x}{\ln x(x^2 + 1)}$

(D) $\dfrac{2x^2}{x^2 + 1}$ (E) none of these.

11. If $f(t) = \dfrac{1}{t^2} - 4$ and $g(t) = \cos t$ then the derivative of

$f(g(t))$ is

(A) $2 \sec^2 t \tan t$ (B) $\tan t$ (C) $2 \sec t \tan t$

(D) $\dfrac{2}{t^3 \sin t}$ (E) $-\dfrac{2}{\cos^3 t}$.

12. If $f(x) = \dfrac{e^{\ln x}}{x}$ then $f(1)$ is

(A) 0   (B) 1   (C) e (D) $\dfrac{e}{2}$ (E) not defined.

13. A particle moves on a line according to the law $s = f(t)$ so

that its velocity $v = ks$, where k is a nonzero constant.

Its acceleration is

(A) $k^2 v$ (B) $k^2 s$ (C) k (D) 0   (E) none of these.

*14. The radius of a sphere is 10 in.; if the radius is increased by

0.01 in., then the approximate change, in in.^{3}, in the volume is

(A) $.4\pi$ (B) $\dfrac{4}{9}\pi$ (C) 4π (D) 8π (E) 40π .

15. A relative maximum value of the function $y = \dfrac{\ln x}{x}$ is

(A) 1   (B) e (C) $\dfrac{2}{e}$ (D) $\dfrac{1}{e}$ (E) none of these.

16. If a particle moves on a line according to the law $s = t^5 + 2t^3$,

then the number of times it reverses direction is

(A) 4   (B) 3   (C) 2   (D) 1   (E) 0 .

*17. A particle moves counterclockwise on the circle $x^2 + y^2 = 25$ with constant speed of 2 ft/sec. Its velocity vector, **v** , when the particle is at $(3,4)$, equals

(A) $-\frac{1}{5}(8\mathbf{i} - 6\mathbf{j})$ (B) $\frac{1}{5}(8\mathbf{i} - 6\mathbf{j})$ (C) $-2\sqrt{3}\mathbf{i} + 2\mathbf{j}$

(D) $2\mathbf{i} - 2\sqrt{3}\mathbf{j}$ (E) $-2\sqrt{2}(\mathbf{i} - \mathbf{j})$.

18. A rectangular pig pen is to be built against a wall so that only three sides will require fencing. If p feet of fencing are to be used, the area of the largest possible pen is

(A) $\frac{p^2}{2}$ (B) $\frac{p^2}{4}$ (C) $\frac{p^2}{8}$ (D) $\frac{p^2}{9}$ (E) $\frac{p^2}{16}$.

*19. Let $R = a \cos kt\mathbf{i} + a \sin kt\mathbf{j}$ be the (position) vector $x\mathbf{i} + y\mathbf{j}$ from the origin to a moving point $P(x,y)$ at time t , where a and k are positive constants. The acceleration vector, $\mathbf{a}$, equals

(A) $-k^2 R$ (B) $a^2 k^2 R$ (C) $-aR$

(D) $-ak^2(\cos t\mathbf{i} + \sin t\mathbf{j})$ (E) $-R$.

20. The region bounded by the parabolas $y = x^2$ and $y = 6x - x^2$ is rotated about the x-axis so that a vertical line segment cut off by the curves generates a ring. The value of x for which the ring of largest area is obtained is

(A) 4   (B) 3   (C) $\frac{5}{2}$ (D) 2   (E) $\frac{3}{2}$.

21. $\displaystyle\int \frac{\cos x}{4 + 2 \sin x}\, dx$ equals

(A) $\sqrt{4 + 2 \sin x} + C$ (B) $-\dfrac{1}{2(4 + \sin x)} + C$

(C) $\ln \sqrt{4 + 2 \sin x} + C$ (D) $2 \ln |4 + 2 \sin x| + C$

(E) $\frac{1}{4} \sin x - \frac{1}{2} \csc^2 x + C$.

22. $\int \dfrac{e^u}{4 + e^{2u}}\, du$ is equal to

    (A) $\ln (4 + e^{2u}) + C$ (B) $\dfrac{1}{2} \ln |4 + e^{2u}| + C$

    (C) $\dfrac{1}{2} \tan^{-1} \dfrac{e^u}{2} + C$ (D) $\tan^{-1} \dfrac{e^u}{2} + C$

              (E) $\dfrac{1}{2} \tan^{-1} \dfrac{e^{2u}}{2} + C$.

*23. $\displaystyle\int_2^4 \dfrac{du}{\sqrt{16 - u^2}}$ equals

    (A) $\dfrac{\pi}{12}$ (B) $\dfrac{\pi}{6}$ (C) $\dfrac{\pi}{4}$ (D) $\dfrac{\pi}{3}$ (E) $\dfrac{2\pi}{3}$.

24. $\int \dfrac{dx}{x \ln x}$ equals

    (A) $\ln (\ln x) + C$ (B) $-\dfrac{1}{\ln^2 x} + C$ (C) $\dfrac{(\ln x)^2}{2} + C$

    (D) $\ln x + C$ (E) none of these.

25. If we replace $\sqrt{x - 2}$ by u then $\displaystyle\int_3^6 \dfrac{\sqrt{x - 2}}{x}\, dx$ is equivalent to

    (A) $\displaystyle\int_1^2 \dfrac{u\, du}{u^2 + 2}$ (B) $2\displaystyle\int_1^2 \dfrac{u^2\, du}{u^2 + 2}$ (C) $\displaystyle\int_3^6 \dfrac{2\,u^2}{u^2 + 2}\, du$

    (D) $\displaystyle\int_3^6 \dfrac{u\,du}{u^2 + 2}$ (E) $\dfrac{1}{2}\displaystyle\int_1^2 \dfrac{u^2}{u^2 + 2}\, du$.

*26. $\displaystyle\int_2^4 \dfrac{du}{(u - 3)^2}$ equals

    (A) 2   (B) 1   (C) -1   (D) -2   (E) none of these.

*27. Which of the following improper integrals diverges?

    (A) $\displaystyle\int_0^\infty e^{-x^2}\, dx$ (B) $\displaystyle\int_{-\infty}^0 e^x\, dx$ (C) $\displaystyle\int_0^1 \dfrac{dx}{x}$

    (D) $\displaystyle\int_0^\infty e^{-x}\, dx$ (E) $\displaystyle\int_0^1 \dfrac{dx}{\sqrt{x}}$.

28. If $\dfrac{dQ}{dt} = \dfrac{Q}{10}$ and $Q = Q_0$ when $t = 0$, then Q , at any time t , equals

  (A) $Q_0 \cdot 10^t$ (B) $Q_0 \cdot e^{10t}$ (C) $Q_0 \cdot t^{1/10}$

  (D) $Q_0 \cdot e^{t/10}$ (E) $\dfrac{10 Q_0}{10 - t}$.

29. If a function $f(x)$ is defined by $f(x) \quad \begin{array}{l} = 2x \qquad \text{for } x \leqq 1 \\ = 3x^2 - 2 \quad \text{for } x > 1 \end{array}$,

  then $\displaystyle\int_0^2 f(x)\, dx$ equals

  (A) 6   (B) 5   (C) 4   (D) 3   (E) none of these.

30. The area bounded by the parabola $y = x^2$ and the lines $y = 1$

  and $y = 9$ equals

  (A) 8   (B) $\dfrac{84}{3}$ (C) $\dfrac{64}{3}\sqrt{2}$ (D) 32   (E) $\dfrac{104}{3}$.

31. The total area bounded by the curves $y = x^3$ and $y = x^{1/3}$

  is equal to

  (A) $\dfrac{1}{2}$ (B) $\dfrac{5}{6}$ (C) 1   (D) 2   (E) none of these.

32. The area under the curve $y = \dfrac{1}{\sqrt{x - 1}}$, above the x-axis and bounded

  vertically by $x = 2$ and $x = 5$ equals

  (A) 1   (B) 2   (C) 4   (D) ln 2   (E) 2 ln 2 .

33. The total area enclosed by the curves $y = 4x - x^3$ and $y = 4 - x^2$

  is represented by

  (A) $\displaystyle\int_{-2}^{2} (4x - x^3 + x^2 - 4)\, dx$ (B) $\displaystyle\int_{-2}^{2} (4 - x^2 - 4x + x^3)\, dx$

  (C) $\displaystyle\int_{-2}^{1} (4x - x^3 + x^2 - 4)\, dx + \displaystyle\int_{1}^{2} (4 - x^2 - 4x + x^3)\, dx$

  (D) $\displaystyle\int_{-2}^{1} (4 - x^2 - 4x + x^3)\, dx + \displaystyle\int_{1}^{2} (4x - x^3 + x^2 - 4)\, dx$

  (E) $\displaystyle\int_{-2}^{1} (4x - x^3 + x^2 - 4)\, dx$.

*34. The region bounded by $y = \tan x$, $y = 0$, and $x = \frac{\pi}{4}$ is rotated about the x-axis. The volume generated equals

(A) $\pi - \frac{\pi^2}{4}$ (B) $\pi(\sqrt{2} - 1)$ (C) $\frac{3\pi}{4}$ (D) $\pi(1 + \frac{\pi}{4})$

(E) none of these.

35. The volume obtained by rotating the region bounded by $x = y^2$ and $x = 2 - y^2$ about the y-axis is equal to

(A) $\frac{16\pi}{3}$ (B) $\frac{32\pi}{3}$ (C) $\frac{32\pi}{15}$ (D) $\frac{64\pi}{15}$ (E) $\frac{8\pi}{3}$.

*36. The first-quadrant region bounded by $y = \frac{1}{\sqrt{x}}$, $y = 0$, $x = q$ $(0 < q < 1)$, and $x = 1$ is rotated about the x-axis. The volume obtained as $q \to 0^+$ equals

(A) $\frac{2\pi}{3}$ (B) $\frac{4\pi}{3}$ (C) 2π (D) 4π (E) none of these.

*37. A curve is given parametrically by the equations $x = 3 - 2 \sin t$ and $y = 2 \cos t - 1$. The length of the arc from $t = 0$ to $t = \pi$ is

(A) $\frac{\pi}{2}$ (B) π (C) $2 + \pi$ (D) 2π (E) 4π .

*38. The area in square inches of the surface of a zone cut from a sphere of radius 4 inches by two parallel planes, one through the center of the sphere and the other one inch away, is equal to

(A) 2π (B) 4π (C) 8π (D) 16π (E) 20π .

39. The average (mean) value of $y = \ln x$ over the interval from $x = 1$ to $x = e$ equals

(A) $\frac{1}{2}$ (B) $\frac{1}{2(e - 1)}$ (C) $\frac{2}{e - 1}$ (D) $\frac{1}{e - 1}$

(E) none of these.

40. A particle moves along a line with acceleration $a = 6t$. If, when $t = 0$, $v = 1$, then the total distance travelled between $t = 0$ and $t = 3$ equals

    (A) 30   (B) 28   (C) 27   (D) 26   (E) none of these.

*41. $\lim\limits_{n\to\infty} \frac{1}{n}(\cos\frac{2}{n} + \cos\frac{4}{n} + \cos\frac{6}{n} + \ldots + \cos\frac{2n}{n})$ equals

    (A) $\sin 2$ (B) $\frac{1}{2}\sin 2$ (C) $-\sin 2$ (D) $\frac{1}{2}(\sin 2 - \sin 1)$

    (E) none of these.

42. If $x = f(t)$ is the law of motion for a particle on a line, the particle is said to be in simple harmonic motion if the acceleration

$\frac{d^2 x}{dt^2} = -k^2 x$, k a constant. Which of the following equations does *not* define a simple harmonic motion?

    (A) $x = e^t + e^{-t}$ (B) $x = 4\cos 2t$

    (C) $x = 2\sin(\pi t + 2)$ (D) $x = \sin 2t + \cos 2t$

    (E) $x = \cos(\omega t + \phi)$, ω and ϕ constants.

43. The graph of the equation $y^2 = 4(x + 1)^2 + 4$ is

    (A) a parabola   (B) an ellipse   (C) two intersecting straight lines   (D) a circle   (E) a hyperbola.

44. The graph of $y = \sin\frac{1}{x}$ is symmetric to

    (A) the x-axis   (B) the y-axis   (C) the line $y = x$

    (D) the origin   (E) none of these.

45. Which of the following functions has a graph which is asymptotic to the y-axis?

    (A) $y = \frac{x}{x^2 - 1}$ (B) $y = \frac{x}{x^2 + 1}$ (C) $y = x - \frac{2}{x}$

    (D) $y = \ln(x - 1)$ (E) $y = \frac{\sqrt{x - 1}}{x}$.

Sample Essay Examinations

Sample Essay Examination: 1

1. Show, by analytic geometry, that the two lines drawn from a vertex of a parallelogram to the midpoints of the opposite sides trisect a diagonal of the parallelogram.

2. (a) Integrate $\int \dfrac{x^3}{x^{n-2}}\, dx$, where n may be any real number.

*(b) Integrate $\int_0^1 \dfrac{2}{2 - e^{-x}}\, dx$. *(c) If $y = \ln \dfrac{1 + \sin x}{\cos x}$, find $\dfrac{dy}{dx}$

and use this result to evaluate $\int_0^{\frac{\pi}{3}} \sec x\, dx$.

3. Prove that if $x > 0$ then $x > \ln (1 + x)$, stating any theorems you use.

4. Sketch the graph of $y = x \ln x$, after finding

   (a) the domain;

   (b) intercepts;

   (c) the coordinates of any relative maximum or minimum points;

   (d) the coordinates of any points of inflection;

   (e) the behavior of y for large x ;

   (f) $\lim y$ as $x \to 0^+$.

*5. The base of a solid is the region in the first quadrant bounded by the axes and the line $2x + 3y = 10$, and each cross-section perpendicular to the x-axis is a semicircle. Find the volume of the solid.

6. Consider the family of straight lines with a given slope m , and the chords whose endpoints are the intersections of these lines with the parabola $y = x^2$. Find an equation of the locus of the midpoints of these chords.

7. Let u and v be functions defined for all real numbers and satisfying the conditions:

(a) $u(x_1 + x_2) = u(x_1) \cdot u(x_2)$ for all reals x_1 and x_2 ;

(b) $u(x) = 1 + xv(x)$;

(c) $\lim\limits_{x \to 0} v(x) = 1$.

Prove that u has a derivative for each x and that $u'(x) = u(x)$.

Sample Essay Examination: 2

---

1. Sketch the graph of $y = \dfrac{x^2}{x - 2}$ after finding

(a) intercepts;

(b) coordinates of any relative maximum or minimum points;

(c) values of x for which the graph is concave upward;

(d) any vertical or horizontal asymptotes.

2. Let the length of one side of a triangle be the constant a and let the measure of the opposite angle be the constant A. Find the proportions of the remaining sides of the triangle of maximum area.

3. (a) Sketch the region in the first quadrant bounded above by the line $y = x + 4$, below by the line $y = 4 - x$, and to the right by the parabola $y = x^2 + 2$.

(b) Find the area of this region.

4. A car is travelling on a straight road at 45 miles per hour when the brakes are applied. The car then slows down at the constant rate of k ft/sec^2 and comes to a stop after travelling 60 ft. Find k.

5. (a) Show, by long division, if $t \geqq 0$, that $1 - t + t^2 \geqq \dfrac{1}{1 + t}$ $\geqq 1 - t + t^2 - t^3$.

   (b) Use the result in (a) to show, if $0 < x \leqq 1$, that

$$x - \frac{x^2}{2} + \frac{x^3}{3} \geqq \ln (1 + x) \geqq x - \frac{x^2}{2} + \frac{x^3}{3} - \frac{x^4}{4} .$$

   (c) Show that it follows from (b) that $0.0954 > \ln 1.1 > 0.0953$.

*6. Prove that the two tangents that can be drawn from any point on the line $y = -1$ to the parabola $x^2 = 4y$ are perpendicular.

7. (a) Evaluate $\displaystyle\int_{1}^{m} \frac{1}{x^2}\, dx$.

   (b) Show that $\displaystyle\sum_{k=2}^{m} \frac{1}{k^2} < 1 - \frac{1}{m}$, m an integer $\geqq 2$.

*(c) Show that $\displaystyle\lim_{m \to \infty} \sum_{k=2}^{m} \frac{1}{k^2} < 1$.

Sample Essay Examination: 3

1. An eaves trough is made by bending a flat piece of tin, which is 6 ft by 16 in., along two lines parallel to its length to form a rectangular cross-section. Find the largest cross-sectional area that can be thus obtained. Justify your answer.

2. (a) Find an equation of the locus of a point $P(x,y)$ for which

the product of the slopes of the lines joining it to (2,-1) and (4,1)

is a constant k.

    (b)   What is the locus if k = -1?

    (c)   What if k < 0 but $k \neq$ -1?

    (d)   What if k = 0?

    (e)   What if k > 0?

3. If the parabola $2y = x^2 - 6$ is rotated about the y-axis it generates a paraboloid of revolution. Suppose a vessel having the shape of this paraboloid contains water to a depth of 4 ft. Determine the amount of water which must be removed to lower the surface by 2 ft.

4. A particle moves along a line so that its displacement from the origin at any time t is given by $x = \frac{7}{2} e^{-4t} \sin 2t$.

    (a) Prove: $a + 8v + 20x = 0$, where v is the velocity and a the acceleration of the particle.

    (b) Show that relative maximum and minimum values of x occur when $\tan 2t = \frac{1}{2}$.

   *5. A curve is given parametrically by

$$\begin{cases} x = 2a \cot \theta \\ y = 2a \sin^2 \theta . \end{cases}$$

    (a) Determine the Cartesian equation of the curve (i.e., find a single equation in x and y).

    (b) Sketch the curve.

    (c) Find the area bounded by the curve and the x-axis.

6. Let the function f be defined by

$$\begin{cases} f(x) = x^2 \sin \dfrac{1}{x} & x \neq 0 \\ f(0) = 0 . \end{cases}$$

(a)　Prove that f is continuous at $x = 0$.

(b)　Prove that $f'(0)$ exists and find it by using the definition of the derivative.

(c)　Prove that f' is *not* continuous at $x = 0$.

7.　(a)　Let the functions f, u, and v be differentiable for all x and let $f'(x) = u(x)v(x)$. Suppose that for a number c, $u(c) = 0$ but $v(c) \neq 0$. Show that if $u'(c)v(c) > 0$ then $f(c)$ is a relative minimum while if $u'(c)v(c) < 0$ then $f(c)$ is a relative maximum. State any theorems you use.

(b)　If $f'(x) = (3x - 3)(x^2 + 2)^3(x^2 - 2x + 3)^{3/2}$ find the x-coordinates of any relative maxima or minima of f by using the theorem in part (a).

Sample Essay Examination: 4

1.　(a)　Find the coordinates of any relative maximum or minimum points of the curve of $y = x^4 - 4x^2$.

(b)　Sketch the curve.

(c)　Find the area bounded by the curve and the x-axis.

2.　The diameter and height of a paper cup in the shape of a cone are both 4 in, and water is leaking out at the rate of $\frac{1}{2}$ in^3/sec. Find the rate at which the water level is dropping when the diameter of the surface is 2 in.

3.　Find the point(s) on the parabola $2x = y^2$ which are closest to the point $(0, \frac{3}{2})$.

4. A particle moves along a straight line so that its acceleration at any time t is given in terms of its velocity v by $a = -2v$.

(a) Find v in terms of t if $v = 20$ when $t = 0$.

(b) Find the distance the particle travels while v changes from $v = 20$ to $v = 5$.

5. Sketch the graph of the function $f(x) = \dfrac{\sin x}{x}$ after considering

(a) the domain;

(b) the intercepts;

(c) any relative maximum or minimum points;

(d) symmetry;

(e) $\lim f$ as $x \to 0$;

(f) continuity of f at $x = 0$;

(g) behavior for large x.

6. An ellipse has center at the origin, a focus at $(0,2)$, and a vertex at $(0,4)$.

(a) Find its equation.

(b) Find the volume of the solid generated by revolving the region in the first quadrant about the major axis of the ellipse.

*7. The current i (in amps) in a certain circuit at time t (in sec) is given by

$$ i = \frac{E}{R} \left(1 - e^{\frac{-Rt}{L}} \right) $$

where E, R, and L are positive constants.

(a) Show that $i < \dfrac{E}{R}$ for all positive t.

(b) Show that $\lim\limits_{t\to\infty} i = \dfrac{E}{R}$.

(c) If $E = 6$, $R = 5$, and $L = 0.1$, find the approximate change in current when t increases from $t = 0$ to $t = 0.01$.

(d) If t, E, and L are held fixed while R varies, find, if it exists, $\lim\limits_{R\to 0} i$.

Sample Essay Examination: 5

1. (a) Sketch the region bounded by the curve of $y^2 = x^3$ and the line segment joining the points $(1,1)$ and $(4,-8)$.

(b) Find the area of this region.

2. (a) Find a rectangular equation of the locus of a point $P(x,y)$ whose distance from the line $x = 2$ is twice its distance from the origin.

(b) Sketch the curve and find a vertex and a focus.

(c) Find a polar equation of the locus.

3. An open box with a capacity of 4 ft^3 and with a square base is to be made from sheet metal costing 50¢ a square foot. If welding costs 10¢ per foot and all the edges will need to be welded,

(a) find the dimensions for the box that will minimize the cost;

(b) show that the dimensions that yield minimum cost are independent of the costs of the sheet metal and of the welding.

4. (a) Prove that the curves of $xy = k$ and $y^2 - x^2 = h$ intersect in two points for every pair of reals k and h provided $hk \neq 0$.

(b) Prove that if $hk \neq 0$, every curve of the first family intersects every curve of the second family at right angles.

*5. (a) Sketch the curve of $y = e^{-x}$ and find, if it exists, the area in the first quadrant under the curve.

(b) Find, if it exists, the volume obtained if this area is revolved about the x-axis.

*6. The motion of a particle in a plane is given parametrically (in terms of time t) by $x = \frac{1}{t}$ and $y = \ln t$, where $t > 0$.

(a) Find the speed of the particle when $t = 1$.

(b) Find the acceleration vector, **a**, when $t = 1$.

(c) Find an equation which expresses y in terms of x and sketch its graph.

(d) Show **v** and **a** when $t = 1$.

7. (a) If $f'(x)$ is positive at each x in the interval $a \leqq x \leqq b$, prove that $f(x)$ is monotonic increasing over the interval. [That is, that if $a \leqq x_1 < x_2 \leqq b$, then $f(x_1) < f(x_2)$.]

(b) Prove that if $0 < x < 2\pi$ then $\frac{\sin x}{x} < 1$.

Sample Essay Examination: 6

1. (a) Sketch the region bounded by the curves of $\sqrt{x} + \sqrt{y} = 3$ and $x + y = 5$.

(b) Find the area of this region.

2. Find the equations of the lines that are tangent to the curve of $y = \frac{x}{1 - x}$ and perpendicular to the line $4x + y + 4 = 0$.

3. The region bounded by the curve of the function $y = f(t)$, the t-axis, $t = 0$, and $t = x$ is rotated about the t-axis. The volume generated for all x is $2\pi(x^2 + 2x)$. Find $f(t)$.

4. A point $P(x,y)$ moves along the curve $y = \ln x$ so that its x-coordinate increases at the rate of $\sqrt{3}$ units per sec. If P is one vertex of an equilateral triangle whose other two vertices are on the x-axis, find how fast the area of the triangle is changing when the y-coordinate of P is 1.

*5. Let P be a fixed point with coordinates (p,q). Prove analytically that the number of tangents that can be drawn from P to the parabola $y^2 = x$ depends on whether q^2 is greater than, less than, or equal to p and determine the number in each of these cases.

*6. (a) Find parametric equations of the locus of $P(x,y)$ if, at any time $t \geq 0$, $\frac{dx}{dt} = y$ and $\frac{dy}{dt} = \sqrt{1 + 2y}$ and if, when $t = 0$, $x = 0$ and $y = 0$.

(b) Find the x- and y-components of the acceleration in terms of y.

(c) Find the speed of P and the magnitude of its acceleration at the instant when $t = 1$.

7. Suppose $F(x) = \displaystyle\int_{1}^{x} \frac{\sin t}{t}\, dt$.

(a) Determine $\displaystyle\lim_{x\to 0} F'(x)$, if it exists.

(b) Prove that $\displaystyle\lim_{x\to 0} F'(\tfrac{1}{x})$ exists and equals zero. State any theorems you use.

Sample Essay Examination: 7

1. (a) Find the area of the region bounded by the curves of $y = x^3 - 2x^2$ and $y = x^2$.

(b) Find the volume of the solid generated by rotating the region in (a) about the y-axis.

2. A tangent drawn to the parabola $y = x^2$ at any point $P(x_1, y_1)$ $(x_1 > 0)$ intersects the axis of the parabola at T. If Q is the foot of the perpendicular from P to the axis of the parabola, prove that the area of the triangle QPT equals $x_1 y_1$.

3. Find the constants a, b, c, d such that the curve of

$$y = ax^3 + bx^2 + cx + d$$

has a relative maximum at the point $(0,1)$ and a point of inflection at the point $(1, 1/3)$. Sketch the curve.

4. Consider, in the first quadrant, the graphs of $y^2 = x$ and $y^2 = 4 - x$. A line segment parallel to the x-axis and with endpoints on these curves is rotated about the x-axis to generate the surface of a cylinder. Show that the cylinder of greatest volume has its height equal to its diameter.

*5. Integrate

(a) $\displaystyle\int \frac{x - 3}{\sqrt{6x - x^2}}\, dx$; (b) $\displaystyle\int \frac{dx}{\sqrt{6x - x^2}}$;

and show how the above can be combined to integrate

(c) $\displaystyle\int \frac{2x + 3}{\sqrt{6x - x^2}}\, dx$.

295

*6.   A cycloid is given parametrically by $x = \theta - \sin\theta$, $y = 1 - \cos\theta$.

(a) Find the slope of the curve at the point where $\theta = 2\pi/3$.

(b) Find the length of one arch of the cycloid.

7.   If a freely falling body starts from rest, then the distance s it falls is given in terms of time t by $s = \frac{1}{2}gt^2$, where g is constant.

(a)   Prove that its velocity $v = \sqrt{2gs}$.

(b)   Prove that the average velocity *with respect to t* from $t = 0$ to $t = t_1$ equals one half v_1 (the velocity when $t = t_1$).

(c)   Prove that the average velocity *with respect to s* from $t = 0$ to $t = t_1$ equals two-thirds v_1.

Sample Essay Examination: 8

---

1.   Sketch the curve of $y = x^3 - 4x^2 + 3x$ and find the area bounded by the curve and the line joining the points $(0,0)$ and $(4,12)$.

2.   A rectangle with sides parallel to the axes has two vertices on the curve of $y = 8 - 2x^2$ and two on the curve of $y = x^2 - 4$. Find the dimensions of the rectangle of largest area. Justify your answer.

3.   Sketch the graph of $y = \ln(4 + x^2)$ after considering (a) intercepts; (b) symmetry; (c) relative maximum or minimum points; (d) possible inflection points.

4. A particle moves along a line so that its position s at time t is given by

$$s(t) = \int_0^t (3w^2 - 6w)\ dw.$$

(a) Find its acceleration at any time t.

(b) Determine the values of t for which the particle is moving in a positive direction.

(c) Find the values of t for which the particle is slowing down.

5. A right triangle RST with hypotenuse ST is inscribed in the parabola $y = x^2$ so that R coincides with the vertex of the parabola. If ST intersects the axis of the parabola at Q, then show that Q is independent of the choice of right triangle.

*6. A point moves on the curve whose parametric equations are

$x = \sqrt{t - 2}$ and $2y = \sqrt{6 - t}$.

(a) Find a single equation in x and y for the path of the point and sketch the part of the curve defined by the parametric equations.

(b) The region bounded by this curve and the axes is rotated about the y-axis. Show that its volume equals $\dfrac{\pi}{2} \displaystyle\int_2^6 \sqrt{6 - t}\ dt.$

(c) Evaluate the integral in (b).

*7. (a) Evaluate, if it exists,

$$\lim_{h \to 0} \frac{1}{h} \int_{\frac{\pi}{4}}^{\frac{\pi}{4}+h} \frac{\sin x}{x}\ dx.$$

(b) By identifying the following with an appropriate definite integral, evaluate

$$\lim_{n \to \infty} \frac{1}{n} \sum_{k=1}^{n} \cos^2 \frac{\pi k}{n}.$$

Sample Essay Examination: 9

1. Sketch the curve of $y = \ln x$ and find the volume of the solid obtained if the region in the first quadrant bounded by the curve and the line $x = e$ is rotated about the y-axis.

*2. Integrate

(a) $\displaystyle\int \frac{dx}{x^3 - x}$ (b) $\displaystyle\int x \cos 3x \, dx$.

3. Let the function f be defined as follows:

$$f(x) = x^3 \qquad x \geq 1$$
$$f(x) = 3x - 2 \qquad x < 1.$$

(a) Show that f is continuous at $x = 1$.

(b) Use the definition of derivative to show that $f'(1)$ exists.

(c) Is f' continuous at $x = 1$? Why?

(d) Evaluate $\displaystyle\int_0^2 f(x) \, dx$.

4. Find a nonzero function, $f(x)$, differentiable for all x and such that if $t \geq 0$, $\displaystyle\int_0^t x \, f(x) \, dx = f^2(t)$.

*5. (a) Sketch the curve whose polar equation is $r = \cos \theta + \sin \theta$.

(b) Find the area enclosed by both the polar curves $r = 4 \sin \theta$ and $r = 4 \cos \theta$.

6. At time $t = 0$ an insect starts crawling along a straight line at the rate of 3 ft/min; two minutes later a second insect starts crawling in a direction perpendicular to that of the first and at a speed of 5 ft/min. How fast is the distance between them changing when the first insect has travelled 12 feet?

*7. The velocity **v** of a particle moving on a curve is given, at time t, by **v** = t**i** - (1 - t)**j**. When $t = 0$, the particle is at the point (0,1).

(a) Find the position vector R at time t.

(b) Find the acceleration vector **a** at time $t = 2$.

(c) For what positive t is the speed of the particle a minimum?

Sample Essay Examination: 10

1. Find the x-coordinate of the point R on the curve of $y = x - x^2$ such that the line OR (where O is the origin) divides the area bounded by the curve and the x-axis into two regions of equal area.

2. Sketch the curve of $y = \sin x \, (1 + \cos x)$, after having found any:

(a) intercepts;

(b) relative maximum or minimum points;

(c) inflection points.

*3. (a) Integrate $\displaystyle\int \frac{dx}{e^x + 1}$.

(b) Evaluate, if possible, $\displaystyle\lim_{b\to\infty} \int_0^b \frac{dx}{e^x + 1}$.

4. The vertices of a triangle are $(0,0)$, $(x, \sin x)$, and $(\cos^3 x, 0)$, where $0 \leq x \leq \frac{\pi}{2}$. Find the value of x for which the area of the triangle is a maximum. Justify your answer.

5. The equation of a curve is $y^2 + ay = \dfrac{x + b}{cx^2 + dx + e}$, where a, b, c, d, e are integers. Determine these integers if the curve exhibits all of the following characteristics:

(a) the curve goes through the origin but has no other intercepts;

(b) the curve is symmetric to the x-axis;

(c) the graph has two horizontal asymptotes, $y = \pm 1$, and one vertical asymptote, $x = 4$.

(d) the graph exists only if $x \leq 0$ or $x > 4$.

*6. A particle moves on the curve of $y^3 = 2x + 1$ so that its distance from the x-axis is increasing at the constant rate of 2 units per second. When $t = 0$ the particle is at $(0,1)$.

(a) Find a pair of parametric equations $x = x(t)$ and $y = y(t)$ which describe the motion of the particle for nonnegative t.

(b) Find $|a|$, the magnitude of its acceleration, when $t = 1$.

7. Let the function f have a derivative for all real x. If $f(a) = 0$ and $f'(x) > 0$ prove that

(a) $f(x)$ is positive if $x > a$;   (b) $f(x)$ is negative if $x < a$.

Sample Essay Examination: 11

1. Sketch the curve of $y^2 = x - x^3$ after finding

(a) intercepts;

(b) symmetry;

(c) asymptotes;

(d) relative maxima and minima.

*2. Find the area which the polar curves of $r = 2 - \cos \theta$ and $r = 3 \cos \theta$ have in common.

3. Let n be an integer greater than 1.

(a) Define $\ln n$ as an integral and interpret $\ln n$ as an **area**.

(b) Show that

$$\frac{1}{2} + \frac{1}{3} + \ldots + \frac{1}{n} < \ln n < 1 + \frac{1}{2} + \frac{1}{3} + \ldots + \frac{1}{n-1} \ .$$

4. A particle moving along the x-axis starts at the origin when $t = 0$. Its acceleration at any time t is $a = -6t$. Find its velocity when $t = 0$ if the maximum displacement of the particle in the positive direction is 16 units.

*5. Integrate:

(a) $\displaystyle \int \frac{dx}{\sqrt{6x - x^2}}$;

(b) $\displaystyle \int x^3 e^{-x^2} \, dx$.

6. A certain chemical substance decomposes at a rate proportional to the amount present. If initially there are 6 gm of the substance and 2 gm decompose in 1 min, how many gm are left after 10 min?

7. Let b be a constant. Find m in terms of b if the line $y = mx + b$ is to be tangent to the curve of $xy = 1$.

Sample Essay Examination: 12

---

1. Sketch, on the same set of axes, the curves of $y = x^3 - 4x$ and of $y = x^2 - 4$, and find the total area bounded by these curves.

2. A cylindrical hole of diameter a is bored through the center of a sphere of radius a. Find the volume that remains.

3. Find the equation of the curve whose slope at any point (x,y) equals $\frac{2y}{x}$ and which passes through the point $(1,1)$.

*4. (a) Integrate $\int \dfrac{2\ dx}{(x - 1)(x^2 + 1)}$.

(b) Evaluate, if possible, $\int_0^\infty xe^{-x^2}\ dx$.

5. Let k and a be positive constants. Let the vertices of the base of a triangle be the origin and $(a,0)$. Find the locus of the vertex of the triangle if

(a) the sum of the tangents of the base angles is k;

(b) the product of the tangents of the base angles is k.

(c) What is each of the above if $a = 1$ and $k = 4$?

*6. A reservoir in the shape of a sphere of radius 4 ft has its center 8 ft above the surface of a pond, and water is pumped into the bottom of the reservoir from the pond. Determine the work done in filling the reservoir to a depth of 6 ft.

*7. A particle starts when $t = 0$ at the point $(4,0)$ and moves counterclockwise on the circle $x^2 + y^2 = 16$. Its speed at time t equals e^t.

(a) Find when it first reaches the point $(-4,0)$.

(b) Write its acceleration a as a vector in terms of the unit vectors i and j at the time found in part (a).

[In handwritten work the clearest and simplest notation for vectors is ordinary letters with an arrow over them: $\vec{a}$, $\vec{\imath}$, $\vec{\jmath}$.]

Sample Essay Examination: 13

1. Sketch the graph of $y = x + \sin x$ after having found

   (a) intercepts;

   (b) relative maximum or minimum points;

   (c) inflection points.

2. A square is inscribed in a circle of radius a. Set up an integral with appropriate limits for the volume obtained if the region outside the square but inside the circle is rotated about a diagonal of the square.

3. (a) Integrate $\int_1^x \frac{dt}{t}$ where $x > 1$.

   (b) Interpret the integral in (a) as an area.

   (c) Show that $x - 1 > \ln x > \frac{x-1}{x}$ if $x > 1$.

4. (a) Find the function y for which $\frac{dy}{dx} = e^{x-y}$, given that when $x = 0$, $y = 1$.

   *(b) For what values of n does $\int_1^{\infty} \frac{dx}{x^{2-n}}$ converge? To what?

*5. A particle moves along a curve so that its position vector and velocity vector are perpendicular at all times. Prove that the particle moves along a circle whose center is at the origin.

*6. Sketch the curve of $y = e^{x/2} + e^{-x/2}$ and find its length from $x = 0$ to $x = 2$.

7. Let the functions f and g be differentiable for all real x.
If $f(a) = g(a)$ and $f'(x) > g'(x)$ for all x, prove that

$$\text{if } \quad x > a, \qquad f(x) > g(x);$$
$$\text{if } \quad x < a, \qquad f(x) < g(x).$$

Sample Essay Examination: 14

1. Find the volume obtained if the trapezoid with vertices at
$(2,0)$, $(2,2)$, $(5,0)$, and $(5,5)$ is rotated about the y-axis.

2. Investigate the curve of $y = \ln \sin x$ on the interval
$-2\pi < x < 2\pi$ for

(a) extent;

(b) intercepts;

(c) relative maximum or minimum points;

(d) concavity;

(e) asymptotes.

Sketch the curve.

3. Assume that the volume of a balloon that is falling decreases
at a rate proportional to its volume. If it loses 10% of its initial
volume during the first minute of fall, find how long it will take to
lose 50% of its initial volume.

4. If a tangent is drawn to the parabola $y = 3 - x^2$ at any point other than the vertex then it forms a right triangle with the axes. At what point on the curve should the tangent be drawn to form the triangle of least area?

*5. The acceleration of a particle is given by the vector $a = e^{-t}\, \mathbf{i} + e^t\, \mathbf{j}$. When $t = 0$, the particle is at the point $(1,2)$ and has velocity $\mathbf{v} = 2\,\mathbf{i}$. Find the position vector R at any time t.

*6. Find the area of the surface obtained by rotating about the x-axis the area of $x = y^2$ between $(0,0)$ and $(4,2)$.

7. (a) Find $\dfrac{1}{x}\dfrac{d^2 x}{dy^2}$ if $y = \displaystyle\int_0^x \dfrac{1}{\sqrt{3 + 2t^2}}\, dt$.

(b) If $f'(x) = (\sin x)\cdot f(x)$ and $f(0) = 3$, find $f(x)$.

Sample Essay Examination: 15

---

1. (a) Sketch the graph of $y = x^4 - 6x^2$, showing any maximum, minimum, or inflection points.

(b) Find the area bounded by this curve and the x-axis.

2.   A cube is contracting so that its surface area decreases at the constant rate of 72 in^2/sec. Determine how fast the volume is changing at the instant when the surface area is 54 ft^2.

3.   Find a function y which satisfies the conditions:

  (1) $\dfrac{y'}{y}$ = $2x$ (2) $y(1)$ = e.

4.   (a) If $f(x)$ = $|x|^3$, find $f'(0)$ by using the definition of derivative.

  (b) Is $f'(x)$ continuous at $x = 0$? Why or why not?

  (c) Is the function $x|x|$ continuous at $x = 0$? Why or why not?

  (d) Evaluate

$$\int_{-1}^{1} (1 - |x|)\ dx.$$

*5.   A rod RS of length c units slides with its ends R and S on the x- and y-axes respectively, as shown in Figure S15-5. A rod SP of length k units is rigidly attached to RS at S so that the points R, S, and P are

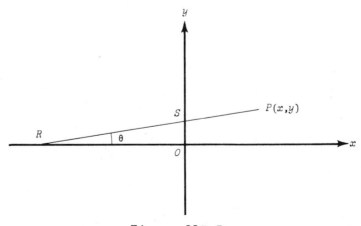

Figure S15-5

collinear at all times. Find the locus of P using as parameter the angle θ shown; find the Cartesian equation of the locus by eliminating θ, and name the curve.

*6. (a) Evaluate, if possible, $\displaystyle\int_0^\infty \frac{dx}{x^2 + 4}$.

(b) Evaluate $\displaystyle\int_1^e x \ln x \, dx.$

(c) Integrate $\displaystyle\int \frac{x - 3}{x^2 - 1} \, dx.$

7. A particle moves along the x-axis so that its acceleration at time t is given by $a = \dfrac{1}{v}$. If its initial velocity v_0 equals 2 and it starts at the origin,

(a) find its velocity at any time t;

(b) find the distance it travels in the first 6 seconds.

Solution Keys

Multiple-Choice Questions

For each of the eleven sets we give first a table showing the correct answers. In each table, some of the indications of correct answer are marked by an asterisk. The asterisk means that some comment or hint about the problem is given below the table.

Set 1 : Limits

1. B.	6. D*.	11. E.	16. E*.	21. C*.
2. D.	7. A.	12. B*.	17. B*.	22. B*.
3. C.	8. E.	13. B.	18. C.	23. A.
4. A.	9. C.	14. A*.	19. D.	24. E*.
5. D*.	10. D.	15. C.	20. C.	25. B*.

5. D. Note that $\dfrac{x^3 - 8}{x^2 - 4} = \dfrac{(x - 2)(x^2 + 2x + 4)}{(x - 2)(x + 2)}$.

6. D. This limit is the derivative of $f(x) = x^6$ at $x = 1$; to see this, use the definition of derivative to write $f'(1)$.

12. B. This is $f'(8)$ where $f(x) = x^{1/3}$.

14. A. As $x \to \infty$, the *function* $\sin x$ does, indeed, oscillate between -1 and 1

16. E. The formula $1 - \cos x = 2 \sin^2 \dfrac{x}{2}$ can be used here to "resolve" the indeterminacy; then we get

$$\lim_{x \to 0} \frac{2 \sin^2 \frac{x}{2}}{x} = \lim_{x \to 0} \frac{\sin^2 \frac{x}{2}}{\frac{x}{2}}$$

$$= \lim_{x \to 0} \left[\sin \frac{x}{2} \cdot \frac{\sin \frac{x}{2}}{\frac{x}{2}} \right]$$

$$= 0 \cdot 1 = 0 .$$

310

17. B. Note $\dfrac{\sin x}{x^2 + 3x} = \dfrac{\sin x}{x(x + 3)} = \dfrac{\sin x}{x} \cdot \dfrac{1}{x + 3}$.

21. C. This is $f'(0)$ where $f(x) = e^{-x}$.

22. B. This is $f'(e)$ where $f(x) = \ln x$.

24. E. Note that $x \sin \dfrac{1}{x}$ can be rewritten $\dfrac{\sin \frac{1}{x}}{\frac{1}{x}}$ and that as

$x \to \infty$, $\dfrac{1}{x} \to 0$.

25. B. Since $\ln x = \displaystyle\int_{1}^{x} \dfrac{1}{t}\, dt$ (which is equal to the area under $y = \dfrac{1}{t}$

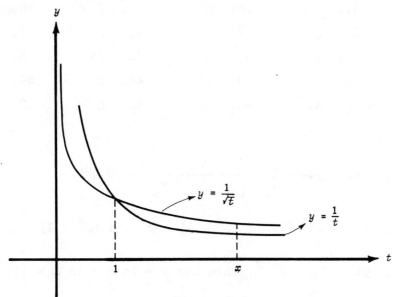

Figure 1-1

from $t = 1$ to $t = x$, shown in Fig. 1-1), and since, for $x > 1$,

$$\int_{1}^{x} \frac{1}{t}\, dt \ \leq \ \int_{1}^{x} \frac{1}{\sqrt{t}}\, dt$$

$$\leq \ 2\sqrt{t}\,\Big]_{1}^{x} \ = \ 2(\sqrt{x} - 1),$$

therefore $\ln x \ \leq \ 2(\sqrt{x} - 1)$. Noting, also, that, for $x > 1$,

$0 < \ln x$, it follows that

$$0 \ < \ \frac{\ln x}{x} \ \leq \ 2\left(\frac{1}{\sqrt{x}} - \frac{1}{x}\right) .$$

Since the expression on the right approaches zero as $x \to \infty$, then

$$\lim_{x \to \infty} \frac{\ln x}{x} = 0 .$$

Set 2 : Differentiation

1. C.	6. D.	11. C*.	16. D.	21. C.
2. A.	7. A.	12. E.	17. B.	22. A.
3. B.	8. E*.	13. A.	18. D.	23. D.
4. B.	9. D.	14. C.	19. A.	24. E*.
5. E.	10. B.	15. D.	20. C*.	25. B.

26. D.	31. C*.	36. E*.	41. B.	46. A.
27. C.	32. C.	37. E.	42. C.	47. B.
28. A.	33. A.	38. A.	43. E*.	48. E.
29. D.	34. D.	39. E*.	44. C.	49. B*.
30. E.	35. B.	40. D.	45. D.	50. A.

8.   E.   The correct answer is $\dfrac{1}{(1 - x^2)^{3/2}}$.

11.   C.   Hint: $y = \ln e^x - \ln (e^x - 1) = x - \ln (e^x - 1)$.

20.   C.   Hint: since $y = x^{\ln x}$, then $\ln y = \ln x \cdot \ln x = (\ln x)^2$.

24.   E.   The correct answer is $3 \ln^2 x + \ln^3 x$.

31.   C.   Since $\dfrac{dy}{dt} = \dfrac{1}{1 - t}$ and $\dfrac{dx}{dt} = \dfrac{1}{(1 - t)^2}$, then $\dfrac{dy}{dx} = 1 - t = \dfrac{1}{x}$.

36.   E.   Hint: $\dfrac{dy}{dx} = 2t^2 - 3t \ \ (t \neq 0)$ and $\dfrac{d^2y}{dx^2} = \dfrac{4t - 3}{2t}$.

39.   E.   The correct answer is $- \dfrac{6}{x^4}$.

43.   E. $f'(x)$ here equals $\dfrac{-x - 1}{(x - 1)^3}$; note that $f'(-1) = 0$.

49.   B.   Since $\dfrac{dy}{dt} = -2 \sin 2t = -4 \sin t \cos t$ and $\dfrac{dx}{dt} = - \sin t$,

then $\dfrac{dy}{dx} = 4 \cos t$. Then, $\dfrac{d^2y}{dx^2} = - \dfrac{4 \sin t}{- \sin t}$.

Set 3: Applications of Differential Calculus

1. D.	6. D.	11. C*.	16. A.	21. E.	26. E*.
2. A.	7. E.	12. B.	17. B*.	22. C.	27. B.
3. E.	8. C.	13. D*.	18. E.	23. B.	28. D.
4. B.	9. D*.	14. E.	19. D*.	24. D.	29. A*.
5. A*.	10. A.	15. C.	20. B.	25. A.	30. D*.

31. C.	36. E.	41. E.	46. A.	51. E*.	56. B.
32. E.	37. A*.	42. C*.	47. E.	52. C.	57. A.
33. B.	38. B*.	43. B.	48. A*.	53. D*.	58. D.
34. A.	39. D.	44. C.	49. B*.	54. B*.	59. E.
35. C.	40. D.	45. D.	50. C*.	55. E.	60. D*.

5.   A.   Hint: at any point on the curve, the slope is $\dfrac{1}{\sqrt{2x + 1}}$.

9.   D.   Since $y' = \dfrac{y}{2y - x}$, the tangent is vertical for $x = 2y$.

Substitute in the given equation.

11. C.   We get, taking differentials, $4x\,dx - 3y^2\,dy = 0$, and use

$x = 3$, $y = 2$, and $dx = .04$ to find dy. The answer is $y + dy$.

13. D.   Since $e = 10$ with a possible error of 1%, $de = \pm.1$. From

$V = e^3$ and $dV = 3e^2\,de$, we get $dV = \pm 30$ or a possible error

of 30 in^3 in the volume.

17. B. $f'(x)$ changes sign only as x passes through zero.

19. D.   Since $f'(x) = 4\cos x + 3\sin x$, the critical values of x are

those for which $\tan x = -\dfrac{4}{3}$. For these values,

when $\dfrac{\pi}{2} < x < \pi$ then $\sin x = \dfrac{4}{5}$ and $\cos x = -\dfrac{3}{5}$

but

when $\dfrac{3\pi}{2} < x < 2\pi$ then $\sin x = -\dfrac{4}{5}$ and $\cos x = \dfrac{3}{5}$.

If these are used to determine the sign of $f''(x)$, we see that the second-quadrant x yield a negative second derivative, but the fourth-quadrant x give a positive second derivative. It follows that the function is a maximum for the former set, for which f has the value 5 . Note that $f(0) = f(2\pi) = -3$.

26. E. The answer is $t < 2$, since for all such t the velocity is positive while the acceleration is negative.

29. A. Since $v = 4t^3 - 18t^2 + 24t$

$$= 2t(2t^2 - 9t + 12)$$

and since $2t^2 - 9t + 12$ is always positive, it follows that the sign of v is the same as that of t.

30. D. See Fig. 3-1, which shows the motion of the particle during the

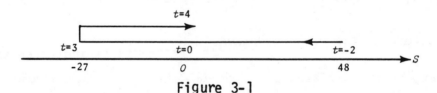

Figure 3-1

time interval $-2 \leqq t \leqq 4$. The particle is at rest when $t = 0$ or 3, but reverses direction only at 3. The endpoints need to be checked here, of course. Indeed, the maximum displacement occurs at one of those, namely when $t = -2$.

37. A. Note that $\mathbf{v} = -\pi \sin \frac{\pi}{3}t\mathbf{i} + \frac{2\pi}{3} \cos \frac{\pi}{3}t\mathbf{j}$.

38. B. $\mathbf{a} = -\frac{\pi^2}{3} \cos \frac{\pi}{3}t\mathbf{i} - \frac{2\pi^2}{9} \sin \frac{\pi}{3}t\mathbf{j}$.

42. C. Hint: when $V = \frac{32\pi}{3}$, $r = 2$ and $\frac{dr}{dt} = \frac{1}{4\pi}$.

48. A. See Fig. 3-2, where V, the volume of the cylinder, equals $2\pi r^2h$. Then $V = 2\pi(R^2h - h^3)$ is a maximum for $h^2 = \frac{R^2}{3}$, and the ratio

of the volumes of sphere

to cylinder is

$$\frac{4}{3}\pi R^3 \ : \ 2\pi \cdot \frac{2}{3}R^2 \cdot \frac{R}{\sqrt{3}} \quad \text{or}$$

$$\sqrt{3} : 1 \ .$$

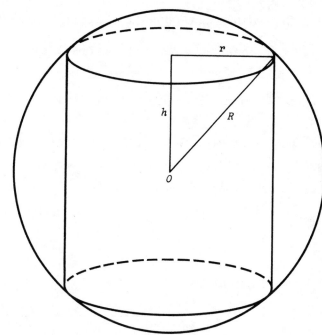

Figure 3-2

49. B.   See Fig. 3-3. If we let m be the slope of the line, then its
equation is $y - 2 = m(x - 1)$ with intercepts as indicated in
the Figure.

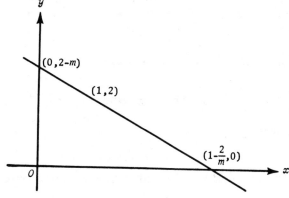

Figure 3-3

The area A of the triangle is given by

$$A \ = \ \frac{1}{2}(2 - m)(1 - \frac{2}{m})$$

$$= \ \frac{1}{2}(4 - \frac{4}{m} - m) \ .$$

Then $\frac{dA}{dm} = \frac{1}{2}(\frac{4}{m^2} - 1)$ and equals 0 when $m = \pm 2$.

50. C.   Hint: let $q = (x - 6)^2 + y^2$ be the quantity to be minimized.

Then $q = (x - 6)^2 + (x^2 - 4)$.

51. E.   No minimum product exists.

53. D.   See Fig. 3-4. At noon, car A is at O, car B at N; the cars are shown

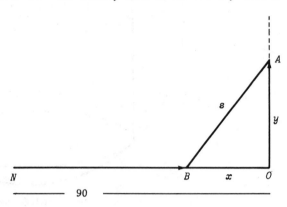

Figure 3-4

t hours after noon. We know that $\frac{dx}{dt}$ = -60 and that $\frac{dy}{dt}$ = 40. Using

$s^2 = x^2 + y^2$, we get

$$\frac{ds}{dt} = \frac{x\frac{dx}{dt} + y\frac{dy}{dt}}{s} .$$

At one P.M., $x = 30$ and $y = 40$.

54. B. $\frac{ds}{dt}$ (from Problem 53) is zero when $y = -\frac{3}{2}x$. Note that $x = 90 - 60t$

and $y = 40t$.

60. D.   Since $f''(x) = 12ax^2 + 2b$ and $ab > 0$, then a and b are both

positive or both negative. Thus, $f''(x)$ never equals zero.

Set 4: Integration

1. C.	6. B.	11. D.	16. A.	21. E.
2. E*.	7. A.	12. C.	17. E*.	22. E.
3. A.	8. E.	13. B.	18. D*.	23. B.
4. D.	9. D.	14. C.	19. A.	24. C.
5. E.	10. A.	15. B.	20. D.	25. A.

26. A.	31. B.	36. C.	41. E.	46. B.
27. E.	32. E.	37. E*.	42. D*.	47. C.
28. B.	33. A.	38. A.	43. A.	48. C.
29. D.	34. D.	39. C*.	44. B.	49. D.
30. C.	35. E.	40. B.	45. C.	50. A.

51. C.	56. D.	61. C*.	66. E*.	71. D*.
52. E*.	57. E.	62. E.	67. B*.	72. C*.
53. B.	58. A*.	63. A*.	68. D.	73. A*.
54. B.	59. B*.	64. D.	69. E*.	74. B*.
55. B.	60. D*.	65. C.	70. B*.	75. E*.

2. E. Hint: expand. The correct answer is $\frac{x^3}{3} - x - \frac{1}{4x} + C$.

17. E. $\int \frac{(x-2)^3}{x^2}\, dx = \int (x - 6 + \frac{12}{x} - \frac{8}{x^2})\, dx = \frac{x^2}{2} - 6x + 12 \ln |x| + \frac{8}{x} + C$.

18. D. Hint: expand.

37. E. If we let $u = \tan^{-1} y$, then we integrate $\int u\, du$. The correct answer is $\frac{1}{2} (\tan^{-1} y)^2 + C$.

39. C. The answer is equivalent to $\frac{1}{2} \ln |1 - \cos 2t| + C$.

42. D. Hint: decompose integrand into partial fractions. The answer is equivalent to $\frac{1}{2}(\ln |x| + \ln |x - 2|) + C$.

52. E. Hint: $\ln \sqrt{x} = \frac{1}{2} \ln x$.

58. A. Hint: the integrand is equivalent to $1 - \frac{2}{y + 1}$.

59. B. Hint: let $u = \sqrt{t + 1}$. Then $u^2 = t + 1$, $2u\, du = dt$, and $t = u^2 - 1$.

60. D. Hint: multiply.

61. C. Hint: use the parts formula twice (that is, $\int u \, dv = uv - \int v \, du$).

Let $u = e^\theta$ both times.

63. A. Hint: use integration by parts.

66. E. Hint: letting $u = 4x - 4x^2$, we see that we are integrating $- \frac{1}{4} \int u^{-\frac{1}{2}} du$.

67. B. Hint: divide, getting $\int \left[e^x - \frac{e^x}{1 + e^x} \right] dx$.

69. E. Hint: use integration by parts, letting $u = \tan^{-1} x$.

70. B. Hint: note that $\dfrac{1}{1 - e^x} = \dfrac{1 - e^x + e^x}{1 - e^x} = 1 + \dfrac{e^x}{1 - e^x}$. Or multiply

integrand by $\dfrac{e^{-x}}{e^{-x}}$, recognizing that the correct answer is equivalent

to $- \ln \left| e^{-x} - 1 \right|$.

71. D. Hint: expand numerator and divide.

72. C. Hint: observe that $e^{2 \ln u} = u^2$.

73. A. If we let $u = 1 + \ln y^2 = 1 + 2 \ln |y|$, we want to

integrate $\frac{1}{2} \int \dfrac{du}{u}$.

74. B. Hint: expand and note that $\int (\tan^2 \theta - 2 \tan \theta + 1) \, d\theta$

$= \int \sec^2 \theta \, d\theta - 2 \int \tan\theta \, d\theta$.

75. E. Multiply by $\dfrac{1 - \sin \theta}{1 - \sin \theta}$. The correct answer is $\tan \theta - \sec \theta + C$.

Set 5: Definite Integrals

1. C.	6. A.	11. D.	16. A*.	21. D.
2. B.	7. D.	12. B.	17. D.	22. A.
3. E.	8. E.	13. B.	18. A.	23. E.
4. B.	9. A.	14. E.	19. C.	24. C.
5. D.	10. C.	15. C.	20. E.	25. C.

26. A.	31. B.	36. E*.	41. C.	46. C.
27. E.	32. A.	37. D.	42. D.	47. B.
28. C.	33. E*.	38. B.	43. A.	48. E.
29. A.	34. C.	39. C.	44. D.	49. C.
30. E*.	35. D.	40. A.	45. E.	50. D.

16. A.   One can, of course, substitute $x = 4 \sin \theta$ to evaluate this

integral; however, the answer is obtained immediately if the

integral is recognized as that for the area of a semicircle

of radius 4.

30. E. $\int_0^e \frac{du}{u} = \lim_{h \to 0^+} \int_h^e \frac{du}{u} = \lim_{h \to 0^+} \ln |u| \Big|_h^e = \lim_{h \to 0^+} (\ln e - \ln h).$ So

the integral diverges to infinity.

33. E. $\int_2^4 \frac{dx}{(x-3)^2} = \int_2^3 \frac{dx}{(x-3)^2} + \int_3^4 \frac{dx}{(x-3)^2}.$ Neither of the

latter integrals converges; therefore the original integral diverges.

36. E.   Note, first, that $\int_0^\infty \frac{dx}{1 + x^2} = \lim_{b \to \infty} \tan^{-1} x \Big|_0^b = \frac{\pi}{2}.$ Since

$Q(b) = \int_0^b \frac{dx}{x^3 + 1}$ increases with b and, further, $Q(b) \leq \int_0^b \frac{dx}{x^2 + 1}$,

$Q(b)$ converges as $b \to \infty$. Similarly, since $\int_0^\infty \frac{dx}{e^x} = 1$ and since,

further, $S(b) = \int_0^b \frac{dx}{e^x + 2}$ increases with b and $\int_0^b \frac{dx}{e^x + 2} \leq \int_0^b \frac{dx}{e^x}$,

$S(b)$ also converges as $b \to \infty$.

Set **6**: Application of Integration: Area

1.	C.	6.	D.	11.	D.	16.	B.	21.	C.
2.	C.	7.	C.	12.	D.	17.	B.	22.	E.
3.	A.	8.	E.	13.	C.	18.	C.	23.	B.
4.	D.	9.	A.	14.	E.	19.	D.	24.	D.
5.	B.	10.	A.	15.	A.	20.	A.	25.	A.

We give below, for each problem, a sketch of the region in question, and indicate a typical element of area.

1.   C.

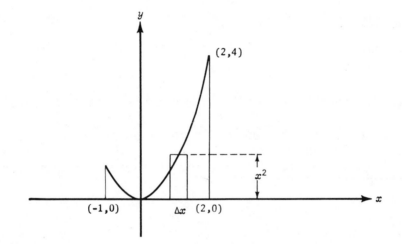

2.   C.

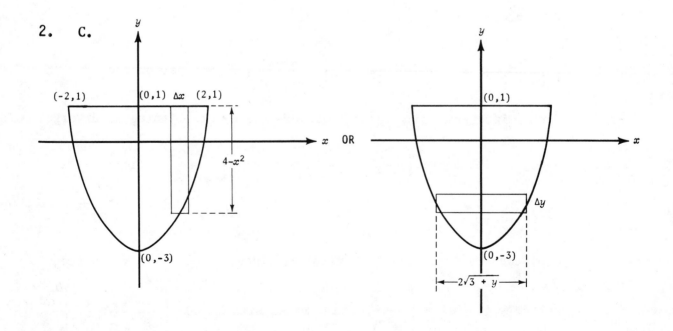

3.   A.

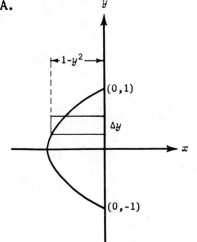 OR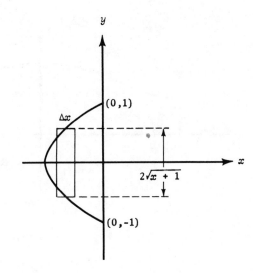

4.   D.

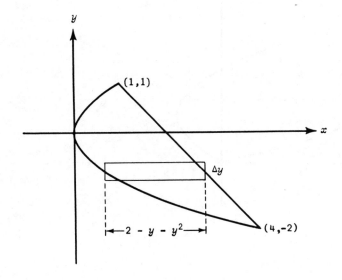

5.   B.

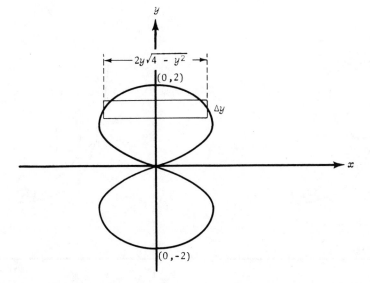

6.   D.

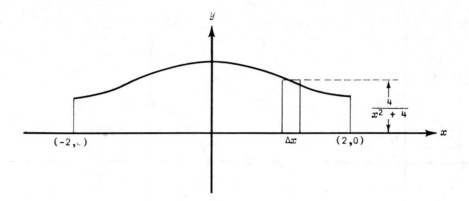

7.   C.

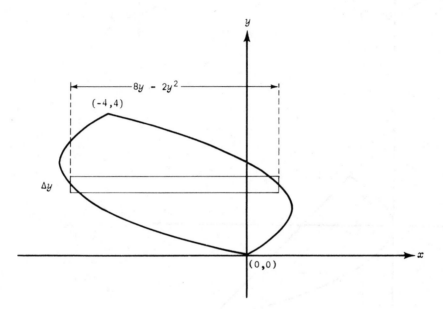

8.   E.

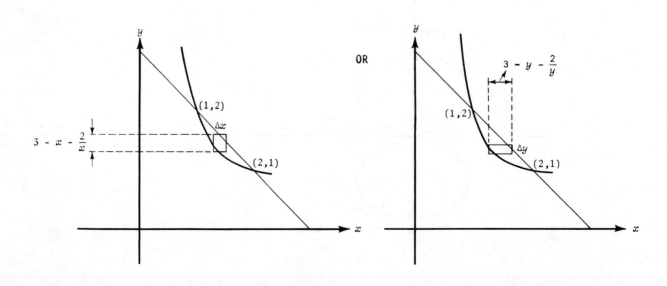

9. A.

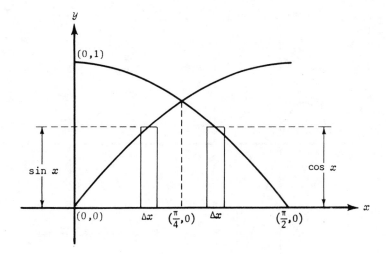

10. A.

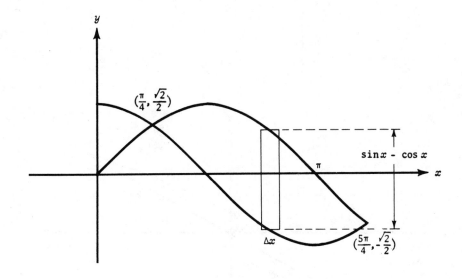

11. D.

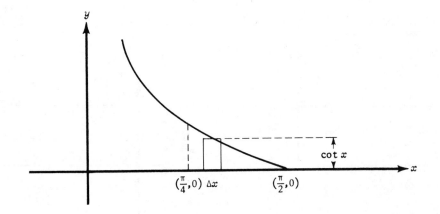

12. D.

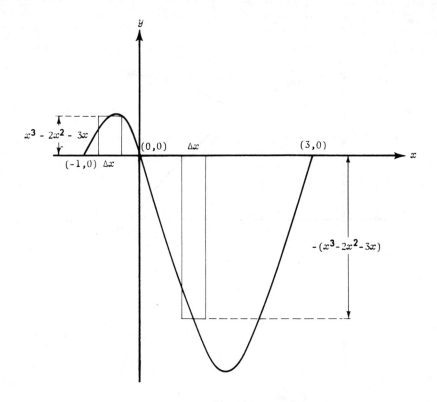

13. C.

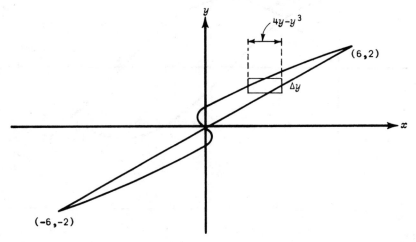

14. E.

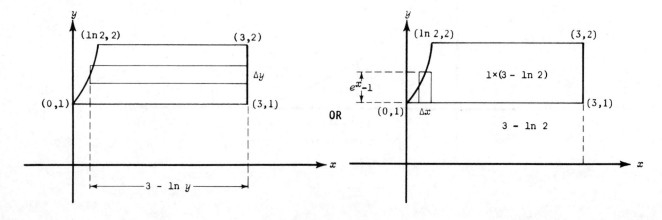

15.   A.

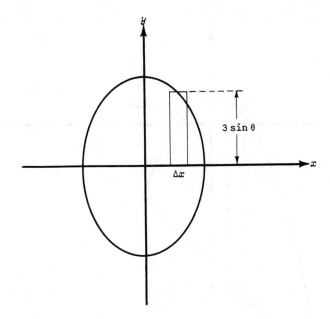

16.   B.

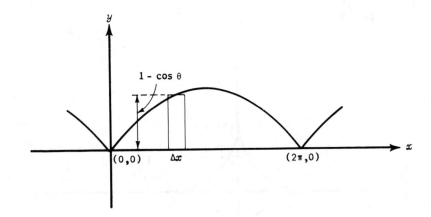

17.   B.

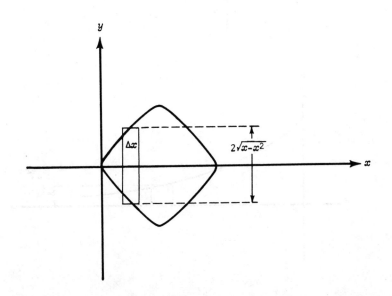

18. C.

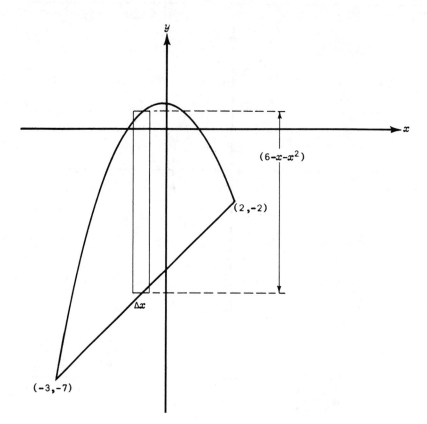

$(6-x-x^2)$

$(2,-2)$

Δx

$(-3,-7)$

19. D.

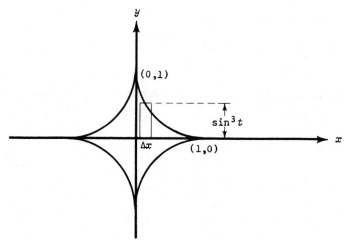

$(0,1)$

$\sin^3 t$

Δx $(1,0)$

20. A.

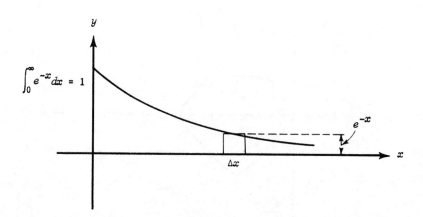

$\int_0^\infty e^{-x}\,dx = 1$

e^{-x}

Δx

21. C.

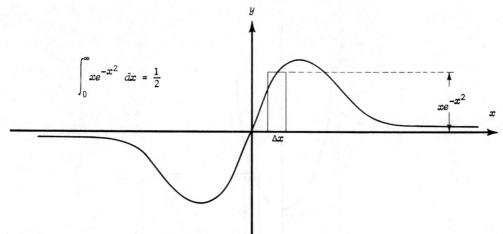

$$\int_0^\infty xe^{-x^2}\,dx = \tfrac{1}{2}$$

22. E.

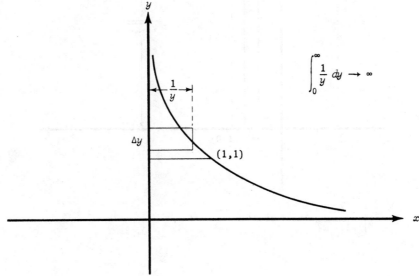

$$\int_0^\infty \frac{1}{y}\,dy \to \infty$$

(1,1)

23. B.

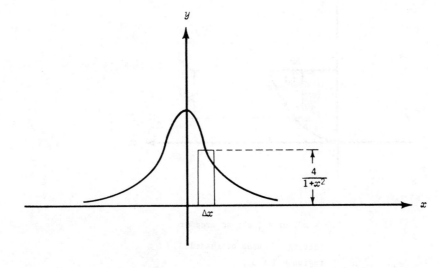

$$\int_{-\infty}^{\infty} \frac{4}{1 + x^2}\,dx = \lim_{b\to\infty} 4\tan^{-1} x \Big|_{-b}^{b} = 4\pi .$$

24.   D.

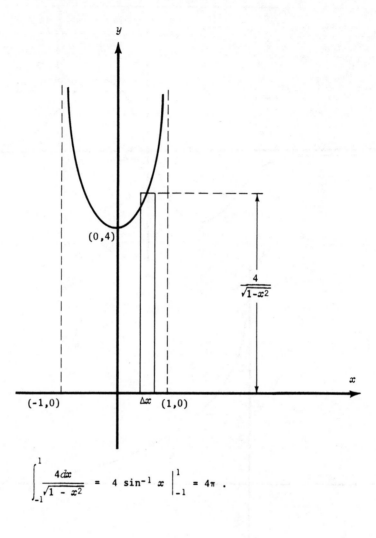

$$\int_{-1}^{1} \frac{4\,dx}{\sqrt{1 - x^2}} \;=\; 4\,\sin^{-1} x \;\Big|_{-1}^{1} \;=\; 4\pi \;.$$

25.   A.

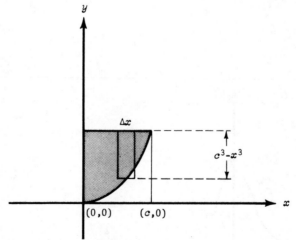

$$\int_{0}^{c} (c^3 - x^3)\, dx = \frac{3}{4}\, c^4; \text{ so area of}$$

rectangle : area of shaded

region = 4 : 3 .

Set 7: Application of Integration: Volume

1. B.	6. A.	11. C.	16. D.	21. B.	26. A.
2. D.	7. D.	12. A.	17. A.	22. E.	27. D.
3. C.	8. D.	13. B.	18. B.	23. D.	28. B.
4. A.	9. E.	14. A.	19. D.	24. C.	29. C.
5. C.	10. B.	15. C.	20. C.	25. A.	30. D.

Sketches and comments are given below for each problem.

1.   B.

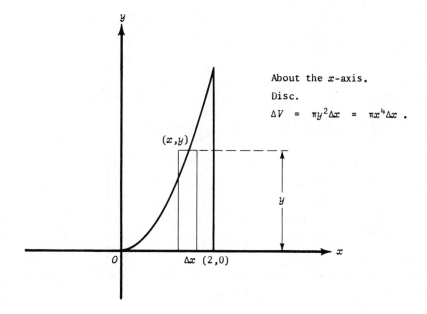

About the x-axis.
Disc.
$\Delta V = \pi y^2 \Delta x = \pi x^4 \Delta x$.

2.   D.

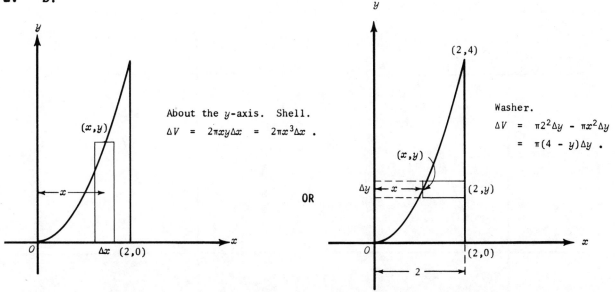

About the y-axis. Shell.
$\Delta V = 2\pi x y \Delta x = 2\pi x^3 \Delta x$.

OR

Washer.
$\Delta V = \pi 2^2 \Delta y - \pi x^2 \Delta y$
$= \pi(4 - y)\Delta y$.

3.   C.

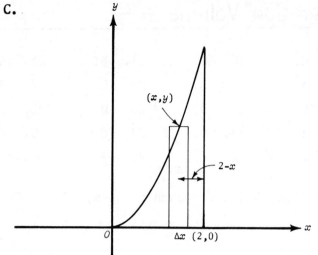

About $x = 2$.

Shell.

$\Delta V = 2\pi(2 - x)y\Delta x$

$\qquad = 2\pi(2 - x)x^2\Delta x$.

4.   A.

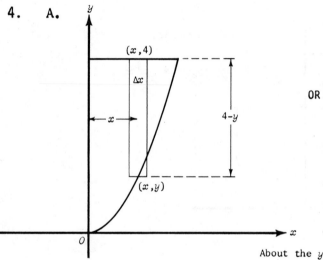

OR

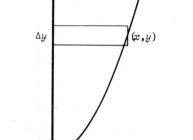

About the y-axis.

Shell.

$\Delta V = 2\pi x(4 - y)\Delta x$

$\qquad = 2\pi x(4 - x^2)\Delta x$.

Disc.

$\Delta V = \pi x^2 \Delta y$

$\qquad = \pi y \Delta y$.

5.   C.

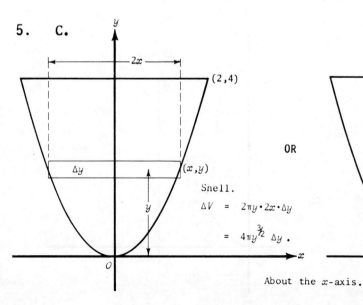

OR

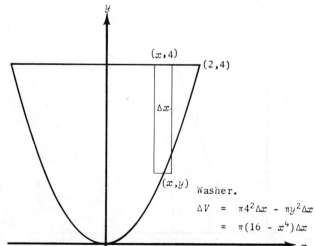

Snell.

$\Delta V = 2\pi y \cdot 2x \cdot \Delta y$

$\qquad = 4\pi y^{\frac{3}{2}}\Delta y$.

Washer.

$\Delta V = \pi 4^2 \Delta x - \pi y^2 \Delta x$

$\qquad = \pi(16 - x^4)\Delta x$

About the x-axis.

6.   A.

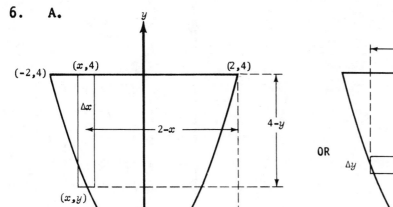

About $x = 2$.

Shell.

$\Delta V = 2\pi(2 - x)(4 - y)\Delta x$

$= 2\pi(2 - x)(4 - x^2)\Delta x$.

Washer (shell).

$\Delta V = 2\pi \cdot 2 \cdot 2x \cdot \Delta y$

$= 8\pi y^{1/2}\, \Delta y$.

7.   D.

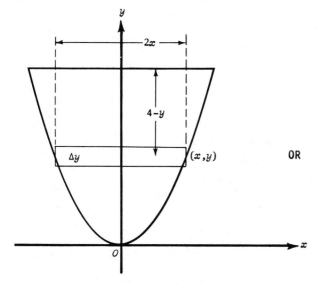

OR

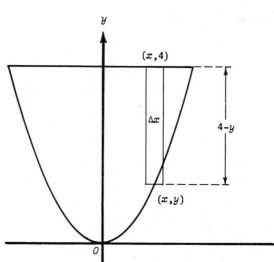

About $y = 4$.

Shell.

$\Delta V = 2\pi(4 - y)2x\Delta y$

$= 4\pi(4 - y)y^{1/2}\, \Delta y$.

Disc.

$\Delta V = \pi(4 - y)^2\Delta x$

$= \pi(4 - x^2)^2\Delta x$.

8.   D.

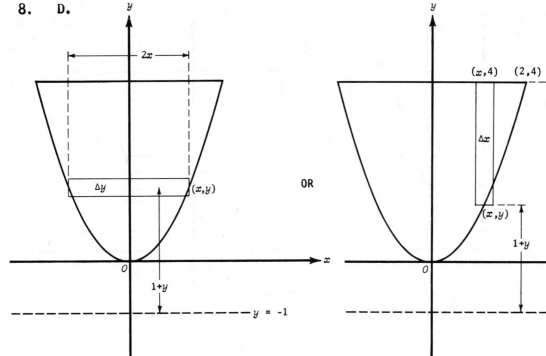

OR

About $y = -1$.

Shell.

$\Delta V = 2\pi(1 + y) \cdot 2x \cdot \Delta y$

$= 4\pi(1 + y)y^{1/2} \Delta y$.

Washer.

$\Delta V = \pi \cdot 5^2 \Delta x - \pi(1 + y)^2 \Delta x$

$= \pi[25 - (1 + y)^2] \Delta x$.

9.   E.

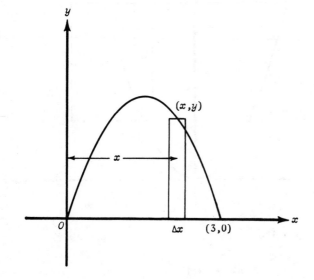

About the y-axis.

Shell.

$\Delta V = 2\pi xy \Delta x$

$= 2\pi x(3x - x^2) \Delta x$.

10. B.

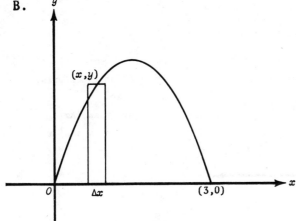

About the x-axis.

Disc.

$\Delta V = \pi y^2 \Delta x$

$\quad\quad = \pi(3x - x^2)^2 \Delta x$.

11. C.

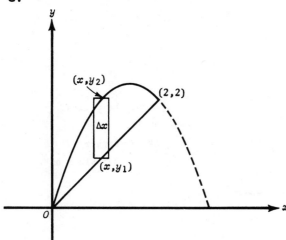

About the x-axis.

Washer.

$\Delta V = \pi y_2^2 \Delta x - \pi y_1^2 \Delta x$

$\quad\quad = \pi[(3x - x^2)^2 - x^2]\Delta x$.

12. A.

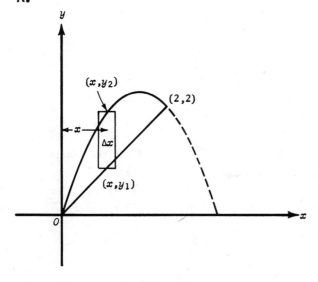

About the y-axis.

Shell.

$\Delta V = 2\pi x(y_2 - y_1)\Delta x$

$\quad\quad = 2\pi x(2x - x^2)\Delta x$.

13. B.

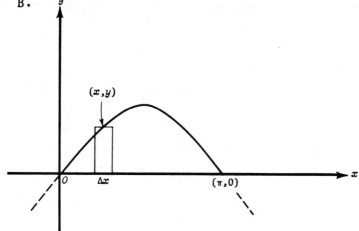

About the x-axis.
Disc.
$$\Delta V \;=\; \pi y^2 \Delta x$$
$$\;=\; \pi \sin^2 x \; \Delta x \;.$$

14. A.

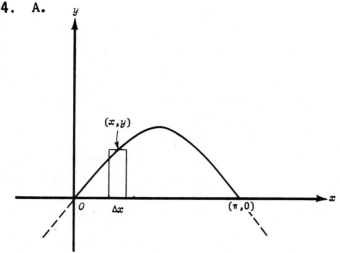

About the y-axis.
Shell.
$$\Delta V \;=\; 2\pi x y \Delta x$$
$$\;=\; 2\pi x \sin x \; \Delta x \;.$$

15. C.

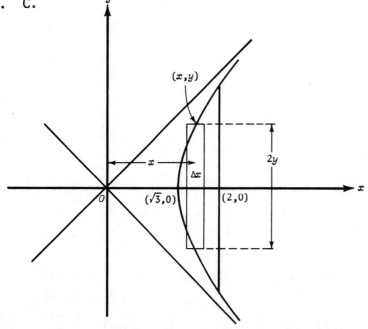

About the y-axis.
Shell.
$$\Delta V \;=\; 2\pi x (2y) \Delta x$$
$$\;=\; 4\pi x \sqrt{x^2 - 3} \; \Delta x \;.$$

16. D.

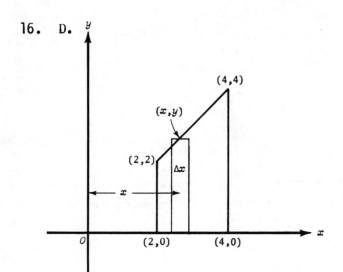

About the y-axis.
Shell.
$$\Delta V = 2\pi x y \Delta x$$
$$= 2\pi x^2 \Delta x .$$

17. A.

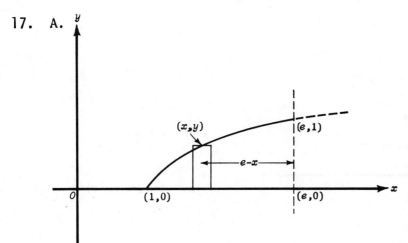

About $x = e$.

Shell.
$$\Delta V = 2\pi(e - x)y\Delta x$$
$$= 2\pi(e - x)\ln x \, \Delta x .$$

OR

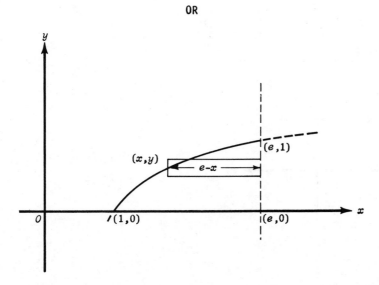

Disc.
$$\Delta V = \pi(e - x)^2 \Delta y$$
$$= \pi(e - e^2)^2 \Delta y .$$

18. B.

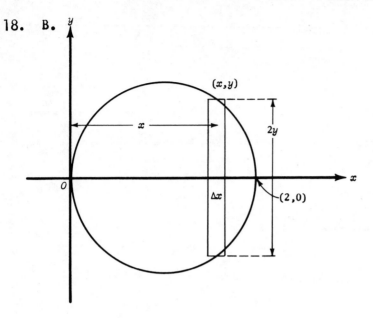

About the y-axis.
Shell.
$$\Delta V = 2\pi x \cdot 2y \Delta x$$
$$= 4\pi x\sqrt{2x - x^2}\ \Delta x\ .$$

19. D.

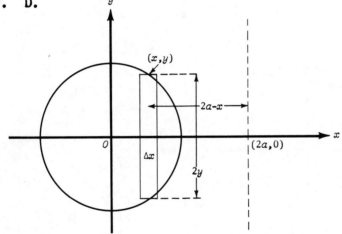

About $x = 2a$.

Shell.
$$\Delta V = 2\pi(2a - x)\cdot 2y\cdot \Delta x\ .$$

OR

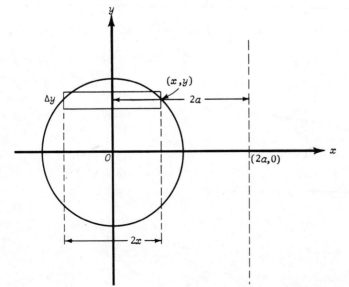

Washer (shell).
$$\Delta V = 2\pi \cdot 2a \cdot 2x \cdot \Delta y\ .$$

20. C.

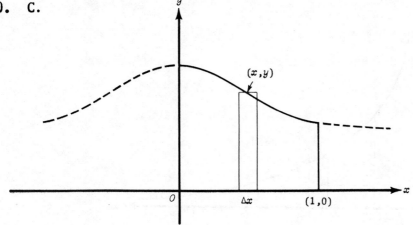

About the x-axis.
Disc.
$\Delta V = \pi y^2 \Delta x$.

21. B.

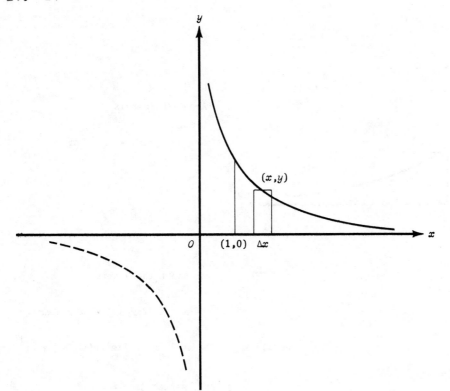

About the x-axis.
Disc.
$\Delta V = \pi y^2 \Delta x = \dfrac{\pi}{x^2} \Delta x$.

22. E.

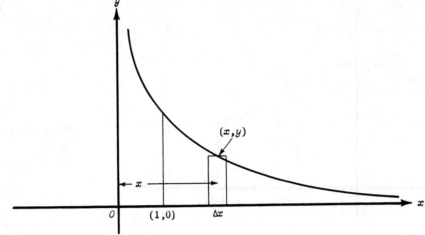

About the y-axis.

Shell.

$\Delta V = 2\pi xy\Delta x = 2\pi\Delta x$.

Note that $2\pi\displaystyle\int_1^\infty dx$ diverges to infinity.

23. D.

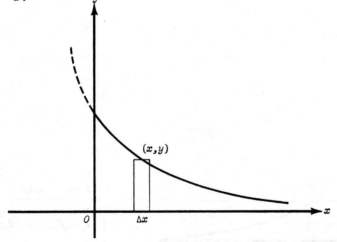

About the x-axis.

Disc.

$\Delta V = \pi y^2\Delta x = \pi e^{-2x}\Delta x$.

24. C.

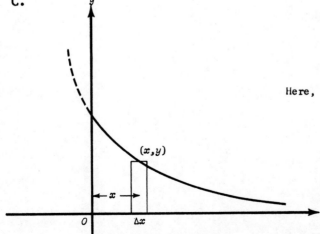

About the y-axis.

Shell.

$\Delta V = 2\pi xy\Delta x = 2\pi xe^{-x}\Delta x$.

Here, $V = 2\pi\displaystyle\int_0^\infty xe^{-x}\,dx = \lim_{b\to\infty} 2\pi(xe^{-x} - e^{-x})\Big|_0^b$

$= 2\pi$, since $\displaystyle\lim_{b\to\infty}\frac{b}{e^b} = 0$.

25. A.

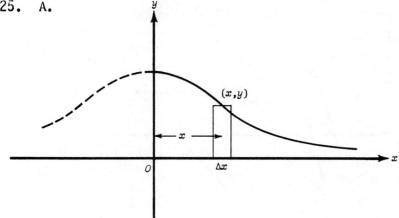

About the y-axis.
Shell.
$\Delta V \;=\; 2\pi xy\,\Delta x \;=\; 2\pi xe^{-x^2}\Delta x$.

26. A.

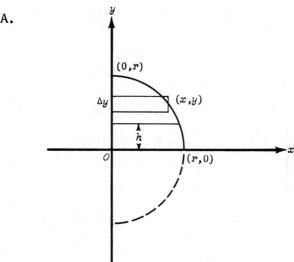

About the y-axis.
Disc.
$\Delta V \;=\; \pi x^2\Delta y \;=\; \pi(r^2 - y^2)\Delta y$.

27. D.

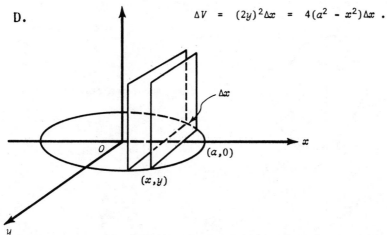

$\Delta V \;=\; (2y)^2\Delta x \;=\; 4(a^2 - x^2)\Delta x$.

28. B.

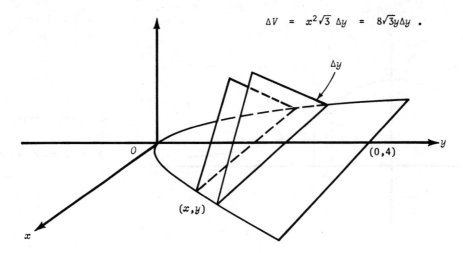

$$\Delta V \;=\; x^2\sqrt{3}\,\Delta y \;=\; 8\sqrt{3}y\Delta y \;.$$

29. C.

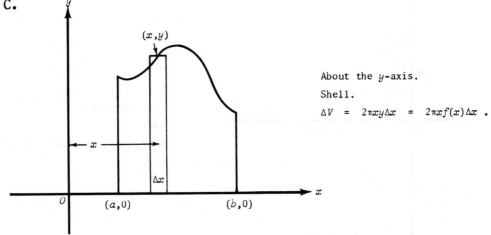

About the y-axis.
Shell.
$$\Delta V \;=\; 2\pi xy\Delta x \;=\; 2\pi xf(x)\,\Delta x \;.$$

30. D.

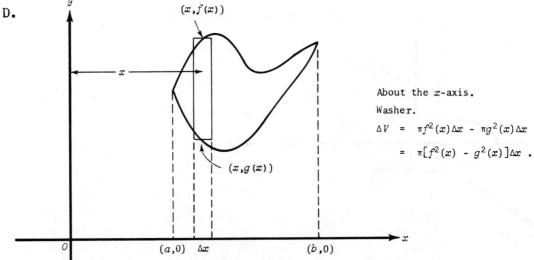

About the x-axis.
Washer.
$$\Delta V \;=\; \pi f^2(x)\,\Delta x \;-\; \pi g^2(x)\,\Delta x$$
$$\;=\; \pi\big[f^2(x) \;-\; g^2(x)\big]\Delta x \;.$$

Set 8: Further Application of Integration

1. C*.	6. E.	11. C.	16. A.	21. E*.	26. A*.
2. A.	7. A.	12. C*.	17. E*.	22. A*.	27. D*
3. D.	8. A.	13. B.	18. B*.	23. B.	OR A*.
4. D.	9. D.	14. E.	19. B*.	24. A*.	
5. B.	10. C.	15. D.	20. C*.	25 C.	

1. C. Note that the curve is symmetric to the x-axis.

12. C. If we let $\bar{v}$ be the average velocity with respect to s, then

$$\bar{v} \;=\; \frac{1}{s(1) - s(0)} \int_{s(0)}^{s(1)} v\,ds \;=\; \frac{1}{16}\int_0^{16} 32t\,ds \;=\; 2\int_0^{16}\frac{\sqrt{8}}{4}\,ds \;=\; \frac{64}{3}.$$

17. E. The answer is 8. Since the particle reverses direction when

$t = 2$, and $v > 0$ for $t > 2$ but $v < 0$ for $t < 2$, therefore

$$s \;=\; -\int_0^2 (3t^2 - 6t)\,dt + \int_2^3 (3t^2 - 6t)\,dt.$$

18. B. Since $v = \sin t$ is positive on $0 < t \leqq 2$, $s = \int_0^2 \sin t\,dt$

$= 1 - \cos 2$.

19. B. $A = 8\int_0^{\frac{\pi}{4}} \frac{1}{2}\cos^2 2\theta\,d\theta \;=\; \frac{\pi}{2}.$

20. C. The small loop is generated as θ varies from $\frac{\pi}{6}$ to $\frac{5\pi}{6}$.

21. E. $s \;=\; \frac{\sqrt{5}}{2}\int_0^{\ln 16} e^{\theta/2}\,d\theta \;=\; 3\sqrt{5}.$

22. A. $s \;=\; \int_{\frac{\pi}{4}}^{\frac{3\pi}{4}} 3\csc^2\theta\,d\theta \;=\; 6.$ Note that this is the length

of the segment of the horizontal line $y = 3$ from $x = -3$ to

$x = 3$.

24. A.   Note that the given limit can be rewritten as

$$\lim_{n\to\infty} \frac{1}{n}\left(\frac{1}{1+\frac{1}{n}} + \frac{1}{1+\frac{2}{n}} + \ldots + \frac{1}{1+\frac{n}{n}}\right) \quad \text{or} \quad \lim_{n\to\infty}\sum_{k=1}^{n} f(x_k)\,\Delta x$$

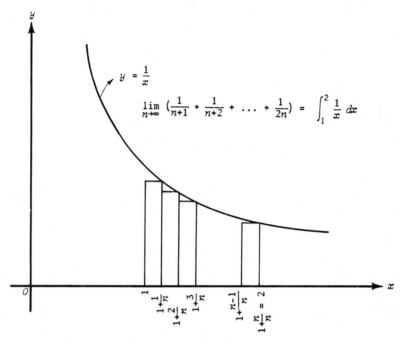

Figure 8-1

where $\Delta x = \frac{1}{n}$, $x_k = 1 + \frac{k}{n}$, $f(x_k) = \frac{1}{x_k}$, and the subdivisions

are made on the interval $1 \leq x \leq 2$. See Figure 8-1 where

the given limit, and the equivalent definite integral $\int_1^2 \frac{dx}{x}$,

are interpreted as the area under $y = \frac{1}{x}$ from $x = 1$ to $x = 2$.

26. A.   Here, $\displaystyle\lim_{n\to\infty}\sum_{k=1}^{n}\frac{1}{\sqrt{kn}}$ equals $\displaystyle\lim_{n\to\infty}\sum_{k=1}^{n}\frac{1}{\sqrt{\frac{k}{n}}}\frac{1}{n}$ or $\displaystyle\lim_{n\to\infty}\sum_{k=1}^{n}f(x_k)\Delta x$

where $\Delta x = \frac{1}{n}$, $x_k = \frac{k}{n}$, $f(x_k) = \frac{1}{\sqrt{x_k}}$, on the interval $[0,1]$.

The equivalent definite integral $\int_0^1 \frac{1}{\sqrt{x}}\,dx$ is improper but

does converge.

27. **D.** This limit can again be recognized as $\displaystyle\lim_{n\to\infty}\sum_{k=0}^{n-1} f(x_k)\Delta x$, where

OR A.

$\Delta x = \dfrac{1}{n}$, $x_k = \dfrac{k}{n}$, and $f(x_k) = \sin \pi x_k$, on the interval $[0,1]$.

The equivalent definite integral is thus $\displaystyle\int_0^1 \sin \pi x \, dx$ which

equals $\dfrac{2}{\pi}$.

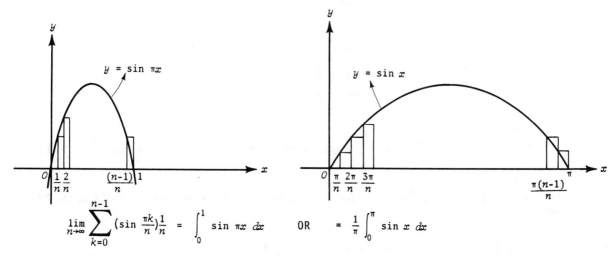

$$\lim_{n\to\infty}\sum_{k=0}^{n-1}\left(\sin \frac{\pi k}{n}\right)\frac{1}{n} = \int_0^1 \sin \pi x \, dx \qquad OR \qquad = \frac{1}{\pi}\int_0^\pi \sin x \, dx$$

Figure 8-2

Alternatively, one can take $f(x_k)$ to be $\sin x_k$ on $[0,\pi]$

with $\Delta x = \dfrac{\pi}{n}$ and $x_k = \dfrac{\pi k}{n}$. Then

$$\lim_{n\to\infty}\sum_{k=0}^{n-1}\sin \frac{\pi k}{n} \cdot \frac{1}{n} = \lim_{n\to\infty}\frac{1}{\pi}\sum_{k=0}^{n-1}\sin \frac{\pi k}{n} \cdot \frac{\pi}{n}$$

which is equivalent to $\dfrac{1}{\pi}\displaystyle\int_0^\pi \sin x \, dx$. The value of this

integral is also $\dfrac{2}{\pi}$. In Figure 8-2 these two equivalent

definite integrals have been interpreted as areas.

Set 9: Sequences and Series

1. D.	6. C*.	11. B.	16. C*.	21. A*.
2. C.	7. C*.	12. A*.	17. B*.	22. C.
3. D.	8. E.	13. E.	18. B*.	23. A*.
4. E*.	9. B*.	14. C.	19. D.	24. C*.
5. A.	10. A*.	15. D*.	20. E*.	25. B*.

26. D*.	31. C.	36. C*.
27. E*.	32. A*.	37. E*.
28. B.	33. C*.	38. A*.
29. D.	34. E.	39. D*.
30. D.	35. A*.	40. C*.

4. E. Note that $\{\frac{2}{e}\}^n$ is a sequence of the type $\{r^n\}$ with $|r| < 1$; also that $\lim \frac{n^2}{e^n} = 0$ by repeated application of L'Hôpital's rule.

6. C. See illustrative Example 11, p. 174.

7. C. $\left|\frac{n}{n+1} - 1\right| < 0.01$ if $\left|-\frac{1}{n+1}\right| = \frac{1}{n+1} < 0.01$; $n + 1 > \frac{1}{0.01}$

or $n > 100 - 1 = 99$.

9. B. $\sum_{n=1}^{\infty} \frac{1}{n(n+1)} = \frac{1}{1 \cdot 2} + \frac{1}{2 \cdot 3} + \frac{1}{3 \cdot 4} + \dots + \frac{1}{n(n+1)} + \dots$;

so $s_n = 1 - \frac{1}{2} + \frac{1}{2} - \frac{1}{3} + \frac{1}{3} - \dots + \frac{1}{n} - \frac{1}{n+1} = 1 - \frac{1}{n+1}$,

and $\lim_{n \to \infty} s_n = 0$.

10. A. $S = \frac{a}{1-r} = \frac{2}{1-(-\frac{1}{2})} = \frac{4}{3}$.

12. A. If $\sum_{k=1}^{\infty} u_k$ converges, so does $\sum_{k=m}^{\infty} u_k$ where m is any positive integer; but their *sums* are probably different.

15. D. $\dfrac{n}{\sqrt{4n^2 - 1}} > \dfrac{n}{\sqrt{4n^2}} = \dfrac{1}{2}$, the general term of a divergent series.

16. C.   The limit of the ratio for the series $\sum \dfrac{1}{n^{3/2}}$ is 1, so this

test fails; note for (E) that $\lim\limits_{n \to \infty} \dfrac{u_{n+1}}{u_n} = \lim\limits_{n \to \infty} \left(\dfrac{n + 1}{n}\right)^n$

$= \lim\limits_{n \to \infty} \left(1 + \dfrac{1}{n}\right)^n = e.$

17. B. $\lim\limits_{n \to \infty} \dfrac{(-1)^{n+1}(n - 1)}{n + 1} = 1$, not zero.

18. B.   A, C, and E all converge absolutely; D is the divergent

geometric series with $r = -1.1$.

19. D. $S = \dfrac{a}{1 - r} = \dfrac{2/3}{1 - 2/3} = \dfrac{2/3}{1/3} = 2.$

20. E.   Note the following counterexamples:

(A) $\sum \dfrac{(-1)^{n-1}}{n}$ (B) $\sum \dfrac{1}{n}$ (C) $\sum \dfrac{(-1)^{n-1} \cdot n}{2n - 1}$

(D) $\sum \left(- \dfrac{3}{2}\right)^{n-1}.$

21. A.   If $f(x) = \sqrt{x - 1}$, then $f(0)$ is not defined.

23. A. $\lim\limits_{n \to \infty} \left|\dfrac{x + 1}{n + 1}\right| = 0$ for all $x \neq -1$; since the given series converges

to zero if $x = -1$ it therefore converges for *all* x.

24. C. $\lim\limits_{n \to \infty} (n + 1)(x - 3) = \infty$ unless $x = 3.$

25. B.   The differentiated series is $\sum\limits_{n=1}^{\infty} \dfrac{(x - 2)^{n-1}}{n}$; so $\lim\limits_{n \to \infty} \left|\dfrac{u_{n+1}}{u_n}\right| = |x - 2|.$

26. D.   The integrated series is $\sum\limits_{n=0}^{\infty} \dfrac{x^{n+1}}{n + 1}$ OR $\sum\limits_{n=0}^{\infty} \dfrac{x^n}{n}.$

27. E. $e^{-x/2} = 1 + \left(- \dfrac{x}{2}\right) + \left(- \dfrac{x}{2}\right)^2 \cdot \dfrac{1}{2!} + \left(- \dfrac{x}{2}\right)^3 \cdot \dfrac{1}{3!} + \left(- \dfrac{x}{2}\right)^4 \cdot \dfrac{1}{4!} + \cdots$

32. A. Use $e^{-x} = 1 - x + \frac{x^2}{2!} - \cdot \ldots$; $e^{-0.1} = 1 - (+0.1) + \frac{(0.01)}{2!} + R_2$.

$|R_2| < \frac{0.001}{3!} < 0.0005$. Or use the series for e^x and let $x = -0.1$

33. C. $e^u = 1 + u + \frac{u^2}{2!} + \ldots$, and $\sin x = x - \frac{x^3}{3!} + \ldots$, so

$e^{\sin x} = 1 + (x - \frac{x^3}{3!} + \ldots) + \frac{1}{2!}(x - \frac{x^3}{3!} + \ldots)^2 + \ldots$

Or generate the Maclaurin series for $e^{\sin x}$.

35. A. $f(x) = x \ln x$
            $f'(x) = 1 + \ln x$
            $f''(x) = \frac{1}{x}$
            $f'''(x) = -\frac{1}{x^2}$
            $f^{(4)}(x) = \frac{2}{x^3}$
            $f^{(5)}(x) = -\frac{3 \cdot 2}{x^4}$. $f^{(5)}(1) = -3 \cdot 2$.

So the coefficient of $(x - 1)^5$ is $-\frac{3 \cdot 2}{5!} = -\frac{1}{20}$.

36. C. $\sin x = x - \frac{x^3}{3!} + \ldots$; $\sin 2° = (0.03490) + R_2$.

$|R_2| < \frac{(0.03490)^3}{3} < \frac{(0.04)^3}{6} < 0.0001$.

37. E. The error, $|R_4|$, is less than $\frac{1}{5!} < 0.009$.

38. A. $\int_0^{0.3} x^2 e^{-x^2} \, dx = \int_0^{0.3} x^2(1 - x^2 + \frac{x^4}{2!} - \ldots) \, dx$

$= \int_0^{0.3} (x^2 - x^4 + \frac{x^6}{2!} - \ldots) \, dx = \frac{x^3}{3} - \frac{x^5}{5} + \ldots \Big|_0^{0.3}$

$= 0.009$ to three decimal places.

39. D. $\displaystyle\int_0^{0.2} \frac{e^{-x} - 1}{x}\, dx = \int_0^{0.2} \frac{(1 - x + \frac{x^2}{2!} - \frac{x^3}{3!} + \ldots) - 1}{x}\, dx$

$\displaystyle = \int_0^{0.2} \left(-1 + \frac{x}{2} - \frac{x^2}{3!} + \ldots\right) dx = \left. -x + \frac{x^2}{2 \cdot 2} - \frac{x^3}{3 \cdot 6} + \ldots \right|_0^{0.2}$

$\displaystyle = -0.190; \quad |R_n| < \frac{(0.2)^3}{18} < 0.0005.$

40. C. $f(x) = a_0 + a_1 x + a_2 x^2 + a_3 x^3 + \ldots$; if $f(0) = 1$, then $a_0 = 1$.

$f'(x) = a_1 + 2a_2 x + 3a_3 x^2 + 4a_4 x^3 + \ldots$; $f'(0) = -f(0) = -1$,

so $a_1 = -1$. Since $f'(x) = -f(x)$, we see that

$1 - x + a_2 x^2 + a_3 x^3 + \ldots = -(-1 + 2a_2 x + 3a_3 x^2 + 4a_4 x^3 + \ldots)$

identically. Thus

$$-2a_2 = -1 \qquad a_2 = \frac{1}{2}$$

$$-3a_3 = a_2 \qquad a_3 = -\frac{1}{3!}$$

$$-4a_4 = a_3 \qquad a_4 = -\frac{1}{4!}$$

$$\vdots \qquad\qquad \vdots$$

We see, then, that

$$f(x) = 1 - x + \frac{x^2}{2!} - \frac{x^3}{3!} + \frac{x^4}{4!} - \ldots;$$

$$(0.2) = 1 - (0.2) + \frac{(0.2)^2}{2!} - \frac{(0.2)^3}{3!} + R_3$$

$$= 0.819, \quad |R_3| < 0.0005.$$

Set 10: Differential Equations

1.	A.	6.	E*.	11.	D*.	16.	C*.	21.	D*.	26.	B*.
2.	E.	7.	E*.	12.	A*.	17.	B*.	22.	C*.	27.	E*.
3.	C.	8.	A.	13.	E*.	18.	E*.	23.	B*.	28.	C*.
4.	B.	9.	C.	14.	A*.	19.	A.	24.	C*.		
5.	D.	10.	B.	15.	D*.	20.	D*.	25.	A*.		

6. E. Since $\int \frac{dy}{y} = \int \frac{dx}{x}$, it follows that $\ln y = \ln x + C$, or

$\ln y = \ln x + \ln k$; so $y = kx$.

7. E. The solution is $y = ke^{x}$, $k \neq 0$.

11. D. The problem gives rise to the differential equation $\frac{dP}{dt} = kP$

where $P = 2P_0$ when $t = 50$. We seek $\frac{P}{P_0}$ for $t = 75$.

We get $\ln \frac{P}{P_0} = kt$ with $\ln 2 = 50k$; then $\ln \frac{P}{P_0} = \frac{t}{50} \ln 2$

or $\frac{P}{P_0} = 2^{t/50}$.

12. A. Let S equal the amount present at time t; using $S = 40$ when

$t = 0$ yields $\ln \frac{S}{40} = kt$. Since, when $t = 2$, $S = 10$, we

get $k = \frac{1}{2} \ln \frac{1}{4}$ or $\ln \frac{1}{2}$ or $-\ln 2$.

13. E. The general solution is $y = k \ln |x| + C$ and the particular

solution is $y = 2 \ln |x| + 2$.

14. A. The given equation is homogeneous; let $y = vx$.

15. D. Let $y = vx$.

16. C. $e^{\int dx} = e^{x}$ is an integrating factor.

17. B. This equation can be put in the form $\frac{dy}{dx} + P(x)y = Q(x)$;

$(x^2 + 1)$ is an integrating factor.

18. E.   Rewriting the equation $\frac{dx}{dy} + 2x \tan y = 2 \sin y$ reveals that it is linear in x and x'; $e^{\int 2 \tan y \, dy} = \sec^2 y$ is an integrating factor.

20. D.   This homogeneous linear equation with constant coefficients has characteristic equation $m^2 - 4m - 5 = (m + 1)(m - 5) = 0$.

21. D.   The auxiliary equation here is $m^2 + 4m = m(m + 4) = 0$.

22. C.   Hint: use the method of undetermined coefficients and let $y_p = ax^2 + bx + c$.

23. B.   Note that the general solution of the associated homogeneous equation is $y = c_1 e^{-3x} + c_2 x e^{-3x}$. Let $y_p = ax^2 e^{-3x}$ and see that $a = \frac{1}{2}$.

24. C. $y = y_c + y_p$ and y_c, here, is $c_1 e^{2x} + c_2 e^{-2x}$.

25. A.   The general solution is $x = A \cos(3t + \alpha)$. Use the given conditions to determine A and α.

26. B.   Here $y_c = c_1 e^{2x} + c_2$. We let $y_p = ax + b$; $a = -2$; b we incorporate into c_2.

27. E.   The differential equation is $m \cdot \frac{d^2 x}{dt^2} = -kx$ or $\frac{w}{g} \cdot \frac{d^2 x}{dt^2} = -kx$. $k = 20$, so the equation becomes $x'' = -64x$ with solution $x = A \cos(8t + \alpha)$. The initial conditions $t = 0$, $x = 1$, $\frac{dx}{dt} = 0$ yield $x = \cos 8t$.

28. C.   The differential equation is $\frac{d^2 x}{dt^2} = -4x$ with particular solution $x = 2 \cos 2t$. Here, $v = \frac{dx}{dt} = -4 \sin 2t$.

Set 11: Miscellaneous

1. D*.	6. E.	11. B*.	16. A.	21. C*.
2. E.	7. A*.	12. A*.	17. E*.	22. A.
3. C*.	8. A.	13. C*.	18. A*.	23. D*.
4. A*.	9. B*.	14. D*.	19. D*.	24. A*.
5. A.	10. B*.	15. C*.	20. B*.	25. E.

26. E*.	31. A*.	36. E*.
27. D*.	32. E*.	37. C.
28. B.	33. B*.	38. B*.
29. C*.	34. C*.	39. A*.
30. D*.	35. A*.	40. D*.

1. D. The equation of the line is $3y + x + 1 = 0$.

3. C. Use the fact that the product of the slopes is -1 .

4. A. Recall that the distance from (x_1, y_1) to the line with equation $ax + by + c = 0$ is
$$\frac{|ax_1 + by_1 + c|}{\sqrt{a^2 + b^2}} .$$

7. A. Hint: if new axes, x'-y', are chosen with origin at $(2,1)$, the equation of the parabola referred to these is $x'^2 = 16y'$.

9. B. Rewrite the equations as $x - 1 = -\sin t$, $\frac{y - 4}{2} = -\cos t$; square and add. The locus is an ellipse with center at $(1,4)$.

10. B. Since $x + 2 = \sin t$ and $y = \cos^2 t$, we get $(x + 2)^2 + y = 1$, where $-3 \leq x \leq -1$ and $0 \leq y \leq 1$.

11. B. The circles have centers at $(2,-1)$ and $(0,3)$ respectively.

12. A. The domain of $|x - 3| \leq 2$ is $1 \leq x \leq 5$, and that of $|x| > 4$ is $-4 < x$ or $x > 4$.

13. C.   The equations may be rewritten $\frac{x}{2} = \sin u$ and $y = 1 - 2 \sin^2 u$,

giving $y = 1 - 2 \cdot \frac{x^2}{4}$.

14. D.   The graph of f is shown in Figure 11-1; f is defined and

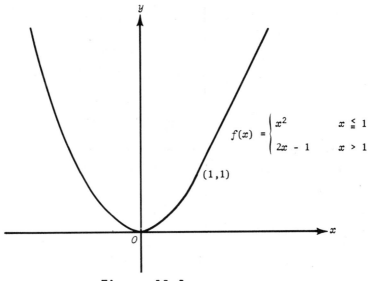

$$f(x) = \begin{cases} x^2 & x \leq 1 \\ 2x - 1 & x > 1 \end{cases}$$

(1,1)

Figure 11-1

continuous at all x including $x = 1$. Since

$\lim_{x \to 1^-} f'(x) = 2 = \lim_{x \to 1^+} f'(x)$, $f'(1)$ exists and is equal to 2.

15. C.   The Cartesian equation is $xy = 2$.

17. E.   The curve has vertical asymptotes at $x = 2$ and $x = -2$ ·and
a horizontal asymptote at $y = -2$.

18. A.   Since $\sin(-\theta) = - \sin \theta$, $f(-x)$ here is equal to $f(x)$ and
the function is even.

19. D.   The relation $y^2 = x + 1$ yields two y's for each x in the domain.

20. B.   The rectangular equation is $x^2 + y^2 - 2y = 0$, that of a circle
with center at (0,1) and radius 1 .

21. C.   The graph of f is shown in Figure 11-2. $f(x) = x|x|$ is equivalent

to
$$f(x) = \begin{cases} x^2 & x \geq 0 \\ -x^2 & x < 0 \end{cases}.$$

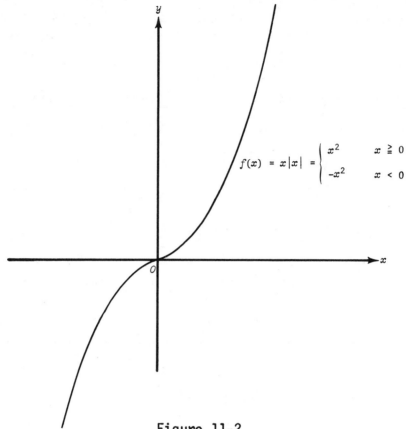

$$f(x) = x|x| = \begin{cases} x^2 & x \geq 0 \\ -x^2 & x < 0 \end{cases}$$

Figure 11-2

Here $\lim\limits_{x \to 0^-} f'(x) = 0 = \lim\limits_{x \to 0^+} f'(x)$, so the derivative

exists at $x = 0$.

23. D.   Using the formula for area in polar coordinates, $A = \dfrac{1}{2} \displaystyle\int_\alpha^\beta r^2 \, d\theta$,

we see that the required area is given by

$$4 \cdot \frac{1}{2} \int_0^{\frac{\pi}{4}} 2 \cos 2\theta \, d\theta \ .$$

24. A.   The required area is shaded in Figure 11-3.

26. E.   Any points of intersection of the two graphs would have

ordinates that satisfy the equation $y^2 - y + 2 = 0$.

Since this equation has no real roots, the graphs do

not intersect.

27. D.   If $f(x) = x \sin \dfrac{1}{x}$ for $x \neq 0$ and $f(0) = 0$, then

$\lim\limits_{x \to 0} f(x) = 0 = f(0)$; thus this function is continuous at 0.

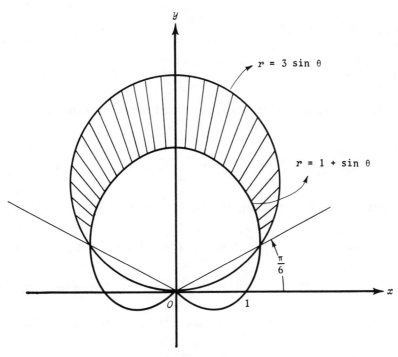

Figure 11-3

29. C. The locus leads to the equation $(x - 1)^2 = 4[(x + 1)^2 + y^2]$.

30. D. The graph shown has the following characteristics: it has no x-intercepts; the y-intercept is -2 ; it has vertical asymptotes $x = 1$ and $x = -1$; and it has the x-axis as horizontal asymptote.

31. A. For the graph shown, since the tangent is horizontal at three points the function must be of fourth degree. Since $f(x) < 0$ when $|x| < \sqrt{2}$, only the function in (A) can be correct.

32. E. The function $f(x) = \dfrac{x^2 - 1}{x - 1}$ is such that $\lim_{x \to 1} f(x) = 2$ but it does not satisfy any of the conditions given in (A), (B), (C), or (D).

33. B. Since $\lim_{x \to 1} f(x) = 1$, to render $f(x)$ continuous at $x = 1$ we must define $f(1)$ to be 1 .

34. C.   Here, $f(g(u)) = e^{\ln u} = u$.

35. A.   The rectangular equation is $y - 2x = 1$.

36. E. $\frac{dy}{dx}$ can be obtained by implicit differentiation as follows:

$$2ky\frac{dy}{dx} + x\frac{dy}{dx} + y = 0 . \quad \text{So} \quad \frac{dy}{dx} = \frac{-y}{2ky + x} = \frac{1}{2 - 2k} \quad \text{at } (-2,1).$$

The equation of the tangent to the curve at $(-2,1)$ is thus

$y - 1 = \frac{1}{2 - 2k}(x + 2)$, and if this line is to pass through

the origin, $(0,0)$ must satisfy the equation, yielding $k = 2$.

38. B.   The radius of the circle is the distance between the point

$(2,-1)$ and the tangent line $x + 2y + 5 = 0$.

39. A.   The equation of the locus is obtained by using $(\frac{y}{x - 2})(\frac{y - 1}{x + 3}) = 1$.

40. D.   Here, since $f(x) = 2x - \frac{2}{x}$, $f(\frac{1}{x}) = \frac{2}{x} - 2x$ which is equal to

$-f(x)$. The function is thus odd.

Practice Examination: 1

1.	C	6.	D*	11.	B*	16.	E	21.	A	26.	E
2.	A	7.	D*	12.	A	17.	C	22.	E	27.	C
3.	D	8.	A*	13.	B	18.	D*	23.	D*	28.	A*
4.	C*	9.	C	14.	D	19.	B	24.	B	29.	D
5.	E	10.	E	15.	A*	20.	C*	25.	B	30.	A

31.	C*	36.	E*	41.	D
32.	B*	37.	A	42.	B*
33.	E*	38.	C*	43.	C
34.	B	39.	B	44.	D
35.	D*	40.	E	45.	E

4. C. The distance between the point (x_1, y_1) and the line $ax + by + c = 0$

is given by $\dfrac{|ax_1 + by_1 + c|}{\sqrt{a^2 + b^2}}$.

6. D. The two lines have equations $(x + 1) \pm (y - 3) = 0$.

7. D. On the interval $[1,4]$, $f'(x) = 0$ only for $x = 3$. Since $f(3)$ is

a relative minimum, we check the end points and find that $f(4) = 6$

is the absolute maximum of the function.

8. A. Let $y = ax^3 + bx^2 + cx + d$; use the equations $y(0) = 0$, $y'(0) = 0$,

$y''(1) = 0$, and $y(1) = -2$ to determine the constants.

11. B.   The curve crosses the y-axis only at the origin.

15. A.   Although $f'(2) = f'(1) = 0$, $f'(x)$ changes sign only as x increases

through 1 and in this case $f'(x)$ changes from negative to positive.

18. D.   The area is given, here, by $\displaystyle\int_0^2 (2 + x - x^2)\ dx$.

20. C.   The graph of $y = \dfrac{x^2 - 4}{x^2 - 1}$ has a horizontal asymptote at $y = 1$ and

two vertical asymptotes at $x = 1$ and $x = -1$.

23. D.   The volume is given by $\pi\displaystyle\int_0^\infty e^{-2x}\ dx = \dfrac{\pi}{2}$.

28. A.   Let $u = x^2$. Then $\dfrac{dy}{dx} = \dfrac{dy}{du} \cdot \dfrac{du}{dx} = \dfrac{df}{du} \cdot \dfrac{du}{dx} = f'(u)\dfrac{du}{dx}$

$= \sqrt{5u - 1} \cdot 2x = 2x\sqrt{5x^2 - 1}$.

31. C.   See Fig. PE1-1. Since $x^2 + y^2 = 26^2$ and since it is given that

$\dfrac{dx}{dt} = 3$, it follows that $2x\dfrac{dx}{dt} + 2y\dfrac{dy}{dt} = 0$

and $\dfrac{dy}{dt} = -\dfrac{x}{y}(3)$ at any time t. When

$x = 10$, then $y = 24$ and $\dfrac{dy}{dt} = \dfrac{-5}{4}$.

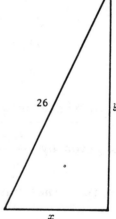

Figure PE1-1

32. B.   The surface area, S, is given by

$$S = 2\pi\int_0^2 y\sqrt{1 + \left(\dfrac{dy}{dx}\right)^2}\ dx.$$

Then

$$S \;=\; 2\pi \int_0^2 \sqrt{x}\,\sqrt{1 + \frac{1}{4x}}\; dx \;=\; 2\pi \int \frac{\sqrt{4x+1}}{2}\; dx$$

$$=\; \frac{\pi}{4} \cdot \frac{2}{3}(4x+1)^{3/2}\Big|_0^2 \;=\; \frac{\pi}{6} \cdot 26 \;=\; \frac{13\pi}{3}.$$

33. E. Separating variables yields $\dfrac{dx}{x} = k\, dt$. Integrating, we get

In $x = kt + C$. Since $x = 2$ when $t = 0$, ln $2 = C$. Then

In $\dfrac{x}{2} = kt$. Using $x = 6$ when $t = 1$, it follows that   ln $3 = k$.

35. D.   Note that $f(g(x)) \;=\; \sqrt{1 - \dfrac{2}{\dfrac{1}{x}}} \;=\; \sqrt{1 - 2x}$ $(x \neq 0)$.

36. E. See Fig. PE1-2, where the generating circle has equation $x^2 + y^2 = 16$, and where the y-axis is taken positive downward. Then the work, W,

$$=\; \pi w \int_0^4 yx^2 dy \;=\; \pi w \int_0^4 y(16 - y^2)dy \;=\; 64\pi w \ .$$

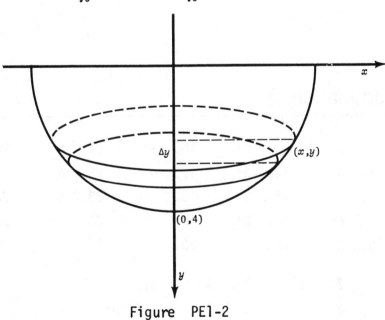

Figure PE1-2

38. C.   The trick here is to recognize that the limit of the sum is

equal to $\int_0^1 x^2 \, dx$. To see this, recall that

$$\lim_{n \to \infty} \sum_{k=1}^{n} f(x_k) \, \Delta x = \int_a^b f(x) \, dx$$

where the interval from a to b has been subdivided (or partitioned).

Here, then, we see that Δx can be replaced by $\frac{1}{n}$, x_k by $\frac{k}{n}$,

and $f(x_k)$ by $x_k{}^2$ to get the given limit. Observing that, as

k varies from 1 to n, x_k takes on the values $\frac{1}{n}$, $\frac{2}{n}$, $\ldots$, $\frac{n}{n}$,

we conclude that the interval in question here is from 0 to 1.

42. B. $\dfrac{1}{\frac{\pi}{3}} \displaystyle\int_0^{\pi/3} \tan x \, dx = \dfrac{3}{\pi} \left[-\ln \cos x \right]_0^{\pi/3} = \dfrac{3}{\pi} \left(-\ln \dfrac{1}{2} \right)$.

Practice Examination: 2

1. C.	6. B	11. C*	16. B*	21. D	26. D*
2. A*	7. A*	12. B*	17. B*	22. A	27. C*
3. B*	8. D	13. D*	18. A*	23. E	28. C
4. C*	9. E*	14. E*	19. D*	24. D*	29. E*
5. E	10. C*	15. C*	20. E	25. B	30. A

31. B*	36. A*	41. A*
32. C*	37. D*	42. D*
33. B*	38. B*	43. E
34. E*	39. C*	44. A*
35. E*	40. D*	45. B

2. A.   Since $\dfrac{\cos x}{x - \frac{\pi}{2}} = \dfrac{\sin\left(\frac{\pi}{2} - x\right)}{x - \frac{\pi}{2}} = \dfrac{-\sin\left(x - \frac{\pi}{2}\right)}{x - \frac{\pi}{2}}$ we can let

$\alpha = \left(x - \frac{\pi}{2}\right)$ and then find $\displaystyle\lim_{\alpha \to 0} \dfrac{-\sin\alpha}{\alpha} = -1$.

3. B.   As $x \to 0$, $\sin\frac{1}{x}$ oscillates between -1 and 1, remaining finite.

Since $-1 \leqq \sin\frac{1}{x} \leqq 1$, we get

$$-x \leqq x \sin\frac{1}{x} \leqq x \qquad \text{when } x > 0 \qquad \text{and}$$

$$-x \geqq x \sin\frac{1}{x} \geqq x \qquad \text{when } x < 0 .$$

In either case $x \sin\frac{1}{x}$ is "squeezed" to 0 as $x \to 0$.

4. C.   Note that $\displaystyle\lim_{h \to 0} \dfrac{\ln(2 + h) - \ln 2}{h} = f'(2)$, where $f(x) = \ln x$.

7. A.   If $f(x) = x \cos\frac{1}{x}$, then $f'(x) = -x\sin\frac{1}{x}\left(-\frac{1}{x^2}\right) + \cos\frac{1}{x}$

$= \frac{1}{x}\sin\frac{1}{x} + \cos\frac{1}{x}$, and $f'\left(\frac{2}{\pi}\right) = \frac{\pi}{2}\cdot 1 + 0$.

9. E.   Here, $\dfrac{dy}{dx} = \dfrac{\frac{dy}{dt}}{\frac{dx}{dt}} = \dfrac{\frac{1}{\sqrt{1 - t^2}}}{\frac{1}{2}\frac{(-2t)}{\sqrt{1 - t^2}}} = -\frac{1}{t}.$

10. C. $\dfrac{d}{dx}\sin^2(x + y) = 2\sin(x + y)\cos(x + y)\left(1 + \dfrac{dy}{dx}\right)$

$$= [\sin 2(x + y)]\left(1 + \dfrac{dy}{dx}\right).$$

11. C.   If $y = e^x \ln x$, then $\dfrac{dy}{dx} = \dfrac{e^x}{x} + e^x \ln x$, which equals e

when $x = 1$. Since also $y = 0$ when $x = 1$, the equation

of the tangent is $y = e(x - 1)$.

12. B.   If we let $f(x) = x^{1/3}$ then we want $[f(64) + df]$ where

df is obtained when $x = 64$ and $dx = -1$.

13. D.   See sketch, Figure PE2-1. It is given that $\frac{dx}{dt} = -2$; we want

$\frac{dA}{dt}$ where $A = \frac{1}{2} xy$. $\frac{dA}{dt} = \frac{1}{2}(x\frac{dy}{dt} + y\frac{dx}{dt}) = \frac{1}{2}\left[3\cdot\frac{dy}{dt} + y\cdot(-2)\right].$

Since $y^2 = 25 - x^2$, it follows that $2y\frac{dy}{dt} = -2x\frac{dx}{dt}$ and when

$x = 3$, $y = 4$ and $\frac{dy}{dt} = \frac{3}{2}$. Then $\frac{dA}{dt} = -\frac{7}{4}$.

Figure PE2-1

14. E.   Since $f'(x)$ exists for all x, it must equal 0 for any x_0 for
which it is a relative maximum, and it must also change sign
from positive to negative as x increases through x_0. For the
given derivative, no x satisfies both of these conditions.

15. C.   Here, $v = 3t^2 + 2t - 1 = (3t - 1)(t + 1)$; when v is positive,
the particle is moving to the right.

16. B. $v = 4(t - 2)^3$ and changes sign exactly once, when $t = 2$.

17. B.   The speed of the particle along the curve is given by

$$|\mathbf{v}| = \sqrt{(\frac{dx}{dt})^2 + (\frac{dy}{dt})^2}.$$

Here,

$$|\mathbf{v}| = \sqrt{36 \sin^2 3t + 9 \cos^2 3t}$$

$$= \sqrt{27 \sin^2 3t + 9 \sin^2 3t + 9 \cos^2 3t}$$

$$= \sqrt{27 \sin^2 3t + 9}.$$

The maximum value of $|\mathbf{v}|$ occurs when $\sin^2 3t = 1$; that is,
when $\sin 3t = \pm 1$. From this we have $3t = \frac{\pi}{2}$ or $\frac{3\pi}{2}$, so that
$t = \frac{\pi}{6}$ or $\frac{\pi}{2}$; but only $\frac{\pi}{2}$ is on the restricted interval.

18. A. $f'(x)$, here, is $e^{-x}(1 - x)$; f has maximum value when $x = 1$.

19. D.   See Figure PE2-2. V, the volume of the cylinder, equals

$\pi x^2 y$, where $2x + 2y = 18$. So $V = \pi x^2 (9 - x)$ and

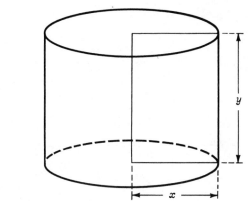

Figure PE2-2

$V' = \pi(18x - 3x^2)$. Since $x = 6$ yields maximum volume,

the area of the rectangle, xy , equals 18.

24. E.   The integral is improper. As $e^x \to 2$, $\lim \dfrac{1}{2 - e^x} = \infty$, so

the integral diverges.

26. D.   **The given integral is equivalent to** $\int \left[1 + \dfrac{2x - 1}{x^2 - x}\right] dx$, **which**

integrates into $x + \ln |x^2 - x| + C$.

27. C.   The given integral is equivalent to $\displaystyle\int_{-1}^{0} (1 + x)\ dx + \int_{0}^{1} (1 - x)\ dx$.

See Figure PE2-3 which shows the graph of $f(x) = 1 - |x|$ on $[-1,1]$.

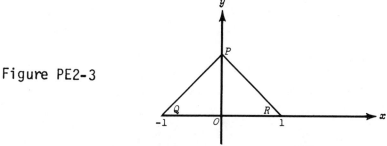

Figure PE2-3

The area of triangle PQR **is equal to** $\displaystyle\int_{-1}^{1} (1 - |x|)\ dx.$

29. E.   **Separating variables we get** $y\ dy = (1 - 2x)\ dx.$ **Integrating**

gives $\frac{1}{2}y^2 = x - x^2 + C$, or $y^2 = 2x - 2x^2 + k$, or

$2x^2 + y^2 - 2x = k$.

31. B.   See Figure PE2-4. The region is divided into two parts by

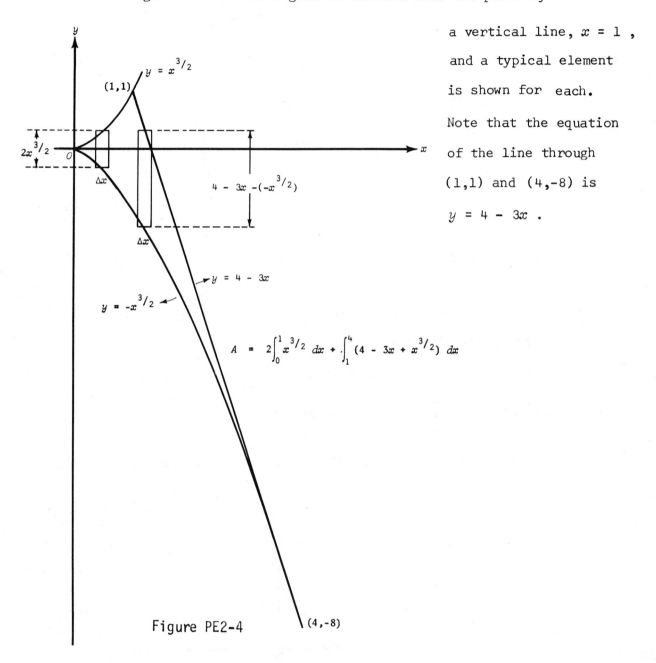

a vertical line, $x = 1$, and a typical element is shown for each. Note that the equation of the line through (1,1) and (4,-8) is $y = 4 - 3x$.

$y = x^{3/2}$

(1,1)

$2x^{3/2}$

Δx

$4 - 3x - (-x^{3/2})$

Δx

$y = 4 - 3x$

$y = -x^{3/2}$

$A = 2\int_0^1 x^{3/2}\, dx + \int_1^4 (4 - 3x + x^{3/2})\, dx$

Figure PE2-4

(4,-8)

32. C.   See Figure PE2-5. A represents the required area.

33. B.   The required area, A, is given by the integral

$$2\int_0^1 \left(4 - \frac{4}{1 + x^2}\right)\, dx = 2(4x - 4\tan^{-1} x)\Big|_0^1 = 2\left(4 - 4\cdot\frac{\pi}{4}\right).$$

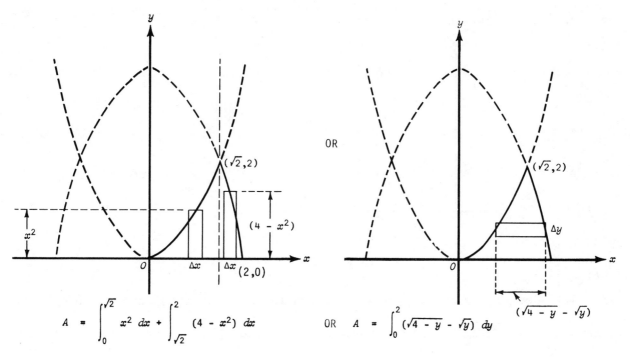

$$A = \int_0^{\sqrt{2}} x^2 \, dx + \int_{\sqrt{2}}^2 (4 - x^2) \, dx \qquad \text{OR} \qquad A = \int_0^2 (\sqrt{4 - y} - \sqrt{y}) \, dy$$

Figure   PE2-5

34. E.   The area, A, is represented by $\displaystyle\int_0^{2\pi} (1 - \cos t) \, dt = 2\pi$.

35. E.   See Figure PE2-6.   The equation of the generating circle

is $(x - 3)^2 + y^2 = 1$, which yields $x = 3 \pm \sqrt{1 - y^2}$.

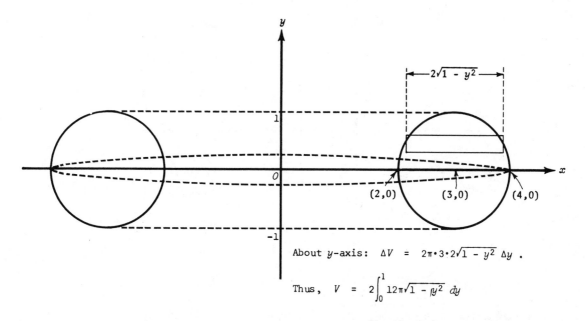

About y-axis: $\Delta V = 2\pi \cdot 3 \cdot 2\sqrt{1 - y^2} \, \Delta y$.

Thus, $V = 2\displaystyle\int_0^1 12\pi\sqrt{1 - y^2} \, dy$

$= 24\pi$ times the area of a quarter
of a unit circle.

Figure   PE2-6

36. A.   See Figure PE2-7.

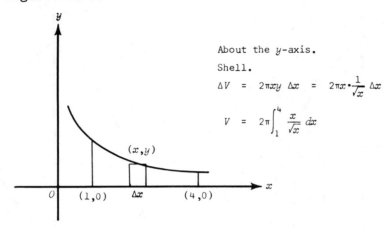

About the y-axis.

Shell.

$$\Delta V = 2\pi xy\ \Delta x = 2\pi x \cdot \frac{1}{\sqrt{x}}\ \Delta x$$

$$V = 2\pi \int_{1}^{4} \frac{x}{\sqrt{x}}\ dx$$

Figure PE2-7

37. D.   See Figure PE2-8, where a sketch is shown of functions f and g satisfying the given conditions. Since $f(x) > g(x)$ for all x, $a < x < b$, $f(x) - g(x) > 0$ and $\int_{a}^{b} (f(x) - g(x))\ dx > 0.$

It follows that $\left[\int_{a}^{b} f(x)\ dx - \int_{a}^{b} g(x)\ dx \right] > 0.$

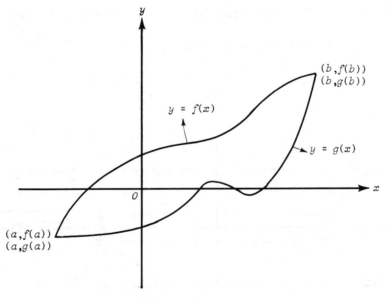

Figure PE2-8

38. B.   Since the length, s, is given by $\int_{a}^{b} \sqrt{1 + (\frac{dy}{dx})^2}\ dx$, then

$$s = \int_0^1 \sqrt{1 + [\tfrac{1}{2}(e^x - e^{-x})]^2} \; dx$$

$$= \int_0^1 \sqrt{1 + \tfrac{1}{4}(e^{2x} - 2 + e^{-2x})} \; dx$$

$$= \int_0^1 \sqrt{\tfrac{1}{4}e^{2x} + \tfrac{1}{2} + \tfrac{1}{4}e^{-2x}} \; dx$$

$$= \int_0^1 \sqrt{\tfrac{1}{4}(e^x + e^{-x})^2} \; dx \;=\; \int_0^1 \tfrac{1}{2}(e^x + e^{-x}) \; dx$$

$$= \tfrac{1}{2}(e^x - e^{-x})\Big|_0^1 \;=\; \tfrac{1}{2}[(e - \tfrac{1}{e}) - (1 - 1)] \;=\; \tfrac{1}{2}(e - \tfrac{1}{e}) \; .$$

39. C.   See Figure PE2-9.

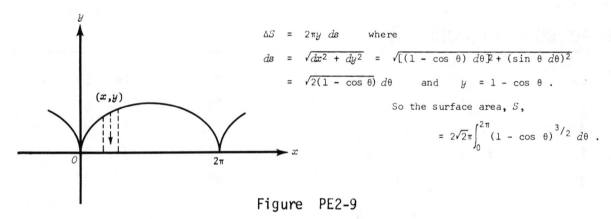

$$\Delta S = 2\pi y \; ds \qquad \text{where}$$

$$ds = \sqrt{dx^2 + dy^2} = \sqrt{[(1 - \cos\theta)\;d\theta]^2 + (\sin\theta\;d\theta)^2}$$

$$= \sqrt{2(1 - \cos\theta)}\;d\theta \qquad \text{and} \qquad y = 1 - \cos\theta \; .$$

So the surface area, S,

$$= 2\sqrt{2}\,\pi \int_0^{2\pi} (1 - \cos\theta)^{3/2}\;d\theta \; .$$

Figure   PE2-9

40. D.   Note that v **is negative from** $t = 0$ **to** $t = 1$ **, but positive from** $t = 1$ **to** $t = 2$ **.   Thus the distance travelled is given by**

$$-\int_0^1 (t^2 - t)\;dt + \int_1^2 (t^2 - t)\;dt \; .$$

41. A.   Recall that $\displaystyle\lim_{n\to\infty}\sum_{k=1}^{n} f(x_k)\,\Delta x = \int_a^b f(x)\;dx$ **where the subdivisions**

are on the interval $[a,b]$ **.   Rewrite the given limit as follows:**

$$\lim_{n\to\infty}\left[\left(\tfrac{1}{n}\right)^{1/2} + \left(\tfrac{2}{n}\right)^{1/2} + \left(\tfrac{3}{n}\right)^{1/2} + \cdots + \left(\tfrac{n}{n}\right)^{1/2}\right]\tfrac{1}{n}$$

and note that $\Delta x = \dfrac{1}{n}$, $x_k = \dfrac{k}{n}$, and $f(x_k) = (x_k)^{1/2}$. The interval in this case is from 0 to 1.

42. D. The work is given by the integral $\displaystyle\int_4^8 5x \; dx$ where 5 is the spring "constant."

44. A. The given equation can be multiplied by r to yield

$r^2 = 2r \sin \theta + 2r \cos \theta$; the Cartesian equation is obtained by using $x = r \cos \theta$, $y = r \sin \theta$, and

$x^2 + y^2 = r^2$.

Practice Examination: 3

1. E*	6. E*	11. B*	16. D*	21. C	26. B*
2. A	7. D	12. C*	17. C*	22. E*	27. C*
3. C*	8. D*	13. B*	18. A*	23. A*	28. E*
4. A*	9. E*	14. E*	19. B*	24. B*	29. D*
5. D*	10. C	15. C*	20. A	25. D*	30. A*

31. C*	36. C*	41. D*
32. B*	37. E*	42. A*
33. A*	38. B*	43. E*
34. D*	39. C*	44. D*
35. C*	40. D*	45. B*

1. E. $\dfrac{x^2 - 2}{4 - x^2} \to \infty$ as $x \to 2$.

3. C. Note that $\dfrac{\sin^2 \frac{x}{2}}{x^2} = \dfrac{\sin^2 \frac{x}{2}}{4 \frac{x^2}{4}} = \dfrac{1}{4} \lim_{\theta \to 0} \left[\dfrac{\sin \theta}{\theta}\right]^2$, where we let $\dfrac{x}{2} = \theta$.

4. A. This is $f'(0)$ where $f(x) = e^x$; or one can use L'Hôpital's Rule here, getting $\lim\limits_{x \to 0} \dfrac{e^x - 1}{x} = \lim\limits_{x \to 0} \dfrac{e^x}{1} = 1$.

5. D. The slope of $y = |x|$ equals 1 for $x > 0$ and -1 for $x < 0$.

6. E. Since $e^{\ln u} = u$, $y = 1$.

8. D. We want $\dfrac{d}{du} \tan^{-1} e^{2u}$ where $\dfrac{d}{dx} \tan^{-1} v$ equals $\dfrac{\frac{dv}{dx}}{1 + v^2}$.

9. E. Differentiating the relation $xy - x + y = 2$ implicitly

yields $\dfrac{dy}{dx} = \dfrac{1 - y}{x + 1}$. Since when $x = 0$, $y = 2$, the slope

at this point is -1 and the equation of the tangent is

thus $y = -x + 2$.

11. B. $\dfrac{d}{dx}(x^2 e^{x^{-1}}) = x^2 e^{x^{-1}}(-\dfrac{1}{x^2}) + 2xe^{x^{-1}}$.

12. C. If we let $y = \sqrt[3]{x}$, we want $y + dy$ where $x = 125$ and $\Delta x = dx = 2$. Then,

$$dy = \dfrac{dx}{3x^{2/3}}\bigg|_{x=125} \approx .03 .$$

13. B. Let s be the distance from the origin: then $s = \sqrt{x^2 + y^2}$

and $\dfrac{ds}{dt} = \dfrac{x \frac{dx}{dt} + y \frac{dy}{dt}}{\sqrt{x^2 + y^2}}$. Since $\dfrac{dy}{dt} = 2x \dfrac{dx}{dt}$ and $\dfrac{dx}{dt} = \dfrac{3}{2}$,

$\dfrac{dy}{dt} = 3x$. Substituting yields $\dfrac{ds}{dt} = \dfrac{3\sqrt{5}}{2}$.

14 E. Here, $\dfrac{dy}{dx} = -12x - 4x^3$ and $\dfrac{d^2y}{dx^2} = -12 - 12x^2 = -12(1 + x^2)$.

Since the second derivative never changes sign (the curve

is everywhere concave down), there are no inflection points.

15. C. $v = 3t^2 + 3$ and is always positive, while $a = 6t$ and is

positive for $t > 0$ but negative for $t < 0$. The speed
therefore increases for $t > 0$ but decreases for $t < 0$.

16. D. The speed, $|v|$, equals $\sqrt{(\frac{dx}{dt})^2 + (\frac{dy}{dt})^2}$, and since

$x = 3y - y^2$ we find $\frac{dx}{dt} = (3 - 2y)\frac{dy}{dt} = (3 - 2y) \cdot 3$. $|v|$ is

then evaluated using $y = 1$, and equals $\sqrt{(3)^2 + (3)^2}$.

17. C. Here, $\frac{dx}{dt} = e^t(\cos t - \sin t)$, $\frac{dy}{dt} = e^t(\sin t + \cos t)$, and

$\frac{d^2x}{dt^2} = -2(\sin t)e^t$, $\frac{d^2y}{dt^2} = 2(\cos t)e^t$, and the magnitude of

the acceleration, $|a|$, is $\sqrt{(\frac{d^2x}{dt^2})^2 + (\frac{d^2y}{dt^2})^2} = 2e^t$.

18. A. See Figure PE3-1. The area, A, of a typical rectangle is

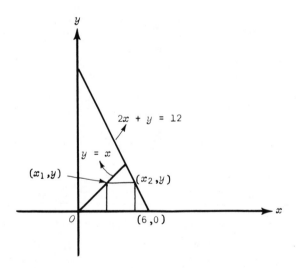

Figure PE3-1

$A = (x_2 - x_1) \cdot y = (\frac{12 - y}{2} - y) \cdot y = 6y - \frac{3y^2}{2}$. For $y = 2$,

$\frac{dA}{dy} = 0$.

19. B. If S represents the square of the distance from $(3,0)$ to
a point (x,y) on the curve, then $S = (3 - x)^2 + y^2$.
Setting $\frac{dS}{dx} = 0$ yields $\frac{dy}{dx} = \frac{3 - x}{y}$, while differentiating

the relation $x^2 - y^2 = 1$ with respect to x yields

$\frac{dy}{dx} = \frac{x}{y}$. These derivatives are equal for $x = \frac{3}{2}$.

22. E. The integral is equal to $\left. \dfrac{\tan^3 x}{3} \right|_{\frac{\pi}{4}}^{\frac{\pi}{3}} = \frac{1}{3}(3\sqrt{3} - 1)$.

23. A. The integral is rewritten

$$\frac{1}{2}\int \frac{y^2 - 2y + 1}{y} \, dy$$

$$\frac{1}{2}\int \left(y - 2 + \frac{1}{y}\right) \, dy$$

$$\frac{1}{2}\left(\frac{y^2}{2} - 2y + \ln y\right) + C .$$

24. B. $\displaystyle\int_{\frac{\pi}{6}}^{\frac{\pi}{2}} \cot x \, dx = \left. \ln \sin x \right|_{\frac{\pi}{6}}^{\frac{\pi}{2}} = 0 - \ln \frac{1}{2}$.

25. D. $\displaystyle\int_{1}^{e} \ln x \, dx$ can be integrated by parts to yield $\left. (x \ln x - x) \right|_{1}^{e}$,

which equals $e \ln e - e - (1 \ln 1 - 1) = e - e - (0 - 1) = 1$.

26. B. Recall that $\dfrac{d}{dx}\displaystyle\int_{a}^{x} f(t) \, dt = f(x)$.

27. C. $\displaystyle\int_{0}^{\infty} \frac{dx}{x^2 + 1} = \lim_{b \to \infty} \left. \tan^{-1} x \right|_{0}^{b} = \frac{\pi}{2}$. The integrals in (A),

(B), and (D) all diverge to infinity.

28. E. $\displaystyle\int_{-a}^{a} f(x) \, dx = 2\displaystyle\int_{0}^{a} f(x) \, dx$ only if $f(x)$ is even ;

$\qquad\qquad\qquad = 0 \qquad\qquad$ only if $f(x)$ is odd ;

$\qquad\qquad\qquad = F(a) - F(-a)$, where $\dfrac{dF(x)}{dx} = f(x)$ represents

the total area bounded by $y = f(x)$, the x-axis, and the vertical

lines $x = -a$ and $x = a$, only if $f(x) \geq 0$ on $[-a,a]$.

29. D. Separate variables to get $\dfrac{dy}{y} = \dfrac{dx}{x}$ and integrate to get

$\ln y = \ln x + C$. Since $y = 3$ when $x = 1$, $C = \ln 3$.

30. A. See Figure PE3-2.

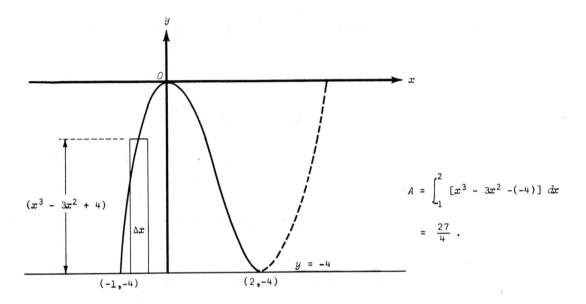

$(x^3 - 3x^2 + 4)$

$y = -4$

$(-1,-4)$ $(2,-4)$

$A = \displaystyle\int_{-1}^{2} [x^3 - 3x^2 - (-4)]\, dx$

$= \dfrac{27}{4}$.

Figure   PE3-2

31. C. See Figure PE3-3.

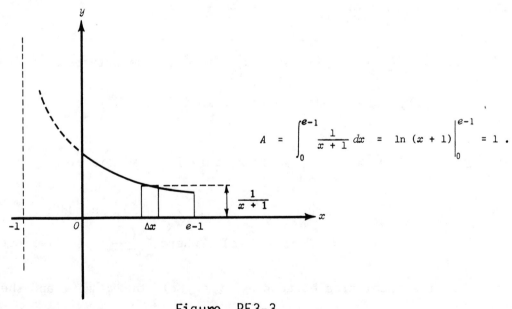

$A = \displaystyle\int_{0}^{e-1} \dfrac{1}{x+1}\, dx = \ln(x+1)\Big|_{0}^{e-1} = 1$.

$\dfrac{1}{x+1}$

Figure   PE3-3

32. B.   See Figure PE3-4.

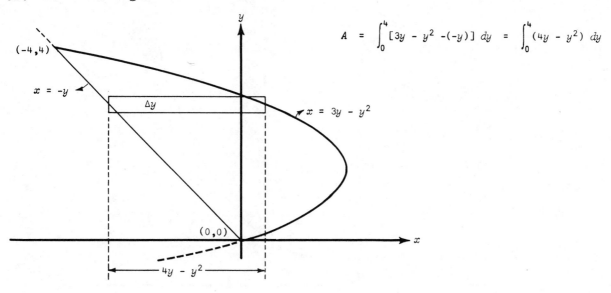

$$A = \int_0^4 [3y - y^2 -(-y)]\, dy = \int_0^4 (4y - y^2)\, dy$$

Figure   PE3-4

33. A.   See Figure PE3-5.

$$A = \int_0^{2a} y\, dx = \int_{\theta=0}^{\theta=\frac{\pi}{4}} 2a\cos^2\theta \cdot 2a\sec^2\theta\, d\theta = 4a^2\theta\,\Big|_0^{\frac{\pi}{4}} = \pi a^2$$

Figure   PE3-5

34. D.   The generating circle has equation $x^2 + y^2 = 4$. The volume,

V, equals $\pi\displaystyle\int_{-1}^{1} x^2\, dy = 2\pi\int_0^1 (4 - y^2)\, dy$.

35. C.   See Figure PE3-6.

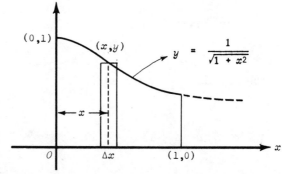

About the y-axis. Shell.

$$V = 2\pi xy\,\Delta x = \frac{2\pi x}{\sqrt{1 + x^2}}\,\Delta x.$$

$$V = 2\pi\int_0^1 \frac{x}{\sqrt{1 + x^2}}\, dx .$$

Figure   PE3-6

36. C. See Figure PE3-7.

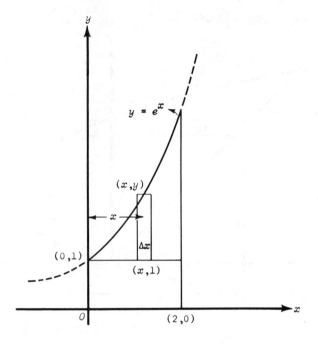

About the x-axis. Washer.

$\Delta V = \pi(y^2 - 1^2)\, \Delta x$.

$V = \pi \displaystyle\int_0^2 (e^{2x} - 1)\, dx$.

Figure PE3-7

37. E. Since $v = \dfrac{ds}{dt} = 4s$, we have $\dfrac{ds}{s} = 4dt$. So $\ln s = 4t + C$, where, using $s(0) = 3$, $C = \ln 3$. Then, since $s = 3e^{4t}$, $s\left(\dfrac{1}{2}\right) = 3e^2$.

38. B. The arc length is $\displaystyle\int_1^4 \sqrt{1 + \left(\dfrac{dy}{dx}\right)^2}\, dx = \int_1^4 \sqrt{1 + \left(x - \dfrac{1}{4x}\right)^2}\, dx$

$= \displaystyle\int_1^4 \sqrt{\left(x + \dfrac{1}{4x}\right)^2}\, dx = \int_1^4 \left(x + \dfrac{1}{4x}\right)\, dx = \dfrac{15}{2} + \dfrac{1}{4}\ln 4 = \dfrac{15}{2} + \dfrac{1}{2}\ln 2$.

39. C. $y_{av} = \dfrac{1}{3 - 1}\displaystyle\int_1^3 (x - 3)^2\, dx$.

40. D. We can rewrite the given limit as $\displaystyle\lim_{n \to \infty} \sum_{k=1}^{n} \ln\left(1 + \dfrac{k}{n}\right) \Delta x$,

where $\Delta x = \dfrac{1}{n}$, or as $\displaystyle\lim_{n \to \infty} \sum_{k=1}^{n} \ln(x_k)\, \Delta x$, where the

partition is made of the interval from 1 to 2. Note that

this is equivalent to $\lim\limits_{n \to \infty} \sum\limits_{k=1}^{n} \ln (1 + x_k) \, \Delta x$ (where the

interval is from 0 to 1), and thus to the integral $\int_0^1 \ln (1 + x) \, dx$.

41. D. $a = \dfrac{dv}{dt} = -t^2$ yields $v = -\dfrac{t^3}{3} + C_1$, and $s = -\dfrac{t^4}{12} + C_1 t + C_2$.

Since $s(0) = 0$, $C_2 = 0$; and since $s(1) = 3$, $C_1 = \dfrac{37}{12}$.

Thus $v(0) = \dfrac{37}{12}$.

42. A. Here $x^2 + y^2 = 4$, whose locus is a circle; but since the
given equations imply x and y both nonnegative the curve
defined is in the first quadrant.

43. E. The point given is *on* the line.

44. D. See Figure PE3-8. The set of x for which $|x + 1| > 2$ is

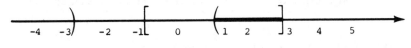

Figure PE3-8

$x < -3$ or $x > 1$, and the set for which $|x - 1| \leq 2$ is
$-1 \leq x \leq 3$. The set which satisfies both inequalities is
shown by a heavy line in the Figure.

45. B. Note that $\lim\limits_{x \to \infty} x e^x = \infty$, that $\lim\limits_{x \to \infty} \dfrac{e^x}{x} = \infty$, that $\lim\limits_{x \to \infty} \dfrac{x}{x^2 + 1} = 0$,

and that $\dfrac{x^2}{x^3 + 1} \geq 0$ for $x > -1$.

Practice Examination: 4

1. A*	6. E*	11. A*	16. E*	21. C	26. E*
2. C*	7. D*	12. B	17. A*	22. C*	27. C*
3. E*	8. A*	13. B*	18. C*	23. D*	28. D*
4. D*	9. C*	14. C*	19. A*	24. A*	29. A*
5. B*	10. D*	15. D*	20. D*	25. B	30. E*

31. C*	36. E*	41. B*
32. B*	37. D*	42. A*
33. D*	38. C*	43. E
34. A*	39. D*	44. D
35. A*	40. A*	45. C*

1. A. $\lim\limits_{x\to 0}\dfrac{x^3 - 3x^2}{x} = \lim\limits_{x\to 0}(x^2 - 3x) = 0$.

2. C. The given limit equals $f'(\frac{\pi}{2})$ where $f(x) = \sin x$.

3. E. Here, $\lim\limits_{x\to 2^-}[x] = 1$, while $\lim\limits_{x\to 2^+}[x] = 2$.

4. D. $\lim\limits_{x\to\infty} x \tan\dfrac{\pi}{x} = \lim\limits_{x\to\infty}\dfrac{\tan\frac{\pi}{x}}{\frac{1}{x}} = \lim\limits_{x\to\infty}\dfrac{\pi \tan\frac{\pi}{x}}{\frac{\pi}{x}}$. Setting $y = \dfrac{\pi}{x}$

this yields $\pi \lim\limits_{y\to 0}\dfrac{\tan y}{y} = \pi \lim\limits_{y\to 0}\left[\dfrac{\sin y}{y}\cdot\dfrac{1}{\cos y}\right] = \pi\cdot 1\cdot 1 = \pi$.

5. B. Since $\ln\dfrac{x}{\sqrt{x^2 + 1}} = \ln x - \dfrac{1}{2}\ln(x^2 + 1)$, then $\dfrac{dy}{dx} =$

$\dfrac{1}{x} - \dfrac{1}{2}\cdot\dfrac{2x}{x^2 + 1} = \dfrac{1}{x(x^2 + 1)}$.

6. E. Rewrite y as $(x^2 + 16)^{1/2}$, yielding $\dfrac{dy}{dx} = \dfrac{x}{(x^2 + 16)^{1/2}}$, and

apply the quotient rule.

7. D. $\dfrac{dy}{dx} = -2\sin^3\theta\cos\theta$.

8. A. Differentiate implicitly to get $4x - 4y^3\frac{dy}{dx} = 0$. Substitute

$(-1,1)$ to find $\frac{dy}{dx}$, the slope, at this point, and write the

equation of the tangent: $y - 1 = -1(x + 1)$.

9. C. Since $f(x) = x \ln x$, $f'(x) = 1 + \ln x$, $f''(x) = \frac{1}{x}$, and

$f'''(x) = -\frac{1}{x^2}$.

10. D. Since $\dfrac{dy^2}{d(\ln x)} = \dfrac{\frac{dy^2}{dx}}{\frac{d(\ln x)}{dx}}$ and $y^2 = \ln (x^2 + 1)$, we find

$\dfrac{dy^2}{d(\ln x)} = \dfrac{\frac{2x}{x^2 + 1}}{\frac{1}{x}} = \dfrac{2x^2}{x^2 + 1}$ $(x > 0)$.

11. A. If $f(t) = \frac{1}{t^2} - 4$ and $g(t) = \cos t$, then $f(g(t)) = \frac{1}{\cos^2 t} - 4$

$= \sec^2 t - 4$, and its derivative is $2 \sec^2 t \tan t$.

13. B. Since $v = ks = \frac{ds}{dt}$, then $a = \frac{d^2s}{dt^2} = k \frac{ds}{dt} = kv = k^2s$.

14. C. V , the volume, equals $\frac{4}{3} \pi r^3$, so that $\Delta V \approx \frac{dV}{dr} dr = 4\pi r^2 dr = 4\pi$.

15. D. Here $y' = \frac{1 - \ln x}{x^2}$, which is zero for $x = e$. Since the

signs change from positive to negative as x increases through

e , this critical value yields a relative maximum. Note that

$f(e) = \frac{1}{e}$.

16. E. Since $v = \frac{ds}{dt} = 5t^4 + 6t^2$ never changes signs, there are no

reversals in motion along the line.

17. A.   Let $\dot{x} = \dfrac{dx}{dt}$ and $\dot{y} = \dfrac{dy}{dt}$. Then $2x\dot{x} + 2y\dot{y} = 0$ and $\dot{y} = -\dfrac{3}{4}\dot{x}$

at the point $(3,4)$. Using, also, the fact that the speed

$|\mathbf{v}| = \sqrt{\dot{x}^2 + \dot{y}^2} = 2$, we have $\dot{x}^2 + \dot{y}^2 = 4$, yielding

$\dot{x} = \dfrac{+8}{-5}$ and $\dot{y} = \dfrac{-6}{+5}$ at the given point. Since the particle

moves counterclockwise the velocity vector, $\mathbf{v}$, at $(3,4)$

must be $-\dfrac{8}{5}\mathbf{i} + \dfrac{6}{5}\mathbf{j}$.

18. C.   Letting y be the length parallel to the wall and x the other

dimension of the rectangle, we have that $p = 2x + y$ and

that $A = xy = x(p - 2x)$. For $x = \dfrac{p}{4}$ we have $\dfrac{dA}{dx} = 0$,

which yields $y = \dfrac{p}{2}$.

19. A. $\mathbf{v} = -ak \sin kt \; \mathbf{i} + ak \cos kt \; \mathbf{j}$, and $\mathbf{a} = -ak^2 \cos kt \; \mathbf{i} - ak^2 \sin kt \; \mathbf{j}$

$= -k^2 \mathbf{R}$.

20. D.   See Figure PE4-1. Since the area, A , of the ring equals

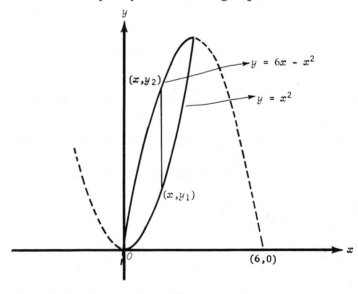

Figure PE4-1

$y_2{}^2 - y_1{}^2$, $A = \pi[(6x - x^2)^2 - x^4] = \pi[36x^2 - 12x^3 + x^4 - x^4]$, and

$\dfrac{dA}{dx} = \pi(72x - 36x^2) = 36\pi x(2 - x)$, where it can be verified

that $x = 2$ produces the maximum area.

22. C.   Note that the given integral is of the type

$$\int \frac{dv}{a^2 + v^2} = \frac{1}{a} \tan^{-1} \frac{v}{a} + C .$$

23. D. $\displaystyle\int_2^4 \frac{du}{\sqrt{16 - u^2}} = \sin^{-1} \frac{u}{4} \bigg|_2^4 = \frac{\pi}{3} .$

24. A.   This is of type $\displaystyle\int \frac{du}{u}$ with $u = \ln x$.

26. E.   We must be careful to note that this is an *improper* integral (for which the function becomes infinite at $x = 3$, on the interval of integration). This integral diverges.

27. C.   Check to verify that each of the other improper integrals converges.

28. D. $\dfrac{dQ}{Q} = \dfrac{dt}{10}$ yields $\ln Q = \dfrac{t}{10} + C$, where $C = \ln Q_0$. So,

$$\ln \frac{Q}{Q_0} = \frac{t}{10} \quad \text{or} \quad Q = Q_0 e^{t/10} .$$

29. A.   Here $\displaystyle\int_0^2 f(x) \, dx = \int_0^1 2x \, dx + \int_1^2 (3x^2 - 2) \, dx$.

30. E.   See Figure PE4-2.

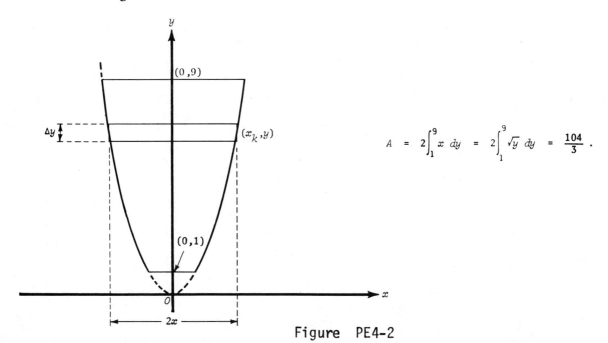

$$A = 2 \int_1^9 x \, dy = 2 \int_1^9 \sqrt{y} \, dy = \frac{104}{3} .$$

Figure PE4-2

31. C.   See Figure PE4-3.

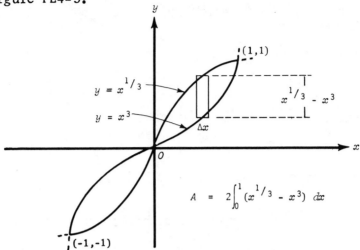

$$A = 2\int_0^1 (x^{1/3} - x^3)\, dx$$

Figure PE4-3

32. B.   See Figure PE4-4.

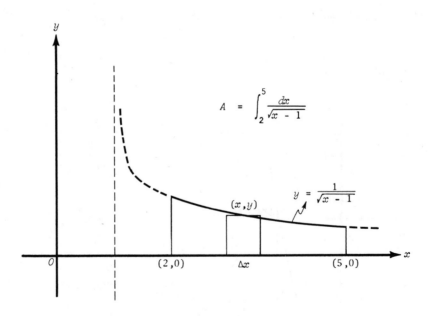

$$A = \int_2^5 \frac{dx}{\sqrt{x-1}}$$

Figure   PE4-4

33. D.   See Figure PE4-5.

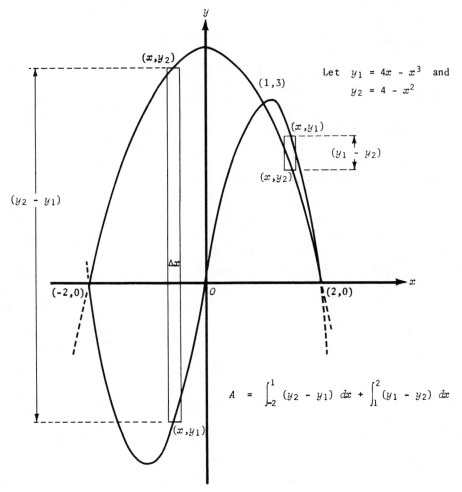

Let $y_1 = 4x - x^3$ and
     $y_2 = 4 - x^2$

$$A = \int_{-2}^{1} (y_2 - y_1) \, dx + \int_{1}^{2} (y_1 - y_2) \, dx$$

Figure   PE4-5

34. A.   See Figure PE4-6.

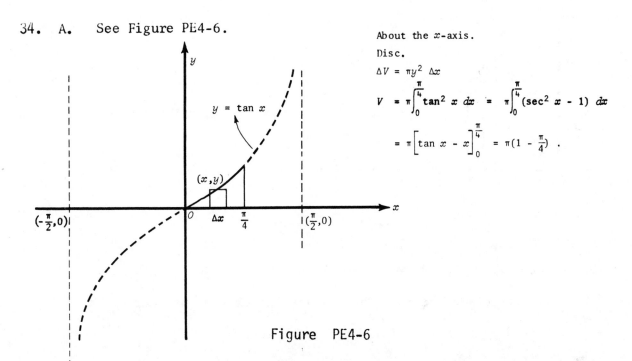

About the x-axis.

Disc.

$\Delta V = \pi y^2 \, \Delta x$

$$V = \pi \int_{0}^{\frac{\pi}{4}} \tan^2 x \, dx = \pi \int_{0}^{\frac{\pi}{4}} (\sec^2 x - 1) \, dx$$

$$= \pi \left[\tan x - x \right]_{0}^{\frac{\pi}{4}} = \pi (1 - \frac{\pi}{4}) \ .$$

Figure   PE4-6

35. A.   See Figure PE 4-7.

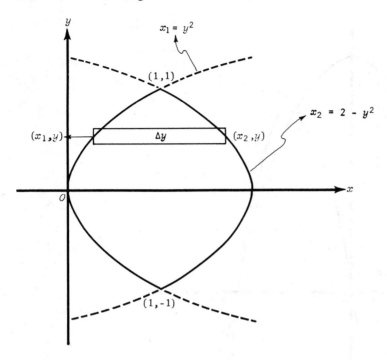

About the y-axis. Washer.

$\Delta V = \pi(x_2{}^2 - x_1{}^2)\, \Delta y$

$V = 2\pi \displaystyle\int_0^1 \left[(2 - y^2)^2 - y^4\right]\, dy$

$= 2\pi \displaystyle\int_0^1 (4 - 4y^2)\, dy$.

Figure   PE4-7

36. E.   See Figure PE4-8.

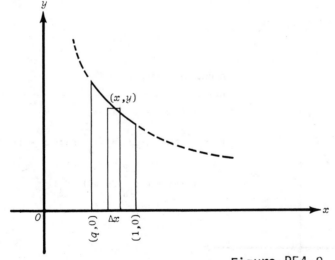

About the x-axis. Disc.

$\Delta V = \pi y^2\, \Delta x = \pi \cdot \dfrac{1}{x}\, \Delta x$.

$V = \lim\limits_{q \to 0^+} \pi \displaystyle\int_q^1 \dfrac{1}{x}\, dx$.

Note that $V \to \infty$ as $q \to 0^+$.

Figure PE4-8

37. D.   See Figure PE4-9, which shows that we seek the length of a

semicircle of radius 2 here. The answer can, of course, be

found by using the formula for arc length:

$$s = \int_0^\pi \sqrt{\left(\frac{dx}{dt}\right)^2 + \left(\frac{dy}{dt}\right)^2}\ dt.$$

The parametric equations

$$\begin{cases} x = 3 - 2\sin t \\ y = 2\cos t - 1 \end{cases}$$

yield the Cartesian equation

$$(x - 3)^2 + (y + 1)^2 = 4\ .$$

$t = 0$

$\cdot (3,-1)$

$t = \pi$

About the y-axis. $\Delta S = 2\pi x\ ds$, where $ds = \sqrt{1 + \left(\frac{dx}{dy}\right)^2}\ dy$

$\Delta S = 2\pi x \sqrt{1 + \frac{y^2}{x^2}}\ dy = 2\pi x \cdot \frac{4}{x}\ dy$, and $S = 8\pi \int_0^1 dy$

Figure PE4-9

38. C. See Figure PE4-10, where the zone of the sphere is shown at the left and the generating arc of the circle at the right.

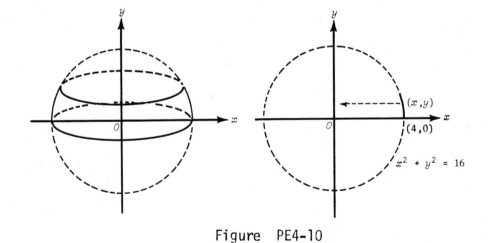

(x,y)

$(4,0)$

$x^2 + y^2 = 16$

Figure   PE4-10

39. D. $(y_{av})_x = \frac{1}{e - 1} \int_1^e \ln x\ dx = \frac{1}{e - 1}\left[x\ln x - x\right]_1^e$, where

$\int \ln x\ dx$ can be obtained by integrating by parts.

40. A.   Since $a = \frac{dv}{dt} = 6t$, $v = 3t^2 + C$, and since $v(0) = 1$, $C = 1$.

Then $v = \frac{ds}{dt} = 3t^2 + 1$ yields $s = t^3 + t + C'$ and we can let

$s(0) = 0$. Then we want $s(3)$.

41. B.   Note that the given limit can be rewritten $\lim\limits_{n \to \infty} \sum\limits_{k=1}^{n} \cos 2x_k \, \Delta x$

where $\Delta x = \frac{1}{n}$ and the partition is over the interval from

0 to 1. Then we evaluate $\int_0^1 \cos 2x \, dx$.

42. A.   Verify that for each of the other equations $\frac{d^2 x}{dt^2} = -k^2 x$,

k a constant, while for $x = e^t + e^{-t}$, $\frac{d^2 x}{dt^2} = x$.

45. C.   Note that although x is a factor of the denominator in (E),

the domain of $\frac{\sqrt{x - 1}}{x}$ is $x \geq 1$.

Sample Essay Examinations

Sample Essay Examination: 1

1. See sketch, Figure S1-1a.

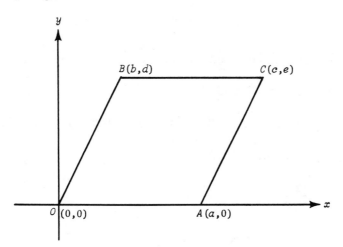

Figure S1-1a

Since $BC \| OA$, $\dfrac{e - d}{c - b} = 0$ and $e = d$; since $OB \| AC$, $\dfrac{e}{c - a} = \dfrac{d}{b}$ and

(using the fact that $d = e$) we see that $c = a + b$. The vertices of

the parallelogram are relabeled in Figure S1-1b and the lines OF and OG

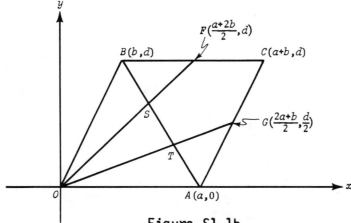

Figure S1-1b

are drawn from O to the midpoints of BC and AC respectively. The coordinates of these midpoints are

$$F(\frac{a + 2b}{2}, d) \qquad \text{and} \qquad G(\frac{2a + b}{2}, \frac{d}{2}).$$

The equations of lines OF, OG, and AB are

$$OF: \quad y = \frac{2d}{a + 2b} x;$$

$$OG: \quad y = \frac{d}{2a + b} x;$$

$$AB: \quad y = \frac{d}{b - a}(x - a).$$

Let S and T be the points of intersection, respectively, of the pair OF and AB and of the pair OG and AB.

If we solve simultaneously the pair of equations for lines AB and OG, we get, for the y-coordinate of T,

$$\frac{2a + b}{d} y = \frac{b - a}{d} y + a.$$

From this, $3ay = ad$, and since $a \neq 0$, $y = \frac{d}{3}$.

Solving the equations of lines AB and OF simultaneously for the y-coordinate of S yields

$$\frac{a + 2b}{2d} y = \frac{b - a}{d} y + a,$$

or $3ay = 2ad$ and $y = \frac{2}{3} d$.

Since the projections of the points T and S on the y-axis trisect the projection of segment AB on the y-axis, it follows that T and S trisect the diagonal of the parallelogram.

2. (a) For $n \neq 6$, $\displaystyle\int \frac{x^3}{x^{n-2}}\, dx = \int x^{5-n}\, dx = \frac{x^{6-n}}{6 - n} + C.$

But if $n = 6$, it equals $\int \dfrac{dx}{x} = \ln |x| + C$.

(b) $\int \dfrac{2}{2 - e^{-x}} \, dx = \int \dfrac{2e^x}{2e^x - 1} \, dx = \int \dfrac{du}{u}$, where $u = 2e^x - 1$.

The definite integral then equals $\ln \left| 2e^x - 1 \right|_0^1 = \ln (2e - 1) - \ln 1$

$= \ln (2e - 1)$.

(c) If $y = \ln \dfrac{1 + \sin x}{\cos x}$, then it equals $\ln (1 + \sin x) - \ln \cos x$,

and

$$\dfrac{dy}{dx} = \dfrac{\cos x}{1 + \sin x} + \dfrac{\sin x}{\cos x} = \dfrac{\cos^2 x + \sin x + \sin^2 x}{(\cos x)(1 + \sin x)}$$

$$= \dfrac{1 + \sin x}{(\cos x)(1 + \sin x)} = \sec x \quad \text{if} \quad \sin x \neq -1 .$$

So $\displaystyle\int_0^{\frac{\pi}{3}} \sec x \, dx = \ln \dfrac{1 + \sin x}{\cos x} \Big|_0^{\frac{\pi}{3}} = \ln \dfrac{1 + \frac{\sqrt{3}}{2}}{\frac{1}{2}} = \ln (2 + \sqrt{3})$.

3. METHOD 1. To show that $x > \ln (1 + x)$ if $x > 0$, let

$f(x) = x - \ln (1 + x)$ and observe that $f'(x) = 1 - \dfrac{1}{x + 1} = \dfrac{x}{x + 1}$

and that $f'(x)$ exists at each positive x . Since f is continuous

at $x = 0$ it follows that $f(x)$ is continuous for each $x \geqq 0$ and

that the Mean Value Theorem holds. Then there is a number c , $0 < c < x$,

such that $\dfrac{f(x) - f(0)}{x} = f'(c)$. So $\dfrac{x - \ln (1 + x) - 0}{x} = \dfrac{c}{c + 1}$.

Since c is positive so is the right-hand member, and since $x > 0$ we

have $x - \ln (1 + x) > 0$, or (for $x > 0$) $x > \ln (1 + x)$.

Theorems used:

(a) The Mean Value Theorem: If f is continuous on the closed

interval $[a,b]$ and its derivative f' exists on the open interval

(a,b) then there is a number c , $a < c < b$, such that $\dfrac{f(b) - f(a)}{b - a} = f'(c)$.

(b) If $p > q$ and $r > 0$, then $pr > qr$.

METHOD 2. Let $f(x) = x - \ln (1 + x)$ and note that $f'(x) =$

$1 - \dfrac{1}{1 + x} = \dfrac{x}{x + 1}$ and that $f''(x) = \dfrac{1}{(1 + x)^2}$. The only critical

value here is $x = 0$, and $f''(0) > 0$ so that this critical value of x

yields a minimum. (In fact, $f'' > 0$ for all x.) Since f and its

derivatives are continuous for all $x \geqq 0$ and since the minimum value

of f at 0 is 0 , then $f(x) > 0$ for all $x > 0$, or $x > \ln (1 + x)$.

Theorems used:

(a) If a function f and its derivative f' are continuous

on an interval $[a,b]$, if $f'(c) = 0$ $(a < c < b)$, and if $f''(c) > 0$,

then $f(c)$ is a relative minimum.

(b) If a function and its derivatives are continuous on an

interval, if its curve is everywhere concave up, and if there is

only one critical value on this interval, then f attains its

absolute minimum at this critical value.

See Figure S1-3a, where the curve of $y = \ln (1 + x)$ and the

line $y = x$ are sketched. It is interesting to observe that

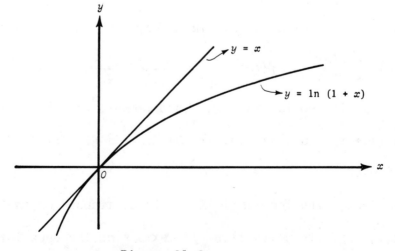

Figure S1-3a

ln $(1 + x)$ may be regarded as the area under the curve $y = \dfrac{1}{1 + t}$

from $t = 0$ to $t = x$; that is, $\displaystyle\int_0^x \dfrac{1}{1 + t}\, dt = \ln(1 + x)$; and

that x may be interpreted as the area of a circumscribed rectangle

of length x and height 1. The latter area is greater than the

former for all $x > 0$. See Figure S1-3b.

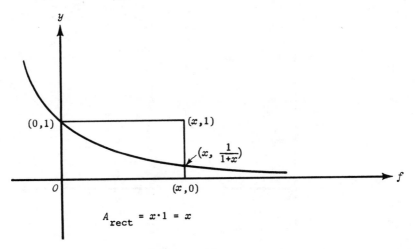

Figure S1-3b

4. Here $y = x \ln x$, $y' = 1 + \ln x$, and $y'' = \dfrac{1}{x}$.

(a) The domain consists of all positive x .

(b) x cannot be 0, but $y = 0$ if $x = 1$.

(c) Since $y' = 0$ for $\ln x = -1$, $x = \dfrac{1}{e}$ is a critical value;

$y''(\frac{1}{e}) > 0$, assuring that $(\frac{1}{e}, -\frac{1}{e})$ is a relative minimum. Since y is

continuous if $x > 0$, the curve has no other maximum or minimum points.

(d) $y'' > 0$ if $x > 0$; the curve is thus concave up and has no

inflection points.

(e) $\displaystyle\lim_{x\to\infty} y = \infty$.

(f) $\displaystyle\lim_{x\to 0^+} x \ln x = 0$. This can best be shown by noting that

$$x \ln x = -x \ln x^{-1} = -\frac{\ln \frac{1}{x}}{\frac{1}{x}}.$$ Then $\displaystyle\lim_{x \to 0^+} x \ln x = \lim_{x \to 0^+} -\frac{\ln \frac{1}{x}}{\frac{1}{x}}$

$$= \lim_{x \to 0^+} \frac{\frac{1}{x}}{-\frac{1}{x^2}} = 0,$$ where L'Hôpital's Rule has been applied.

The curve is sketched in Figure S1-4.

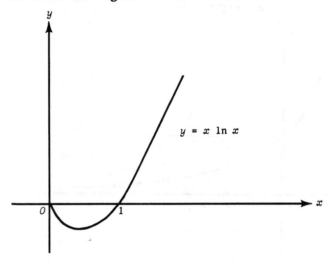

$y = x \ln x$

Figure S1-4

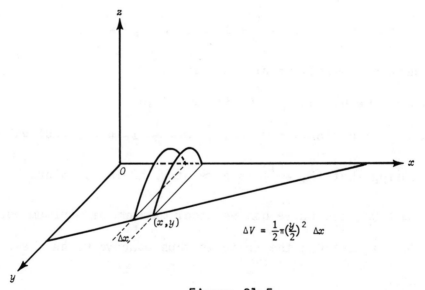

(x, y)

Δx

$\Delta V = \frac{1}{2}\pi\left(\frac{y}{2}\right)^2 \Delta x$

Figure S1-5

5. The solid is sketched in Figure S1-5. The volume of the slice

$$\Delta V = \pi \cdot \frac{1}{2}\left(\frac{y}{2}\right)^2 \Delta x \quad \text{and}$$

$$V = \frac{\pi}{8} \int_0^5 y^2 \, dx$$

$$= \frac{\pi}{8} \int_0^5 \left(\frac{10 - 2x}{3}\right)^2 \, dx$$

$$= \frac{\pi}{72} \int_0^5 (100 - 40x + 4x^2) \, dx$$

$$= \frac{\pi}{18} \left[25x - 5x^2 + \frac{x^3}{3} \right]_0^5 = \frac{125\pi}{54} \, .$$

6. See the sketch, Figure S1-6, where the parabola $y = x^2$ is shown together with some chords whose slope is m . To find the endpoints

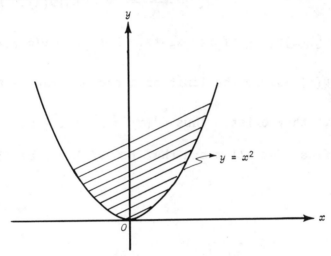

Figure S1-6

of these chords, we solve simultaneously $y = x^2$ and $y = mx + b$, where the latter is the family of lines of slope m . Thus $x^2 - mx - b = 0$ and $x = \frac{m \pm \sqrt{m^2 + 4b}}{2}$. So the abscissas of the endpoints are

$$\frac{m + \sqrt{m^2 + 4b}}{2} \qquad \text{and} \qquad \frac{m - \sqrt{m^2 + 4b}}{2} \, .$$

The x value of the midpoint of any of these chords is m . The locus of the centers of the chords, then, is the line $x = m$.

7. The definition of $u'(x)$ is $\lim\limits_{h\to 0} \dfrac{u(x+h) - u(x)}{h}$ if this limit

exists. We know (1) $u(a+b) = u(a)\cdot u(b)$ for all real a and b; (2)

$u(x) = 1 + xv(x)$; and (3) $\lim\limits_{x\to 0} v(x) = 1$. So

$$\frac{u(x+h) - u(x)}{h} \;=\; \frac{u(x)\cdot u(h) - u(x)}{h} \qquad \text{by (1);}$$

$$=\; u(x)\frac{[u(h) - 1]}{h}$$

$$=\; u(x)\frac{[1 + hv(h) - 1]}{h} \qquad \text{by (2);}$$

$$=\; u(x)\frac{[hv(h)]}{h} \;=\; u(x)v(h), \quad h \neq 0.$$

Now $u'(x) = \lim\limits_{h\to 0} \left[u(x)v(h)\right]$ if it exists. But $\lim\limits_{h\to 0} \left[u(x)v(h)\right]$

$= \lim\limits_{h\to 0} u(x) \lim\limits_{h\to 0} v(h)$, since the limit of a product equals the product

of the limits, if they exist. Thus $u'(x) = u(x)\cdot 1 = u(x)$, since we

know $u(x)$ is defined for all x and that $\lim\limits_{h\to 0} v(h) = 1$ by (3).

Sample Essay Examination: 2

1. (a) The origin is the only intercept.

(b) Note that y' and y'' can be found easily if we rewrite

$y = \dfrac{(x^2 - 4) + 4}{x - 2} = \dfrac{x^2 - 4}{x - 2} + \dfrac{4}{x - 2}$. Then $y = (x + 2) + 4(x - 2)^{-1}$,

$y' = 1 - 4(x - 2)^{-2}$, and $y'' = 8(x - 2)^{-3}$. To find any maxima or

minima note that $y' = \dfrac{x^2 - 4x}{(x - 2)^2}$ and that $x = 0$ and $x = 4$ are both

critical values. Since $y'' = \dfrac{8}{(x - 2)^3}$ and is negative for $x = 0$

but positive for $x = 4$, the points $(0,0)$ and $(4,8)$ are respectively

a maximum and a minimum.

(c) Since $y'' > 0$ when $x > 2$, the curve is concave up for $x > 2$.

(d) $x = 2$ is a vertical asymptote. The graph has no horizontal asymptote, but does approach the line $y = x + 2$ as $|x|$ becomes large. Note that the domain is all real numbers except 2.

The curve is sketched in Figure S2-1.

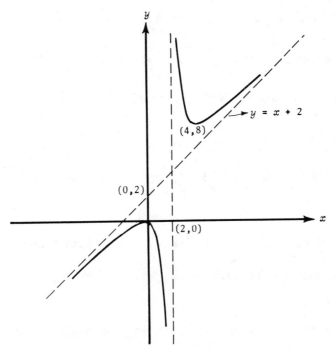

Figure S2-1

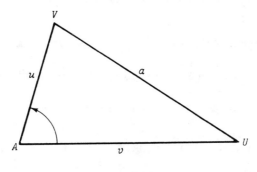

Figure S2-2

2. The triangle is sketched in Figure S2-2, where u and v represent the lengths of the remaining sides. The area

$$S = \frac{1}{2} uv \sin A \qquad (1)$$

and by the law of cosines,

$$a^2 = u^2 + v^2 - 2uv \cos A . \qquad (2)$$

Differentiating S in (1) with respect to u yields $\frac{dS}{du} = \frac{1}{2} \sin A \ (u \frac{dv}{du} + v)$; differentiating implicitly with respect to u in (2), we get

$$0 \ = \ 2u + 2v\frac{dv}{du} - 2 \cos A \ (u \frac{dv}{du} + v) \qquad (3)$$

where $\frac{d}{du} a^2 = 0$ because a^2 is a constant.   Since we seek a maximum area for the triangle, we set $\frac{dS}{du} = 0$.   Since $\frac{1}{2} \sin A$ is constant and is different from zero it follows that $\frac{dv}{du} = - \frac{v}{u}$.   Using this in (3) we get

$$0 \ = \ 2u + 2v(- \frac{v}{u}) - 2 \cos A \ [u(- \frac{v}{u}) + v]$$

or $u^2 - v^2 = 0$.

Since u and v must both be positive, it follows that the triangle has maximum area when it is isosceles, i.e., when $u = v$.

3. (a) The region is sketched in Figure S2-3. The pertinent points of intersection are labelled.

(b) The required area consists of two parts. The area of the triangle is represented by $\int_0^1 [(x + 4) - (4 - x)] \ dx$ and is equal to 1, while the area of the region bounded at the left by $x = 1$, above by $y = x + 4$, and at the right by the parabola is represented by $\int_1^2 [(x + 4) - (x^2 + 2)] \ dx$. This equals $\int_1^2 (x + 2 - x^2) \ dx = \frac{x^2}{2} + 2x - \frac{x^3}{3} \Big|_1^2$ $= \frac{7}{6}$. The required area, thus, equals $2 \frac{1}{6}$ or $\frac{13}{6}$.

4. Since 45 mi/hr is equivalent to 66 ft/sec, we know that the acceleration $a = -k$ and that when $t = 0$, the velocity $v = 66$ and the distance $s = 0$. Since $a = \frac{dv}{dt}$, we integrate to get $v = -kt + C$,

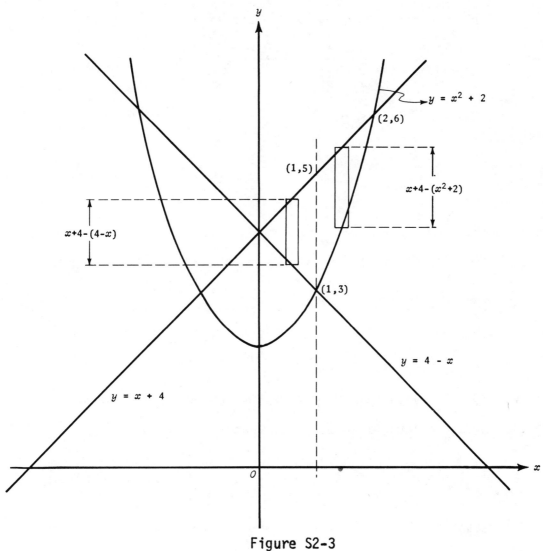

Figure S2-3

and use the initial velocity to get $C = 66$, so that

$$v = -kt + 66. \qquad (1)$$

Since $v = \dfrac{ds}{dt}$ we integrate again, getting $s = -\dfrac{1}{2} kt^2 + 66t + C'$, and

use the initial distance to get

$$s = -\dfrac{1}{2} kt^2 + 66t.$$

To find k, note that v, in (1), equals zero when the car comes to a

stop, i.e. when $t = \dfrac{66}{k}$, and that $s = 60$ when $v = 0$. Thus, in (2),

$$60 = -\dfrac{1}{2} \left(\dfrac{66}{k}\right)^2 + 66\left(\dfrac{66}{k}\right) = \dfrac{1}{2} \dfrac{(66)^2}{k},$$

and $k = \dfrac{363}{10}$ or 36.3 ft/sec^2.

5. (a) Long division of 1 by $(1 + t)$ begins as follows:

$$
1 + t \mid \overline{
\begin{array}{l}
1 - t + t^2 - t^3 \\
1 \\
\underline{1 + t} \\
- t \\
\underline{- t - t^2} \\
+ t^2 \\
\underline{+ t^2 + t^3} \\
- t^3 \\
\underline{- t^3 - t^4} \\
+ t^4
\end{array}}
$$

Observe that

$$
1 - t + t^2 - \frac{t^3}{1 + t} = \frac{1}{1 + t} = 1 - t + t^2 - t^3 + \frac{t^4}{1 + t}
$$

and that, if $t \geq 0$, $-\dfrac{t^3}{1 + t} \leq 0$ while $\dfrac{t^4}{1 + t} \geq 0$. Thus, if $t \geq 0$, we have

$$
1 - t + t^2 \geq \frac{1}{1 + t} \geq 1 - t + t^2 - t^3.
$$

(b) If $0 \leq t \leq 1$, each member of the inequality in (a) is positive and it follows, if $0 \leq x \leq 1$, that

$$
\int_0^x (1 - t + t^2)\, dt \geq \int_0^x \frac{dt}{1 + t} \geq \int_0^x (1 - t + t^2 - t^3)\, dt.
$$

Integrating gives

$$
t - \frac{t^2}{2} + \frac{t^3}{3} \Big|_0^x \geq \ln(1 + t) \Big|_0^x \geq t - \frac{t^2}{2} + \frac{t^3}{3} - \frac{t^4}{4} \Big|_0^x
$$

or

$$
x - \frac{x^2}{2} + \frac{x^3}{3} \geq \ln(1 + x) \geq x - \frac{x^2}{2} + \frac{x^3}{3} - \frac{x^4}{4}.
$$

(c) We let $x = 0.1$ in (b) to approximate $\ln 1.1$, and see that

$$
0.1 - \frac{.01}{2} + \frac{.001}{3} \geq \ln 1.1 \geq 0.1 - \frac{.01}{2} + \frac{.001}{3} - \frac{.0001}{4}.
$$

Since 0.0954 is slightly greater than the left member here while 0.0953 is slightly less than the right, it follows that $0.0954 \geq \ln 1.1 \geq 0.0953$.

6. The parabola is sketched in Figure S2-6. Let p be the x-coordinate of the random point on the line $y = -1$ from which the tangents are drawn

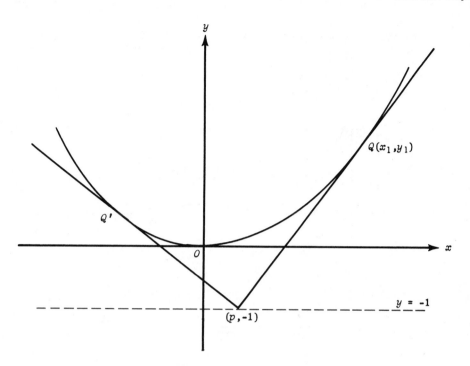

Figure S2-6

to the parabola.   Let the coordinates of a point of tangency be (x_1, y_1).

We wish to find the slopes of the two tangents and show that their product

equals -1.

The equation of a tangent is $y - y_1 = \frac{x_1}{2}(x - x_1)$, where $\frac{x_1}{2}$ is the slope

of the tangent and is obtained from $\frac{dy}{dx}$ evaluated at $x = x_1$.   Since

$(p, -1)$ is on the tangent, it follows that $- 1 - y_1 = \frac{x_1}{2}(p - x_1)$.

Letting $y_1 = \frac{x_1^2}{4}$, we have $- 1 - \frac{x_1^2}{4} = \frac{x_1}{2}(p - x_1)$, or, simplifying,

$x_1^2 - 2px_1 - 4 = 0$.   By the quadratic formula we get two solutions

for x_1: $x_1 = p \pm \sqrt{p^2 + 4}$.

We thus have the abscissas of the two points of tangency, Q and Q',

and the slopes $\frac{p + \sqrt{p^2 + 4}}{2}$ and $\frac{p - \sqrt{p^2 + 4}}{2}$.   Since their product

$\frac{p^2 - (p^2 + 4)}{4} = -1$, the two tangents are perpendicular and this fact

is independent of our choice of point on the line $y = -1$.

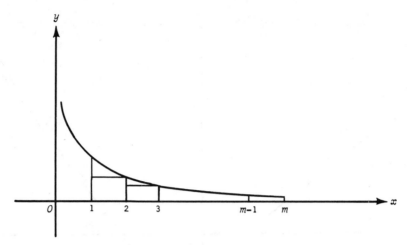

Figure S2-7

7. (a) $\int_1^m \frac{1}{x^2}\, dx \;=\; -\frac{1}{x}\Big|_1^m \;=\; -\left(\frac{1}{m} - 1\right) \;=\; 1 - \frac{1}{m}.$

(b) If m is an integer ≥ 2, $\displaystyle\sum_{k=2}^{m} \frac{1}{k^2}$ can be interpreted as the sum

of the areas of inscribed rectangles of width 1 and height $\frac{1}{k^2}$ (see Figure

S2-7) for the region under the curve and above the x-axis from $x = 1$ to

$x = m$. Since this sum is clearly less than the actual area under the

curve of $y = \frac{1}{x^2}$ from $x = 1$ to $x = m$, it follows that

$$\sum_{k=2}^{m} \frac{1}{k^2} \;<\; \int_1^m \frac{1}{x^2}\, dx \;=\; 1 - \frac{1}{m}.$$

(2) The inequality in (b) is true for all $m \geq 2$ and so

$$\lim_{m\to\infty} \sum_{k=2}^{m} \frac{1}{k^2} \;<\; \lim_{m\to\infty} \int_1^m \frac{1}{x^2}\, dx.$$

The latter defines an improper integral which converges to 1.

Therefore

$$\lim_{m\to\infty} \sum_{k=2}^{m} \frac{1}{k^2} \;<\; 1.$$

Sample Essay Examination: **3**

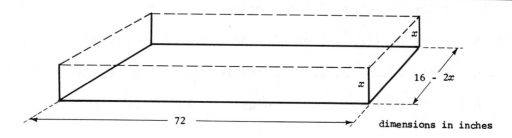

Figure S3-1

1. See Figure S3-1.   The area A of a cross-section is

$A(x) = x(16 - 2x) = 2(8x - x^2)$. Then $\frac{dA}{dx} = 2(8 - 2x)$, which is 0

if $x = 4$.   Note that $0 < x < 8$, that $A(x)$ is continuous, that

$\frac{d^2A}{dx^2} = -4$ which indicates that the curve is concave down.   It

follows that the area is a maximum when $x = 4$ and that it equals 32 in^2.

Note that the length of the trough is irrelevant for this problem.

2. (a) See Figure S3-2.   An equation of the locus is

$\frac{y - 1}{x - 4} \cdot \frac{y + 1}{x - 2} = k$, or $y^2 - 1 = k(x^2 - 6x + 8)$.

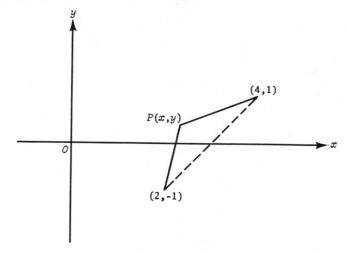

Figure S3-2

(b) If $k = -1$, we get $y^2 - 1 = -x^2 + 6x - 8$, or $x^2 - 6x + y^2 = -7$.

Completing the square in x yields $(x - 3)^2 + y^2 = 2$. This curve is a

circle with center at (3,0) and radius $\sqrt{2}$. Note that if $k = -1$ the angle formed at P is a right angle and the given fixed points are the extremities of the diameter of the circle.

(c) If $k < 0$ but different from -1, the curve is an ellipse.

(d) If $k = 0$ the locus consists of the two lines $y = \pm 1$.

(e) If $k > 0$ the curve is a hyperbola: $y^2 - kx^2 + 6kx = 8k + 1$.

3. See Figure S3-3. The amount of water that must be removed to lower the surface by 2 ft equals the volume of the paraboloid

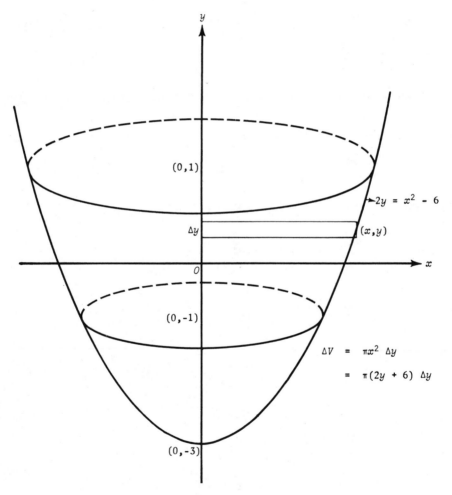

Figure S3-3

contained between the planes $x = -1$ and $x = 1$. Thus

$$V = \pi \int_{-1}^{1} x^2 \, dy = \pi \int_{-1}^{1} (2y + 6) \, dy$$

which equals 12π ft^3.

4.   Since $x = \frac{7}{2} e^{-4t} \sin 2t$, $v = 7e^{-4t} (\cos 2t - 2 \sin 2t)$ and

$a = 14e^{-4t}(3 \sin 2t - 4 \cos 2t)$.

(a)   Then it can be verified directly that $a + 8v + 20x = 0$.

(b)   Since $e^{-4t} > 0$ for all t, $v = 0$ when $\cos 2t = 2 \sin 2t$, or

when $\tan 2t = \frac{1}{2}$.

The triangles drawn in Figure S3-4 show the cases possible when

$\tan 2t = \frac{1}{2}$.

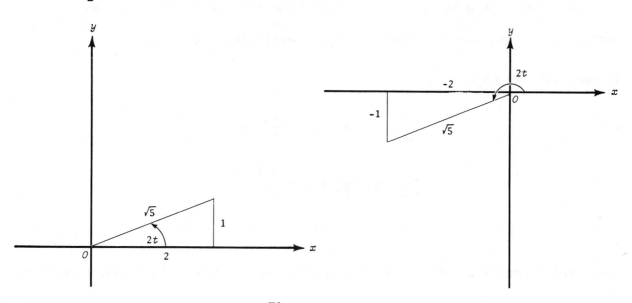

Figure S3-4

If $0 < 2t < \frac{\pi}{2}$, $\sin 2t = \frac{1}{\sqrt{5}}$ and $\cos 2t = \frac{2}{\sqrt{5}}$; if $\pi < 2t < \frac{3\pi}{2}$, $\sin 2t = -\frac{1}{\sqrt{5}}$

and $\cos 2t = -\frac{2}{\sqrt{5}}$.   In the first case $a < 0$ so that x is a relative maximum;

in the second case $a > 0$ so that x is a relative minimum.

5.   (a)   Since $x = 2a \cot \theta$, $x^2 = 4a^2 \cot^2 \theta = 4a^2(\csc^2 \theta - 1)$;

since $y = 2a \sin^2 \theta$, $\sin^2 \theta = \frac{y}{2a}$ and $\csc^2 \theta = \frac{2a}{y}$.   So

$x^2 = 4a^2\left(\frac{2a}{y} - 1\right)$ or $x^2 + 4a^2 = \frac{8a}{y}$ and $y = \frac{8a^3}{x^2 + 4a^2}$.

(b) The curve is sketched in Figure S3-5.

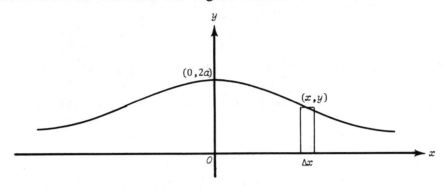

Figure S3-5

(c) The area A bounded by the curve and the x-axis can be given either in rectangular coordinates or parametrically. In rectangular coordinates, we have

$$A \;=\; 2\int_0^\infty y \; dx \;=\; 2\int_0^\infty \frac{8a^3}{x^2 + 4a^2} \; dx$$

$$=\; \lim_{b\to\infty} 16a^3\cdot\frac{1}{2a} \; \tan^{-1} \frac{x}{2a}\Big|_0^b$$

$$=\; 8a^2\cdot\frac{\pi}{2} \;=\; 4\pi a^2 \;,$$

where the symmetry of the curve with respect to the y-axis has been exploited. Parametrically, we have

$$A \;=\; 2\int_0^\infty y \; dx \;=\; 2\int_{\frac{\pi}{2}}^0 2a \sin^2 \theta \; (-2a \csc^2 \theta) \; d\theta$$

$$=\; -8a^2\cdot\theta\,\Big|_{\frac{\pi}{2}}^{0} \;=\; 4\pi a^2$$

as before.

6. **(a)** To prove that f is continuous at $x = 0$ we must show that

$$\lim_{x\to 0} f(x) \text{ exists and equals } f(0).$$

If $x \neq 0$ note that $-1 \leqq \sin \frac{1}{x} \leqq 1$ and that $-x^2 \leqq x^2 \sin\frac{1}{x} \leqq x^2$.

Since $\lim\limits_{x\to 0} (-x^2) = \lim\limits_{x\to 0} x^2 = 0$, it follows from the Squeeze Theorem

(p. 3) that $\lim\limits_{x\to 0} x^2 \sin \frac{1}{x} = 0$; i.e., $\lim\limits_{x\to 0} f(x) = f(0)$.

(b) The definition of $f'(0)$ is $\lim\limits_{h\to 0} \dfrac{f(0 + h) - f(0)}{h}$. Thus

$f'(0) = \lim\limits_{h\to 0} \dfrac{h^2 \sin \frac{1}{h}}{h} = \lim\limits_{h\to 0} h \sin \frac{1}{h}$. Since $-1 \leqq \sin \frac{1}{h} \leqq 1$ $(h \neq 0)$,

it follows that $h \sin \frac{1}{h}$ is squeezed between $-h$ and h as $h \to 0$, so

that $\lim\limits_{h\to 0} h \sin \frac{1}{h} = f'(0) = 0$.

(c) $f'(x)$ can be obtained for nonzero x by using the product rule.

Thus $f'(x) = x^2 \cos \frac{1}{x} \left(- \frac{1}{x^2}\right) + 2x \sin \frac{1}{x} = - \cos \frac{1}{x} + 2x \sin \frac{1}{x}$.

If f' is to be continuous at $x = 0$ then $\lim\limits_{x\to 0} f'(x)$ must exist and be

equal to $f'(0)$. Note, however, since $\lim\limits_{x\to 0} \cos \frac{1}{x}$ fails to exist, that

$f'(x)$ is not continuous at 0.

7. (a) Since f' exists for all x, it follows that f is continuous

for all x. Since $f'(x) = u(x)v(x)$, we can apply the product rule for

a derivative to obtain $f''(x) = u(x)v'(x) + u'(x)v(x)$. If $u(c) = 0$

but $v(c) \neq 0$, then $f''(c) = u'(c)v(c)$. Thus, if $u'(c)v(c) > 0$, $f''(c) > 0$

and the critical value c yields a minimum for f, while if $u'(c)v(c) < 0$

then f is a maximum at c.

Theorems used:

1. If the function f has a finite derivative at $x = a$, then f

is continuous at $x = a$.

2. If r and s are differentiable functions of x then $\frac{d}{dx}(rs)$

$= r\frac{ds}{dx} + s\frac{dr}{dx}$.

3. Let f be continuous, let f' and f'' exist on some open interval containing c and let $f'(c) = 0$. Then $f(x)$ has a relative minimum at $x = c$ if $f''(c)$ is positive; it has a relative maximum at $x = c$ if $f''(c)$ is negative.

(b) Since $f'(x) = (3x - 3)(x^2 + 2)^3(x^2 - 2x + 3)^{3/2}$ the only critical value is $x = 1$. (Note that $x^2 + 2$ and $x^2 - 2x + 3$ are positive for all x.) We can thus apply the theorem in part (a), letting $u(x) = 3x - 3$ and letting $v(x) = (x^2 + 2)^3(x^2 - 2x + 3)^{3/2}$.

Then $u'(x)v(x) = 3(x^2 + 2)^3(x^2 - 2x + 3)^{3/2}$, and since $u'(1)v(1) > 0$, $f(1)$ is a relative minimum.

Sample Essay Examination: 4

1. (a) Since $y = x^4 - 4x^2$, $y' = 4x^3 - 8x$ and $y'' = 12x^2 - 8$. Then $y' = 4x(x^2 - 2)$, and $0, \pm\sqrt{2}$ are critical values. Since $y''(0) < 0$ while $y''(\pm\sqrt{2}) > 0$, the graph has a relative maximum point at $(0,0)$ and minima at $(\pm\sqrt{2}, -4)$.

(b) The curve is sketched in Figure S4-1.

(c) The area bounded by the curve and the x-axis is given by

$$A = 2\int_0^2 -(x^4 - 4x^2)\ dx$$

where we use the symmetry about the y-axis. Thus

$$A = 2\int_0^2 (4x^2 - x^4)\ dx = \frac{128}{15}\ .$$

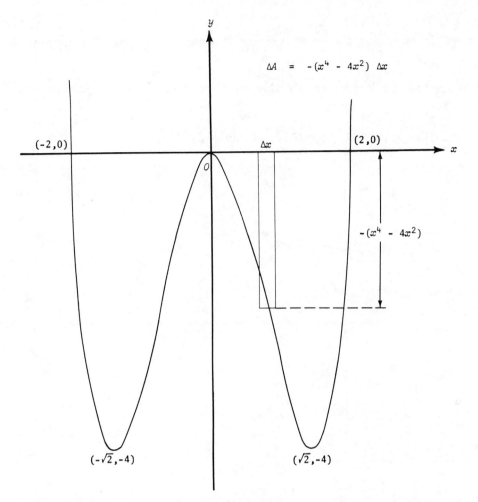

$$\Delta A \ = \ - (x^4 \ - \ 4x^2) \ \Delta x$$

Figure S4-1

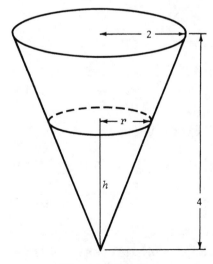

Figure S4-2

2. See Figure S4-2. We know that $\frac{dV}{dt} = -\frac{1}{2}$ and that $h = 2r$.

Here, $V = \frac{1}{3}\pi r^2 h = \frac{\pi h^3}{12}$. So $\frac{dV}{dt} = \frac{\pi h^2}{4}\frac{dh}{dt}$ and $\frac{dh}{dt} = -\frac{1}{2}\frac{4}{\pi h^2} = -\frac{2}{\pi h^2}$ at any time.

When the diameter is 2 in, so is the height, and $\frac{dh}{dt} = -\frac{1}{2\pi}$. The water

level is thus dropping at the rate of $\frac{1}{2\pi}$ in/sec.

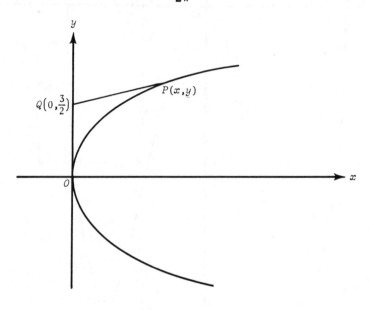

Figure S4-3

3. The parabola $2x = y^2$ is shown in Figure S4-3. If we let

$s = \overline{PQ}^2 = x^2 + (y - \frac{3}{2})^2$ then $\frac{ds}{dx} = 2x + 2(y - \frac{3}{2})\frac{dy}{dx}$. Since $2x = y^2$,

$2 = 2y\frac{dy}{dx}$ and $\frac{dy}{dx} = \frac{1}{y}$. Setting $\frac{ds}{dx}$ equal to 0 yields $x + (y - \frac{3}{2})\frac{1}{y} = 0$,

and (since P is on the curve) $\frac{y^2}{2} + \frac{y - \frac{3}{2}}{y} = 0$. Then $y^3 + 2y - 3 = 0$,

and $y = 1$ is the only critical value.

Note that (1) the distance $\overline{PQ}$ cannot be maximized; (2) if P is

the origin, $\overline{PQ} = \frac{3}{2}$; (3) if P is $(\frac{1}{2},1)$, $\overline{PQ} = \frac{\sqrt{2}}{2}$. We see that $(\frac{1}{2},1)$ is

the point on the curve of $2x = y^2$ closest to the point $(0,\frac{3}{2})$.

4. (a) Since $a = \frac{dv}{dt} = -2v$, we have, separating variables,

$\dfrac{dv}{v}$ = -2 dt.   Integrating, we get

$$\ln v = -2t + C, \qquad (1)$$

and since $v = 20$ when $t = 0$ we get $C = \ln 20$.   Then (1) becomes

$\ln \dfrac{v}{20}$ = -2t or, solving for v,

$$v = 20e^{-2t}. \qquad (2)$$

(b)   The second part of the problem can be done in any of the following three ways:

METHOD 1.   Since, from (2), $v = \dfrac{ds}{dt} = 20e^{-2t}$, we can integrate to get

$$s = -10e^{-2t} + C_1. \qquad (3)$$

If we let $s = 0$ when $t = 0$ (i.e., when $v = 20$), then $C_1 = 10$.   So (3) becomes

$$s = -10e^{-2t} + 10. \qquad (4)$$

When $v = 5$, we see from (2) that $e^{-2t} = \dfrac{1}{4}$.   Then, in (4), $s = -10\left(\dfrac{1}{4}\right) + 10$

$= \dfrac{15}{2}$.

METHOD 2.   The above method is entirely equivalent to the following.   Let s be the required distance travelled (as v decreases from 20 to 5); then

$$s = \int_{v=20}^{v=5} 20e^{-2t}\, dt = \int_{t=0}^{\ln 2} 20e^{-2t}\, dt \qquad (5)$$

where, when $v = 5$, we get, using (2), $\dfrac{1}{4} = e^{-2t}$ or $-\ln 4 = -2t$.   Evaluating s in (5) gives

$$s = -10e^{-2t}\Big|_0^{\ln 2} = -10\left(\dfrac{1}{4} - 1\right) = \dfrac{15}{2}.$$

METHOD 3.   Since $a = \dfrac{dv}{dt} = \dfrac{ds}{dt}\dfrac{dv}{ds}$, we have $v\dfrac{dv}{ds} = -2v$, which yields

$dv = -2ds$.   Integrate to get $v = -2s + C_2$, and let $s = 0$ when $v = 20$.

Then $C_2 = 20$ and $v = -2s + 20$.   When $v = 5$, s, again, equals $\dfrac{15}{2}$.

This last method is especially neat because s is given directly in terms of v and the data of the second part of the problem involve only these two variables.   However, either of the first two methods for solving part (b) follows naturally from the solution of part (a).

5.   (a)   The domain of the function is all nonzero reals.

(b) $\dfrac{\sin x}{x} = 0$ where $\sin x = 0$; i.e., for $x = n\pi$, n a nonzero integer.

(c)   If $x \neq 0$, $f'(x) = \dfrac{x \cos x - \sin x}{x^2}$ and $f'(x) = 0$ when $x \cos x - \sin x = 0$, i.e., when $\tan x = x$.

(d)   Since $f(-x) = f(x)$, the graph is symmetric to the y-axis.

(e) $\lim\limits_{x \to 0} \dfrac{\sin x}{x} = 1$.

(f)   Although $\lim\limits_{x \to 0} f(x)$ exists, f is not continuous at $x = 0$, because $f(0)$ does not exist.

(g)   Since $\sin x$ oscillates between -1 and 1, remaining finite, as $|x| \to \infty$, $\dfrac{\sin x}{x} \to 0$.

The graphs of $y = x$ and $y = \tan x$ are sketched lightly in Figure S4-5. R, O, and S are three points of the infinite set of intersections of these graphs.   The graph of f is sketched in a heavy line; the slope of the curve equals zero at 0, and at R, S, and all other points for which $\tan x = x$.

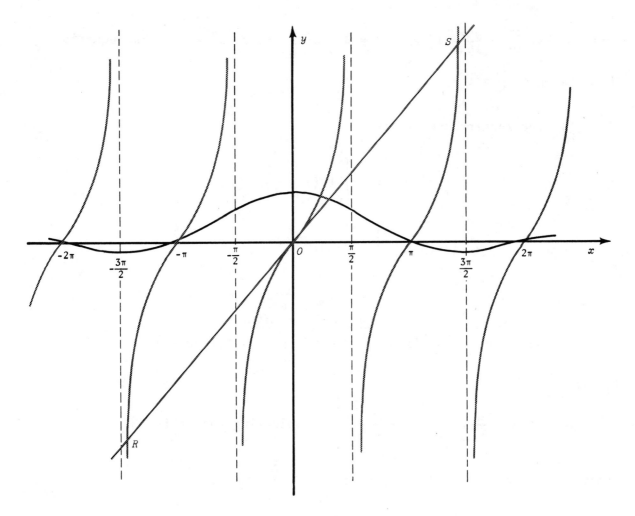

Figure S4-5

6.   See Figure S4-6.

(a)   The equation of the

given ellipse is of the form

$\dfrac{x^2}{b^2} + \dfrac{y^2}{a^2} = 1$, where the vertices

are $(0,\pm a)$, the foci are

$(0,\pm c)$, and $c^2 = a^2 - b^2$.

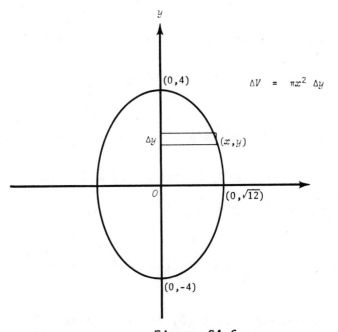

Figure S4-6

Then we have $\frac{x^2}{b^2} + \frac{y^2}{16} = 1$, and $c^2 = 4 = a^2 - b^2$, so $b^2 = 12$. The equation, then, is $\frac{x^2}{12} + \frac{y^2}{16} = 1$.

(b)   The required volume is

$$V = \pi \int_0^4 x^2 \, dy = \pi \int_0^4 12\left(1 - \frac{y^2}{16}\right) \, dy$$

$$= 12\pi \left[y - \frac{y^3}{48} \right]_0^4 = 32\pi.$$

7.   (a)   Since $i = \frac{E}{R}(1 - e^{\frac{-Rt}{L}})$ and $e^{\frac{-Rt}{L}} < 1$ if $t > 0$,

then $i < \frac{E}{R}$.

(Note that $\frac{d}{dt} e^{\frac{-Rt}{L}} = -\frac{R}{L} e^{\frac{-Rt}{L}}$, indicating that this

function decreases for all t; when $t = 0$, $e^{\frac{-Rt}{L}} = 1$.)

(b)   As $t \to \infty$, $e^{\frac{-Rt}{L}} \to 0$; so $\lim_{t \to \infty} i = \frac{E}{R}$.

(c)   For small changes in t, the change in i is approximately

equal to di. Thus $\Delta i \approx di = \frac{d}{dt} i \, \Delta t$, where $\frac{di}{dt}$ is to be evaluated

for $t = 0$ and $\Delta t = 0.01$. So $\Delta i \approx \frac{R}{L} \cdot \frac{E}{R} e^{\frac{-Rt}{L}} \Delta t = \frac{E}{L} e^0 (0.01) = 0.01 \frac{E}{L} = 0.6$.

(d)   If E, L, and t are all held fixed, while R varies, we

can write

$$\lim_{R \to 0} i = \lim_{R \to 0} (-E) \frac{(e^{-\frac{t}{L}R} - 1)}{R} = -E \lim_{R \to 0} \frac{e^{-\frac{t}{L}R} - 1}{R}.$$

Recalling that $f'(0)$ is defined as $\lim_{h \to 0} \frac{f(h) - f(0)}{h}$ or

$\lim\limits_{R \to 0} \dfrac{f(R) - f(0)}{R}$, we see that $\lim\limits_{R \to 0} i$ equals $-Ef'(0)$, where $f(R) = e^{-\frac{t}{L}R}$.

Remember that t and L are constants here. Thus

$$\lim_{R \to 0} i \;=\; -E\left(\frac{-t}{L}\right)e^{-\frac{t}{L}R} \;,$$

and when $R = 0$ this is $\dfrac{Et}{L}$.

Alternatively, we may note that

$$\lim_{R \to 0} i \;=\; E \lim_{R \to 0} \frac{1 - e^{-\frac{t}{L}R}}{R} \;=\; E \lim_{R \to 0} \frac{u(R)}{v(R)},$$

where $u(R)$ and $v(R)$ both approach 0 as R does. We can then apply L'Hôpital's rule:

$$E \lim_{R \to 0} \frac{1 - e^{-\frac{t}{L}R}}{R} \;=\; E \lim_{R \to 0} \frac{\frac{t}{L}e^{-\frac{t}{L}R}}{1} \;=\; \frac{Et}{L} \;.$$

Sample Essay Examination: 5

1. (a) See Figure S5-1.

(b) The required area is labelled ROQ. The equation of the line RQ through $(1,1)$ and $(4,-8)$ is $y - 1 = -3(x - 1)$, or $x = \dfrac{4 - y}{3}$. We describe two methods for finding the area.

METHOD 1. If the area is found by summing horizontal elements, then

$$A \;=\; \int_{-8}^{1} (x_2 - x_1)\; dy$$

where x_2 is an abscissa on the line and x_1 on the curve. So

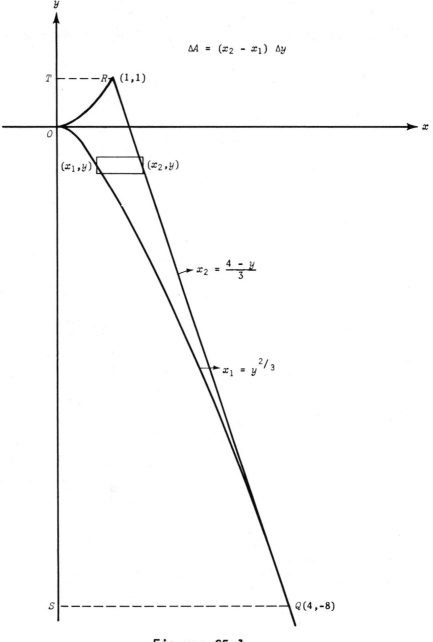

Figures S5-1

$$A = \int_{-8}^{1} \left(\frac{4 - y}{3} - y^{2/3} \right) \, dy$$

$$= \left. \frac{4y}{3} - \frac{y^2}{6} - \frac{3}{5} y^{5/3} \right|_{-8}^{1} = \frac{27}{10}.$$

METHOD 2. *A* can also be found by subtracting from trapezoid *RQST*

the area bounded by the curve, the *y*-axis, and the horizontal lines

y = -8 and y = 1.   Then A = $\frac{1}{2}(1 + 4)\cdot 9 - \int_{-8}^{1} y^{2/3}\,dy = \frac{45}{2} - \frac{99}{5} = \frac{27}{10}$.

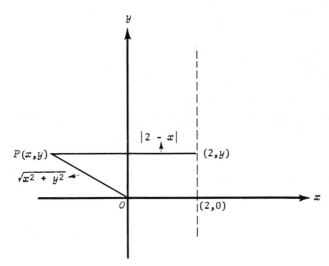

Figure S5-2a

2.   (a)   See Figure S5-2a.   It is given that $|2 - x| = 2\sqrt{x^2 + y^2}$;
then $4 - 4x + x^2 = 4(x^2 + y^2)$ and

$$4 = 3x^2 + 4x + 4y^2 \tag{1}$$

(b) Equation (1) can be written in more convenient form if we
complete the square in x.   Then $4 + \frac{4}{3} = 3(x^2 + \frac{4}{3}x + \frac{4}{9}) + 4y^2$, or

$\frac{16}{3} = 3(x + \frac{2}{3})^2 + 4y^2$, or

$$1 = \frac{(x + \frac{2}{3})^2}{\frac{16}{9}} + \frac{y^2}{\frac{4}{3}}. \tag{2}$$

Equation (2) is that of an ellipse with center at $(-\frac{2}{3}, 0)$, a vertex at

$(\frac{2}{3}, 0)$, and a focus as $(0,0)$.   The ellipse is sketched in Figure S5-2b.

(c)   The polar equation of the ellipse can be found directly from
the statement of the locus.   Let the coordinates of P be r, θ.   Then

$2 - r \cos \theta = 2r$, or $r = \dfrac{2}{2 + \cos \theta}$.

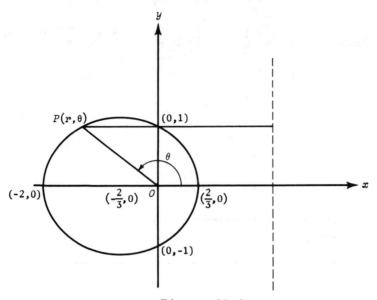

Figure S5-2b

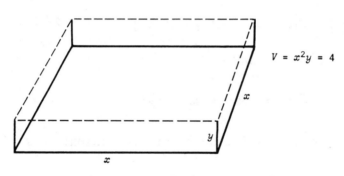

Figure S5-3

3. (a) In Figure S5-3 we let the dimensions of the box be $x \times x \times y$. The volume $x^2y = 4$. The cost $C = 50(x^2 + 4xy) + 10(4x + 4y)$. Using the expression for the volume we get

$$C = 50\left(x^2 + \frac{16}{x}\right) + 10\left(4x + \frac{16}{x^2}\right), \qquad (1)$$

whence

$$\frac{dC}{dx} = 50\left(2x - \frac{16}{x^2}\right) + 10\left(4 - \frac{32}{x^3}\right).$$

Setting this equal to zero yields $10\left[10 \,\frac{x^3 - 8}{x^2} + 4 \,\frac{x^3 - 8}{x^3}\right] = 0,$

$$\frac{20\,(x^3 - 8)\,(5x + 2)}{x^3} \;=\; 0.$$

If $x > 0$, note that $x = 2$ is the only critical value, that C is a continuous function of x, and that $\frac{dC}{dx}$ changes from negative to positive as x increases through 2. Thus $x = 2$ yields minimum cost and the and the dimensions of the box are 2×2×1.

(b)   To show that the specific costs of the sheet metal and welding do not affect the dimensions that yield a minimum total cost, let p be the cost per ft^2 of the sheet metal and q the cost per ft of the welding. Then (1) above becomes

$$C \;=\; p\!\left(x^2 + \frac{16}{x}\right) + q\!\left(4x + \frac{16}{x^2}\right)$$

and

$$\frac{dC}{dx} \;=\; p\!\left(2x - \frac{16}{x^2}\right) + q\!\left(4 - \frac{32}{x^3}\right)$$

$$=\; 2p\frac{x^3 - 8}{x^2} + 4q\frac{x^3 - 8}{x^3}$$

$$=\; \frac{2\,(x^3 - 8)\,(px + 2q)}{x^3}\,.$$

Since x must be positive, note that the only x for which $\frac{dC}{dx} = 0$ is, as before, $x = 2$; furthermore, this does not depend on p or q.

4.   (a)   In Figure S5-4 a curve of each family is sketched, with h and k both taken as positive. To find possible points of intersection we solve simultaneously the equations $xy = k$ and $y^2 - x^2 = h$, getting $\frac{k^2}{x^2} - x^2 = h$ or

$$x^4 + hx^2 - k^2 = 0. \tag{1}$$

The quadratic formula here yields

$$x^2 \;=\; \frac{-h \pm \sqrt{h^2 + 4k^2}}{2}. \tag{2}$$

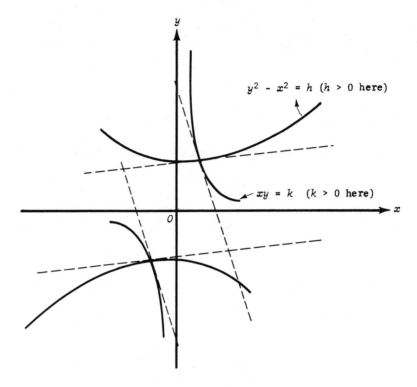

Figure S5-4

If $hk \neq 0$, $\sqrt{h^2 + 4k^2} > |h|$ and $-h + \sqrt{h^2 + 4k^2}$ is positive. There are, thus, if $hk \neq 0$, 2 distinct reals which satisfy (1) and therefore two distinct points of intersection of every pair of the given families of curves.

(b)   Note that for $xy = k$ the slope $\frac{dy}{dx} = -\frac{y}{x}$, while for $y^2 - x^2 = h$ the slope $\frac{dy}{dx} = \frac{x}{y}$. At a point of intersection (x_1, y_1), the existence of which is guaranteed by (2) above, the product of these slopes is

$-\frac{y_1}{x_1} \cdot \frac{x_1}{y_1} = -1$, indicating that the curves intersect at right angles.

5.   (a)   The curve is sketched in Figure S5-5. The area A in the first quadrant under the curve, if it exists, is given by the improper integral

$$A = \int_0^\infty e^{-x}\, dx = \lim_{b \to \infty} \int_0^b e^{-x}\, dx$$

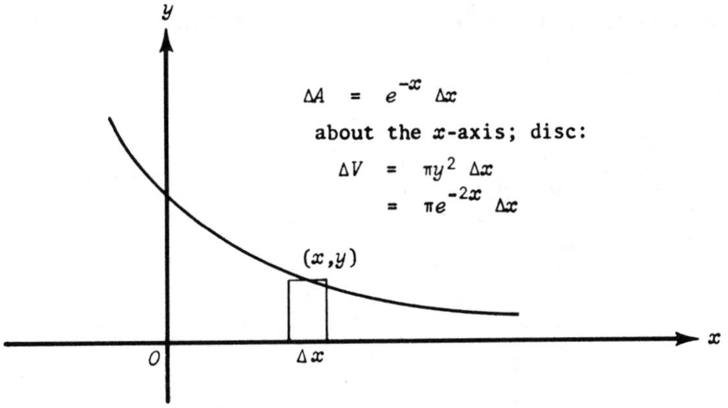

$$\Delta A = e^{-x}\,\Delta x$$

about the x-axis; disc:

$$\Delta V = \pi y^2\,\Delta x$$
$$= \pi e^{-2x}\,\Delta x$$

(x, y)

Δx

Figure S5-5

$$= \lim_{b\to\infty} -e^{-x}\Big|_0^b = -\lim_{b\to\infty}\left(\frac{1}{e^b} - 1\right) = 1.$$

So the area does exist and equals 1.

(b)   The volume V obtained by rotating the first-quadrant area about the x-axis is given by

$$V = \pi\int_0^\infty e^{-2x}\,dx = \pi\lim_{b\to\infty}\int_0^b e^{-2x}\,dx$$

$$= -\frac{\pi}{2}\lim_{b\to\infty} e^{-2x}\Big|_0^b$$

$$= -\frac{\pi}{2}\lim_{b\to\infty}\left[\frac{1}{e^{2b}} - 1\right] = \frac{\pi}{2}.$$

So the volume also exists.

6.   Note that

$$x = \frac{1}{t}; \qquad \frac{dx}{dt} = -\frac{1}{t^2}; \qquad \frac{d^2x}{dt^2} = \frac{2}{t^3};$$

$$y = \ln t; \quad \frac{dy}{dt} = \frac{1}{t}; \qquad \frac{d^2y}{dt^2} = -\frac{1}{t^2}.$$

Thus:

(a)   The speed, $|\mathbf{v}| = \sqrt{\dfrac{1}{t^4} + \dfrac{1}{t^2}}$ at any time t, and equals $\sqrt{2}$ when

$t = 1$.

(b)   The acceleration $a = \frac{2}{t^3}i - \frac{1}{t^2}j$ at any time, and equals $2i - j$ when $t = 1$.

(c)   Since $t = \frac{1}{x}$, $y = \ln \frac{1}{x} = -\ln x$. The curve is sketched in Figure S5-6.

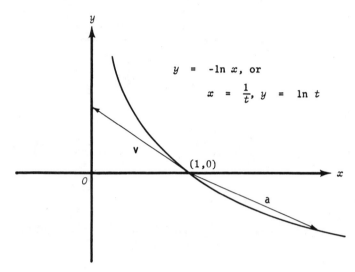

$y = -\ln x$, or

$x = \frac{1}{t}$, $y = \ln t$

$(1,0)$

Figure S5-6

(d)   The particle is at $(1,0)$ when $t = 1$ and travels in a clockwise direction along the curve as t increases. v and a when $t = 1$ are shown in the Figure.

7.   (a)   To show that $f(x)$ is monotonic increasing on the closed interval $[a,b]$ we must show, if $a \leq x_1 < x_2 \leq b$, that $f(x_1) < f(x_2)$. Since $f'(x)$ is positive at each x in the given interval, the function is continuous at each x and we may apply the Mean Value Theorem. Thus, since $x_1 < x_2$ there exists a number c, $x_1 < c < x_2$, such that

$$\frac{f(x_2) - f(x_1)}{x_2 - x_1} = f'(c).$$

Since both $(x_2 - x_1)$ and $f'(c)$ are positive, so is $f(x_2) - f(x_1)$, and $f(x_1) < f(x_2)$.

(b) To prove $\dfrac{\sin x}{x} < 1$ if $0 < x < 2\pi$, note that $\sin x$ and its derivative, $\cos x$, are both continuous. By the Mean Value Theorem, then, there is a number c, $0 < c < x$, such that

$$\frac{\sin x - 0}{x - 0} = \cos c.$$

Since, if $0 < c < x < 2\pi$, then $\cos c < 1$, it follows that $\dfrac{\sin x}{x} < 1$.

Actually this implies that $\dfrac{\sin x}{x} < 1$ for all positive x since

$$\lim_{x \to \infty} \frac{\sin x}{x} = 0.$$

Sample Essay Examination: 6

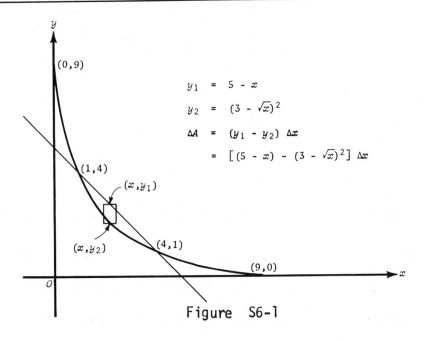

$$y_1 = 5 - x$$
$$y_2 = (3 - \sqrt{x})^2$$
$$\Delta A = (y_1 - y_2)\,\Delta x$$
$$= \left[(5 - x) - (3 - \sqrt{x})^2\right]\Delta x$$

Figure S6-1

1. (a) The region is sketched in Figure S6-1. To determine where the graphs intersect, we solve simultaneously $y = 5 - x$ and $y = (3 - \sqrt{x})^2$. Then $5 - x = 9 - 6\sqrt{x} + x$, $6\sqrt{x} = 2x + 4$ or $3\sqrt{x} = x + 2$, $9x = x^2 + 4x + 4$, and $0 = x^2 - 5x + 4$, with roots $x = 1$ and $x = 4$. The points are $(1,4)$ and $(4,1)$, as shown in the Figure.

(b) For the area we thus have

$$A = \int_1^4 [5 - x - (3 - \sqrt{x})^2]\, dx \quad \int_1^4 5 - x - (9 - 6\sqrt{x} + x)\, dx$$

$$= \int_1^4 (6\sqrt{x} - 2x - 4)\, dx = 4x^{3/2} - x^2 - 4x \Big|_1^4$$

$$= 4(8 - 1) - (16 - 1) - 4(4 - 1) = 1.$$

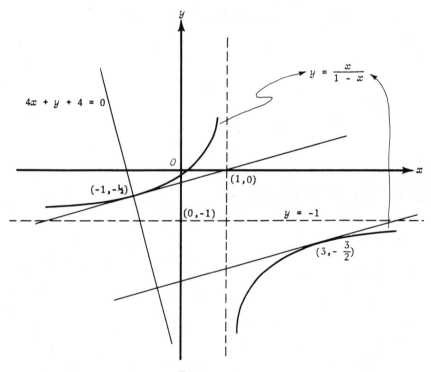

Figure S6-2

2. The graph of $y = \dfrac{x}{1 - x}$ and the line $4x + y + 4 = 0$ are shown

in Figure S6-2. Note that the curve has a vertical asymptote at $x = 1$

and a horizontal asymptote at $y = -1$. To find the points on the curve

at which the tangent is perpendicular to the given line, we find the

slope of the curve and set it equal to the negative reciprocal of the

slope of the line.

Since $\dfrac{dy}{dx} = \dfrac{1}{(1 - x)^2}$, we seek x_1 such that $\dfrac{1}{(1 - x_1)^2} = \dfrac{1}{4}$. We get

$(1 - x_1)^2 = 4$ or $1 - x_1 = \pm 2$. Then $x_1 = -1$ or 3, with corresponding ordinates on the curve $-\frac{1}{2}$ and $-\frac{3}{2}$, respectively. The required lines

have equations $y + \frac{1}{2} = \frac{1}{4}(x + 1)$ and $y + \frac{3}{2} = \frac{1}{4}(x - 3)$.

A reasonably careful sketch will expose unreasonable answers.

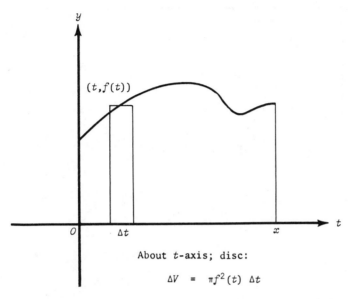

$(t, f(t))$

Δt

About t-axis; disc:

$$\Delta V = \pi f^2(t) \Delta t$$

Figure S6-3

3. See Figure S6-3. The volume is given by the integral

$$V = \pi \int_{t=0}^{x} y^2 \, dt = \pi \int_0^{x} f^2(t) \, dt.$$

Since $\frac{dV}{dx} = \pi f^2(x)$ and since $V = 2\pi(x^2 + 2x)$ then $\pi f^2(x) = 2\pi(2x + 2)$

and $f^2(x) = 4x + 4$. Thus $f(x) = 2\sqrt{x + 1}$ and $f(t) = 2\sqrt{t + 1}$.

4. See Figure S6-4, where the length of a side of the equilateral

triangle equals $2s$.

Since $(2s)^2 = s^2 + y^2$, $s = \frac{y}{\sqrt{3}}$. The area, A, of the triangle is

ys or $\frac{y^2}{\sqrt{3}}$ or $\frac{1}{\sqrt{3}}(\ln x)^2$. Then $\frac{dA}{dt} = \frac{2}{\sqrt{3}} \cdot \frac{\ln x}{x} \cdot \frac{dx}{dt} = \frac{2}{\sqrt{3}} \cdot \frac{\ln x}{x} \cdot \sqrt{3} = \frac{2 \ln x}{x}$

at any time t. When $y = 1$, i.e., $\ln x = 1$, $x = e$ and $\frac{dA}{dt} = \frac{2(1)}{e}$ units/sec.

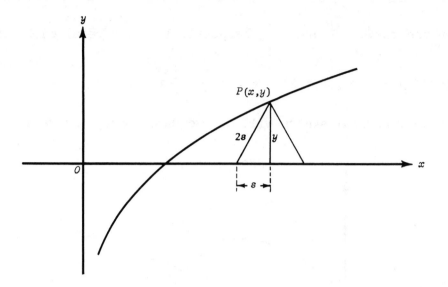

Figure S6-4

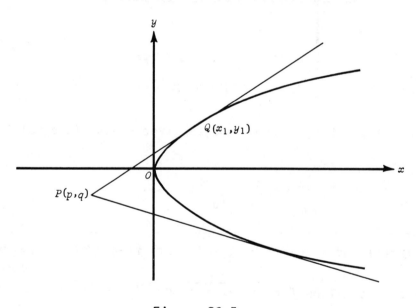

Figure S6-5a

5. The parabola is sketched in Figure S6-5a. If we let $Q(x_1, y_1)$ be a point of tangency then we can find Q by using the fact that it is both on the tangent PQ and on the curve $y^2 = x$. The equation of the tangent from P to the curve is

$$y - q = \frac{1}{2y_1}(x - p) \qquad (1)$$

where the slope is the derivative of $y^2 = x$ when $y = y_1$. Since $Q(x_1, y_1)$
is on this tangent, (1) becomes

$$y_1 - q = \frac{1}{2y_1}(x_1 - p)$$

or

$$2y_1^2 - 2qy_1 = x_1 - p. \tag{2}$$

Since Q is on the parabola, we can use $y_1^2 = x_1$ in (2) to get

$2y_1^2 - 2qy_1 = y_1^2 - p$, or

$$y_1^2 - 2qy_1 + p = 0. \tag{3}$$

Applying the quadratic formula to solve (3), we see that

$$y_1 = \frac{2q \pm \sqrt{4q^2 - 4p}}{2} = q \pm \sqrt{q^2 - p}. \tag{4}$$

The number of possible solutions for y_1 thus depends on q and p.
There are none, one, or two according as q^2 is less than, equal to,
or greater than p.

In Figure S6-5b the three cases are shown, and demonstrate the
following:

> If $q^2 < p$ P is within the parabola; no tangents may be
> drawn from P to the parabola.

> If $q^2 = p$ P is on the parabola; one tangent may be drawn
> to the parabola at P.

> If $q^2 > p$ P is outside the parabola; two tangents may be
> drawn from P to the parabola.

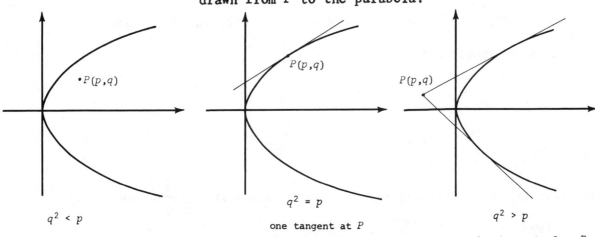

$q^2 < p$

no tangents from P

$q^2 = p$

one tangent at P

Figure S6-5b

$q^2 > p$

two tangents from P

6. (a) Since $\frac{dx}{dt} = y$ and $\frac{dy}{dt} = \sqrt{1 + 2y}$, one can separate variables

in the latter to get $\frac{dy}{\sqrt{1 + 2y}} = dt$. Integrating yields $\sqrt{1 + 2y} = t + C_1$.

Since $y = 0$ when $t = 0$, this gives $1 = 0 + C_1$, and $C_1 = 1$. So

$\sqrt{1 + 2y} = t + 1$, and we can square this to get $1 + 2y = (t + 1)^2$. Then

$$y = \frac{t^2}{2} + t. \tag{1}$$

Using (1) in $\frac{dx}{dt} = y$, it follows that $\frac{dx}{dt} = \frac{t^2}{2} + t$, and we can again

separate and integrate to get $x = \frac{t^3}{6} + \frac{t^2}{2} + C_2$. Using $x = 0$ when $t = 0$

shows that $C_2 = 0$. Thus

$$x = \frac{t^3}{6} + \frac{t^2}{2} \qquad \text{and} \qquad y = \frac{t^2}{2} + t. \tag{2}$$

(b) For this we describe two alternatives.

ALTERNATIVE 1. We can find the x- and y-components of the acceleration

in terms of y by differentiating the given equations with respect to t.

Thus $\frac{d^2x}{dt^2} = \frac{dy}{dt}$ and $\frac{d^2y}{dt^2} = \frac{2}{2\sqrt{1 + 2y}} \frac{dy}{dt}$. Since it is given that $\frac{dy}{dt} = \sqrt{1 + 2y}$,

it follows that $\frac{d^2x}{dt^2} = \sqrt{1 + 2y}$ and $\frac{d^2y}{dt^2} = 1$.

ALTERNATIVE 2. Or we can differentiate twice in (2) to get the

components of acceleration in terms of t:

$$\frac{dx}{dt} = \frac{t^2}{2} + t \qquad\qquad\qquad \frac{dy}{dt} = t + 1$$

$$\frac{d^2x}{dt^2} = t + 1 \qquad\qquad\qquad \frac{d^2y}{dt^2} = 1.$$

Note that these are equivalent to those obtained in Alternative 1,

since, from (a), $t + 1 = \sqrt{1 + 2y}$.

(c)   Alternative 2 of (b) can be used to obtain the speed $|\mathbf{v}|$ and magnitude of acceleration when $t = 1$ immediately.   Thus

$$|\mathbf{v}| = \sqrt{(\tfrac{dx}{dt})^2 + (\tfrac{dy}{dt})^2}$$

and when $t = 1$ this is

$$\sqrt{(\tfrac{3}{2})^2 + 2^2} = \tfrac{5}{2}.$$

The magnitude of the acceleration equals

$$\sqrt{(\tfrac{d^2x}{dt^2})^2 + (\tfrac{d^2y}{dt^2})^2}$$

and when $t = 1$ this is

$$\sqrt{2^2 + 1^2} = \sqrt{5}.$$

Or we may note, from (1), that when $t = 1$, $y = \tfrac{3}{2}$.   Then we can use the given equations to get, when $t = 1$, $\tfrac{dx}{dt} = \tfrac{3}{2}$ and $\tfrac{dy}{dt} = \sqrt{4} = 2$, and proceed to use Alternative 1 of (b) to get $\tfrac{d^2x}{dt^2} = \sqrt{4} = 2$ and $\tfrac{d^2y}{dt^2} = 1$. Again, then, when $t = 1$ the speed of P is $\tfrac{5}{2}$ and its acceleration has magnitude $\sqrt{5}$.

7.   Here, $F(x) = \displaystyle\int_{1}^{x} \frac{\sin t}{t}\, dt.$

(a) $F'(x) = \dfrac{\sin x}{x}$ and $\displaystyle\lim_{x \to 0} F'(x) = \lim_{x \to 0} \frac{\sin x}{x} = 1.$

(b)   From (a), $F'(\tfrac{1}{x}) = \dfrac{\sin \tfrac{1}{x}}{\tfrac{1}{x}}$ and thus $\displaystyle\lim_{x \to 0} F'(\tfrac{1}{x}) = \lim_{x \to 0} \dfrac{\sin \tfrac{1}{x}}{\tfrac{1}{x}}$

$= \displaystyle\lim_{x \to 0} x \sin \tfrac{1}{x}.$ Note that, since $-1 \leqq \sin \tfrac{1}{x} \leqq 1$ for all $x \neq 0$,

if $x > 0$, $-x \leqq x \sin \tfrac{1}{x} \leqq x$, while

if $x < 0$, $-x \geqq x \sin \tfrac{1}{x} \geqq x.$

In either case, since $x \sin \frac{1}{x}$ is "squeezed" between two quantities each

of which approaches zero as x does, so must $x \sin \frac{1}{x}$.   Thus

$$\lim_{x \to 0} \frac{\sin \frac{1}{x}}{\frac{1}{x}} = 0.$$

Theorems used:

(1)   If $a < b$ and $c > 0$, $ac < bc$, while if $c < 0$, $ac > bc$.

(2)   The "Squeeze" theorem: if $f(t) \leqq g(t) \leqq h(t)$ for all values of t

near c and if $\lim_{t \to c} f(t) = \lim_{t \to c} h(t) = L$, then $\lim_{t \to c} g(t) = L$.

(3)   If $\lim_{t \to c^-} g(t) = \lim_{t \to c^+} g(t) = L$, then $\lim_{t \to c} g(t) = L$.

Sample Essay Examination: 7

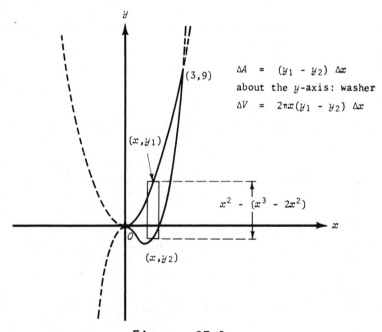

Figure   S7-1

1.   The region is sketched in Figure S7-1.

(a)   We solve $y = x^3 - 2x^2$ and $y = x^2$ simultaneously: $x^3 - 2x^2 = x^2$

or $x^2(x - 3) = 0$. The curves intersect, then, for $x = 0$ and $x = 3$.
For the area A we have

$$A = \int_0^3 (y_1 - y_2)\ dx = \int_0^3 x^2 - (x^3 - 2x^2)\ dx$$

$$= \int_0^3 (3x^2 - x^3)\ dx = x^3 - \frac{x^4}{4}\Big|_0^3 = \frac{27}{4}.$$

(b)   If the region in part (a) is rotated about the y-axis, a typical element of volume is a washer for which $\Delta V = 2\pi RHT$. The volume V of the solid obtained is given by

$$V = 2\pi \int_0^3 x(y_1 - y_2)\ dx = 2\pi \int_0^3 x(3x^2 - x^3)\ dx$$

$$= 2\pi \int_0^3 (3x^3 - x^4)\ dx = 2\pi \left[\frac{3x^4}{4} - \frac{x^5}{5}\right]_0^3$$

$$= 2\pi \left(\frac{3^5}{4} - \frac{3^5}{5}\right) = 2\pi \cdot 3^5 \left(\frac{1}{20}\right) = 24.3\pi.$$

2.   The parabola and a tangent to it at P are sketched in Figure S7-2. The equation of the tangent at P is $y - y_1 = 2x_1(x - x_1)$, where the slope $2x_1$ is the derivative of $y = x^2$ at $x = x_1$.   To find the ordinate of T,

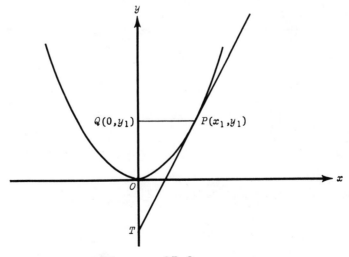

Figure   S7-2

we let $x = 0$, getting $y - y_1 = -2x_1^2$ or $y = y_1 - 2x_1^2$. Since (x_1, y_1) is on the parabola, $y_1 = x_1^2$ and the ordinate of T is $-y_1$. The area of triangle QPT equals $\frac{1}{2}\overline{QP}\cdot\overline{TQ} = \frac{1}{2}x_1 \cdot (2y_1) = x_1 y_1$.

3. Since $y = ax^3 + bx^2 + cx + d$, $y' = 3ax^2 + 2bx + c$ and $y'' = 6ax + 2b$. If the curve is to have a relative maximum at $(0,1)$ and a point of inflection at $(1, \frac{1}{3})$, then it must follow that

$$y'(0) = 0 \qquad\qquad\qquad\qquad c = 0$$
$$y''(1) = 0 \qquad\qquad\qquad 6a + 2b = 0$$
$$y(0) = 1 \qquad\qquad\qquad\qquad d = 1$$
$$y(1) = \frac{1}{3} \qquad\qquad a + b + c + d = \frac{1}{3}.$$

The values for c and d given by the first and third of the equations on the right enable us to solve the second and fourth of the equations simultaneously, yielding $a = \frac{1}{3}$ and $b = -1$.

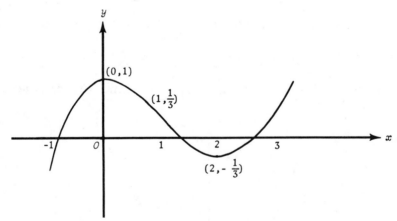

Figure S7-3

The graph of $y = \frac{1}{3}x^3 - x^2 + 1$ is sketched in Figure S7-3. Note that the curve has a relative minimum at $(2, -\frac{1}{3})$.

4. See Figure S7-4. Since the volume V of the cylinder is $\pi R^2 H$

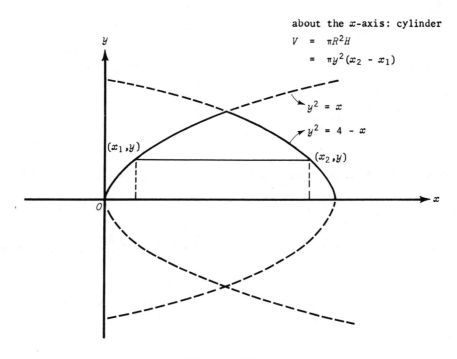

Figure S7-4

and the radius R, here, equals y, while the height H equals $x_2 - x_1$,

we have $V = \pi y^2 (x_2 - x_1) = \pi y^2 (4 - y^2 - y^2) = \pi y^2 (4 - 2y^2) = \pi (4y^2 - 2y^4)$.

Then $\frac{dV}{dy} = \pi (8y - 8y^3) = 8\pi y (1 - y^2)$, and the only possible y here for which

$\frac{dV}{dy} = 0$ is $y = 1$. Since $\frac{d^2 V}{dy^2} = \pi (8 - 24y^2)$ and this is negative when $y = 1$,

the volume of the cylinder is a maximum for this radius. Thus the

diameter is 2 and the height, $4 - 2y^2$, is also 2.

5. (a) Let $A = \displaystyle\int \frac{x - 3}{\sqrt{6x - x^2}} \, dx$. Then $A = -\frac{1}{2} \displaystyle\int \frac{6 - 2x}{\sqrt{6x - x^2}} \, dx$

$= -\frac{1}{2} \displaystyle\int (6x - x^2)^{-1/2} (6 - 2x) \, dx = -\frac{1}{2} \displaystyle\int u^{-1/2} \, du$, where $u = 6x - x^2$.

Then $A = -\frac{1}{2} \frac{u^{1/2}}{\frac{1}{2}} + C_1 = -\sqrt{6x - x^2} + C_1$.

(b)   Let $B = \int \dfrac{dx}{\sqrt{6x - x^2}}$.   This equals $\int \dfrac{dx}{\sqrt{9 - (x^2 - 6x + 9)}}$

$= \int \dfrac{dx}{\sqrt{3^2 - (x - 3)^2}} = \int \dfrac{du}{\sqrt{a^2 - u^2}}$, where $a = 3$ and $u = x - 3$.   Since

$\int \dfrac{du}{\sqrt{a^2 - u^2}} = \sin^{-1} \dfrac{u}{a} + C$, we see that $B = \sin^{-1} \dfrac{x - 3}{3} + C_2$.

(c)   Let $C = \int \dfrac{2x + 3}{\sqrt{6x - x^2}}\, dx$ and note that this equals $\int \dfrac{2x - 6 + 9}{\sqrt{6x - x^2}}\, dx$

$= 2 \int \dfrac{x - 3}{\sqrt{6x - x^2}}\, dx + 9 \int \dfrac{dx}{\sqrt{6x - x^2}} = 2A + 9B$.   So, from (a) and (b) above,

$C = -2\sqrt{6x - x^2} + 9 \sin^{-1} \dfrac{x - 3}{3} + C_3$.

6.   Since $x = \theta - \sin \theta$ and $y = 1 - \cos \theta$, $dx = (1 - \cos \theta)\, d\theta$ and $dy = \sin \theta\, d\theta$.

(a)   The slope at any point is given by $\dfrac{dy}{dx}$, which here equals

$\dfrac{\sin \theta}{1 - \cos \theta}$.   When $\theta = \dfrac{2\pi}{3}$, $\dfrac{dy}{dx} = \dfrac{\dfrac{\sqrt{3}}{2}}{1 - \left(-\dfrac{1}{2}\right)} = \dfrac{\sqrt{3}}{3}$.

(b)   The differential of arc length ds satisfies the equation $ds^2 = dx^2 + dy^2$.   So $ds^2 = (1 - 2 \cos \theta + \cos^2 \theta + \sin^2 \theta)\, d\theta^2$, and $ds = \sqrt{2 - 2 \cos \theta}\, d\theta$.   Since y equals zero when $\theta = 2n\pi$, n an integer, one arch of the cycloid is completed as θ varies from 0 to 2π.   Then

$$s = \sqrt{2} \int_0^{2\pi} \sqrt{1 - \cos \theta}\, d\theta = \sqrt{2} \int_0^{2\pi} \sqrt{2} \sin \dfrac{\theta}{2}\, d\theta$$

$$= 2 \cdot 2 \left(-\cos \dfrac{\theta}{2}\right) \Big|_0^{2\pi} = -4(-1-1) = 8 \text{ units.}$$

7. (a)   We know that

$$s = \frac{1}{2}gt^2 \tag{1}$$

and thus that

$$v = \frac{ds}{dt} = gt. \tag{2}$$

Solving (1) for t yields $\sqrt{\frac{2s}{g}} = t$ $(t \geqq 0)$, and (2) becomes

$$v = g\sqrt{\frac{2s}{g}} = \sqrt{2gs}. \tag{3}$$

Note, from (2), that $v_1 = gt_1$, and, from (3), that $v_1 = \sqrt{2gs_1}$.

(b)   The average velocity v_t with respect to t over the time interval $[0, t_1]$ is given by

$$v_t = \frac{1}{t_1 - 0}\int_0^{t_1} gt\,dt = \frac{1}{t_1}\left[\frac{1}{2}gt^2\right]_0^{t_1}$$

$$= \frac{1}{t_1}\frac{gt_1^2}{2} = \frac{1}{2}gt_1 = \frac{1}{2}v_1.$$

(c)   The average velocity v_s with respect to s over the time interval $[0, t_1]$ is given by

$$v_s = \frac{1}{s_1 - 0}\int_0^{s_1} \sqrt{2gs}\,ds = \frac{\sqrt{2g}}{s_1}\left[\frac{2}{3}s^{3/2}\right]_0^{s_1}$$

$$= \frac{2}{3}\sqrt{2g}\cdot s_1^{1/2} = \frac{2}{3}\sqrt{2gs_1} = \frac{2}{3}v_1.$$

Sample Essay Examination: 8

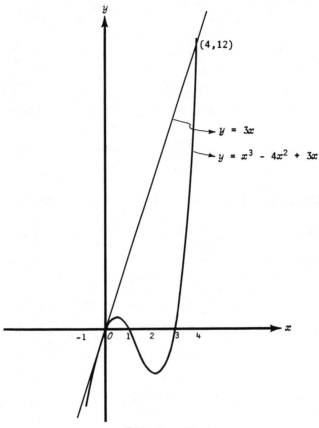

Figure S8-1

1. See Figure S8-1. Area = $\frac{64}{3}$.

2. $\frac{4\sqrt{3}}{3}$ by 8.

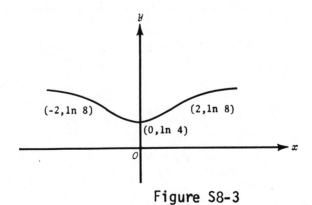

Figure S8-3

3. See Figure S8-3. (a) $x = 0$, $y = \ln 4$. (b) Symmetric to y-axis.

(c) Relative minimum at $(0, \ln 4)$. (d) Inflection points at $(\pm 2, \ln 8)$.

4. (a) Since $v = \dfrac{ds}{dt} = 3t^2 - 6t$, $a = \dfrac{dv}{dt} = 6t - 6$.

(b) $v > 0$ if $t < 0$ or $t > 2$.

(c) The particle is slowing down if $t < 0$ or if $1 < t < 2$.

5. Hint: Find the coordinates of S and T by solving simultaneously $y = x^2$ with $y = mx$ and with $y = -\dfrac{1}{m} x$. Q is the point $(0,1)$ for all nonzero m.

6. (a) $x^2 + 4y^2 = 4$. The curve is sketched in Figure S8-6; note that $2 \leqq t \leqq 6$.

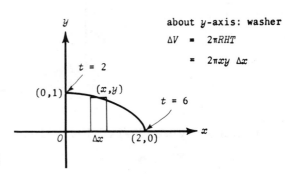

Figure   S8-6

(b) Since a typical element of volume about the y-axis is a washer,
$V = 2\pi RHT$ and
$$V = 2\pi \int_{x=0}^{2} xy\ dx = 2\pi \int_{t=2}^{6} \sqrt{t-2} \cdot \frac{\sqrt{6-t}}{2} \cdot \frac{dt}{2\sqrt{t-2}}$$
$$= \frac{\pi}{2} \int_{2}^{6} \sqrt{6-t}\ dt.$$

(c) $V = \dfrac{8\pi}{3}$.

7. (a) The given limit is equivalent to
$$\lim_{h \to 0} \frac{F\left(\frac{\pi}{4} + h\right) - F\left(\frac{\pi}{4}\right)}{h} = F'\left(\frac{\pi}{4}\right)$$
where $F'(x) = \dfrac{\sin x}{x}$. The answer is $\dfrac{2\sqrt{2}}{\pi}$.

(b) $\lim\limits_{n \to \infty} \dfrac{1}{n} \sum\limits_{k=1}^{n} \cos^2 \dfrac{\pi k}{n} = \dfrac{1}{\pi} \int_{0}^{\pi} \cos^2 x\ dx = \dfrac{1}{2}$.

Sample Essay Examination: 9

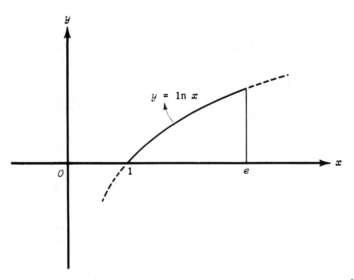

Figure S9-1

1. See Figure S9-1. The volume equals $\frac{\pi}{2}(e^2 + 1)$.

2. (a) Hint: use partial fractions. $\ln \dfrac{\sqrt{(x - 1)(x + 1)}}{x} + C$.

    (b) Hint: use integration by parts. $\frac{1}{3} x \sin 3x + \frac{1}{9} \cos 3x + C$.

3. (b) $f'(1) = 3$.

    (c) Yes. $\displaystyle\lim_{x \to 1^+} f'(x) = \lim_{x \to 1^-} f'(x) = 3 = f'(1)$.

    (d) $\dfrac{13}{4}$.

4. Hint: differentiate with respect to t. $f(x) = \dfrac{x^2}{4} + C$ (C a constant).

5. (a) See Figure S9-5.

The curve is a circle.

    (b) $2(\pi - 2)$.

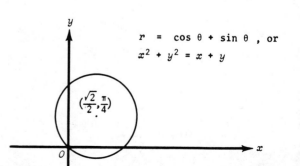

Figure S9-5

6. $\dfrac{43\sqrt{61}}{61}$ ft/min.

7. (a) $R = \dfrac{t^2}{2}\,\mathbf{i} + \dfrac{t^2 - 2t + 2}{2}\,\mathbf{j}$.

(b) $\mathbf{a} = \mathbf{i} + \mathbf{j}$ for all t.

(c) The speed is a minimum when $t = \dfrac{1}{2}$.

Sample Essay Examination: **10**

1. Hint: Let R have coordinates (a,b), where $b = a - a^2$. Then

we seek a such that $\displaystyle\int_0^a (x - x^2 - \dfrac{b}{a}\,x)\,dx = \dfrac{1}{2}\,ab + \int_0^1 (x - x^2)\,dx$.

$a = \dfrac{1}{\sqrt[3]{2}}$ or $\dfrac{1}{2}\sqrt[3]{4}$.

2. (a) $y = 0$ if $x = n\pi$, n an integer.

(b) The curve has maximum and minimum points respectively at

$\left(2n\pi + \dfrac{\pi}{3}, \dfrac{3\sqrt{3}}{4}\right)$ and $\left(2n\pi - \dfrac{\pi}{3}, \dfrac{-3\sqrt{3}}{4}\right)$, where n is an integer.

(c) The coordinates of the inflection points are $(n\pi,\ 0)$, n an integer,

and $\left(\cos^{-1} - \dfrac{1}{4},\ \pm\dfrac{3\sqrt{15}}{16}\right)$.

The curve is sketched in Figure S10-2.

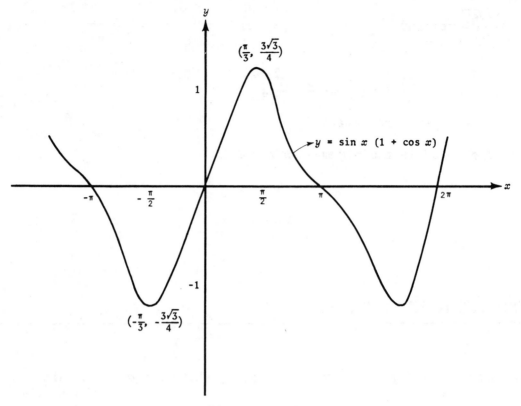

Figure S10-2

3.   (a) Hint: $\displaystyle\int \frac{dx}{e^x + 1} = \int \frac{e^x + 1 - e^x}{e^x + 1}\, dx = x - \ln (e^x + 1) + C.$

(b) We seek $\displaystyle\lim_{b\to\infty} [b - \ln (e^b + 1) + \ln 2].$ Since

$$\lim_{b\to\infty} [\ln e^b - \ln (e^b + 1)] = \lim_{b\to\infty} \ln \frac{e^b}{e^b + 1} = \ln \lim_{b\to\infty} \frac{e^b}{e^b + 1} = \ln 1 = 0,$$

the answer to this part is $\ln 2$.

4. The area A of the triangle equals $\frac{1}{2} \cos^3 x \sin x$, and this is a maximum when $x = \frac{\pi}{6}$. Note that $\frac{d^2 A}{dx^2}$ is negative for this value of x.

5. The equation of the curve is $y^2 = \dfrac{x}{x - 4}$.

6. (a) Since $\frac{dy}{dt} = 2$, $y = 2t + 1$ and $x = 4t^3 + 6t^2 + 3t$.

(b) Since $\frac{d^2y}{dt^2} = 0$ and $\frac{d^2x}{dt^2} = 24t + 12$, then when $t = 1$, $|a| = 36$.

7. Hint: Apply the Mean Value Theorem twice, first to $f(x)$ on $[a,x]$ where $x > a$, then to $f(x)$ on $[x,a]$ where $x < a$.

Sample Essay Examination: 11

1. (a) The intercepts are $(0,0)$, $(\pm 1,0)$.

(b) The domain is $\{x \mid x \leq -1 \text{ or } 0 \leq x \leq 1\}$.

(c) The curve is symmetric to the x-axis.

(d) There are no vertical or horizontal asymptotes.

(e) The curve has a relative maximum at $(\frac{\sqrt{3}}{3}, \frac{\sqrt{2\sqrt{3}}}{3})$ and a relative minimum at $(\frac{\sqrt{3}}{3}, -\frac{\sqrt{2\sqrt{3}}}{3})$.

The curve is sketched in Figure S11-1.

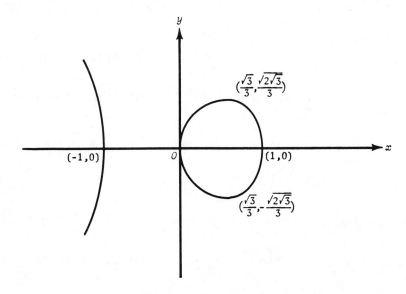

Figure S11-1

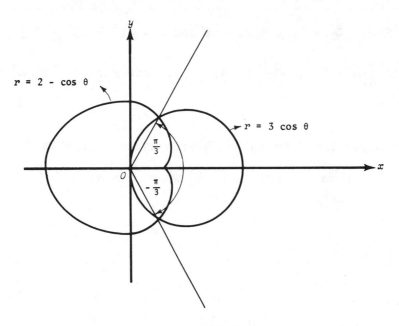

Figure S11-2

2. See Figure S11-2. The required area A is twice the sum of the following areas: that of the limaçon from 0 to $\frac{\pi}{3}$, and that of the circle from $\frac{\pi}{3}$ to $\frac{\pi}{2}$. Thus

$$A = 2\left[\frac{1}{2}\int_{0}^{\frac{\pi}{3}}(2 - \cos\theta)^2\ d\theta\ +\ \frac{1}{2}\int_{\frac{\pi}{3}}^{\frac{\pi}{2}}(3\cos\theta)^2\ d\theta\right]$$

$$= \frac{9\pi}{4}\ -\ 3\sqrt{3}.$$

3. (a) $\ln n = \int_{1}^{n}\frac{1}{t}\ dt.$ $\ln n$ may be interpreted as the area under the curve of $y = \frac{1}{t}$ (and above the t-axis) from $t = 1$ to $t = n$.

(b) $\frac{1}{2} + \frac{1}{3} + \ldots + \frac{1}{n}$ can be regarded as the sum of the areas of inscribed rectangles, each of width 1 and of heights $\frac{1}{2}, \frac{1}{3}, \ldots, \frac{1}{n}$, as indicated by the broken lines in Figure S11-3a. $1 + \frac{1}{2} + \frac{1}{3} + \ldots + \frac{1}{n-1}$ can be regarded as the sum of the areas of circumscribed rectangles, each of width 1 and of heights $1, \frac{1}{2}, \frac{1}{3}, \ldots, \frac{1}{n-1}$, as shown in Figure S11-3b. Clearly, the inequality given in 3(b) holds.

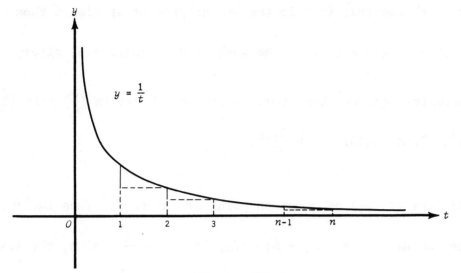

Figure S11-3a

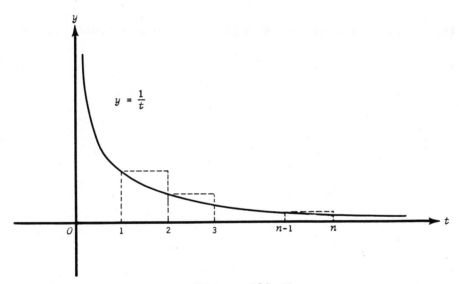

Figure S11-3b

4. Since $a = -6t$, it follows that $v = -3t^2 + C$ and $s = -t^3 + Ct + C'$. Note also that $s(0) = 0$ and that s must equal 16 when $v = 0$. The initial velocity is 12.

5. (a) $\sin^{-1} \dfrac{x - 3}{3} + C.$

(b) *Hint*: Use the parts formula, letting $u = x^2$ and $dv = xe^{-x^2} dx$. The answer is $-\dfrac{1}{2} e^{-x^2}(x^2 + 1) + C.$

6. *Hint*: We know that if s is the amount present at time t then $\frac{ds}{dt} = -ks$, $s(0) = 6$, and $s(1) = 4$. We seek $s(10)$. Integrate, after separating variables, and use the given conditions to get $\ln\left(\frac{s}{6}\right) = \ln\left(\frac{2}{3}\right)^t$, or $\frac{s}{6} = \left(\frac{2}{3}\right)^t$. Thus, $s(10) = 6\left(\frac{2}{3}\right)^{10}$.

7. *Hint*: Let (x_1, y_1) be a common point of tangency. Then the following three equations hold: $y_1 = mx_1 + b$; $x_1 y_1 = 1$; $-\frac{1}{x_1^2} = m$, the last of these deriving from the fact that the slope of the curve at (x_1, y_1) equals the slope of the line. Simultaneous solution of the equations yields

$$m = -\frac{b^2}{4}.$$

Sample Essay Examination: **12**

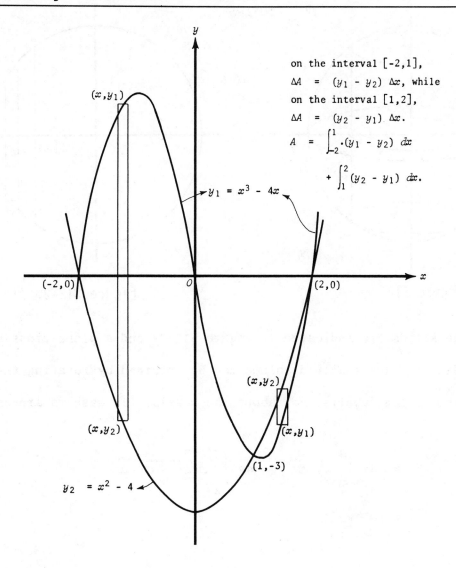

on the interval $[-2,1]$,
$\Delta A = (y_1 - y_2) \Delta x$, while
on the interval $[1,2]$,
$\Delta A = (y_2 - y_1) \Delta x$.

$$A = \int_{-2}^{1} \cdot (y_1 - y_2) \, dx$$

$$+ \int_{1}^{2} (y_2 - y_1) \, dx.$$

(x, y_1)

$y_1 = x^3 - 4x$

$(-2,0)$

O

$(2,0)$

(x, y_2)

(x, y_2)

(x, y_1)

$(1,-3)$

$y_2 = x^2 - 4$

Figure S12-1

1. See Figure S12-1. Note that simultaneous solution of the
two equations yields the points of intersection $(-2,0)$, $(1,-3)$, and
$(2,0)$. The total area

$$A = \int_{-2}^{1} \left[(x^3 - 4x) - (x^2 - 4) \right] \, dx + \int_{1}^{2} \left[(x^2 - 4) - (x^3 - 4x) \right] \, dx$$

$$= \frac{71}{6}.$$

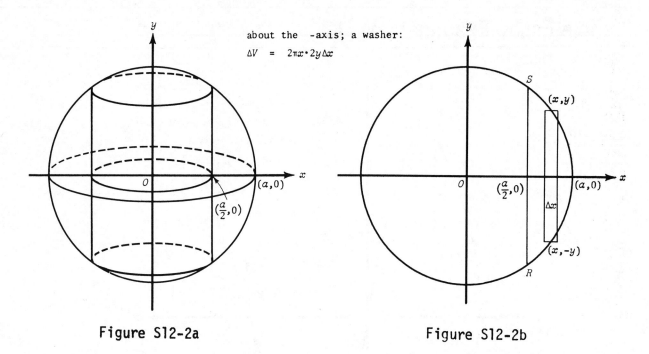

about the -axis; a washer:

$$\Delta V = 2\pi x \cdot 2y \, \Delta x$$

Figure S12-2a   Figure S12-2b

2. The solids are indicated in Figure S12-2a and a plane cross-section in Figure S12-2b. The required volume can be obtained by rotating the region of the circle labelled RST about the y-axis. If washers are used, then

$$V = 4\pi \int_{\frac{a}{2}}^{a} xy \, dx = 4\pi \int_{\frac{a}{2}}^{a} x\sqrt{a^2 - x^2} \, dx$$

$$= \frac{\sqrt{3}}{2} \pi a^3.$$

3. $y = x^2$.

4. (a) *Hint*: Use the partial fraction theorem. If we let

$$\frac{2}{(x - 1)(x^2 + 1)} = \frac{A}{x - 1} + \frac{Bx + C}{x^2 + 1}$$

then $A = 1$, $B = -1$, $C = -1$. So

$$\int \frac{2 \, dx}{(x - 1)(x^2 + 1)} = \frac{\ln |x - 1|}{\sqrt{x^2 + 1}} - \tan^{-1} x + C'. \quad .$$

(b) $$\int_{0}^{\infty} xe^{-x^2} \, dx = \lim_{b \to \infty} -\frac{1}{2} e^{-x^2} \Big|_{0}^{b} = \frac{1}{2}.$$

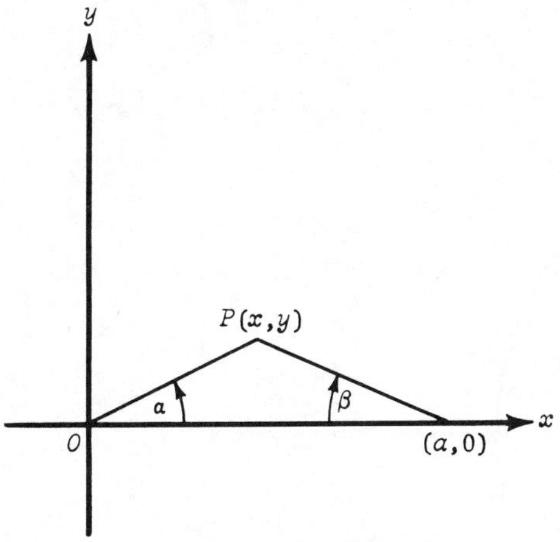

Figure S12-5a

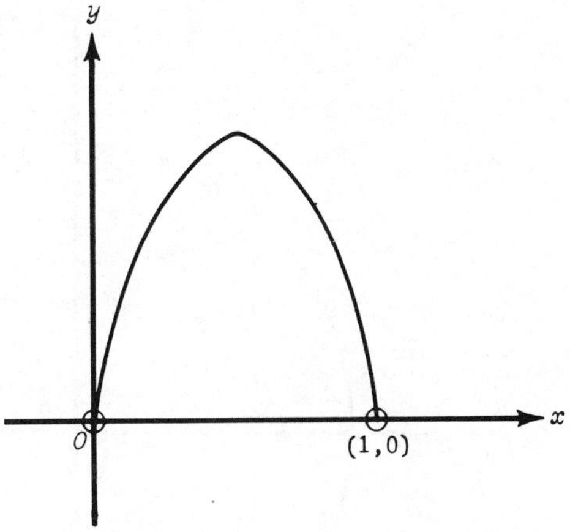

Figure S12-5b

5. See Figure S12-5a. Let the vertex have coordinates (x,y).

(a) Then $\dfrac{y}{x} - \dfrac{y}{x-a} = k$ (where we have used the fact that tan β

equals the negative of the slope of AP). The simplified equation is

equation is

$$-ay = kx^2 - akx \qquad\qquad (1)$$

which is that of a parabola.

(b) Here $\left(\dfrac{y}{x}\right)\cdot\left(-\dfrac{y}{x-a}\right) = k$, and this becomes

$$y^2 + kx^2 - akx = 0 \qquad\qquad (2)$$

which is the equation of an ellipse provided $k > 0$.

(c) If $a = 1$ and $k = 4$, we get for (1)

$$-y = 4x^2 - 4x,$$

sketched in Figure S12-5b, and, for (2),

$$y^2 + 4x^2 - 4x = 0,$$

sketched in Figure S12-5c. In each case, the

origin and $(a,0)$, which satisfy the equations

found, must be omitted from the locus since

neither point can be the required vertex.

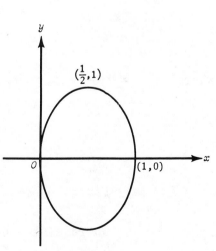

Figure S12-5c

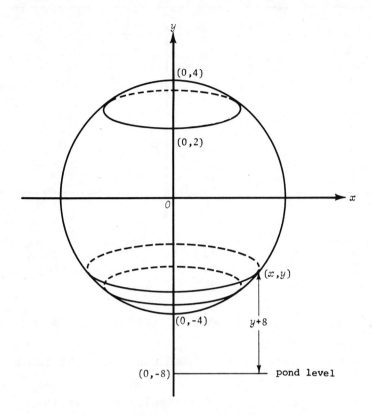

Figure S12-6

6. See Figure S12-6. ΔW, an element of work, equals the weight, $w\Delta V$ (where w is the weight in lb per ft^3 of volume and ΔV is the volume of an element) times the distance through which the element is to be moved.

Thus

$$\Delta W = w \cdot \pi x^2 \Delta y \cdot (y + 8);$$

$$W = \pi w \int_{4}^{2} x^2 (y + 8) \ dy,$$

where $x^2 = 16 - y^2$. The work W equals $540\pi w$ ft-lbs.

7. (a) *Hint*: Since it is given that $\dfrac{ds}{dt} = e^t$, it follows that $s = e^t + C$, where $s(0) = 0$. So $s = e^t - 1$, and when the particle reaches $(-4,0)$ first we note that $s = 4\pi$. Thus $t = \ln(4\pi + 1)$.

(b) Note that

$$v_x^2 + v_y^2 = e^{2t} \qquad\qquad (1)$$

$$xv_x + yv_y = 0, \qquad\qquad (2)$$

where the latter is obtained by differentiating the equation of the circle with respect to t. At $(-4,0)$ we get from (2) that $v_x = 0$ and thus, from (1), that $v_y = -e^t$. Differentiate (1) with respect to t, getting $v_x a_x + v_y a_y = e^{2t}$, so that a_y at $(-4,0)$ equals $-e^t$ or $-(4\pi + 1)$.

If we differentiate (2) with respect to t, we get $xa_x + ya_y + v_x^2 + v_y^2 = 0$, and $xa_x + ya_y = -e^{2t}$. At $(-4,0)$, then, $-4a_x = -e^{2t}$, t, so $a_x = \dfrac{e^{2t}}{4} = \dfrac{(4\pi + 1)^2}{4}$.

Thus

$$\mathbf{a} = \frac{(4\pi + 1)^2}{4} \mathbf{i} - (4\pi + 1) \mathbf{j}.$$

Sample Essay Examination: **13**

1. (a) The origin is the only intercept.

(b) There are no relative maxima or minima. Although $y' = 1 + \cos x$ is zero for $x = (2n + 1)\pi$, n an integer, note that y' does not change sign ($y' \geqq 0$ for all x).

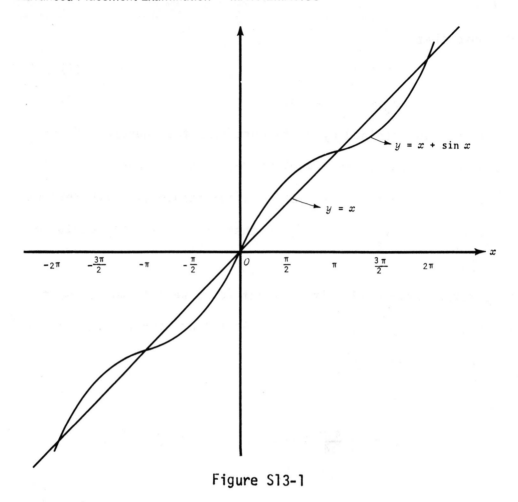

Figure S13-1

(c)   The curve has inflection points when $x = n\pi$, n an integer.
See Figure S13-1.

2.   See Figure S13-2. The equation of the circle is $x^2 + y^2 = a^2$;
the equation of RS is $y = a - x$. If y_2 is an ordinate of the circle and y_1
of the line, then $\Delta V = \pi y_2{}^2 \Delta x - \pi y_1{}^2 \Delta x$, and

$$V = 2\pi \int_0^a \left[(a^2 - x^2) - (a - x)^2 \right] \, dx.$$

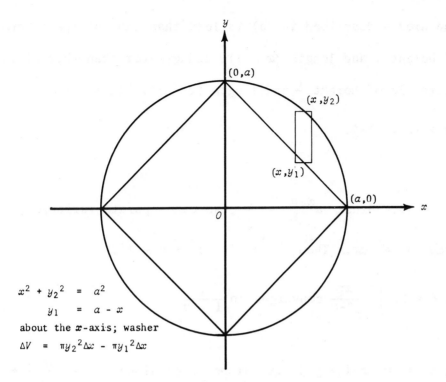

$$x^2 + y_2{}^2 = a^2$$
$$y_1 = a - x$$

about the x-axis; washer

$$\Delta V = \pi y_2{}^2 \Delta x - \pi y_1{}^2 \Delta x$$

Figure S13-2

3. (a) $\ln x$.

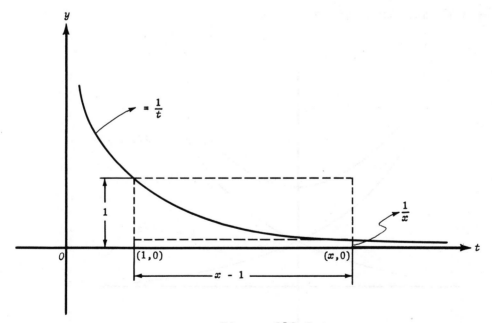

Figure S13-3

(b) See Figure S13-3. $\ln x$ is the area above the t-axis below the

curve $y = \frac{1}{t}$ and bounded by $t = 1$ and $t = x$.

(c) The **area** A described in (b) is less than that of the circumscribed rectangle of height 1 and length $(x - 1)$, and greater than that of the inscribed rectangle of height $\frac{1}{x}$ and length $(x - 1)$. Thus, if $x > 1$, then

$$x - 1 > \ln x > (x - 1) \cdot \frac{1}{x}.$$

4. (a) *Hint*: Since $e^{x-y} = \dfrac{e^x}{e^y}$, we can separate variables, getting $e^y \, dy = e^x \, dx$. Then $y = \ln \left| e^x + e - 1 \right|$.

(b) If $n < 1$, $\displaystyle\int_1^\infty \frac{dx}{x^{2-n}}$ converges to $\dfrac{1}{1 - n}$.

5. Since $\mathbf{R} = x \, \mathbf{i} + y \, \mathbf{j}$, its slope is $\frac{y}{x}$; since $\mathbf{v} = \dfrac{dx}{dt} \mathbf{i} + \dfrac{dy}{dt} \mathbf{j}$, its slope is $\dfrac{dy}{dx}$. If $\mathbf{R}$ is perpendicular to $\mathbf{v}$, then $\dfrac{y}{x} \cdot \dfrac{dy}{dx} = -1$. So,

$$\frac{y^2}{2} = -\frac{x^2}{2} + C, \text{ and } x^2 + y^2 = k \quad (k > 0).$$

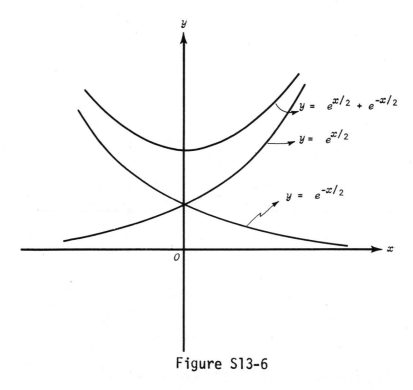

Figure S13-6

6. See Figure S13-6.   Recall that $ds^2 = dx^2 + dy^2$. So

$$s = \int_0^2 \sqrt{dx^2 + \frac{1}{4}(e^x - 2 + e^{-x})\ dx^2}$$

$$= \int_0^2 \sqrt{\frac{1}{4}(e^{x/2} + e^{-x/2})^2\ dx^2}$$

$$= \int_0^2 \frac{1}{2}(e^{x/2} + e^{-x/2})\ dx$$

$$= e^{x/2} - e^{-x/2}\Big|_0^2 = e - \frac{1}{e}.$$

7. Let $H(x) = f(x) - g(x)$, and note that H satisfied the hypotheses of the Mean Value Theorem on $[a,x]$. Thus there is a number c, $a < c < x$, such that $\dfrac{H(x) - H(a)}{x - a} = H'(c)$. Since $H'(c) = f'(c) - g'(c)$, and $f'(c) > g'(c)$ for all c, it follows that $H'(c) > 0$. Then, if $x > a$, $H(x) - H(a) = (x - a)H'(c) > 0$. Since $H(x) - H(a) = [f(x) - g(x)] - [f(a) - g(a)]$ and $f(a) = g(a)$, we see that if $x > a$ then $f(x) - g(x) > 0$, so that $f(x) > g(x)$. The proof that $f(x) < g(x)$ if $x < a$ is similar.

Sample Essay Examination: **14**

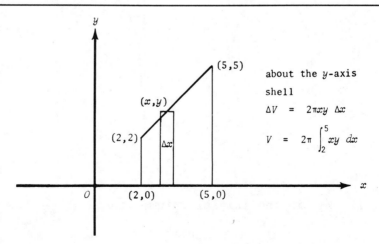

Figure S14-1

1. See Figure S14-1, and note that the equation of the line through (2,2) and (5,5) is $y = x$. $V = \dfrac{234\pi}{3}$.

2. (a) Since $\ln u$ is defined only if $u > 0$, the domain of $\ln \sin x$ is $-2\pi < x < -\pi$ or $0 < x < \pi$; since $0 < \sin x \leqq 1$ on this domain, $\ln \sin x \leqq 0$.

(b) $\ln \sin x = 0$ if $x = -\dfrac{3\pi}{2}$ or $\dfrac{\pi}{2}$.

(c) Note, since $y' = \cot x$, that it is zero when $x = -\dfrac{3\pi}{2}$ or $\dfrac{\pi}{2}$. Since $y'' = -\csc^2 x$, we see that y'' is always negative, so that $(-\dfrac{3\pi}{2},\ 0)$ and $(\dfrac{\pi}{2},\ 0)$ are relative maxima.

(d) The curve is everywhere concave down.

(e) Since $\sin x$ is 0 at -2π, $-\pi$, 0, and π, we see that $\ln \sin x$ becomes negatively infinite as x approaches any of these numbers. The curve has vertical asymptotes corresponding to each of these x's.

See Figure S14-2 for a sketch of the function.

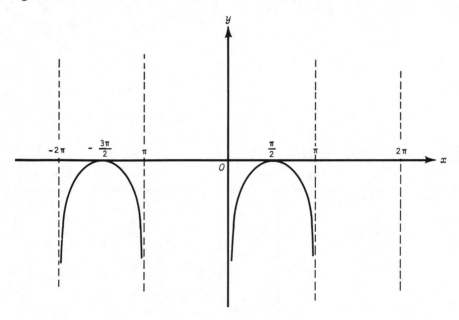

Figure S14-2

3. If V_0 is the initial volume, then $\ln \dfrac{V}{V_0} = t \ln .9$. So $V = \dfrac{1}{2}V_0$ when $t = \dfrac{\ln .5}{\ln .9}$.

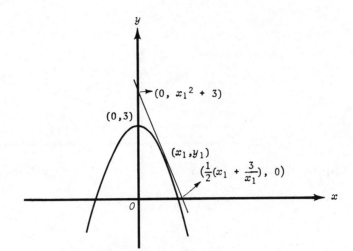

Figure S14-4

4. See Figure S14-4, where an arbitrary point $P(x_1, y_1)$ has been chosen, $x_1 > 0$.

Hint: The equation of the tangent at P is $y - y_1 = -2x_1(x - x_1)$, and the intercepts of this tangent are $x = \dfrac{x_1^2 + 3}{2x_1}$, $y = x_1^2 + 3$.

The area A of the triangle is thus

$$A = \frac{1}{4}(x_1 + \frac{3}{x_1})(x_1^2 + 3).$$

Note that

$$\frac{dA}{dx} = \frac{1}{4}(x_1^2 + 3)(3 - \frac{3}{x_1^2})$$

and that A is a minimum when $x_1 = 1$.

5. We have $\mathbf{v} = (3 - e^{-t})\,\mathbf{i} + (e^t - 1)\,\mathbf{j}$. So $\mathbf{R} = (3t + e^{-t})\,\mathbf{i} + (e^t - t + 1)\,\mathbf{j}$. (*Hint*: when $t = 0$, $\mathbf{v} = 2\mathbf{i} + 0\mathbf{j}$, $\mathbf{R} = \mathbf{i} + 2\mathbf{j}$.)

6. See Figure S14-6, where S is the required surface area.

$S = \frac{\pi}{6}(17^{3/2} - 1).$

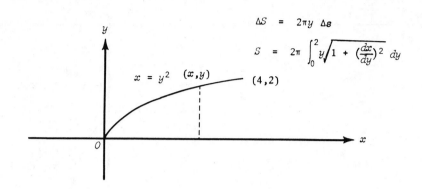

Figure S14-6

7. (a) *Hint*: Find $\frac{dy}{dx}$, then $\frac{dx}{dy}$, and finally $\frac{d^2x}{dy^2}$ using the chain rule. $\frac{1}{x}\frac{d^2x}{dy^2} = 2$.

(b) *Hint*: Solve $\frac{dy}{dx} = (\sin x)\cdot y$. $y = f(x) = 3e^{1-\cos x}$.

Sample Essay Examination: 15

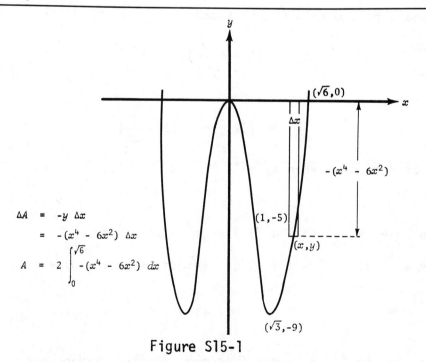

Figure S15-1

1. (a) The curve has a relative minimum at (0,0), relative maxima at $(\pm\sqrt{3},-9)$, and inflection points at $(\pm 1,-5)$. It is sketched in Figure S15-1.

(b)   The area bounded by the curve and the x-axis equals $\frac{48\sqrt{6}}{5}$.

2.   *Hint*: $\frac{dS}{dt}$ = -72 in²/sec, or - $\frac{1}{2}$ ft²/sec, where the surface area S = $6x^2$. Find $\frac{dV}{dt}$ (V is the volume) when S = 54 (ft²).

Answer: - $\frac{3}{8}$ ft³/sec.

3. y = e^{x^2}.

4.   (a) *Hint*: $f'(0)$ = $\lim\limits_{\Delta x \to 0} \frac{|\Delta x|^3}{\Delta x}$; consider the two cases,

$\Delta x \to 0^+$ and $\Delta x \to 0^-$. Answer: $f'(0)$ = 0.

(b)   Yes: $\lim\limits_{x \to 0} f'(x)$ = $f'(0)$ = 0.

(c)   Yes: $\lim\limits_{x \to 0^-} f(x)$ = $\lim\limits_{x \to 0^+} f(x)$ = $f(0)$ = 0.

(d)   The curve of $f(x)$ = 1 - $|x|$ is sketched in Figure S15-4.

$\int_{-1}^{1} (1 - |x|)\ dx$ = $2 \int_{0}^{1} (1 - x)\ dx$ = 1.

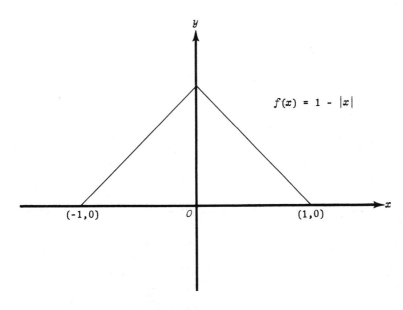

Figure S15-4

5. The parametric equations are $x = k \cos \theta$, $y = (c + k) \sin \theta$.

Eliminating θ yields $\dfrac{x^2}{k^2} + \dfrac{y^2}{(c + k)^2} = 1$; the curve is an ellipse with major axis vertical.

6. (a) $\dfrac{\pi}{4}$.

   (b) $\dfrac{e^2}{4} + \dfrac{1}{4}$.

   (c) $\ln \left| \dfrac{(x + 1)^2}{x - 1} \right| + C$.

7. (a) Since $\dfrac{dv}{dt} = \dfrac{1}{v}$, or $v \, dv = dt$, it follows that $\dfrac{v^2}{2} = t + C$.

Thus $v = \sqrt{2t + 4}$.

   (b) The distance travelled in the first six seconds is

$$\int_0^6 \sqrt{2t + 4} \, dt = \frac{56}{3}.$$

Appendix: Formulas for Reference

Algebra

1. **QUADRATIC FORMULA.** The roots of the quadratic equation

$$ax^2 + bx + c = 0 \quad (a \neq 0)$$

are given by

$$x = \frac{-b \pm \sqrt{b^2 - 4ac}}{2a}.$$

2. **BINOMIAL THEOREM.** If n is a positive integer, then

$$(a + b)^n = a^n + na^{n-1}b + \frac{n(n-1)}{1\cdot2}a^{n-2}b^2 + \frac{n(n-1)(n-2)}{1\cdot2\cdot3}a^{n-3}b^3$$

$$+ \ldots + nab^{n-1} + b^n.$$

3. **REMAINDER THEOREM.** If the polynomial $Q(x)$ is divided by $(x - a)$ until a constant remainder R is obtained, then $R = Q(a)$. In particular, if a is a root of $Q(x) = 0$, then $Q(a) = 0$.

Geometry

In the following formulas,

A	is area	B	is area of base
S	surface area	r	radius
V	volume	C	circumference
b	base	l	arc length
h	height or altitude	θ	central angle in radians
s	slant height.		

4. **triangle:** $A = \frac{1}{2}bh$

5. **trapezoid:** $A = \frac{1}{2}(b_1 + b_2)h$

6. **parallelogram:** $A = bh$

7. circle: $\qquad C = 2\pi r; A = \pi r^2$

8. circular sector: $\qquad A = \frac{1}{2}r^2\theta$

9. circular arc: $\qquad l = r\theta$

10. right circular cylinder: $V = \pi r^2 h; S(\text{lateral}) = 2\pi rh$

11. right circular cone: $\qquad V = \frac{1}{3}\pi r^2 h; S(\text{lateral}) = \pi rs$

12. sphere: $\qquad V = \frac{4}{3}\pi r^3; S = 4\pi r^2.$

Trigonometry

BASIC IDENTITIES.

13. $\qquad \sin^2\theta + \cos^2\theta = 1$

14. $\qquad 1 + \tan^2\theta = \sec^2\theta$

15. $\qquad 1 + \cot^2\theta = \csc^2\theta.$

SUM AND DIFFERENCE FORMULAS.

16. $\qquad \sin(\alpha \pm \beta) = \sin\alpha\cos\beta \pm \cos\alpha\sin\beta$

17. $\qquad \cos(\alpha \pm \beta) = \cos\alpha\cos\beta \mp \sin\alpha\sin\beta$

18. $\qquad \tan(\alpha \pm \beta) = \dfrac{\tan\alpha \pm \tan\beta}{1 \mp \tan\alpha\tan\beta}.$

DOUBLE-ANGLE FORMULAS.

19. $\qquad \sin 2\alpha = 2\sin\alpha\cos\alpha$

20. $\qquad \cos 2\alpha = \cos^2\alpha - \sin^2\alpha$

21. $\qquad \tan 2\alpha = \dfrac{2\tan\alpha}{1 - \tan^2\alpha}.$

HALF-ANGLE FORMULAS.

22. $\qquad \sin\dfrac{\alpha}{2} = \pm\sqrt{\dfrac{1 - \cos\alpha}{2}}$

23.
$$\cos \frac{\alpha}{2} = \pm \sqrt{\frac{1 + \cos \alpha}{2}}.$$

REDUCTION FORMULAS.

24. $\sin (-\alpha) = -\sin \alpha;$ $\cos (-\alpha) = \cos \alpha$

25. $\sin (90° - \alpha) = \cos \alpha;$ $\cos (90° - \alpha) = \sin \alpha$

26. $\sin (90° + \alpha) = \cos \alpha;$ $\cos (90° + \alpha) = -\sin \alpha$

27. $\sin (180° - \alpha) = \sin \alpha;$ $\cos (180° - \alpha) = -\cos \alpha$

28. $\sin (180° + \alpha) = -\sin \alpha;$ $\cos (180° + \alpha) = -\cos \alpha.$

If a, b, c are the sides of triangle ABC and A, B, C are respectively the opposite interior angles, then:

29. LAW OF COSINES. $c^2 = a^2 + b^2 - 2ab \cos C.$

30. LAW OF SINES. $\dfrac{a}{\sin A} = \dfrac{b}{\sin B} = \dfrac{c}{\sin C}.$

31. The area $A = \frac{1}{2}ab \sin C.$

Analytic Geometry

RECTANGULAR COORDINATES

DISTANCE.

32. The distance d between two points $P_1(x_1, y_1)$ and $P_2(x_2, y_2)$ is given by
$$d = \sqrt{(x_2 - x_1)^2 + (y_2 - y_1)^2}.$$

EQUATIONS OF THE STRAIGHT LINE.

33. POINT-SLOPE FORM. Through $P_1(x_1, y_1)$ and with slope m:
$$y - y_1 = m(x - x_1).$$

34. SLOPE-INTERCEPT FORM. With slope m and y-intercept b:

$$y = mx + b.$$

35. TWO-POINT FORM. Through $P_1(x_1, y_1)$ and $P_2(x_2, y_2)$:

$$y - y_1 = \frac{y_2 - y_1}{x_2 - x_1}(x - x_1).$$

36. INTERCEPT FORM. With x- and y-intercepts of a and b respectively:

$$\frac{x}{a} + \frac{y}{b} = 1.$$

37. GENERAL FORM. $Ax + By + C = 0$, where A and B are not both zero. If $B \neq 0$, the slope is $-\frac{A}{B}$, the y-intercept $-\frac{C}{B}$.

DISTANCE FROM POINT TO LINE.

38. Distance d between a point $P(x_1, y_1)$ and the line $Ax + By + C = 0$ is

$$d = \left| \frac{Ax_1 + By_1 + C}{\sqrt{A^2 + B^2}} \right|.$$

EQUATIONS OF THE CONICS.

CIRCLE

39. With center at $(0,0)$ and radius r: $x^2 + y^2 = r^2$.

40. With center at (h,k) and radius r: $(x - h)^2 + (y - k)^2 = r^2$.

PARABOLA

41. With vertex at $(0,0)$ and focus at $(p,0)$: $\quad y^2 = 4px$

42. With vertex at $(0,0)$ and focus at $(0,p)$: $\quad x^2 = 4py$

With vertex at (h,k) and axis

43. parallel to x-axis, focus at $(h{+}p, k)$: $(y - k)^2 = 4p(x - h)$

44. parallel to y-axis, focus at $(h, k{+}p)$: $(x - h)^2 = 4p(y - k).$

ELLIPSE

With major axis of length $2a$, minor axis of length $2b$, and distance between foci of $2c$:

45. Center at $(0,0)$, foci at $(\pm c,0)$, and vertices at $(\pm a,0)$:

$$\frac{x^2}{a^2} + \frac{y^2}{b^2} = 1.$$

46. Center at $(0,0)$, foci at $(0,\pm c)$, and vertices at $(0,\pm a)$:

$$\frac{y^2}{a^2} + \frac{x^2}{b^2} = 1.$$

47. Center at (h,k), major axis horizontal, vertices at $(h\pm a,k)$:

$$\frac{(x-h)^2}{a^2} + \frac{(y-k)^2}{b^2} = 1.$$

48. Center at (h,k), major axis vertical, vertices at $(h,k\pm a)$:

$$\frac{(y-k)^2}{a^2} + \frac{(x-h)^2}{b^2} = 1.$$

For the ellipse, $a^2 = b^2 + c^2$, and the eccentricity $e = \frac{c}{a}$, which is *less* than 1.

HYPERBOLA

With real (transverse) axis of length $2a$, imaginary (conjugate) axis of length $2b$, and distance between foci of $2c$:

49. Center at $(0,0)$, foci at $(\pm c,0)$, and vertices at $(\pm a,0)$:

$$\frac{x^2}{a^2} - \frac{y^2}{b^2} = 1.$$

50. Center at $(0,0)$, foci at $(0,\pm c)$, and vertices at $(0,\pm a)$:

$$\frac{y^2}{a^2} - \frac{x^2}{b^2} = 1.$$

51. Center at (h,k), real axis horizontal, vertices at $(h\pm a,k)$:

$$\frac{(x-h)^2}{a^2} - \frac{(y-k)^2}{b^2} = 1.$$

52. Center at (h,k), real axis vertical, vertices at $(h,k\pm a)$:

$$\frac{(y-k)^2}{a^2} - \frac{(x-h)^2}{b^2} = 1.$$

For the hyperbola, $c^2 = a^2 + b^2$, and the eccentricity $e = \frac{c}{a}$, which

is *greater* than 1.

POLAR COORDINATES

RELATIONS WITH RECTANGULAR COORDINATES.

53.

$$x = r \cos \theta$$

$$y = r \sin \theta$$

$$r^2 = x^2 + y^2$$

$$\tan \theta = \frac{y}{x}.$$

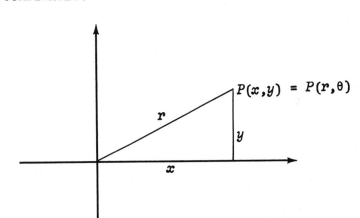

$P(x,y) = P(r,\theta)$

SOME POLAR EQUATIONS.

54. $r = a$ circle, center at pole, radius a.

55. $r = 2a \cos \theta$ circle, center at $(a,0)$, radius a.

56. $r = 2a \sin \theta$ circle, center at $(0,a)$, radius a.

57. $r = a \sec \theta$ line, $x = a$.

    or $r \cos \theta = a$

58. $r = b \csc \theta$ line, $y = b$.

    or $r \sin \theta = b$

59. $r = \cos 2\theta$ rose of four leaves symmetric about the axes.

60. $r = \sin 2\theta$ rose of four leaves symmetric about the quadrant

               bisectors.

61. $r = 1 \pm \cos \theta$ cardioids, cusp at pole, symmetric to x-axis.

62. $r = 1 \pm \sin \theta$ **cardioids, cusp at pole, symmetric to y-axis.**

63. $r^2 = \cos 2\theta$ **lemniscate, symmetric to x-axis.**

64. $r = \theta$ **double spiral passing through the pole.**

65. $r\theta = a$ $(a > 0)$ **hyperbolic spiral asymptotic to the horizontal line $y = a$.**